FRENCH BA
Centre for Language Studies and
Applied Linguistics
Canterbury Christ Church University
Canterbury, Kent
CT1 1QU

Muslims and Jews
in France

Muslims and Jews in France

History of a Conflict

Maud S. Mandel

PRINCETON UNIVERSITY PRESS
Princeton and Oxford

Library of Congress Cataloging-in-Publication Data

Mandel, Maud, 1967– author.
    Muslims and Jews in France : history of a conflict / Maud S. Mandel.
        pages cm
    Includes bibliographical references and index.
    ISBN 978-0-691-12581-7 (alk. paper)
    1. Muslims—France—Social conditions—20th century. 2. Muslims—France—
Social conditions—21st century. 3. Jews—France—Social conditions—20th century.
4. Jews—France—Social conditions—21st century. 5. Muslims—Cultural assimilation—
France. 6. Jews—Cultural assimilation—France. 7. Social integration—France. 8. France—
Ethnic relations. I. Title.
    DC34.5.M87M36 2014
    305.6′970944–dc23   2013020112

British Library Cataloging-in-Publication Data is available

This book has been composed in Minion

Printed on acid-free paper ∞

Printed in the United States of America

10 9 8 7 6 5 4 3 2 1

For my family

CONTENTS

Acknowledgments   ix

INTRODUCTION   1

CHAPTER ONE. Colonial Policies, Middle Eastern War,
and City Spaces: *Marseille in 1948*   15

CHAPTER TWO. Decolonization and Migration:
Constructing the North African Jew   35

CHAPTER THREE. Encounters in the Metropole:
*The Impact of Decolonization on Muslim-Jewish Life in France
in the 1950s and 1960s*   59

CHAPTER FOUR. The 1967 War and the Forging of
Political Community   80

CHAPTER FIVE. Palestine in France: *Radical Politics and
Hardening Ethnic Allegiances, 1968–72*   100

CHAPTER SIX. Particularism versus Pluriculturalism:
The Birth and Death of the Anti-Racist Coalition   125

CONCLUSION   153

Abbreviations   157

Notes   159

Index   241

ACKNOWLEDGMENTS

As all authors, I owe a tremendous intellectual debt to the many people and institutions that have guided and supported me as this book project has evolved. The deeply gifted scholars with whom I have worked at Brown University both in the Program in Judaic Studies and the Department of History have profoundly shaped the way I write and think. While space limitations prevent me from naming the many colleagues who have offered feedback throughout this process, I would like to thank in particular Omer Bartov, Lynn Davidman, Carolyn Dean, Calvin Goldscheider, Mary Gluck, Elliott Gorn, and Michael Steinberg for guidance at critical stages in the writing process. In addition, Ethan Pollock and Robert Self read almost every chapter of this book. These two insightful and creative scholars have not only helped me improve the manuscript but have also made the process far more enjoyable. Deborah Cohen's feedback and, additionally, her sustained friendship gave me confidence when I needed it most.

Also at Brown, I have had the opportunity to interact with a group of intelligent, articulate, and dynamic undergraduate and graduate students, several of whom have aided in the research of this book. For their tremendous help in this capacity, I would like to thank Flannery Berg, David Beyer, Kathryn Boonstra, Kelly Colvin, Rebecca Russo, David Rudin, Stephen Wicken, and Audrey von Maluski.

Several colleagues at other institutions have been extremely supportive over the many years that I have been working on this project and sometimes long before. Phyllis Cohen Albert, Leora Auslander, Vicki Caron, Todd Endelman, Nancy Green, Robin Judd, and Aron Rodrigue have invited me to present work in progress, and/or written letters of recommendation and encouraged me along the way. I was extremely lucky to become acquainted with Ethan Katz shortly after I had begun my research and as he was embarking on his own study of Muslims and Jews in France. An exceptionally generous colleague with boundless energy, Ethan has offered extensive feedback on written work, shared source material, and joined me in several collective endeavors. This fruitful partnership has been one of the most rewarding aspects of this project. Cécile Vidal continues to offer me a home away from home in France and a stunning model of intellectual rigor that I have sought to emulate; she will forever be a source of my profound admiration and affection.

Numerous institutions have made this book possible. At Brown University, the Cogut Center for the Humanities, the Pembroke Center for Teaching and Research on Women, and the Watson Institute for International Studies all provided aid for the initial stages of this project. I would also like to thank the American Council of Learned Societies, the American Philosophical Association, the American Historical Association, the Memorial Foundation for Jewish Culture, and the National Endowment for the Humanities for their crucial aid.

How does one thank the "inner core" adequately for all the help and love they provided? Words fail. Barrett Mandel, Ruth Mandel, and Jeff Lucker not only supplied the TLC on which I have come to depend, but they moved to Paris for stretches of time to help care for my young children and gave me the precious gift of time to carry out my research and writing. My children, Lev and Ava Simon, do not remember a moment when I was not working on this book. Although their presence meant there were long stretches when I was unable to work on it, their love sustained me throughout. Steve Simon has not only been at my side for all endeavors since long before this book began, he also shared a home office with me as I wrote the pages that follow. Indeed, he sits at his own desk a few feet away as I write these very sentences, unaware of my efforts to find words to express my gratitude. But he knows. I dedicate this book to the people who make up this paragraph. It takes a family.

Muslims and Jews
in France

Introduction

In autumn 2000, Muslim-Jewish relations in France captured national attention following a dramatic spike in anti-Jewish violence. Largely the work of Muslim youth from the country's most disadvantaged sectors, the violence raised alarms over rising antisemitism and emerging ethno-religious conflict in France. Periodic moments of dramatic bloodshed such as the 2006 torture and murder of twenty-three-year-old Ilan Halimi, and Mohammed Merah's March 2012 shooting of a rabbi and three children at Ozar Hatorah, a Jewish school in Toulouse, have kept such fears alive, while studies of increasing French Jewish intolerance toward "Arabs" suggest that relations between France's two largest ethno-religious minorities have been forever damaged.[1]

Explanations for the discord have ranged widely. According to some, anti-Jewish attacks have been encouraged by the media's "methodical stigmatization" of Israel and an intensifying anti-Jewish bias in France.[2] Most others, however, have focused on a timeless Muslim Judophobia rooted in the conflict between Islam and Judaism, a ubiquitous European antisemitism that has penetrated Arab culture, or the combustible fusion of radical Islam and anti-Zionism.[3] For still others, the conflict is entirely contemporary: either a by-product of the Arab-Israeli conflict or an expression of the frustrations of disenfranchised French Muslim youth and an increasingly ethnically enclosed Jewish minority.[4] While often diametrically and even angrily opposed to one another, the overall tone of all these analyses is that Muslims and Jews in France are on an explosive collision course.[5]

I envisioned this book as a challenge to that assumption. Polarization, I believed, was a gross simplification of the much richer and more varied range of Muslim-Jewish relations in France. I therefore began my research most drawn to the cultural and historical connections linking these two populations, of which there are many. Indeed, France houses the largest Jewish and Muslim populations living side by side outside of Israel (current estimates number 4,000,000–6,000,000 Muslims and 500,000–600,000 Jews), thanks to the many in both communities who left North Africa following decolonization.[6] Sharing certain linguistic and cultural traditions and a common experience of displacement, these newcomers also experienced similar pressures to assimilate while also often feeling rejected by the nation seeking to integrate them.[7] These multifaceted cultural, linguistic, residential, and historical connections meant that

Muslim-Jewish relations in France were never defined solely as a bitter war over Palestine and Israel, Islam and Judaism, or any other set of binary divisions.

Conflict, nevertheless, dominates the archival record of Muslim-Jewish relations in postwar France. Indeed even if such relations have been multiple and variegated, it was the episodic interethnic political disagreements—whether over French policies in the Middle East and North Africa or over domestic issues related to minority integration in France—that most often caught the attention of a diverse range of social actors, including international Jewish representatives, anti-Zionist Algerian nationalists, French police, Jewish student activists, and second generation Muslim anti-racist organizers. In following these sources, this book thus evolved from a straightforward challenge to narratives of Jewish-Muslim conflict into an examination of how such narratives emerged and in time helped produce the very conflicts they purported to recount.

The result is a study of the evolution and political meaning of conflict. It traces the process through which "Jew" and "Muslim" became political symbols, even as actual Jews and Muslims rarely clashed. Indeed, the very terms "Jew" and "Muslim" hide as much as they reveal, because they cluster various national and ethnic origins under broad religious categories that imply homogeneity and communal identifications in place of the profound heterogeneity that characterizes each population. As I argue throughout these pages, however, heterogeneity is largely irrelevant to the hardening of the political binary *Muslim-Jewish*. Beginning with the birth of Israel and North African anti-colonial warfare and continuing through the failed efforts of the 1980s anti-racist campaigns to bridge ethno-political divisions between activists in France, episodic moments of Muslim-Jewish conflict cemented a narrative of polarization.[8] This book asks why this narrative has proven so powerful and enduring.

Central to this account is France. While global developments, particularly in the Middle East, created fault lines around which activists began to mobilize, the nature of this mobilization (i.e., who was involved), the political rhetoric employed, and the success or lack thereof of their appeal emerged from French political transformations—especially the decolonization of North Africa, the 1968 student uprisings, and the 1980s experiments in multiculturalism. Moreover, the impact of Middle Eastern war was never straightforward. As one relocated Algerian Jew told a researcher in the early 1990s, "When we say 'the Arabs,' I feel hatred, but those are Middle Eastern Arabs. I am not talking about the Arabs who live [in France], because they don't do us any harm. They work, they earn their living, they have children and families like us, *à la française*. That's fine. If we could live together and get on well as we used to back there, it would be perfect. But the problem in Israel is still not solved. So since I've known the Israeli problem, I am anti-Arab, but not against the Arabs of France."[9] As such a remark suggests, focusing *solely* on the Middle East in an effort to understand Muslim-Jewish politics in France misses key aspects of the story.[10] The goal here, then, is not to remove the Middle East from the equation; indeed, the repercussions of conflict between Israel and its neighbors will be a central analytic thread throughout. Rather I will underscore the way global dynamics, both in the Middle East and in French North Africa, *came together* with national and even local factors to shape Muslim-Jewish relations in postcolonial France.

This focus on the postcolonial is far from incidental. From the standpoint of demography alone, decolonization was monumental in the historical trajectories of France's Muslim and Jewish populations.[11] Not only were one million French citizens "repatriated" as a direct outcome of the violence (including many Muslims and Jews), but the dramatic growth of the metropolitan economy meant tens of thousands of former colonial subjects also came to France as immigrants.[12] While Algerian Muslims had begun arriving in the early nineteenth century, their numbers grew from 130,000 in 1930 to over 600,000 by 1965 in a "veritable hemorrhaging of Algeria to France."[13] By 1982 the number had grown to more than 800,000, while Moroccan and Tunisian Muslim populations had grown to 440,000 and 190,000, respectively.[14] Jewish immigration brought 240,000 new arrivals to France between 1944 and 1979, more than half from Algeria and the rest from Morocco and Tunisia.[15] These newcomers more than doubled France's Jewish population, forever transforming its socioeconomic, cultural, political and religious contours and creating new and visible subgroups within a population primarily made up of those with roots in France since before the French Revolution and those who had migrated from war-torn Eastern Europe.[16]

While similar origins and settlement patterns at times forged bonds between different kinds of migrants from North Africa, the juridical and social inequities embedded in French colonization policies and the vastly different levels of Muslim and Jewish communal development in the metropole created sharply divergent integration processes.[17] Beginning with the invasion of Algeria in 1830, colonial administrators, scholars, and legislators constructed categories for understanding North African society that emphasized regional, ethnic, religious, social, and economic divisions over indigenous unity.[18] Jews, in these constructions, were often held to be more intelligent and "assimilable" than the Muslims among who they lived. In Algeria, where such thinking took legal form, the 1870 Crémieux Decree granted French citizenship to all Algerian Jews, juridically cutting them off from most Algerian Muslim subjects.[19] In Tunisia and Morocco, which remained nominally under Muslim control throughout the colonial period, no mass naturalizations occurred. Nevertheless, the "Frenchification" of local Jewish populations took place through more informal administrative practices and the schools of the *Alliance israélite universelle*, meaning Jews had greater opportunities to acculturate to European social and cultural norms than the Muslim populations amidst which they lived, and this contributed to the formation of new social hierarchies.[20] Although the post–World War II French government granted citizenship to Algerian Muslims in an effort to diminish support for the growing independence struggle, those in France continued to face systematic discrimination, particularly after 1954 when the outbreak of FLN (Front de libération nationale) armed protest transformed Algerian Muslims into "the central and even unique symbol of 'the enemy within.'"[21] France's decision to recognize the French citizenship of Jewish Algerians in the war's final negotiations at the very moment when Muslim Algerian French citizens were permanently excluded enfolded Jews into the wider "European" family.[22] Jews fleeing newly independent Algeria thus benefited from all the subsidies and aid available to repatriating citizens, while Muslims from Morocco, Tunisia, and particularly Algeria faced administrative structures that distinguished them from other incoming migrants.[23] For example, while most arriving Tunisian and Moroccan Jews did not share the benefits of citizenship like their Algerian co-religionists, they reported that authorities "bent over backward" to help them obtain French nationality while doing nothing to aid Muslim newcomers.[24]

These inequities had profound economic, cultural, and political consequences in 1960s France, among which were sharply divergent processes of Muslim-Jewish integration. Arriving Jews thus joined a long-rooted French Jewish community, which although deeply undermined by Vichy legislation during World War II, had been engaged by the mid-1950s in a decade-long rebuilding process that had given rise to a highly developed communal infrastructure.[25] While encounters between incoming Jews and those already settled in France were never smooth, the new arrivals benefited from institutional structures geared to facilitating their integration and a communal leadership determined to defend Jewish interests, particularly when Jewish lives were understood to be endangered.[26] Arriving Muslims not only had no equivalent infrastructure in place, but also the organizations that sought to speak for them were profoundly distrusted by French authorities as sources of political instability.[27]

The combined impact of this asymmetrical integration and communal development process was that compared to their Muslim counterparts, French Jewish spokesmen had a far more developed apparatus with which to articulate a group politics and greater access to national and local officials for promoting the causes important to them. Thus while this book seeks to trace Muslim-Jewish political exchange, it does not proceed as an equal tale of two halves. The divergent histories of Muslims and Jews in France's colonial project and the more integrated position of Jews in the metropole necessarily gave the organized French Jewish community more opportunities to shape public discourse and greater access to the hallways of power. In addition, they cast a longer shadow, leaving a larger body of French language sources behind. Indeed, if many of the Jews and Muslims under study spoke Arabic, the public sphere in which they interacted was conducted primarily in French—another arena in which Jews were better schooled.[28]

We should be careful, however, not to assume that the relative ease of Jewish integration into post–World War II France meant they could dictate the terms of that integration. Although by the early twenty-first century, Jews proved more economically mobile, better educated, and professionally better placed than the general population and certainly than French Muslims, the organized community was often criticized for failing to defend Jewish interests successfully (however they were defined in a given moment), particularly with regard to foreign policy around Israel.[29] Dramatic moments of anti-Jewish hostility, such as the October 1980 explosion at the rue Copernic synagogue or the May 1990 desecration of the Jewish cemetery in Carpentras were also raw reminders of Jewish leaders' ongoing inability to use their social capital to end violence and bigotry against them. Moreover, whatever the asymmetry between the stature of Jewish and Muslim spokesmen, respectively, the latter were neither passive nor without political agency, also seeking to influence political culture in France on matters of concern to themselves and their Jewish interlocutors.

The following pages, then, explain when and why certain voices predominated over others and how the combined result created a political landscape so often understood as inevitably polarized. Each of the six main chapters addresses a moment in which Muslim-Jewish conflict became a matter of concern whether to French police charged with maintaining social order, to media sources, or to a wide array of self-appointed communal spokesmen. Beginning in 1948 when war in the Middle East caused minor unrest in the city of Marseille, chapter 1 traces the way in which disagreements over Israel became a way to debate inequities in French minority policies at home and in North Africa. Chapter 2 builds on the link between French colonial policies and Muslim-Jewish relations in the metropole by tracing how decolonization throughout North Africa changed the way a diverse set of social actors, including French colonial administrators, international Jewish spokesmen, and a wide range of indigenous nationalist groups conceptualized Jewish belonging throughout the region. The process, I argue, led to the emergence of the "North African Jew," a category to which no individual ascribed but that worked rhetorically to unite the diverse Moroccan, Tunisian, and Algerian Jewish populations into a collective often understood to be in conflict with "North Africans," "Muslims," or "Arabs." Chapter 3 then examines how these new ways of conceptualizing Muslim-Jewish interactions, and the longer term inequities built into French colonial and minority polices, shaped integration into the metropole in the late 1950s and early 1960s.

In these chapters, and in those that follow on the impact of the 1967 Arab-Israeli War, the 1968 student uprisings in France, and the effort to establish a multiethnic anti-racist campaign in 1980s France, I look closely at the way

Muslim-Jewish conflict unfolded—who participated and why—and I examine how rather isolated episodes of conflict created new binary frameworks often despite the intentions of those involved. Chapter 4 thus considers the impact in France of the 1967 Arab-Israeli War showing that while conflict between France's large Muslim and Jewish populations was, in fact, quite rare, the story of two polarized ethno-religious political units hardened as new political actors, particularly university students, began to use the French campus as a space in which to engage matters of foreign policy. Student uprisings in France in 1968, the subject of chapter 5, then brought the story of Muslim-Jewish polarization to France's national conversation as student radicals began to link the occupation of Palestinian territories evermore fully to leftist politics at home. While many Jewish and Muslim leftists worked together in these endeavors, highly visible moments of discord, such as a riot in the Parisian immigrant neighborhood of Belleville in June 1968 and ongoing conflictual encounters between Muslim and Jewish university students, continued to fuel perceptions of polarization. Indeed, paradoxically, even those who emphasized the cultural connections and shared histories binding Muslims and Jews contributed to this process, since in seeking to counter more polarizing rhetoric, they unwittingly legitimized the boundaries of political discourse as it was taking shape: to deny Muslim-Jewish polarization was to acknowledge the problem, thereby reinforcing the very categories they were seeking to dismantle.

It was not until the 1980s, however, when a new generation of Muslim and Jewish French nationals came of age, that polarization emerged as the central motif for understanding Muslim-Jewish relations. During that decade, a surge of anti-minority violence gave rise to large and widely celebrated anti-racist campaigns that brought Muslim and Jewish youth together in a common struggle. Born in the period following François Mitterand's 1981 election to the presidency on a pro–immigrant rights and decentralization platform, the anti-racist coalition took advantage of the political establishment's unprecedented willingness to recognize the nation's cultural and linguistic diversity. Within a few years, however, growing electoral support for Jean Marie Le Pen's anti-immigrant and nationalist political agenda and a mounting fear of international terrorism meant that officials from across the political spectrum began adopting a more conservative discourse toward religious and cultural difference. "Integration" rather than the "right to be different" once again became the watchword of the day.[30] This mounting conservatism, while mostly directed at France's Muslim population, could conflate the nation's religious minorities,[31] and some Jewish figures began backing away from public connections to Muslims.[32] Meanwhile, some Muslim activists, who had seen value in underscoring a common anti-racist agenda, began reasserting the particular nature of their own community's struggle.

By decade's end, the much-celebrated efforts at cross-ethnic cooperation had given way to distrust and bitterness; interethnic conflict was henceforth presumed. During the 1991 Gulf War, for example, journalists, government officials, and religious leaders predicted widespread Muslim-Jewish conflict in response to unfolding events in the Middle East. The fact that such fears never materialized is one of the paradoxes at the heart of this book. Indeed, whatever their links to the Middle East (and such ties were never homogeneous or frozen in time), Muslims and Jews related to each other *also* as former residents of French North Africa, immigrants competing for limited resources, employers and employees, victims of racist aggression, religious minorities in a secularizing state, and citizens. These multiple and complex interactions were often lost, however, as a narrative of polarization took root, thereby helping to erase them.

The Dilemmas of Terminology

Writing of "Muslims" and "Jews" creates two distinct but overlapping problems for the historian. First, these terms risk collapsing significant diversity under essentializing labels, and second, they seemingly privilege ethno-religious over ethno-political categories of analysis. I will address each of these problems in turn.

As the wide-ranging scholarship on Jews and Muslims in France has made clear, neither population formed an organized or homogeneous body in ethnic, national, religious, social, economic, or political terms. The post–World War II Jewish population included citizens with roots in France prior to the French Revolution as well as large numbers of immigrants or newly minted citizens from Central and Eastern Europe, North Africa, and the Levant. Although a handful of important organizations claimed to speak for all French Jews, the population held a wide range of views on national minority policies, war in the Middle East, racism in France, religious practice, and everything else.[33] Nor was France's Muslim population any more unified, made up as it was of migrants from Algeria, Tunisia, Morocco, Egypt, West Africa, Syria, and Lebanon.[34] In the 1990s, sub-Saharan African, Bosnian, and Central Asian Muslims also came to France.[35] Not surprisingly in a migration this large and spanning numerous decades, national, religious, ethnic, cultural and socioeconomic diversity was the rule.[36]

If recent work has stressed this heterogeneity, however, it has also underscored a certain "community of experience."[37] In the words of Jonathan Laurence and Justin Vaïsse: "Despite their ethnic and national diversity, what Muslims in France increasingly do have in common is their 'lived experience,' which includes the bitterness of exclusion as well as successful efforts to integrate."[38] Scholarship on French Jews has also begun emphasizing bridges linking the diverse Jewish collective. Dominique Schnapper, Chantal Bordes-Benayoun, and Freddy Raphaël, for example, have stressed a social homogenization process from the 1970s to the 1990s. While refusing to use the language of "community," given ongoing French discomfort with recognizing ethno-religious political groupings, they stress how shared experiences of democratic life and economic homogenization have diminished prior differences among Jews.[39]

The existence of communities of experience reminds us that overarching terms like "Jew" or "Muslim" reflect a certain—if partial—lived reality. Moreover, despite the constructed nature of collectives based around these terms and the fact that some who might be considered Jews or Muslims would object to being classified primarily as such, we should not deny their power to shape historical outcomes. As Joyce Dalsheim argues,

> [T]he ways in which we order, divide, and categorize our socio-political world are not innocent. . . . These divisions have very real outcomes, including the constitution of categories of identity, religion, and politics, the delimitation of the contours of action and debate in the present, and the construction of boundaries within which we might imagine possible futures. The narratives that emerge through these divisions become familiar to us, taking the form of common knowledge upon which we base our judgments and take action in the world.[40]

To site but one example of this process: According to Naomi Davidson, beginning in the early twentieth century, French politicians, colonial administrators, intellectuals, and urban planners elaborated a notion of "*Islam français*" that functioned as an essential and eternal marker of difference in French society. While Islam français posited certain compatibilities between French secular republicanism and Islam, it also articulated a "reductionist, totalizing religio-cultural category 'Muslim'" that served to racialize religious difference. Nor was this articulation of an Islam français simply a discursive move, as it became the primary administrative medium through which the French state interacted with Muslim residents in the metropole.[41] This process gathered steam with the decolonization of Algeria. As Todd Shepard has shown, French juridical and bureaucratic practices at the end of the Algerian War of Independence divided "Muslims" from "Europeans," as eight million of the former were stripped of their French citizenship and several hundred thousand non-Muslims—many of whom had never lived in Europe—were claimed as "French."[42] The media then reified these divisions.

As such scholarship has made clear, socially constructed categories had legal, administrative, and cultural implications for those categorized as "Muslims" whether they embraced the label or not. Likewise, if post–World War II

French authorities rejected Vichy legal distinctions, "Jews" never disappeared into a neutral public sphere. Indeed, governmental archives abound with references to "Jews" and the "Jewish community," and self-appointed spokesmen and media outlets repeatedly confirmed the boundaries of such a collective regardless of individual ascription. The categories "Muslim" and "Jew" thus had social meaning for those inside and outside of the "communities" collapsed therein. Muslim-Jewish political conflict evolved in and helped define this discursive space. Assertions of polarization—whatever the reality on the ground— helped legitimate social understandings of group belonging. To understand the evolution of polarization, therefore, is also to understand the way categories calcify, obscuring and flattening the social complexity therein.

Recognition of calcifying political categories raises the second dilemma that the terms "Jew" and "Muslim" create for the historian. As scholarship on both has made clear, the meaning of these terms has changed over time as understandings of the groups they represent have shifted. French Jews were thus known as "*israélites*" from the time of the French Revolution until the middle of the twentieth century, a construction that emphasized Jewish religious affiliations over ethnic or racial identifications so as not to challenge categories of belonging within the French nation. Nazi and Vichy racializing practices coupled with the nationalizing claims of the Zionist movement challenged such constructions of Jewishness. By the mid-twentieth century, the term "*juif*" had replaced "*israélite*" in spoken French and even for most French Jews, who, while rejecting Nazi racial categories, nevertheless emerged from World War II with a reinvigorated sense of ethnic identification.[43]

The term "*musulman*" has had a similarly complex history in France. Indeed, despite the emerging historiographical consensus that the category "Muslim" has been more powerful in colonial and post-colonial French history than previously recognized, it is also true that until the 1970s, French authorities often used the terms "*Musulmans*," "*Algériens*," "*Nord-Africains*," "*Arabes*," "*Musulmanes nord-africains*," and "*indigènes*" interchangeably, a lexical confusion that reflected colonial conflations of geographic, religious, ethnic, and legal categories.[44] In the sources upon which this book is drawn, and particularly those from the 1940s through the 1970s, Algerian, Moroccan, and Tunisian Muslim migrants in France were most typically—although never exclusively—referred to as "*Arabes*," a category that at least some adopted for themselves as part of wider political struggles that sought to link Muslim North Africans with Arab national liberation struggles.[45] It was only in the late 1970s, after the Iranian Revolution spurred fears of spreading Muslim fundamentalism and as French society became increasingly aware of a generation of French-born children of North African immigrants living on the edges of national, social, and cultural life, that media outlets and the wider public began to speak more consistently of musulmans.[46]

Despite this relatively recent development, I have opted to use the term "Muslim" even when analyzing citations that refer directly to Arabes, Nord Africaines, or Algériens. This choice should not be understood to imply that for the migrants themselves religion was more important than ethnic, racial, or national identification, nor does it suggest that theology lay at the heart of evolving Muslim-Jewish relations.[47] Rather, the term works to distinguish Algerian, Tunisian, and Moroccan Muslim migrants from Jews and Christians coming from the same regions (since all were, in fact, Algerians, Tunisians, or Moroccans) and is preferable to the term "Arab," which not only glosses over the varying national and ethnic origins of the migrants collapsed therein but also reflects assumptions about their political allegiances and foreign status that this book seeks to challenge. Put differently, whatever the limitations of the term "Muslim," it shifts the focus away from the Israeli-Palestinian conflict and re-centers our gaze on France, the context in which this term has come to stand in for at least two generations of French-born citizens pushed to the national margins.

Geography and Politics: Harmony and Conflict in One French City

To tell a French story is often to tell a Parisian story, and this book is no exception. Not only does the highly centralized nature of state bureaucracy and cultural production in France focus attention on the nation's capital, but Paris houses the country's largest Muslim and Jewish populations and their most visible institutional structures. Insofar as there have been signs of Muslim-Jewish conflict, they have often been in Parisian immigrant neighborhoods, whether in Belleville in 1968 and 1973 or Sarcelles in 2000. Anti-racist demonstrations have famously ended their marches at the Place de la République and the Place de la Bastille.

If Paris stands at the heart of this study, however, it is in a second French city where de-colonization and Middle Eastern war had their most profound impact. As France's largest port and its gateway to the Mediterranean, Marseille had a front-row seat to the various crises in North Africa and the Middle East. French soldiers departed from this city for Algeria, tanks and guns were shipped to Israel from her ports, "repatriates" fleeing newly emerging independent North African states sought refuge in her neighborhoods, and colonial soldiers and laborers all poured into Marseille in search of exit or work, respectively. While most departed again, the city's identity as a center of transit profoundly marked its political, social, and cultural development and shaped the way Muslims and Jews interacted therein.

Decolonization was particularly unsettling for Marseille. Not only did the city serve as the main arrival point for most of the 1.5 million "returning" French nationals from 1954 to 1964, but its population also grew from 650,000 to 900,000 by 1975 (a 40 percent increase).[48] Although Marseille had attracted large numbers of immigrants before (nearly one quarter of the city's population before diminishing significantly during World War II), those arriving in tandem with France's withdrawal from North Africa transported shared cultural memories of trauma and rupture with them to their new city. Approximately 100,000 French Algerian settlers (*pieds-noirs*) shared the space with large numbers of mostly Algerian Muslim immigrants also fleeing economic and political upheaval, whose numbers grew from 10,000 in 1949 to 35,860 in 1968, and 50,000 by 1974.[49]

The Jewish population also grew dramatically. With a surviving remnant of 4,000–5,000 at the end of World War II, migrations from Egypt, Tunisia, Morocco, and Algeria brought the Jewish population to between 12,000 and 15,000 by 1955.[50] In 1962, with the full-scale Jewish flight from Algeria, the numbers soared, reaching approximately 65,000 by the 1970s, the largest Jewish population in France after Paris.[51]

The encounter between Muslims and Jews in Marseille reflected the specificities of this ethnically heterogeneous postwar urban landscape. Three factors in particular made Marseille distinctive. The first was the port, which as the city's major economic engine, served as a highly visible indication of France's link to the Mediterranean. Carrying migrants, arms, and soldiers to and from the city center, Marseille's port created sites of conflict for those with vested interest in French actions in the Middle East and North Africa.[52]

Second was the visible diversity of Marseille's landscape in a period when other French cities were directing immigrant laborers to the urban periphery.[53] Like all French cities, Marseille experienced an acute postwar housing crisis that posed problems for settling tens of thousands of incoming migrants. Most were pushed into the most squalid residential quarters near the city's industrial and harbor districts (14th, 15th, and 16th *arrondissements*) and in the industrial suburbs (9th arrondissement). Built out of planks and corrugated iron and without electricity, running water, or adequate transport, these slums (*bidonvilles*) were a world apart from Marseille's urban core.[54] Unlike other French cities where a similar process took place, however, downtown Marseille also saw new arrivals move into the overcrowded unventilated apartments in the 1st and 2nd arrondissements. Centrally located between the Old Port and the main train station, these immigrant neighborhoods abutted the Hôtel de Ville (city hall), the Bourse (chamber of commerce and industry), and the Canebière, the city's main commercial district. Symbolically cutting the city's northern industrial sectors from its middle-class and upper-middle-class neighborhoods to the south, the Old Port was the heart of commercial Marseille.[55] No matter where one lived in the city, all residents spent time in or passed through this area regularly, bringing the city's mixed ethnic life into public view and giving it a cosmopolitan flavor.[56]

These mixed neighborhoods—marked by an immigrant-centered commercial culture—provided opportunities for Muslim-Jewish interactions. If by 1975, Muslim immigrants made up 35 percent of the population of the Belsunce area, for example, numerous Jews conducted business in the neighborhood's commercial streets, and Jewish merchants—particularly jewelers—continued to populate the rue d'Aix and the neighboring markets on the rue Sainte Barbe.[57] While such neighborhoods were not unique to Marseille (Belleville, in Paris, for example, was similarly integrated),[58] the acute nature of the housing crisis meant that incoming repatriates and immigrants often lived for years in the same areas. As one anthropologist described the neighborhood around the porte d'Aix in 1972: "Jews, Arabs, Blacks, Italians, French of modest means . . . all live together. It's their complementarity that permeates the area."[59] Although wealthier repatriates—Jews among them—moved out as soon as was economically feasible, ethnic intermingling continued to mark Marseille's urban development, as those remaining in the commercial districts continued to work in a sophisticated economic trading zone that linked the central port regions of the city with secondary markets in other parts of the city.[60]

The third factor that made Marseille distinct was its relatively stable political landscape. Dominated by one figure, Marseille's postwar political life was linked directly with socialist Gaston Defferre. Mayor for thirty-three years (1944–45; 1953–86), Defferre controlled the city's political establishment, the local socialist party, and the major center-left newspaper Le Provençal (which he co-founded following the Liberation). Nationally visible due to his long-standing participation in the National Assembly (1945–58, 1962–86), Senate (1959–62), ministerial positions, and bid for the presidency, Defferre maintained unchallenged control over Marseille's political establishment, a position he used to confront national political figures when it suited him. Defferre felt particularly strongly about Israel. A vocal advocate for the young state, he used his position to speak out in its defense and worked closely with the local Jewish leadership to create links between Marseille and Israel. When war broke out in the Middle East in 1967 and 1973, much of Marseille's response as well as the way Muslim-Jewish relations unfolded were a product of the climate he created.

Due to the three factors described above, Muslim-Jewish relations in Marseille were clearly distinct from that in other French cities. The focus on the southern port city, however, serves more than as a counterpoint to generalizations derived from Paris, because Marseille can be understood as the space in which all the major factors influencing Muslim-Jewish conflict in France—decolonization, Middle Eastern politics, and French minority politics—came together in their most combustible form. As such, it serves less as a case study and more as the physical meeting point of all this book's central themes. And yet, despite its potentially explosive interethnic landscape, Muslims and Jews in Marseille also have a history of harmonious and even convivial exchange. As one Jewish cab driver remarked to a journalist in 2005, "I'm a Jew, my neighbors, they're Arabs, we understand each other fine."[61] Although the city experienced some of the most heightened fears of polarization during the 1991 Gulf War, widespread conflict did not break out; likewise in the post-2000 period when Muslim-Jewish relations garnered so much popular attention in France, relations in Marseille remained largely calm. A focus on Marseille thus captures the way fears of growing Muslim-Jewish conflict could take on a life of their own, divorced from the more variegated social landscape.

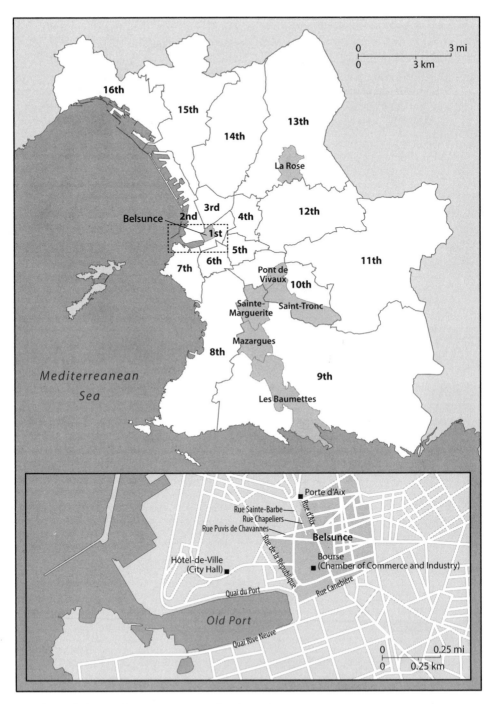

City of Marseille by arrondissement. Inset: 1st and 2nd arrondissements.

1

Colonial Policies, Middle Eastern War, and City Spaces

Marseille in 1948

In June 1948, North African Muslim dockworkers in Marseille refused to load freight onto boats transporting Jews or arms to the Middle East. As one official reported, "They consider Marseille to be one of the principle supply bases for the state of Israel."[1] Others complained that complaisant French officials were turning a blind eye to the thousands of Jewish migrants traveling through the city en route to Israel who, upon arrival, sent their passports to their co-religionists in Morocco and Tunisia for re-use.[2]

As such comments suggest, the 1948 war over the declaration of Israeli independence had repercussions in France. The war coincided with the growth of North African anti-colonial movements in the metropole, which at times criticized British and Jewish control of Palestine as a symbol of wider European efforts to dominate the Arab world, and the growth of Jewish nationalism in the aftermath of the Holocaust. These elements gave the struggle between Israel and her neighbors a powerful local resonance. Interestingly, however, while Paris held much larger Muslim and Jewish populations, that city saw few of the tensions evident in Marseille in the same period. Rather, animosities in Marseille were linked to charged city spaces and specific sites associated with Jewish migration, including the port and transit camps that housed large numbers of refugees en route to Palestine. The former gave the distant war a local immediacy; the latter highlighted contradictions in French policies toward its Jewish and Muslim populations. Indeed, a focus on these tumultuous months in Marseille makes clear the degree to which local clashes over Palestine were as much about wider questions related to French minority policies at home and in North Africa as they were about war in the Middle East. Put differently, for the demonstrating dockworkers cited above, France's willingness to condone the passage of Jewish people and arms through its port became part of a criticism of France's relationship to its Muslim subjects and citizens writ large and of the inequalities built into French colonial policies. That criticism was about Israel and Palestine to be sure, but it was also, in equal measure, about France.

As France's largest port and its gateway to the Mediterranean, Marseille saw a significant transient population of twenty thousand Jews travel through the city between March 1946 and May 1948 en route to Palestine.[3] To facilitate the migration, Jewish welfare and Zionist organizations established local offices, transforming Marseille into one of the most vibrant and politicized Jewish institutional landscapes in postwar Europe. The same period saw anti-colonial activities expand in the city as well, as approximately ten thousand Algerian Muslims took advantage of migration reforms to settle in the area.[4] Promised the same rights as all French citizens by the law of 20 September 1947, these impoverished, mostly male laborers nevertheless suffered from discrimination and heavy police surveillance.[5] In response, Marseille saw the establishment of several Algerian nationalist organizations, some of which promoted pan-Arab and pro-Palestinian causes as part of their wider anti-colonial agenda.[6]

Animosities in Marseille in spring 1948 emerged from the combustible encounter between these Jewish and pan-Arab nationalists over who would be victorious in Palestine. Equally divisive, however, was the way *French* policies in the Middle East seemed to favor one minority over the other. Disagreements among policymakers marked French approaches to the Palestine issue, reflecting fears of spreading pan-Arab nationalism, on the one hand, and postwar discomfort over further limiting Jewish movement, on the other.[7] The Ministry of Foreign Affairs, anxious to keep North Africa stable in the face of mounting Arab nationalism, saw Palestine as a tinderbox capable of exploding in unpredictable ways.[8] In the words of one official: "One cannot forget that there is no Jewish problem in France; [however] a Muslim problem is emerging which does not allow us to participate in a settlement to the feud that . . . violently antagonizes the Arab states. It is to be feared that once the Palestinian affair is settled, the Arab League will turn its attention toward 'the Liberation of their North African brothers.'"[9] The irony that a "Muslim problem" had so rapidly erased France's "Jewish problem" seems to have escaped notice; clearly, however, concern that Arab nationalism could spread to North Africa and endanger French rule encouraged some authorities to prioritize appeasement of Muslim subjects and citizens over their Jewish counterparts.

Such an outlook meant that despite sympathy for Jewish victims of Nazism, North African policymakers cautioned against allowing migration to Palestine, which, it was feared, would galvanize Arab nationalism throughout the Maghreb.[10] As one official wrote in 1947, "One cannot underestimate the disadvantages, notably in North Africa, of being on poor terms with England on the one hand and with the Arab countries on the other regarding the Palestinian matter."[11] Such thinking caused considerable French equivocation around the November 1947 United Nations partition plan for Palestine, as the government first supported and then withdrew support for the plan.[12] Likewise, authorities held off for nearly a year before granting Israel recognition after its declaration the following May, in part due to warnings from the major Tunisian, Moroccan, and Algerian nationalist movements, Neo Destour, Istiqlal, and the MTLD, over France's pro-Zionist and anti-Arab policies.[13]

Yet if those foreign ministry officials focused on North Africa were worried about the impact of supporting Zionist aims in Palestine, not all French policymakers shared such perspectives. Many in the government, particularly those in the Ministry of the Interior, were sympathetic toward the plight of Jewish survivors, disgruntled with British efforts to oust France from the Middle East, and committed to a political liberalism that mandated tolerance for Zionism.[14] Such beliefs, as well as a concern that North African Jewish migrants might come to France if Israel was forbidden, encouraged many to turn a blind eye to refugee movements. As a result, thousands of illegal Jewish refugees traveled though French ports between 1946 and 1948, mostly through Marseille.[15] This choice transformed Jewish outmigration into a symbol of French duplicity and a source of considerable bitterness in North Africa.[16] Algerian Muslim spokesmen thus complained to diplomatic officials over French complicity in migration schemes, and French officials recorded significant discontent in Morocco over the same issue.[17]

In Marseille, the gathering point for Jewish clandestine migration to Palestine, such anger was compounded by frustrations that French officials seemed to be favoring Jewish refugees over newly minted French Algerian Muslim citizens. Conflicts around war in the Middle East thus became an opportunity for politically active Muslims and Jews to negotiate their relationship with the French state, as the former established new parameters for political participation in the aftermath of the Holocaust by pushing the French government to support Israel, and the latter tested the limitations on a citizenship that never made good on its promises.

Palestine and Postwar Muslim-Jewish Politics in France

Before turning to clashes in Marseille related to the 1948 war in the Middle East, it is important to understand the relatively circumscribed ways in which the Palestine issue shaped interethnic relations elsewhere in France both prior to and during the 1948 war. While the burgeoning Algerian Muslim nationalist movement in France, and certain segments from within the Jewish population, particularly newly arriving immigrants from Eastern Europe, displayed growing interest in their co-religionists in the Middle East well before World War II, clashes between them were rare given the relatively restrained public activism in both populations and their limited contact with each other. As in Marseille, however, when conflicts *did* emerge, they were often entangled in wider questions related to French minority policies at home and in North Africa. Put differently, disagreements over Palestine were rarely ever *only* about Palestine. Rather, such conflicts became one way that Muslim and Jewish nationalists negotiated their relationship with the wider polity in a period when both Jews and Algerian Muslim residents were experiencing radical changes in their political status.

By the late 1930s, France's Jewish population numbered 300,000, and was made up largely of Eastern European immigrant families and French-born Jewish citizens.[18] The Muslim population, which had begun growing significantly during World War I, hitting a peak of nearly 140,000 in 1937, was comprised largely of young seasonal workers from Algeria.[19] Differing in culture, language, place of origin, and status in the polity, members of the two populations had little contact with one another. Moreover, those Muslims and Jews who did interact regularly had far more that united than divided them. Indeed, among the 150,000 Jewish immigrants who came to France before and after World War I were 35,000 Jews from North Africa and the Levant.[20] Having more in common with other North Africans than with East European or French Jews, these new arrivals often lived in similar neighborhoods as incoming Muslims, where cafes, stores, kosher butcher shops (Muslims sometimes purchased ritually slaughtered meat), and markets brought together those with a common North African background.

Insofar as Palestine *did* emerge as a source of interethnic tensions, it was often entangled with the wider issues of French colonial and minority policies, in which both Muslims and Jews had a significant stake in the tumultuous period preceding and following World War II.[21] As Ethan Katz has recently shown, the contours of Muslim-Jewish relations in France were established in these years.[22] World War I, which brought colonial soldiers and laborers to the metropole in unprecedented numbers and which forever changed the European and Middle Eastern landscape, introduced new debates on the future of Palestine, French colonial policies, and the status of immigrants, establishing the parameters of Muslim-Jewish interactions in France for the next several decades. The interwar growth of both populations, coupled with debates over fascism, mounting xenophobia, and the emerging Algerian crisis, ensured that such interactions could be charged.

World War II radically transformed the hierarchies that had previously shaped the parameters of interethnic relations. French Jews were stripped of a wide range of rights, as Nazi officials sought to win Muslim allegiances with promises of increased autonomy and possible independence. For colonial subjects seeking to better their sociocultural status, the new racialized discourse provided one way to curry favor with the authorities, and helps explain the marked hostility toward Jews that emerged from France's Muslim population even as some helped Jewish friends and neighbors to hide. With the return of republican rule, however, and the abolition of Vichy's antisemitic policies, Jews returned to their former status in the polity while North African Muslim struggles for political recognition began to intensify.[23] General de Gaulle's decision to sign the Roosevelt-Churchill Atlantic Charter in September 1942

committed France in principle to the right of self-determination, giving politically active Muslim nationalists hope that once the war was over, France would
be forced to make concessions with regard to its colonial holdings. For the
leaders of the Provisional Government and the IVth Republic, however, maintaining France's colonial territories was essential to reestablishing the nation's
strength and vitality. Rather than dismantling the empire, therefore, political
leaders instituted a series of reforms that reaffirmed France's commitment to
colonial rule while removing some of its worst political abuses.[24] Beginning
with the ordinance of 7 March 1944 that abolished special penal statutes for
Muslim subjects and offered citizenship to those who met certain criteria
and gave up their rights to native or Muslim courts (about sixty thousand),
subsequent statutes and ordinances, particularly that of 20 September 1947,
broadened voting rights, extended citizenship to all Algerian Muslims, and
dismantled travel restrictions between France and Algeria, opening the door
to significant emigration.[25] The post-1944 reforms promised more rights than
were granted, however, establishing unequal political representation for Algerian Muslim citizens. Moreover, legislative transformations did little to change
practices of exclusion either in Algeria or in the metropole.[26] Violent repression
of a mounting nationalist momentum in Algeria, most notably in the 8 March
1945 massacre at Sétif, proved an additional reminder that Algerian Muslim
citizens were citizens of a different order.

Given the tremendous disruptions of the war and the concomitant transformations in political status, most Jews and Muslims had far more to worry
about in the years immediately following World War II than developments in
Palestine. Among Jews, support for Zionism had certainly grown after an initial period of profound wariness at the end of the nineteenth century, while
Muslims too saw a growing interest in Palestine among key sectors of the
pro-independence movements. A primary focus on the struggle for national
independence, however, kept Muslim attentions focused elsewhere, while
Jews—traditionally reticent to voice a visible ethnic politics in France and primarily consumed with rebuilding their disrupted communities—kept much of
their pro-Zionist activism behind the scenes. As a result, Muslim-Jewish conflict around the Palestine issue was rare.

For French Jews, interest in Zionism had begun to increase with the 1930s
refugee crisis in Central and Eastern Europe, which pushed many Jewish immigrants to France; such Zionist activism intensified following the expropriations, mass arrests, and deportations of the Second World War.[27] East European
Jewish immigrants, already more sympathetic to Zionist ideology and dis-
proportionately targeted by the war's antisemitic persecutions, also became
the movement's most ardent supporters, as did new refugees—often en route
to Palestine—who held small but regular pro-Zionist rallies in Yiddish.[28] In
this context, French Jewish organizations began cautiously voicing support for
Jewish nationalism, most notably in the declarations of the newly formed

Conseil représentatif des israélites de France (CRIF), which brought together leaders of the native French Jewish establishment and immigrant Jews of Zionist, Communist, and Bundist affiliation. While political disagreements undermined the CRIF's initial unity, and representatives of the traditionally anti-Zionist Jewish left continued to criticize Jewish nationalism, the new organization remained steadfast in its support of Palestine as a home for Jewish refugees.[29] Zionism now had the mainstream institutional legitimacy it had lacked. As one French official noted, even those "in the circles most removed from Zionism generally support the energetic attitude of Zionists of all tendencies and of Jewish patriots who call for the creation of an independent Jewish state in Palestine."[30] Likewise, the president of the Consistoire, the primary Jewish religious body and a former bastion of anti-Zionism, reported in spring 1945 that while "before the war, Zionism held no attraction for French Jews who, above all, sought to mark their belonging to the French community," the recent persecutions had created new solidarity.[31] Such increased support for Zionism did not, however, translate into widespread public activism, and few French Jews considered migrating to Israel after 1948.[32]

In late 1940s France, the growing if muted support for Zionism among French Jews was mirrored by a mounting interest in the Palestinian question among Algerian Muslim nationalists. Nevertheless, the issue did not become a central social or political question for most Muslim immigrants. Living on the margins of their host nation and absorbed with the daily tasks of providing for themselves and the families they had left behind, most did not involve themselves in the domestic or international controversies of the day.[33] As one Marseille police official noted in 1949 describing local North African populations, "The Muslims are apolitical. They rarely take an interest in the nation's political life, and only a tiny minority, insignificant one might say, is affiliated with the parties."[34] Although a highly politicized sector of Algerian Muslim activists did emerge during the late 1940s and early 1950s, their efforts focused intensely on Algerian independence.[35] Insofar as the Palestinian issue made headway, it did so through Messali Hadj's Parti du peuple algérien (PPA), which expressed profound sympathy for Palestinian struggles. Denouncing Jewish colonization of Palestine as an extension of European imperialism against Muslims, the PPA placed Zionism at the heart of its support of the Arab fight against domination.[36] Disagreement among Algerian Muslim migrants in France, however— between those who viewed Algeria as an integral part of the Arab world and those in the majority Berber population who stressed an Algerian Algeria over an Arab or Muslim Algeria—kept support for an Arab Palestine second to other concerns.[37]

Muted public activism around the question of Palestine meant that there was little Muslim-Jewish interaction around this issue in the 1940s. When Palestine *did* emerge as a source of tension, it was often enmeshed with the wider issues of French colonial and minority policies characterizing the period. For example, in October 1944, 200–300 Muslim protestors shouted anti-Zionist slogans during a meeting of the Organisation sioniste de France (OSF) in Paris.[38] The debates that day, while ostensibly about the future of Palestine, became a forum for establishing political legitimacy in France. Joseph Fischer, the OSF's secretary general, responded to the demonstrators by accusing them of harboring pro-German sentiments and undermining national harmony. In a context in which France was rebuilding from Nazi occupation and in which Jews were reclaiming their citizenship after years of debilitating exclusionary legislation, this linkage of Muslims to the enemy worked to cast them as outsiders at a moment when Jews were asserting their Frenchness. The protestors were equally quick to draw on war symbolism. According to one circulating flyer, "these people who suffered the most from deportation and forced expropriations have brutally changed face; from the persecuted that they were, they have become persecutors, deporting and expropriating an innocent and peaceful people on a very large scale." Protesters cautioned the French government that supporting Zionist aspirations would anger millions of Arabs in the empire who "consider Palestine the most beautiful and most sacred part of their *patrie* and who are ready to defend it against all imperialist efforts no matter their origin."[39]

The accusations of racism, national destabilization, and anti-imperialism flying around the room suggest that debates around Palestine were inextricably linked to key questions shaping France's broader political landscape in the postwar years. Fischer's accusation of pro-German sympathies among the Muslim demonstrators (implicitly underscoring Jewish loyalty to the republic) and the protestors' counterclaim that supporting Zionist aspirations would enrage France's Muslim subjects, allowed both to proclaim their place in the nation. Debates over Palestine thus became one way for Muslim and Jewish activists to claim their political legitimacy in France.

Such assertions also accompanied direct efforts to influence French policies in the Middle East. Here, though, French Jews' deep roots in the Republic, reclaimed after the years of Vichy persecution, provided them with greater access to the centers of French diplomatic power than was true for Muslim supporters of Arab Palestine.[40] Indeed, while Zionists and friends of the movement often worked from within the political establishment, Arab interests were represented by ambassadors and diplomats from abroad.[41] These efforts rarely overlapped, and interlocutors of the two "sides" had little contact. Moreover, while Zionists had significant organizational representation in France, those supporting Palestinian Arab interests did not have the same institutional strength, a fact that was a matter of commentary in the Arab world. The Egyptian newspaper, *Al Afif*, for example called France "the main center of Zionist political activity" and bemoaned the inability of Arab representatives to challenge Zionist influence.[42] Thus while the Association des amis de la palestine arabe in Paris protested to the Ministry of Foreign Affairs that the 1947 partition plan in Palestine would result in a "politics of division" between Arabs and Jews, and the ambassador of Egypt and the archbishop of Galilee argued that support for partition would threaten French interests in North Africa and the Middle East, they did so from outside the French political establishment.[43] Supporters of Jewish interests in Palestine, in contrast, used their connections in government circles to push for Jewish migration and later for partition.[44] In May 1945, for example, when a pan-Arab demonstration in Paris invited sympathetic French politicians to speak in opposition to Zionism, CRIF officials were concerned enough to petition foreign ministry authorities to support Jewish settlement in Palestine.[45] Likewise, during the 1947 UN debate over the partition of Palestine, various prominent Jewish politicians, such as René Cassin, René Mayer, Daniel Mayer, and Léon Blum, worked behind the scenes to obtain official French support, despite warnings from diplomats and foreign ministry officials over compromising national interests in the Arab world.[46]

Once the United Nations had voted on partition and the British began to withdraw, such activism increased. In January 1948, for example, the Fédération des sociétés juives de France (FSJF), the umbrella organization for East European Jewish immigrants in France, invited its participant organizations to register volunteers for the Jewish fighting forces in Palestine.[47] Likewise, Algerian Muslim nationalist circles solicited funds and recruited volunteers for combat, with the PPA providing anyone interested with a passport to Belgium from where they would be transported to Palestine.[48] While neither effort yielded significant results, passions were mounting. On 13 April 1948, at a meeting of the Comité hébreu de la libération nationale, for example, two hundred "Arab" protestors occupied the chairs until police emptied the premises.[49]

As the numbers of protestors suggests, however, the Palestine issue hardly galvanized North African Muslim populations in France. While Jewish residents in Paris welcomed Israel's declaration of independence on 18 May 1948 with great enthusiasm, and thirty thousand flocked to the Vel d'Hiv to celebrate, such passion did not translate into discord with local Muslim workers.[50] Although Jewish anti-racist organizations called for the immediate cessation of hostilities and for "Arab-Jewish cooperation," such appeals were directed to the Middle East rather than to Paris where 1948 came and went with little interethnic unrest.[51]

Marseille in 1948: Urban Space, Colonial Politics, and the Arab-Israeli Conflict

Unlike in Paris, officials in Marseille predicted a general Muslim-Jewish standoff around the 1948 Arab-Israeli conflict. A close examination, however, makes clear that conflict was quite limited and focused on specific, highly charged sites—the port from which armaments and refugees departed; the cinemas in immigrant neighborhoods where newsreels relayed information from the war zone; and camps where Jewish and Muslim migrants cohabited. The nature of these sites should not surprise, as they displayed directly France's contradictory policies with regard to the newly declared state of Israel—refusing, on the one hand, to recognize the new nation out of fear of alienating Muslim subjects in the empire, while on the other allowing arms and refugees to travel to Israel through French ports.

Post–World War II Marseille was a center of international transit for thousands, serving as a portal for the conflicts of the wider French empire. Five years of bombardment, pillaging, and occupation had destroyed nine kilometers of docks (out of twenty-five) and thousands of buildings, and caused massive demographic dislocation.[52] To facilitate reconstruction, the Provisional Government concentrated initial resources on rebuilding the port and central rail lines. With the reestablishment of regular maritime relations, crucial supplies and people were able to travel to the city while those trapped in Europe began to leave. By the late 1940s, then, Marseille served as a key transit site for liberated French soldiers, prisoners of war, survivors of labor brigades, returning deportees, Jewish refugees, displaced colonial soldiers, immigrant laborers, Syrian exiles fleeing the first wave of decolonization, "repatriating" Armenians, and North African Jews en route to Palestine.[53]

For most, Marseille was a stopping point on a journey elsewhere.[54] Even a several-week sojourn in the city, however, brought many voyagers into contact with one another. An acute postwar housing crisis and an enormous transient population led local authorities to settle tens of thousands of migrants in transit camps on the city's periphery.[55] Distanced both physically and culturally from the city center, thousands of East European (and to a lesser extent Moroccan and Tunisian) Jews awaited departure for Palestine from these camps; similar camps housed North African Muslim soldiers and laborers trapped in France during the war and awaiting repatriation.[56] Incoming Algerian Muslims, fleeing difficult economic conditions and surging inflation at home and seeking opportunities in the expanding postwar metropolitan economy, often moved into the same areas. In the largest such camp, Grand Arénas, many of these Muslims and Jewish refugees actually cohabited, albeit in separate barracks. Others resided in the crowded streets of the city's traditional immigrant neighborhoods or near the factories that employed them on the city's outskirts. Centrally located between the Old Port and the main train station, the city's first and second districts had earned the moniker *quartier arabe* due to the large numbers of Algerian Muslims who had settled there. The neighborhood was, however, mixed, and a number of Jewish agencies opened offices there to facilitate refugee movement from the train station, just north of the quarter, to the port on its western edge.[57]

The combination of postwar housing shortages and port life thus brought significant visibility to Jewish migratory movements in the very neighborhoods where Algerian Muslim laborers were heavily concentrated, focusing local attention on the distant Middle Eastern conflict and underscoring the French government's willingness to support the Israeli side in the conflict despite equivocation by the Foreign Ministry. Already during the Exodus Affair of July 1947, when the French government allowed 4,515 European Jews to sail from its shores to Palestine, Algeria's Arabic-language press accused the government of being "propagandists for Zionism not only in France but also in North Africa."[58] As tensions emerged in Marseille around the Palestine issue, anti-Zionist hostility was also often directed at the French. Like arguments at the Zionist rally in Paris in October 1944, those in 1948 Marseille reflected a postwar moment in which Muslim and Jewish subjects of the French empire were renegotiating their position within the polity and in which the Jewish victims of Vichy were rebuilding from a period of significant dislocation and loss. Tensions often reflected these negotiations of status, born during the war itself and far from settled in its immediate aftermath.

As noted earlier, the racial politics of the Nazi and Vichy years stripped Jews of their place in French society while providing Muslims with new opportunities to promote their communal self-interest. In Marseille, the largest city of the Unoccupied Zone and free from Nazi occupation until November 1942, the port and railroad had linked Switzerland with Spain, attracting large numbers of fleeing Jews. By 1941, fifteen thousand Jews lived in the city, a quarter to a half of whom were of North African and Mediterranean origin.[59] The city also housed France's second largest Muslim population, also numbering approximately fifteen thousand, as well as a large apparatus for administering North African and Muslim affairs.[60] Common origins and immigrant commercial life brought the two populations into regular contact. When war broke out, a few Muslims protected Jewish acquaintances, and some North African Jews relied on their knowledge of Arabic to "pass" as Muslims. At other times, however, Muslims denounced their Jewish neighbors. As the Service of Algerian Affairs of Marseille reported in December 1941, "Hardly a [Muslim] conversation in Marseille takes place without complaints expressed against the Jews," a state of affairs the report attributed to the success of German propaganda in convincing Algerian Muslims that Jews were manipulating French colonial control of their homeland.[61] Indeed, Nazi propagandists emphasized links between Jews and the European imperialist project as part of their campaign to win support in North Africa. Such efforts seem to have yielded results in France when coupled with the anti-Semitic context of the Vichy years and decades of Muslim nationalist rhetoric regarding Jewish colonial designs in Palestine. At the very least, World War II strengthened discursive links between Jews and European colonialism in certain strands of North African nationalist rhetoric.[62]

With the war's end and the restoration of Jewish citizenship, the Provisional Government quickly repudiated the racist politics of its predecessors, but Vichy's downfall did not end questions about the place of ethnic and religious minorities within the polity. Although Jewish citizens quickly regained all the rights of which they had been stripped, officials downplayed the specificity of their war losses, making restitution difficult.[63] For severely weakened Jewish communities, such as the one in Marseille, rebuilding was a slow and arduous process. Dramatically depleted due to deportations and dislocations, the local Jewish population had dropped from 18,000 to 4,000–5,000 by 1945.[64] With no infrastructure in place, those who remained had significant difficulty reconstituting a robust communal structure. These problems were exacerbated by the heterogeneous nature of the Jewish population, which was made up of native Jews with long-term regional roots, North African and other Mediterranean Jews who had arrived in the century's first decades, and Central and Eastern European refugees. Jewish dispersion throughout the city also impeded communal development.[65] As one returning Jewish POW described:

> [A]ll the persons of a certain age who had responsibilities had been deported. . . . Thus we find ourselves in the months of June and July in Marseille . . . with a community that could be deemed nonexistent in terms of leadership. The Chief Rabbi of Marseille is all alone. . . . [T]here is no money, and the new president of the Consistoire, Monsieur Fedia Cassin . . . paid from his own pocket the entire reconstruction of the community, all of the organization, the staff of the Consistory and the rabbis.[66]

The influx of thousands of illegal Jewish refugees in 1946 and 1947 exacerbated the sense of crisis. Although many officials turned a blind eye to their movements, others were less sanguine, particularly in Marseille where such migration created new social tensions. Thus if the war's end had reestablished Jewish citizenship, it was several years before those in Marseille felt secure.

Algerian Muslims, who made up the majority of Marseille's Muslim population in the late 1940s, found themselves in an even more tenuous position, since while French Jews may have continued to feel insecure in the decade following World War II, the government had, in fact, restored to them the rights of which they had been stripped. For Algerian Muslims, in contrast, the end of the Second World War raised anew the question of French colonial control in North Africa at a moment when both Britain and France were seeking to reconcile the victory of democracy in Europe with their desire to justify ongoing control of their empires.[67] As we have seen, the result was a series of political and economic reforms that culminated in the 1947 Statute of Algeria granting—among other things—citizenship to Algerian Muslim men in mainland France and establishing unregulated migration between France and Algeria. Employment, settlement, and policing practices, however, continued to discriminate against them, helping to explain why incoming Algerian Muslims were interned until 1946 in transit camps under military supervision.[68] That year, the Ministry of Interior reminded local authorities that practices that "appear to establish distinctions among the French" could no longer be tolerated.[69] Discrimination nevertheless continued: The caution was reiterated in 1947, demonstrating that legal equality had not translated fully into administrative practice.[70]

Nor did many Algerian Muslims take advantage of the full range of new rights available to them. Working to stay solvent in a context where housing shortages and a struggling postwar labor market made their position precarious, in the late 1940s, only one thousand Algerian Muslims had registered on electoral rolls.[71] While some joined the Confédération générale du travail (CGT), such affiliations seem to have reflected a hope of assuring work rather than a commitment to participating in French political life.[72] Insofar as Algerian Muslims in Marseille expressed their political engagement with France, they did so as elsewhere in the country by participating in the burgeoning nationalist movement. In 1945 the Parti du peuple algérien created four federations in France, one of which was in Marseille.[73] In 1946, after its leaders had been arrested and the party reconstituted as the Mouvement pour le triomphe des libertés démocratiques (MTLD), its charismatic leader, Messali Hadj, received an enthusiastic welcome in Marseille.[74] Over the next several years, the pro-independence movement spread.[75] Although city officials sought to counter its appeal by improving living and working conditions and relaunching prewar discussions on the construction of a mosque and welcome center, political frustrations continued to mount.[76] At the annual 1 May 1950 Labor Day Parade, for example, several hundred Algerian Muslims followed behind the CGT calling for the abolition of colonialism.[77] Eight days later, the MTLD organized a commemoration of the Sétif massacre.[78] While police believed a handful of Muslim elites were provoking their co-religionists who were concerned primarily with material issues, anti-French rhetoric was clearly on the rise.[79]

Pro-Palestinian activism, while hardly widespread among Algerian Muslims in the 1940s, increased as part of this wider nationalist movement. Most notably, the MTLD-PPA—which as we saw above condemned Zionism as part of its larger anti-colonial vision—promoted Palestinian rights. In December 1947, for example, copies of its newspaper, L'Emigré, circulated in the city's North African quarters. Given a ban against the publication, we can assume its diffusion was limited. Nevertheless, a glance at the paper points to the centrality of anti-Zionism in the movement's rhetoric. While the first article stressed the nationalist movement's commitment to creating a state for all Algerians irrespective of race or religion, the second, entitled, "The Arab States and the Palestinian Question," railed against Zionism. Although "the Arab states hope that the Jewish communities in their countries will not suffer," the authors insisted, they would fight Zionism's outrages "by all means at their disposition."[80] Such rhetoric came to Marseille in other forms as well. In a wide-ranging speech at the Cinema Colibri on 5 May 1950, for example, Larbi Bouhali, the secretary general of the Algerian communist party, called for (among other things) the suppression of colonialism, the banning of the atomic bomb, and support for the Palestinian people.[81] Pro-Palestinian appeals were not unique to Marseille.

It was in Marseille, however, that pro-Palestinian Muslims and pro-Zionist Jews began confronting each other thanks to certain characteristics distinctive of the city. In particular, Maresille's close proximity to North Africa and the Middle East, its position as a leading port city with thousands of Jewish and Muslim transits, and its city spaces all brought the two into contact with each other and drew attention to the contradictions in French policy regarding the intensifying struggle for Palestine.

The first Zionist and pro-Palestinian activities in Marseille in May and June 1948 were focused on France's role, or lack thereof, in the conflict. On 6 May 1948, for example, fifteen hundred Zionist activists gathered to promote the Jewish struggle, raise funds for arms and supplies, and criticize French neutrality in the conflict.[82] Early June saw Muslim dockworkers protest when trade union leaders tried to enforce this neutrality by telling members not to load a ship sailing for Syria, one of the belligerents in the conflict.[83] It was only later in June, however, when tensions began to mount. According to police accounts, anti-Jewish hostility became evident when "Arab circles" that had initially been optimistic about eliminating the Jewish state began fearing the reverse would occur.[84] Such interpretations, however, overlooked the primary trigger for mounting hostilities—riots in the Moroccan town of Oujda on 7 June during which five Jews were killed and another fifteen injured. That evening during further rioting in the nearby mining town of Djérada, thirty-seven more Jews were murdered. These events, which others have covered ably and at length, need not be revisited here.[85] Of central concern for our purposes, however, is the riots' origins, which were directly related to Moroccan nationalist efforts to win adherents to the anti-French cause and which channeled anger against French officials for turning a blind eye to Jewish migrations from Morocco to Palestine into energy for the nationalist movement. Most work on the riots has overlooked Jewish migration to Palestine as a spark for local animosity, emphasizing only that agents of the Moroccan nationalist movement, Istiqlal, fomented the violence in an effort to channel anti-Zionist sentiment into support for their movement.[86] Contemporary observers offered similar impressions. Alphonse Juin, for example, the French resident general, stressed Istiqlal's involvement: "Disjointed and dormant for a year, [Istiqlal] found in anti-Zionism a means of re-building strength and cohesion by exploiting a widely shared sentiment among Muslims. After having organized a boycott, they provoked the riots with the secret hope that we would respond violently thereby strengthening their propaganda."[87]

Many Moroccan Jews seconded the notion that the riots had been preplanned. The president of the Jewish community in Oujda, for example, noted: "For about a month, tendentious rumors circulated among the Muslim population; they accused Jews of allegedly placing a bomb in the new Medina. These false rumors were spread to create agitation. Jews were molested, insulted in the streets, calls for boycotts circulated."[88] The stress on nationalist agitation allowed locals to blame outsiders for disrupting a generally peaceful social landscape. According to a local Jewish school director, for example, "one wonders how such acts could take place in a city where Jews and Arabs have always lived on such good terms."[89] The answer, agreed many, was Moroccan nationalism, which had used the Palestine issue for its own ends.[90]

While these arguments make clear how anti-colonialism and anti-Zionism became further entangled in Morocco in 1948, they overlook the specific role of Jewish migration in intensifying passions. A border town between Morocco and Algeria, Oujda not only attracted "propaganda agents of all ideological stripes," but it also served as a transit point for young Zionists en route to Palestine.[91] It was this fact, above all else, that allowed Moroccan nationalists to use the anti-Zionist criticism as a way to forward their anti-French agendas. Already in the weeks prior to the riot, Jewish outmigration from Oujda had angered local Istiqlal representatives who had organized patrols to prevent suspicious passengers from departing. In a region that had been galvanized by massive strikes (particularly in Djérada), tensions were high.[92] According to the regional head, M. Brunel, the riot began when a Jewish barber attempted to cross the border from Morocco to Algeria, en route to Palestine with explosives.[93] In his account, while the war had enflamed passions everywhere, what "overheated" the local atmosphere was "the clandestine passage over the border of a large number of young Zionists from all regions of Morocco trying to get to Palestine via Algeria."[94] Juin too stressed the intersections of geography, anger over Jewish migration, and nationalist-inspired efforts to rile the population. Claiming that the proximity of the Algerian border was one crucial factor in the rioting, he noted "the clandestine departure of Jews for Palestine ignited the anger already inflamed by professional agitators."[95] Similarly, the French Ministry of Foreign Affairs believed Jewish migration to be a significant irritant: "It is characteristic that those in this region near to the Algerian border consider all Jews who depart as combatants for Israel."[96] Anti-Zionism, then, however present in an abstract sense in 1948 Morocco, only became a source of violent local conflict when Jewish Moroccans started leaving to fight in Palestine. In this sense, the transnational mobilization of certain Jews provoked a transnational countermobilization on the part of some Moroccan Muslims, entangling the anti-colonial movement with the anti-Zionist movement in tangible ways.

I have focused at length on the riot in Oujda and its causes because it was this event and not the 1948 war in Palestine, as such, that first brought passions to a head in Marseille. Indeed, local police reports on interethnic conflict all date from 9 June or after. For Jewish and Muslim observers in Marseille—many with family and friends in North Africa—the riots suggested that the war between Israel and its Arab neighbors was spreading to their *own* communities. Marseille's North African Muslim dockworkers thus accused Jews of starting the Moroccan riots and vowed revenge.[97] Meanwhile Marseille's Jewish leadership organized a day of mourning, arguing that recent events were the "logical conclusion of the tension in North Africa between Muslims and Jews."[98] As such rhetoric suggests, Muslim and Jewish political discourse in Marseille was intimately connected with North African politics, leading local French authorities to fear that rioting would spread to the metropole. They thus increased protection around all Jewish institutions accordingly, warning that given "the sudden and violent excesses to which [Muslim laborers] are accustomed," conflict was a distinct possibility and that further departures to Palestine should be curtailed until spirits had calmed.[99]

The biases evident in such assertions and the acknowledgment that Jewish migration through French ports was a trigger for North African Muslim nationalist politics remind us that French officials were not bystanders in an ongoing drama between Muslims and Jews, but were, in fact, helping to shape the context in which conflict was emerging. Indeed, the first near confrontation between Jewish and Muslim residents in Marseille focused primarily on the way the war in Palestine was underscoring inequalities between them in France. On 10 June at the cinema on rue Canebière (directly abutting Marseille's immigrant districts), Algerian Muslim spectators complained of biased newsreels. While Jewish attendees clapped exuberantly at portrayals of heroic Israeli combatants and the valiant Zionist struggle, Muslims criticized a general silence on the Arab struggle, which—when covered—presented Arab soldiers as rebels. While no violence broke out, Algerian Muslim attendees complained that foreign-born Jews had no business taunting French Muslims.[100]

This assertion of "Frenchness" in contradistinction to the "foreignness" of Jewish refugees was a fascinating attempt to assert Algerian Muslim's status as citizens at a moment when many authorities still treated them as immigrants. To the frustration of many, in summer 1948, officials monitored the comings and goings of North African Muslims even more so than that of Jewish refugees, arguing that a growing Muslim presence was problematic at a moment when so many refugees were also traveling through the city en route to Israel.[101] That Jewish refugees enjoyed greater recognition than Algerian-born Muslim French citizens proved galling to the latter who also complained angrily when French Jewish politicians used their position to support the Zionist struggle against the Arabs.[102] For them, Jewish inclusion (so recently returned) in contradistinction to their own marginalization was an ongoing source of irritation, and for us, such motivations serve as a reminder of how inequities in political access can stoke interethnic clashes.

Such frustrations were also clear in Muslim responses to the transfer of arms and immigrants to Palestine through Marseille's ports with the apparent acquiescence of French officials. By the end of World War II, Marseille had become a visible center of Zionist activity, as Jewish welfare agencies flocked there to support the transient refugee population.[103] Keren Kayemet LeIsrael (KKL), for example, one of the fund-raising arms of the Zionist movement whose activities had been suspended under Vichy, quickly reestablished a presence, raising funds to buy land in Palestine and aiding clandestine migration.[104] Arms made their way through the city, mainly via the efforts of the Zionist paramilitary group, Ha'Irgun HaTzva'i HaLe'umi BeEretz Yisra'el, or the Irgun, which established a local branch in spring 1947.[105] Jewish agencies from Great Britain and the United States created local affiliates to help clandestine refugees find housing, resources, medical aid, and temporary employment, and the communist organization, Union des juifs pour la résistance et l'entraide (UJRE), opened centers to tend to refugee needs. Most visibly, the Fédération des sociétés juives de France, the umbrella association uniting the myriad Eastern European Jewish compatriotic organizations into one cooperative, opened offices on 24 rue des Convalescents, near the train station and in the heart of what was already called the "Arab quarter."[106] Under the direction of Frédéric Thau, the FSJF became the primary intercessor between the municipal government and the Jewish Agency (the body responsible for organizing migration to Palestine/Israel), establishing an active if financially precarious network to provide food, legal aid, child care, and employment to Jewish refugees.[107] Relying on the good will of local authorities, it also ran several regional refugee camps (the largest in Trets, Pélissanne, and La Ciotat) as well as two welcome centers in Marseille (Roucas-Blanc and Caillols).

With the declaration of Israeli independence, clandestine migration operations moved into the open, and Marseille's ports began "packing them in from all sides."[108] While the FSJF continued to facilitate refugee care, Israeli and international Jewish agencies now openly participated in receiving, housing, and feeding migrants, establishing fourteen camps in the Marseille region for those en route to Israel, two of which the French government owned but made available to the Jewish Agency (Grand Arénas and St. Chamas) and twelve of which the American Joint Distribution Committee rented or purchased for the FSJF and the Jewish Agency. The former generally served as welcome and transit centers while the latter (often run by religious and secular youth movements) housed those between the ages of sixteen and eighteen for three to six months as they studied agricultural techniques, elementary Hebrew, and Jewish history before embarking for Israel.[109]

May and June 1948 were the "coming out" of this Jewish migration program, causing resentment for Algerian Muslim activists who saw Jewish fortunes reverse so successfully while their own deteriorated. The anger, not surprisingly, was focused on the two sites where such activities were most visible. The first was the port, the symbolic "door" to France for both populations and a visible reminder of the munitions, supplies, and bodies traveling to Palestine. For Algerian Muslim laborers—many of whom worked on the docks—the port was a site of war, and activists threatened to sabotage ships they feared were supplying Jewish fighters.[110] Conflict around port activities intensified on 11 June when the *Altalena*, an Irgun-owned ship, sailed from the Port-de-Bouc—thirty miles from Marseille—loaded with one thousand Jewish volunteers and stockpiles of weapons. Although Irgun agents attempted to maintain secrecy around the operation, hiding such a large vessel proved impossible. Given the heightened tensions in Marseille, word of the *Altalena*'s departure caused considerable consternation, particularly since the ship—originally scheduled to sail in early June—did not depart until 11 June, the first day of the truce between Arab and Israeli forces in Palestine. Calling a dockworker strike, the Syndicat des ouvriers musulmans de Port-de-Bouc refused to load the ship,[111] while Muslim protesters in Marseille threatened sabotage, and local nationalists called for Arab unity.[112] Fearing the consequences of significant unrest to the well-being of the already distrusted Algerian Muslim laboring population, Marseille's Muslim communal leaders implored their compatriots to remain calm while appealing to French authorities to prevent infractions of the truce.[113] Meanwhile, Jews from Marseille traveled to Port-de-Bouc to load the ship while the FSJF and Jewish student groups called for donations of binoculars, sleeping bags, backpacks, and other objects to aid Jewish combatants.[114]

A second site of conflict in June 1948 was the refugee and labor camps on the city's periphery in which Jewish refugees and Algerian Muslim transients often resided. For Algerian Muslims, angry that local Jews had established "a veritable framework for aiding their co-religionists in Palestine," Marseille's refugee centers appeared to be military schools that used the cover of their agricultural and educational facilities to train Jewish recruits. For such critics, Jewish transients were not needy refugees but "soldiers who would soon be fighting Arab armies," while the FSJF's refugee center was an arms-smuggling hub, as evidenced by the comings and goings of trucks between midnight and 4:00 A.M. and the armed guard at the door.[115] Spying on these camps became one expression of Algerian Muslim anger, as were PPA calls for volunteers to fight in Palestine or to donate funds to supply Arab armies. The PPA also criticized the opening of a consulate in Marseille to facilitate Jewish immigration. While the Office palestinien d'immigration had in fact already functioned for two years as a quasi-clandestine body, its transformation into the Office d'immigration de l'État d'Israël in May 1948 made Jewish migratory activities highly visible, angering PPA adherents.[116]

In spite of these simmering tensions, the only incidents of interethnic violence (and these rather mute) broke out in June 1948 in the Grand Arénas transit camp. Constructed by the French government in 1939 to hold prisoners of war, by 1946 Grand Arénas sheltered thousands of displaced persons and immigrant laborers. In June 1948, Vietnamese migrants and four hundred Jewish refugees (the latter funded and cared for by the Jewish Agency) shared the camp with several dozen Algerian Muslim laborers who resided in barracks operated by the Ministry of Labor. Living side by side with no barrier between them, Muslim and Jewish migrants largely ignored each other, and the camp experienced no disruptions in May 1948 despite daily combat exercises by the camp's Jewish inhabitants. In mid-June, however, when two Muslim workers wandered separately into the Jewish barracks while hunting for their own, tensions mounted. While the first was "unceremoniously" dismissed, the second was detained for the morning and forced to work in the Jewish canteen, raising passions in the Muslim barracks.[117] Two weeks later another lost Muslim laborer wandered into the Jewish camp and was roughed up after insulting several residents. Shortly thereafter, two or three seemingly drunk Jewish residents entered the Muslim barracks where they attacked the French guard.[118] The next few days brought similar small-scale harassments leading Mohamed Talmoudi, president of the Association des Musulmans algériens, to request separation of camp residents.[119] No separation occurred.[120] By late October, a labor ministry official was still lamenting the problems caused by the presence of Jewish and Arab elements in the camp, warning that "serious incidents" might result.[121]

Despite such concerns and the charged environment around Jewish refugee camps, however, summer 1948 saw no serious violence between Marseille's Muslim and Jewish migrant populations. With the exception of the few incidents described above, daily police reports indicated peaceful intercommunal relations throughout the charged days of June *even* in mixed residential areas like Grand Arénas.[122] With the war's second ceasefire from 18 July to 15 October, tensions continued to dissipate.[123] If police continued to document Muslim support for "their Arab brothers in Palestine" well into 1949, the previous summer's passions had cooled.[124] Tellingly, however, if "slogans of 'Arab victors throwing Jews in the sea' have given way bit by bit to peaceful and amicable understandings between Jews and Arabs," what remained was profound resentment over French complaisance to Jewish departures for Palestine. Indeed, ongoing anger and frustration over the Arab defeat was henceforth channeled almost entirely toward French policymakers who it was believed had favored the Zionists despite assertions to the contrary.[125]

That police continued to document Muslim resentment toward French support for Jewish migration is revealing. For many Muslims, Jewish migration was not only an indication that Middle Eastern war was locally relevant but it also signaled the inherent inequities facing Muslim migrants in France. Marseille's Zionist organizations seem to have understood these dynamics. Seeking to avoid igniting passions around migration, they maintained as low a profile as possible even after the previously clandestine Palestinian immigration office was allowed to move into the open.[126] Although the city's ports continued to be major sites of Jewish departures, a formal Israeli consulate did not open until July 1950. In the interim the FSJF continued to operate as a link between the French government and the Jewish Agency, but its officials conducted migrations with considerable discretion.[127] Moreover, the French government's decision to withhold formal recognition of Israel for several months created little protest among Marseille's otherwise vocal pro-Zionist organizations. Cognizant of the problems facing "a power whose influence extends over a vast Muslim empire," the Jewish leadership remained silent, and fewer than one hundred participants attended a meeting organized by the Jewish communist group, the UJRE, in November criticizing such policies.[128] Even members of the city's most ardently Zionist circles proved sensitive to the way their support for Israel could irritate local conditions. In May 1949, for example, the FSJF celebrated Israel's first anniversary. So as to avoid sparking controversy, organizers chose to show a film stressing Israel's efforts to incorporate Holocaust survivors rather than one on the recent war.[129] Such choices helped ensure that tensions that had mounted in Marseille in summer 1948 would diminish quickly in the war's aftermath.

The city's distinctive profile had nevertheless allowed conflict to emerge in ways that were atypical for France. The reasons, as we have seen, were threefold: First, although Marseille was a French city, its political culture was deeply affected by events in North Africa. Although the Mediterranean divided the colonies and protectorates from the metropole, the line was porous, meaning that anti-colonial, nationalist, and Zionist politics in North Africa had repercussions in Marseille. Second, the specific contours of Marseille's urban landscape brought Jews and Muslims together in ways that drew attention to France's willingness to support the Zionist side of the struggle even while claiming neutrality. Transit camps, the port, and even the Cinema Colibri, located on the edge of a mixed immigrant neighborhood, were shared spaces in which migrants of all kinds came together, making the issue of Jewish migration and the war in Palestine particularly visible. Third, World War II had raised vexing questions as to the place of both Jews and colonial subjects in the French polity, the repercussions of which lasted well into the postwar period. With Algerian Muslim citizenship so fragile and contested, and with Jewish citizenship having been so recently tested, the issue of French support for Palestine became a highly charged barometer of the country's fluctuating and contradictory commitments to some of its most insecure citizens. It was in Marseille's port and transit camps that these fluctuations and contradictions were most visible.

With the end of the 1948 war and France's formal recognition of Israel the next spring, whatever tensions had existed between largely transient Muslim and Jewish populations receded. While the MTLD-PPA continued to sympathize with the Palestinian plight, by the early 1950s most politically active North African Muslim migrants in France were focused on their own liberation struggles. For Jews, Israel was of more sustained interest. The Jewish press and mainstream institutional bodies focused heavily on strengthening Israel's economy and social structure and promoting political and cultural exchanges between France and Israel.[130] The depth of communal engagement, however, is hard to gauge. Many local activists complained of paltry numbers at pro-Israel events, and Israeli hopes that France would become the center of European Zionism gave way to understandings that most Jews continued to view France as their home despite the traumas of World War II.[131] Furthermore, prominent Jewish intellectuals, such as Raymond Aron, took issue with the notion of a unified Jewish people, expressing public discomfort at being seen as anything other than French.[132] If most French Jews looked favorably on Israel, their support was largely passive and private, expressed around dinner tables and as part of intercommunal dialogue. Even financial contributions to the new state, which increased throughout the 1950s, compared poorly to those from Great Britain, despite the smaller size of the latter's Jewish community.[133] Given the rather latent interest of most French Jews in Israel and the focus of Algerian Muslim migrants on North African politics and the struggles of daily life, by the late 1940s, Israeli statehood—never a major source of intercommunal tension— posed even fewer problems.

In two crucial respects, however, sources of tension in 1948 France extended beyond a narrow focus on war in Israel: first, by making clear that French commitment to its Muslim or Jewish subjects/citizens could be understood through its relationship to Palestine-Israel, and second by underscoring the way ethnic politics in French North Africa could influence Muslim-Jewish political discourse in the metropole. As French decolonization pushed ever larger numbers of North Africans (Muslims and Jews) to France, these dynamics intensified, a process to which we will now turn.

2

Decolonization and Migration

Constructing the North African Jew

The emigration of Moroccan and Tunisian Jews, already a source of tension in 1948 despite the small numbers, surged during French decolonization. Sixty-one thousand Moroccan Jews thus left for Israel between 1955 and the first half of 1956, as did 15,300 Tunisian Jews.[1] In addition, approximately 20,000 Algerian Jews departed from 1954 to 1961 (after which most others left), although their destination was almost always France where they held citizenship.[2] By 1984, North Africa, which had once housed 470,000 Jews, held 16,700.[3]

The complex push factors behind this migration, which coincided with France's violent withdrawal from the region, included poverty and economic upheaval, bloodshed, and fear of independence.[4] Yet if motivations were diverse, departures came to be understood as "Jewish" for many with a vested interest in the region. One key legacy of this process was the construction of the "North African Jew," a discursive category to which no individual ascribed as such, but that framed the diverse Moroccan, Tunisian, and Algerian Jewish populations into a collective often understood to be in conflict with "North Africans," "Muslims," or "Arabs."

This way of thinking emerged through three channels. The first was through French administrators charged with governing the nation's colonial territories and increasingly fearful of the threat that pan-Arab nationalism and Zionism posed to regional peace.[5] The reports and letters warning of this danger often imagined North Africa's diverse populations as two polarized cross-regional ethno-religious factions. While never the only way of conceptualizing ethnic relations in Morocco, Tunisia, and Algeria, local French officials regularly referred to North African Jews as a collective and hypothesized that developments in one country were likely to undermine Muslim-Jewish relations elsewhere. Certainly, as Todd Shepard has made clear, by the time of the 1962 negotiations between the FLN and the French, the latter had rejected distinctions between Jews and other "Europeans" thereby juridically sealing the "Frenchness" of Algeria's Jewish population and marking them off from Jews elsewhere in North Africa.[6] And yet this juridical move never fully erased competing conceptualizations of Jews as a distinct political unit increasingly at odds with the region's Muslim majority.

The endurance of this way of understanding Muslim-Jewish relations in North Africa came secondly from international Jewish organizations that began focusing on the region in the late 1940s as part of their wider post-Holocaust efforts to save Jewish life. Such interest had roots in the nineteenth century when the Alliance israélite universelle, established in Paris in 1860 to fight for Jewish political rights and modernization worldwide, established an educational network in Morocco and Tunisia.[7] The Alliance continued this work after World War II, while expanding its mandate to a range of juridical and social issues, particularly in Morocco.[8] The growing international Jewish philanthropic network, which reached its apogee after World War II in the American Jewish Joint Distribution Committee, initially showed little interest in North Africa given its post-Holocaust efforts to rebuild European Jewish communities. The struggle in Palestine, however, refocused the international Jewish gaze on Muslim lands, particularly on Iraq, Libya, and Syria where anti-Jewish violence spiked in response to the 1948 war. North Africa—removed as it was from both the site of the Holocaust's worst devastations and from the center of the Middle Eastern conflict—received less attention. Soon, however, both the size and poverty of the local Jewish population caught the attention of agencies focused on the Jewish future. While not always concerned with "North African Jews" as a whole—mitigating poverty, disease, and education in Morocco received the most sustained attention—the legacy of the recent devastation in Europe combined with the mounting conflict in other regions of the Middle East meant that Jewish life in Algeria, Tunisia, and Morocco was often interpreted in a much wider context.[9] Moreover, for those rebuilding Jewish life after World War II, local tensions were often viewed as an indication of likely future violence, a problem to be solved before the fact, often through migration to Israel. If for many international Jewish agencies a pro-Zionist agenda existed in tension with efforts to ensure minority rights in the emerging independent states of North Africa, meaning migration was never their sole priority, other expressly Zionist organizations sought actively to encourage Jewish departures, emphasizing their co-religionists' alienation and exclusion from the entire Arab world.[10]

A third source for the more homogenized image of the "North African Jew" came from indigenous nationalist movements. Here too, the crystallization of this category was never straightforward and, indeed, often contrary to the stated aims of the mainstream Algerian, Tunisian, and Moroccan nationalist parties whose leaders downplayed quarrels with local Jews in their efforts to build united national fronts. Thus, the FLN, Neo Destour, and Istiqlal, the major Algerian, Tunisian, and Moroccan independence movements, respectively, all declared Jews to be equal partners in the struggle against the French and integral members of their respective nations. All three movements, however, had spokesmen that blurred the lines between Jews and Zionists. Warning Jews that emigration, particularly to Israel, was a sign of disloyalty to their birth nations, nationalist rhetoric in all three countries helped establish new binaries around which those monitoring Jewish life took note.[11]

The combined voices of French colonial administrators, international Jewish organizations, and nationalist activists meant that by the end of the decolonization process there was a North African Jewish story to tell, a story that rendered less visible the diverse ways in which Jews and Muslims interacted on the ground or alternative political visions of Muslim-Jewish cooperation.[12] This chapter will trace the emergence of this story by looking closely at Jewish departures and the way a whole host of actors came to see particularistic meanings within them. While I will concentrate heavily on Algeria both because nearly 90 percent of that nation's Jewish population relocated to France and because recent scholarship has emphasized the "Frenchness" of these departures, a narrow focus on one country overlooks the way many of the political actors considered here came to see Jewish emigration as a sign of a broader Muslim-Jewish crisis.[13] While not the only way of understanding the impact of decolonization on North Africa's diverse Muslim and Jewish populations, this narrative proved powerful and enduring in subsequent decades in France.

Decolonization and the Renewal of Jewish Migration

In August 1954, just after the first anniversary of France's exile of Morocco's Sultan Muhammad V to Madagascar for his nationalist sympathies, seven Jews were killed in the town of Petitjean. Part of the wider violence associated with challenging French rule in the region, the murders reflected the escalating nature of the conflict. Indeed, although the French premier, Pierre Mendès-France, proposed granting greater autonomy for Tunisia and gradual internal reforms for Morocco in 1954, the early 1950s were characterized by widespread nationalist resistance and concomitant economic, political, and social breakdown.[14] Likewise, in Algeria, the outbreak of anti-French agitation in November 1954, ultimately pitting Front de liberation nationale terrorism against the French military's ruthless tactics, undermined the lives of many residents. In response, thousands of Muslims, Christians, and Jews left the region, often for France but also for Canada, South America, Israel, and elsewhere in Europe.

Jewish migration was very much a part of this wider collapse of colonial control and the social, economic, and cultural change that followed. In the eyes of many contemporaneous observers, however, these departures were all too Jewish. French officials, in particular, watched Jewish migration with profound ambivalence. Indeed, the 2,075 Jews who requested to leave Morocco after the murders in Petitjean, a dramatic increase from the 561 during the same period in 1953, appeared to Regency officials as misguided. In the opinion of Francis

Lacoste, Morocco's resident general, the ethnicity of the Petitjean victims was coincidental, terrorism rarely targeted Jews, and fears about their future were unwarranted.[15] In fall 1955, foreign ministry officials asserted that Jews had suffered comparatively fewer troubles than the wider European population.[16] Rather, they argued, it was migrations themselves that stirred animosity.

Such concerns first appeared in 1948 when French colonial officials began reporting strong opposition from Muslims in Algeria, Tunisia, and Morocco to immigration to Israel. Between 1948 and November 1951, approximately 46,000 Moroccan and Tunisian Jews had emigrated (after which Israeli selective immigration policies reduced numbers).[17] According to French military and diplomatic correspondence, these departures were highly provocative. In February 1949, for example, the Ministry of the Interior informed the Ministry of Foreign Affairs that "a massive exodus of Moroccan and Tunisian Jews to Palestine, even after hostilities between Jews and Arabs have ended, is likely to provoke serious discontentment among the Muslim populations we govern."[18] While France's ability to object to migrations to Israel, now legally recognized, had diminished, officials in the Foreign Ministry warned that "departures should not be so large as to irritate our Muslim subjects."[19] Throughout the spring, colonial administrators were thus told to provide "no encouragement" to migrating Jews.[20] Similarly, officials argued against awarding international refugee status to Moroccan Jews, insisting that the 1948 riots in Oujda and Djérada had been "absolutely localized." It was, they warned, migration itself—and not widespread anti-Jewish animosity—that had sparked Muslim anger.[21] As Alphonse Juin, the French resident general commented in April 1949 when commenting on a proposal by the French Jewish organization, the Alliance israélite universelle (AIU), to both rationalize Moroccan Jewish outmigration and improve the juridical position of those remaining, "It will be difficult to prevent the Sultan's subject from seeing Jewish émigrés as disloyal to the state to which they have belonged for time immemorial."[22]

As such fears suggest, migration to Israel—already considered a sign of French duplicity during the 1948 war—continued to irritate in its aftermath, and not only in Morocco.[23] In January 1949, for example, the Prefect in Alger complained that migrants traveling through the country "can lead to frictions and difficulties for which it is difficult to determine the repercussions."[24] Similarly, in the International Zone of Tangiers, which had seen no disturbances in 1948, the Minister Plenipotentiare reported growing anger to spreading Zionism and particularly emigration. During one incident, several hundred Jews, hoping to bid farewell to departing co-religionists, "invaded the docks" after breaking through police barriers. Muslim activists responded by publically condemning "Jewish provocations." In the minister's view, European Zionists were to blame for spreading propaganda and ignoring warnings of moderation.[25]

Because Jewish departure rates diminished in light of French caution, Israeli migration laws, and rumors of the poor conditions facing migrants upon

arrival, hostility diminished somewhat after 1951.[26] Following Petitjean, however, concerns over the implications of departures resurfaced.[27] As the resident
general in Rabat reported, "This movement is spreading to the North African
Jewish communities more generally."[28] As his reference to the wider Maghreb
make clear, while French officials were well aware that most migrants were
coming from Morocco, and from the poorest sectors of the Moroccan Jewish
population at that, many saw in the departures a wider peril: "Jews" spurred
by "Zionists" were leaving, and "Muslims" were angry.[29] This problem, while at
times framed in national or local terms, was often referred to in broader terms,
and numerous reports spoke of "North African Jews" or "Muslims" when framing the conflict they understood to be emerging.[30]

International Jewish organizations, far more likely than French administrators to see Jews qua Jews as the targets of nationalist ire, also often framed
North Africa as a single unit, particularly after Petitjean. The French Zionist
newspaper, La Terre retrouvée, for example, asserted that, "the situation of Jews,
drowning in a mass of Arab fanatics, is becoming more tragic by the day."[31] The
Board of Deputies of British Jews, while focused specifically on Morocco, similarly likened the murder in Petitjean to violence in other Arab countries where
"feeling against Jews has been stirred up" and worried that any future in which
Moroccan nationalists held power would "bode ill for the fate of the Jews."[32]

Such framing of North African nationalism as dangerous for Jews—often
in some future rendition that had yet to be articulated—was widespread in the
early 1950s. The World Jewish Congress (WJC), founded in 1936 to improve
the status of international Jewry, for example, remained nervous about how
the shifting political situation in Morocco would affect Jewish life. Having welcomed Moroccan Jewish delegates to its November 1944 congress, the WJC
was one of the first international Jewish organizations to pressure the French
government to rethink Jewish legal status in its protectorate.[33] Events in Oujda
in 1948 increased the WJC's sense of urgency.[34] As WJC delegate Sylvain Cahn
Débra reported that month: "One can say without exaggeration that Moroccan
Jews live in a kind of terror and are convinced that they must at all costs avoid
giving the Arabs the slightest pretext for new serious incidents."[35] With its attention drawn to the region, the WJC established a section in Morocco in 1949,
the head of which was Jacques Lazarus, a former member of the French resistance and the Hagana, and head of the Comité juif algérien d'études sociales
(CJAES), which represented Algerian Jews to the French administration. Although Lazarus and WJC leaders assumed a future for Jews in Morocco, they
insisted on the "urgent necessity of maintaining the French presence in North
Africa."[36] By early 1954, WJC representatives had established a good working
relationship with Istiqlal leaders in the hopes of ensuring protection for Jewish residents in a new Moroccan state.[37] Following Petitjean, however, the head
of the WJC's international affairs bureau, Maurice Perlzweig, attributed Jewish
safety to the French and accused Istiqlal of doing "absolutely nothing to purge

anti-Jewish tendencies from Arab nationalism."[38] Meetings in March and June 1955 between WJC and Istiqlal representatives did little to assuage Perlzweig's concerns.[39] If later meetings proved more fruitful,[40] WJC leaders continued to fear that inexperience and lack of pragmatism within Istiqlal opened the door to religious fanaticism and xenophobia within the party.[41] The WJC's efforts to ensure a North African Jewish future and to prevent antagonizing the French or the nationalists over the emigration issue were thus tempered by attempts to promote Jewish departures, particularly from isolated areas.[42]

Migration, thus, which had been until then on the periphery (if never absent entirely) from Jewish political strategies in North Africa, began moving to the center. As Herb Katzki summarized, reflecting a general consensus among American Jewish Joint Distribution Committee (AJDC) leaders: "While some regard [events in Petitjean] as an isolated incident which will not be repeated, others fear it is a first step in what may be a concerted anti-Jewish program." Or according to another Joint colleague, "there is no doubt in anyone's mind that the days of Jews in Morocco are numbered, and that sooner or later, many will have to be moved out."[43] The Joint, like the WJC, had been drawn to Morocco in the late 1940s. Although already working in North Africa during the Vichy years, in 1947 the Joint established a small North African department in its Parisian headquarters. The 1948 violence in Oujda and Djérada increased interest dramatically. Herman Stein, employed in the Joint's Welfare Department in Paris, was subsequently given resources to help "Jewish victims of Arab hostility," as well as to provide feeding centers for infants and children, medical care, nurseries, summer camps, vocational training and education.[44] Aid increased again in 1949.[45] As one Joint official noted, "It is not too late for American Jewry to make amends for the many years that their eyes were shut to the crying needs of our sorely stricken North African brethren."[46]

As such comments suggest, growing aid was driven by the perception of a dangerous political context primarily in Morocco but throughout the region as well. As one Joint official lamented in October 1948: "These people are leaving Morocco for fear of their lives. The political situation there is very bad and they are almost entirely unprotected." According to this perspective, after the declaration of Israeli statehood, "the Arabs manifested their nationalist feeling very strongly. . . . [The French] find themselves powerless against them and now they make hardly any attempts to stop Arab acts of violence until they are completely out of hand."[47] By 1950 the Joint's representative for North Africa, Hélène Cazes-Benatar, was arguing that "there is the certain DANGER which menaces this Jewish minority of half a million souls, lost in a mass of about twenty million Arabs, whose scorn and hidden hostility towards the Jew has been transformed to open hate since the establishment of the State of Israel."[48] By spring 1955 such views were circulating widely. According to the AJDC's Moses Beckelman, "long range prospect for Jews in [North Africa was] not satisfactory" and "gradual emigration of substantial numbers of Jews" was essential.[49] Samuel Haber, who emphasized poverty rather than politics as the major factor behind Moroccan Jewish departures, nevertheless predicted that "time may be running out" and that only swift action could prevent disaster.[50] Even André Blumel, president of France's Zionist Federation who downplayed antisemitism among the Moroccan and Tunisian nationalist parties, Istiqlal and Neo Destour, nevertheless warned that widespread anti-Zionism made it "absolutely indispensible" to organize migration to Israel "if you really want to save the Jews."[51] So central was migration to organizational thinking that representatives expressed mystification at French opposition to such an obvious solution.[52]

Given that post–World War II Jewish organizational and philanthropic bodies had directed significant resources to resettling Holocaust survivors, it is not surprising that they saw relocation as the obvious solution in North Africa as well. Indeed, even the profoundly assimilationist French Jewish Alliance israélite universelle, while never abandoning its commitment to ensuring Jewish educational and political opportunities at home, began to advocate for orderly, selective migration to Israel—long rejected as antithetical to the AIU's project of ensuring Jewish emancipation in their home nations. Yet as Yaron Tsur has argued, the AIU leadership came out of the Second World War rethinking its assimilationist commitments. While more narrowly focused on easing poverty and discrimination in the Moroccan *mellah* than on "Arab" antisemitism, the AIU, like Jewish organizations, saw in migration one reasonable solution to a wider Jewish problem.[53]

Just as French colonial officials and Jewish agencies saw a specifically Jewish story in the political unrest and migration from North Africa in the early 1950s, so too did Moroccan, Tunisian, and Algerian nationalist activists. Here, the historical narrative is hardly straightforward, since all the major nationalist parties went out of their way to reach out to Jews and all had indigenous Jewish supporters who fought alongside their Muslim co-nationalists to dislodge the French and to establish independent states for all citizens regardless of faith or ethnicity.[54] However, as noted in the last chapter, the FLN, Neo Destour, and Istiqlal all warned the French Ministry of Foreign Affairs not to recognize Israel, called France's pro-Zionist policies anti-Arab, and warned their Jewish minorities to steer clear of Zionism. At times, these calls dangerously blurred the lines between Jews and Zionism, such as boycotts of Jewish businesses in Morocco or Istiqlal's instigation of the riots in Oujda and Djérada.[55] And while nationalist rhetoric was very careful not to target Jews qua Jews, Jewish émigrés were increasingly a source of frustration.

Interestingly, in the initial surge of Jewish departures after Petitjean, neither the sultan nor the Istiqlal spokesmen expressed any objections, perhaps due to French colonial administrators' efforts to restrain the migration wave.[56] Thus it was largely radio broadcasts from Egypt and Damascus that attacked Jewish migrants for leaving.[57] Very soon, however, local French officials began reporting growing tensions.[58] In June the leader of Istiqlal, Allal el Fasi, strongly denounced collusion between Zionist organizations and the French government and warned Moroccan Jews not to leave.[59] Istiqlal's Abderkader Benjelloun later insisted that el Fasi had been misunderstood, and the goal had not been to threaten Moroccan Jews but to encourage them to stay. Promising equal rights in an independent Morocco, he insisted that "emigration of Moroccan Jews to Israel is due in part to a lack of confidence in the future and we have the impression that it is being encouraged by unjustified propaganda."[60] Whether meant as threat or enticement, Istiqlal's discomfort with Jewish departures was palpable. As two Istiqlal officials, Omar Abdjellil and Abdelkhalek Torres, made clear, emigration and the transfer of capital to Israel was "double treason."[61] A similar ambivalence toward migration was evident in Neo Destour's pronouncements. Thus, in 1954 Neo Destour's Habib Bourguiba met with WJC representative Alexander Easterman, promising equal rights for all citizens be written into the Tunisian constitution while expressing profound ambivalence toward Israel. While several months later he made clear that Jewish Tunisians would have the same right to emigrate as all other Tunisians, he nevertheless asked that Jews be discreet so as to avoid provoking tensions.[62]

Independence in both Morocco and Tunisia dramatically changed the context once again, and thus lies outside this chapter's purview. As should be clear, however, while Jewish departures were certainly the response to a broad range of push-and-pull factors, including fear, lack of opportunity, poverty, anti-Jewish oppression, encouragement by some Jewish and Israeli officials, and Israel's relaxation of migration restrictions, the very fact that some Jews started to leave helped create the reality that so many feared. Namely, while migration may have been a response to hostility it also *sparked* hostility, making Jews seem more foreign. Whether migrants opted to go to Israel, to Paris, or elsewhere, their departures were often understood by French officials, Jewish observers, and Muslim nationalists to be a Jewish flight. Although this conclusion may seem unremarkable when discussing departures from Morocco and Tunisia, the historiography of Algerian Jewish migration has downplayed this component. Yet, as I will argue, in Algeria, too, a Jewish story emerged that—while often being submerged in the story of a wider European flight—nevertheless provided a powerful and enduring counternarrative for understanding Jewish departures from the region.

Migration and the Algerian War: A Jewish Story

While most Moroccan and Tunisian Jews went to Israel prior to 1967, nearly 76,000 went to France.[63] There they were met by nearly 140,000 Algerian Jews who left as part of a much wider flight of the 925,000 French, Spanish, Italian, Maltese, and Algerian Muslims (140,000 of the so-called Harkis who contributed to the French war effort and who subsequently fled to the metropole).[64] Recent assessments have concluded that because Jews were included in the wider category of French repatriates, their departure should be understood as "not a Jewish exodus but [a] *pied noir* exodus."[65] Yet if Jewish departures were similar in kind to others caught up in the process of decolonization, they were not identical in meaning. Although Algerian Jewish representatives insisted that their French citizenship entitled them to access to any protective legislation negotiated for Europeans, this juridical move never fully hid their concern over a distinctly Jewish fate. Both French *and* Jewish, their loyalty to the nation that had emancipated them and their concerns about living under Muslim control merged during decolonialization.[66]

To be sure, the Jewish population was not monolithic, and opinions about the Algerian Revolution ranged according to social status, age, economic milieu, geographic context, political formation, and relationship to France, meaning that some Jews supported or even joined the FLN's struggle, while others were committed members of the Communist party (which ultimately also supported independence), and still others fought with those defending Algérie française. Indeed, one Joint official who toured Algiers, Constantinople, and Oran in 1961 noted so much communal diversity that it was like visiting three distinct countries.[67] As I will argue, however, the organizations and individuals who spoke publicly for Algerian Jews, while on the one hand consistently insisting upon that diversity, on the other, saw more unified Jewish meanings in the unraveling of French North Africa.[68] Moreover, the presence of international Jewish agencies dedicated to encouraging emigration meant this issue was part of communal discussions from the outset of the Algerian crisis even when only small numbers of Jews had left. The combined result was that from early in the FLN's struggle, key figures were articulating particular dangers for Jews under Muslim rule, insisting on the importance of French control for maintaining communal life, speculating on the necessity of Jewish departure, and articulating "specific problems" that affected only them, "like it or not."[69]

Most depictions present the Algerian Jewish leadership as apolitical—loyal French citizens, who due to their sympathy with the Muslim plight and fears about endangering their delicate position, declared neutrality in the conflict.[70] While many disapproved of Muslim political subjugation and felt deeply attached to Algeria, they felt grateful to France for their improving social, economic, and civil status.[71] Stuck between a "rock and a hard place," as André Narboni, president of the Fédération sioniste d'Algérie, later commented, Algerian Jewish spokesmen sought to protect their citizenship without publically identifying with either side.[72] As the CJAES under Jacques Lazarus insisted after the outbreak of hostilities in November 1954, "The majority of this assembly declares itself in favor of caution: nothing must suggest that the Jews have taken a specific position in response to events."[73] Arguing in 1956 that Jews were not a political body but a set of individuals each with his or her own political affinities, the CJAES asserted that no organization could speak on be-half of a Jewish collectivity.[74]

Proclamations of neutrality did not, however, prevent key communal leaders from expressing unabashedly pro-French politics behind closed doors (while explaining the dangers of adopting "inopportune" positions too publicly).[75] As early as 1950—several years before the formal outbreak of war—Algerian Jewish representatives *already* reported that Muslim-Jewish cooperation was no lon-ger possible, and that Jews would be "compelled to collaborate with France . . . to defend, when necessary, their lives and property."[76] Or as representatives of the major Algerian Jewish organizations informed a visiting American con-gressman in November 1954, "We are unanimous in underscoring the absolute necessity of maintaining a French presence for the future of North Africa's Jew-ish communities."[77] As in Morocco and Tunisia, such broad assessments were echoed by international Jewish observers, such as in the 1953 *American Jewish Yearbook*, which reported that although Algerian Jews supported reforms to raise Muslim residents' standard of living, they nevertheless "remain[ed] unan-imously faithful to the principle of a French presence in North Africa."[78]

Such pro-French comments from both Algerian and international Jew-ish representatives mirrored those circulating throughout the wider settler population, while still mapping out distinctly *Jewish* political concerns as well.[79] For such observers, developments in post-independence Morocco and Tunisia—where emigration continued to be a touchstone issue—raised signifi-cant concerns about the Jewish future. In 1956 the new Moroccan government dismantled the Zionist organization charged with coordinating migration. Al-though individuals could still depart on their own, by 1957 all citizens, whether Jewish or Muslim, had difficulty obtaining a passport. The Tunisian govern-ment permitted emigration and—as in Morocco—initially incorporated Jews into its governing bureaucracy. But in both countries, increased identification with the wider Arab world and efforts to break down communal autonomy and to Arabize educational institutions promoted clandestine migration.[80] Given that refugees often stopped first in Algeria, their plight was particularly vis-ible.[81] Stories on the Moroccan and Tunisian Jewish experience began filling the main Algerian Jewish paper, *Information juive*, and communal leaders made regular references to events throughout the Maghreb when speculating on their own future in Algeria.[82]

This message of Jewish particularity was reinforced by developments in the wider Middle East, most notably in November 1956 during the Suez crisis, when Nasser's nationalization of the canal sparked Franco-British-Israeli military in-tervention and significant anti-Jewish activities.[83] The forced departure of many Egyptian Jews led French foreign-ministry officials and reporters to speculate over deteriorating Muslim-Jewish relations throughout the Middle East and North Africa, including in Algeria where elements within the FLN maintained close links with Nasser.[84] Algerian Jewish representatives claimed otherwise.

Information juive thus proclaimed the strength of local Muslim-Jewish relations, and the CJAES insisted on Algerian Jewish distance from events in the Middle East. The very act of engaging in such discussions, however, if only to deny their relevance, reaffirmed a Jewish collectivity.

In the early years of the Algerian crisis, Lazarus, the CJAES, and the Joint also began tracking anti-Jewish violence in ways that defined a Jewish experience within the wider anti-colonial struggle.[85] One informant wrote to Lazarus, for example, of the two hundred Jews of M'Sila who had reportedly lived "on good terms" with their Muslim neighbors but whose fortunes changed in 1955 "when FLN agents took possession of the city." Within a year, a boycott of local businesses coupled with increasing social distance and violence led all but two of the town's Jews to depart.[86] Similarly, a May 1956 bomb in a Constantine café reportedly to punish Jewish cooperation with the French police and a counterattack by Jewish self-defense forces, promoted fears of targeted anti-Jewish activities.[87] By early 1957 Benjamin Heler, president of Algeria's Fédération des sociétés juives, was warning that a "very great physical danger" threatened all the "30,000 Jews in the hinterland of Algeria . . . [who] should be moved either into the cities on the coast or to France and other countries."[88] That summer, Jacques Attal reported to Lazarus that Jews in Bône were seeking French protection from the FLN.[89] As such statements suggest, public proclamations of Jewish "neutrality" coexisted with internal communal discussions underscoring the need for a strong French presence and even migration.

To suggest that communal leaders saw Jewish meanings in Algeria's fight for independence is not to suggest that all Algerian Jews agreed or that social reality always reflected these perceptions.[90] In July 1957, for example, after four grenades were thrown at Oran's Jewish quarter, a local informant insisted that violence had emerged when rebels were pushed into that part of the city, not from anti-Jewish sentiment.[91] In September 1958, after a bomb exploded during synagogue services in Boghari, the rabbi emphasized "the feelings of disgust, revulsion and even hate expressed by all, and particularly by Boghari's Muslims, due to the place where the attack was carried out."[92] Similarly, following a 1960 attack on the main synagogue in Algiers, Muslim residents offered sympathy and protection to their Jewish neighbors, and local Jewish leaders, including those directing the Algerian Zionist Federation, "admitted that there was no organized Moslem movement against the Jews."[93]

Even those who emphasized the enduring friendship between religious communities, however, acknowledged the *possibility* of interethnic clashes in order to dismiss them. In other words, the very claim that Jews and Muslims could live in harmony was always shadowed by its opposite, ultimately reenforcing notions of a distinctive Jewish experience within the independence struggle. Moreover, even those who saw Muslim-Jewish relations as stable, often stressed the importance of ongoing French control to ensure peaceful relations. In the words of Henri Chemouilli, an Algerian Jewish teacher writing in a French

Jewish magazine: "if relations between Jews and Arabs were excellent here and less strong there, they were, overall, good." Yet, "if France is defeated, then we would all, the Jews of Algeria and the Jews of France, bear the consequences."[94]

This sense that there was a Jewish dimension to the Algerian struggle meant that by the late 1950s, the question of departure—if not the act itself—was increasingly discussed in communal gatherings.[95] Most scholarship has focused on de Gaulle's visit to Algeria in 1960 and the desecration of the synagogue of Algiers as the moment when Jews began seriously considering leaving.[96] David Cohen argues, for example, that in 1956 "departure for the Hexagone had not crossed anyone's mind. The Jews envisioned living harmoniously in Algeria with both Christians and Muslims for many years."[97] Much evidence backs up this claim.[98] As Daniel Timsit, a Jewish medical student who joined the FLN, recounted of these years: "[Algerian Jews] did not think that they had to leave. . . . [T]hey did not consider themselves a particularly threatened community."[99] Similarly, Jean Bensimon—who later migrated to France—wrote that although Algerian independence seemed likely in 1954, he did not feel obliged to leave "a country that was mine."[100] Israeli and American Jewish representatives concurred after being rebuffed in efforts to encourage departure.[101] The director of Constantine's Service social de l'association consistoire israélite reported in 1956 that there was no interest in emigration planning, an observation that the chief rabbi in Bône shared.[102]

Such comments have, however, misled historians. True, most Jews were not standing on the docks in the 1950s. Emigration was nevertheless a topic of communal conversation, often driven by the Joint and other international organizations.[103] The very Jews in Constantine and Bône who refused to discuss rescue plans thus told their American and Israeli interlocutors that future emigration was a real possibility.[104] Likewise, the Joint's Stanley Abromovitch noted in June 1956 that talk of departure was the "topic of the day. People discuss this problem at home, in business, everywhere. It was the only subject I heard constantly." In his view—one he spread in his travels—an independent Algeria boded ill for Jews, who would lose civil service positions, businesses and customers. Security questions were also a concern: While "Arabs . . . have no interest in massacring the Jews," Abromovitch explained, "[t]his does not exclude the possibility of a pogrom. In a tense situation, the smallest spark may cause a conflagration. . . . At the present time, any incident may easily cause a panic, a flight from Algeria to France, and to a much lesser extent to Israel. . . . They see no future in Algeria and want to leave. They want to emigrate."[105]

As a Joint representative, it is not surprising that Abromovitch saw danger everywhere; international Jewish agencies, as we have seen, encouraged migration out of fear of future violence. Tellingly, however, the CJAES—the local body so vested in Jewish neutrality—also informed the AJDC and various French Jewish organizations in June 1956 that they should prepare for a large emergency migration to France, "even if it should . . . cause political repercussions either among the French or the Arabs." In their view, "the Jews . . . felt themselves in danger."[106] The following January, the CJAES established a commission to help those of modest means leave for the metropole.[107]

To say that emigration was the "topic of the day" does not contradict previous assertions that Jews hoped to stay. Indeed, this very same CJAES commission had not met by June presumably due to lack of candidates. What should be clear, though, is how essential French control was to the decision to remain. In 1956 most still believed "that the French will protect them; that France will remain in Algeria." As Abromovitch reported, "as long as France intends to stay . . . there will be a possibility to live in Algeria."[108] Given that faith in France's ability to withstand the FLN fluctuated, so did migration plans. In 1957, departures thus increased in conjunction with fears over security.[109] After de Gaulle returned to power in June 1958, security improved, the economy stabilized, and violence subsided, meaning that some who had previously left returned, and migration numbers dropped.[110] Violence and uncertainty surged again, however, after de Gaulle's 16 September 1959 promise to grant Algerian self-determination.[111] On Yom Kippur that October, a grenade in a synagogue killed the rabbi's granddaughter and wounded eleven others. Offering the mirror reflection of Boghari's rabbi a year previously, Rabbi Sellem of Bou Saada commented, "The Muslims express their condolences to us, blaming the so-called criminals and offering a lot of clap trap that makes us not believe them."[112] Or as the *American Jewish Yearbook* described the atmosphere that year, "Confronted by an apparently endless war and mindful of what had happened in Tunisia and Morocco, many Jewish families solved their personal problems by leaving Algeria for France or Israel. Others made preparations to leave if things got worse. In general, a wait-and-see attitude prevailed."[113] These fluctuations reflected hopes that France could renegotiate its colonial relationship in ways that would ensure safety for all; in the eyes of Jewish observers, however, they also demonstrated distinctly Jewish meanings. As one member of the CJAES board noted in June 1957, "one day or another we will be overwhelmed by the Arab world."[114]

Such perspectives shaped Jacques Lazarus's views of the political and economic risks facing Algerian Jews qua Jews, proclamations of their Frenchness notwithstanding. As he warned the WJC's Nehemiah Robinson in June 1957, "In addition to ethnic and religious [prejudices] can be added a nationalist prejudice based in race, meaning that increasingly Arabs buy from Arabs and go to Arab doctors and lawyers, even if, in certain cases, the services offered by Jews proves more advantageous."[115] Born in Alsace in 1920 and having joined the French resistance after escaping a deportation train during World War II, Lazarus's view was undoubtedly influenced by recent European events. In 1946 he moved to Algeria on behalf of the Jewish vocational agency, the Organization for Rehabilitation and Training (ORT). After marrying a woman from a prominent local family, he became active in Algerian Jewish politics, becoming general secretary of the CJAES in 1948 and, as we have seen, director of the WJC's North African division.[116]

Given this background, it is not surprising that Lazarus saw a Jewish story within Algeria's political chaos (he underlined Jewish names in dozens of newspaper articles of murders and terrorist attacks).[117] In 1957, before the UN's debate on the Algerian issue, Lazarus confidentially insisted to the WJC's Maurice Perlzweig that the organization must protest any challenge to France's hold on Algeria. While acknowledging the WJC's broader commitment to justice and equality, Lazarus held that it must support France "without reserve" because "the future of the Jewish collectivity in North Africa is predicated, in large measure, on the maintenance of the French presence in Algeria."[118] These were striking words from a man who had repeatedly asserted there *was no* Jewish collectivity! In fact, while Lazarus insisted that, "there is not a Jewish politics," he also believed that to be Jewish was "a political and not only a religious or social phenomenon."[119] This nuance means that he devoted his life to Jewish politics while claiming they did not exist.

This "Jewish politics" was deeply embedded by 1957. If Algerian Jewish spokesmen fought desperately to protect their citizenship by stressing their integration into French colonial society, the story of Jewish distinctiveness was equally potent and part of their assessment of future opportunities (or lack thereof) in North Africa as a whole.[120] Jewish emigration, while still not widespread, was intrinsically linked to this analysis and became all the more so as the war intensified.

The FLN and the Solidification of an Algerian Jewish Question

By the late 1950s, the FLN had also come to see a Jewish dimension within the wider independence struggle. To be sure, for most of those engaged in a broader struggle, the concerns of the Jewish minority were largely irrelevant. Nevertheless, Jews posed a problem for Algerian nationalists. As indigenous members of Algerian society, Jewish participation in the independence struggle was a potentially valuable way to grant legitimacy to the movement's claim that its struggle pitted oppressed colonial subjects against their imperial masters rather than Muslims against Christians or Arabs against Europeans.[121] Jewish support for the French made such efforts far more complicated.[122] Moreover, as Jews threw in their lot with the French, they did more than side with the despised colonial oppressors; rather, as an indigenous population, they, like the Muslim soldiers who fought with the French army and who were despised as traitors, had—in the eyes of many—committed treason.[123]

Such views were not preordained in 1954 when the FLN first rebelled. Nor did social reality necessarily reflect the increasingly polarizing rhetoric regarding the place of Jews in the Algerian nationalist struggle. As in all such movements, nationalist doctrine did not spread evenly to all social categories or regions, and many associated themselves with family, clan, ethnic group, or tribe over nation.[124] Muslim-Jewish relations "on the ground" reflected this diversity. Moreover, while FLN rhetoric toward Jews played a key role in defining who stood within and who outside the nation, this rhetoric was itself fluid, evolving in response to power struggles within the organization and growing awareness of the pro-French biases behind Jewish neutrality. Put differently, Jewish political discourse influenced nationalist attitudes and vice versa in a dynamic process that redefined how each saw the other.[125] Yet even a cursory glance at hardening FLN rhetoric shows the way nationalist political discourse, despite stressing Jewish Algerianness, actually pointed to their distinctiveness.

In its earliest incarnation, anti-colonial activists collapsed Jews into broader categories of the nation.[126] After the 1956 violence in Constantine, however, and CJAES declarations to the WJC of Jews' commitment to their French citizenship, FLN assertions of Jewish "Algerianness" coexisted with public recognition of their distinctive political status. During his April press conference acknowledging his collaboration with the FLN, for example, moderate Ferhat Abbas distinguished Jews from other Algerian nationals because they benefited from French nationality.[127] Two months later, the FLN asked Jews to join their struggle by similarly underscoring their differences from other Algerians: After having been raised on "cheap patriotism" and "respect for imperial grandeur," Jews now faced "the moment of choice and big decisions," while "for us, Algerians, the choice is made."[128]

With the FLN's recognition of Jewish particularity came a more targeted outreach to join the nationalist camp coupled with a sharp criticism of Jewish silence on colonial injustice. These two facets emerged mostly clearly at the Congrès de la Soummam in August 1956, where the FLN established its platform. Favoring a secular and democratic Algeria, the Congrès de la Soummam represented a moment when more moderate members of the FLN triumphed over those calling for a more religiously inflected political vision. The result, therefore, was a platform that temporarily created space for Jews within the movement.[129] This outreach, however, did not address Jews as Algerians like all others, but rather as those with questionable loyalties. The platform thus posited that while Jews had not gone "definitively into the enemy's camp," they had not chosen a side. The FLN also criticized the chief rabbi who, unlike the archbishop, had not spoken out against colonialism. A letter to Algerian Jewish leaders the following fall similarly criticized this silence. While recognizing that individual Jews supported the revolutionaries, the mainstream Jewish leadership needed "to solemnly confirm their belonging to the Algerian nation" in order to "dispel all misunderstandings and eradicate the seeds of hatred planted by French colonialism." Calling Jewish Algerians "sons of the nation," the FLN nevertheless underscored a growing frustration with Jewish silence.[130]

For the FLN, the 1956 declaration at the Congrès de la Soummam was a culminating point, both a concerted effort—in light of the violence in Constantine—to prove that the national movement was neither religiously fanatical nor an instrument of the Arab League, and to win over a small but influential constituency.[131] Reminding Jewish Algerians that a common indigenous heritage should unite them against the colonial regime, the FLN publicly rejected civil and juridical categories that established Jews as French. By stressing their particular choices, however, and critiquing their position on colonial injustice, the FLN also emphasized Jewish difference from other Algerians.

Such contradictions continued to influence FLN approaches throughout late 1950s.[132] Arguing before the United Nations, on the one hand, that independence in Morocco and Tunisia had brought full political, economic, and social inclusion for Jews, the FLN insisted that the same would be true in a future Algeria. Criticizing certain Jewish spokesmen, they lauded those who supported the nationalist movement and promised equality to all.[133] On the other hand, public invitations to come together were accompanied by more aggressive tactics; some wealthy Jews, for example, received threatening letters "requesting" their support for the nationalist cause, and violence against Jews and Jewish institutions increased.[134] Moreover, periodic pronouncements on Jews continued to stress both their integral position within the nation *and* their particularity. A November 1959 statement (published in February 1960 in *Le Monde*), for example, proclaimed, "You are an integral part of the Algerian people; you do not have to choose between France and Algeria but to become actual citizens of your real country," while noting the distinctive choice before Jews: "Do you want to exercise fully in this country . . . rights that nobody will ever challenge or will you accept living under a reign of contempt and to content yourselves with a citizenship conferred upon you by your oppressors." This recognition of Jewish choice echoed the 1956 declaration if ending somewhat more threateningly by encouraging Jews "to resolve any ambiguity that risks compromising our future relations."[135]

If similarities with the 1956 declaration were palpable, it was the threat to which Jewish leaders responded, underscoring how the give and take between FLN and Jewish spokesmen pushed both into more polarized camps. The CJAES thus publicly condemned the FLN's attempt to impose a collective status on all Jews. Even more upsetting to Jewish leaders, however, was that the FLN's statement appeared in *Le Monde* on the same page as an article asserting de Gaulle's support for a federated Algerian state with rights for Kabyles, Arabs, Chaouias, Mozabites, Jews, and French.[136] The coupling of nationalist assertions of Jews' "Algerianness" with an emerging political consensus that Jews were not French but a separate ethnic community sent the CJAES into overdrive.[137] Establishing that Jews were indistinguishable from other French citizens henceforth became the organization's main goal.

Paradoxically, however, all efforts to prove Jewish Frenchness ended up very much entangled with particularistic ethno-religious concerns. CJAES delegates, for example, asserted the *collective* importance of French citizenship to Algerian Jews, which—in their words—had been their "essential safeguard" (an ironic claim given the Vichy years). As Lazarus explained: "[T]he situation of our co-religionists in Arab countries having won independence, even neighbors like Morocco, should be a subject of interest and bitter reflection for us. How can we believe nationalist leaders who, once independence of their countries has been won, have been eager to forget—whatever the reason given—the solemn promises made regarding the total legal equality that would be granted to their Jewish citizens?"[138] Or as one French Jewish lawyer wrote to the Secrétariat d'état aux affaires algériennes, "Because of its atavistic anxiety and because of the attitude of the Arab world toward the Jewish world, the Jewish minority, fears a Holocaust by the European and Muslim communities."[139] In such missives, we see the reflex not only to assert a collective Jewish politics, but also to collapse Algerian Muslims into broader North African and Arab political categories.

Jewish efforts to protect their French citizenship flew in the face of FLN efforts to claim Jews as Algerians, and in June 1960, Ferhat Abbas warned of a growing alienation among Muslim Algerians.[140] While the FLN disavowed the destruction of Algier's central synagogue on 12 December and condemned antisemitism,[141] criticisms intensified against the "collusion" of some with the colonial regime, as well as "the wait-and-see attitude" of the communal leadership.[142] Such proclamations allowed FLN spokesmen to deny charges of antisemitism while still insisting that there was a price to pay for helping the French.[143] As a March 1961 FLN booklet threatened, the time for decision had come: "For a long time, we have understood and even excused our Jewish friends, deceived by colonial maneuverings, for the difficulty of resolving this division, this 'internal tearing,' this uncertainty. . . . Today, the Algerian people must know on what side its true children will fall."[144] Abdel Kader Chanderli, the United States' FLN representative, likewise warned American Jewish organizations that Jews' retention of French citizenship would be viewed as treason.[145]

Jewish citizenship was, then, a touchstone issue around which debates over loyalties played out. Paradoxically, however, as Jews insisted that they were French like all others and the FLN insisted that Jews were Algerian like all others, both ended up underscoring Jewish distinctiveness. Lazarus admitted this openly to Louis Joxe, Algerian-affairs minister, in March 1961 when he insisted that Jews were asking for no particular guarantees as Jews while still noting that they experienced "anxiety that was perhaps deeper than that of other elements in the population because of their Jewishness, the declarations of the FLN claiming them as Algerian in contempt of the right of auto-determination, and the excessiveness of independent Arab states, most recently Morocco."[146]

International Jewish organizations also underscored this particularity. As one AJDC official put it, "there is a real problem *which only the Jews face* and not the other French nationals in Algeria from who[m] French citizenship cannot be taken away. Under the circumstances, there is a far greater urge to have the Jews of Algeria leave the country before they are caught and trapped as are the Jews in Morocco."[147] Similarly, observers from the American Jewish Committee commented, "If, in an about to become independent Algeria, [Jews] positively dissociate themselves from the Algerian mass whose leaders consider them as Algerian, they may very well be considered as traitors. The attitude of Algerian Moslems toward them would, therefore, be different than to other Frenchmen for who[m] the act of remaining French would seem natural to the Algerians."[148] After visiting Algeria that spring, Max Lapides of the Joint's Geneva Office, described Jews as "surrounded . . . in a sea of Arabs. Today France and the Army afford them the necessary protection and bolster the dikes which keep the sea from all but drowning them." Traveling throughout the country, he spread word of Jewish dilemmas in all Muslim lands and stressed the importance of "tak[ing] positive action while the gates remained open."[149] In Algeria, as in Morocco and Tunisia, then, international Jewish agencies disseminated a "Jewish story" within the wider political chaos and encouraged emigration as a solution.

Unsurprisingly, such efforts angered Algerian nationalists, as Jewish migration once again became a political football. Although on 10 September 1957, Ferhat Abbas, hoping to win Israeli support in United Nations' deliberations over Algeria, promised that as equal citizens, Jews would have the right to emigrate, a spokesman of the Gouvernement provisoire de la république algérienne (GPRA), the political arm of the FLN formed in September 1958, later declared that the future Algerian government would not authorize such departures.[150] These contradictions reflected divisions in the FLN between a moderate group, including Benyoucef Benkhedda, Krim Belkacem, and Mohamed Boudiaf, who pushed for discreet relations with Israel as a means of distancing the Algerian revolution from Egypt, and a second group, headed by Ben Bella, that was close to Nasser and aggressively anti-Zionist.[151] Although the FLN made no formal statements regarding Jewish migration to Israel, particularly given the small numbers involved, Jewish Agency efforts to encourage departures irritated them.[152] In April 1961, Abdelkader Chanderli complained vigorously to AJC representatives over campaigns that "give the impression that the Jews in Algeria are in peril." Somewhat contradictorily, however, he made clear that any migration should take place before Algerian independence, since subsequent departures would reflect poorly on the new state.[153] The ambivalence evident in Chanderli's complaint continued to surface as Jewish migration accelerated, even when the final destination was France. As Henri Chemouilli described, "We didn't leave for Israel, you see, but our departure from Algeria was also a mark of our allegiances [in the minds of Algerian nationalists]."[154]

While limited sources make it difficult to ascertain the prevalence of such views, by the early 1960s there were certainly few illusions about Jewish loyalties. As one Algerian Muslim political leader told a reporter, "It must be said that the Jews have not always had a very favorable attitude toward us. They were fully engaged in support of French Algeria."[155] An exchange between the Muslim deputy from Bône, Abdelbaki Mosbah Chibi, and Jacques Lazarus provides further evidence of concern over Jewish loyalties.[156] Following the violence in Constantine, Chibi, known for his outreach to the Jewish community and his pronouncements on the necessity of Arab-Israeli collaboration, nevertheless expressed concern that Jews had instigated the violence.[157] Lazarus reassured him that no Jews had been involved and praised Muslim outreach in the aftermath. The good will between the men wavered, however, when Chibi requested public Jewish support for the Algerian republic, a gesture that would go a long way in repairing misunderstandings. Lazarus responded by reiterating the CJAES's neutrality and refusing any initiative likely to be misinterpreted.[158]

This exchange points to the way Jews remained outside both Algerian and French political collectivities despite assertions by various actors to the contrary. Indeed, paradoxically enough, proclamations of Jewish inclusion in these wider groups often served to underscore their distinctiveness, a process that became all the more evident in the last two years of the Algerian Revolution as migration numbers soared for all European setters. Even here, where Jewish behavior seemingly mirrored patterns of the wider settler population, distinctive Jewish patterns emerged, patterns that forced changes in FLN policies toward them and once again emphasized a Jewish story within the Algerian independence struggle.

Migration, Jewish Politics, and the Unraveling of French Algeria

In spring 1961, as the first Evian negotiations between the GPRA and the French government began to establish the terms of a cease-fire, the FLN changed its position regarding non-Muslims. Accepting Jews as part of the so-called European minority, the FLN applied the principle of self-determination, which had been so central to their own nationalist struggle, to the Jewish minority. As Krim Belkacem specified in July 1961, "They are indigenous, but we will not force anyone to take a stance one way or another."[159] This move, which French negotiators also promoted, meant that over the last year of the Algerian conflict, Jews "disappeared" juridically into the European majority.[160] Subsequent violence among counterrevolutionary paramilitary forces, the FLN, and the French army similarly deemphasized differences between Jews and non-Jews. As one Joint informant commented in October 1961, "[W]hen one leaves home in the morning, one is never sure of getting back alive and, if one does, of finding the apartment intact and the family safe and sound. This is true throughout the country . . . and applies to all—Moslems, Christians and Jews alike."[161]

And yet the very process that allowed Jews to blend into the pieds noirs population—seemingly detaching them from their particularistic identities—continued to hold powerful lessons about where Jewishness fit in the newly emerging North African political landscape. As one Joint official noted, "The underlying and basic Algerian nationalist feeling about Jews is . . . that they are, if not traitors to independent Algeria, at least collaborators. This sentiment comes through, and Jews feel it, despite any statements that Algerian nationalists may make, in their olive branch moments, that they wish and hope that Jews, like other Europeans, will stay."[162] Moreover, as violence against Jewish victims surged in 1961, the view that Algerian Muslims were Arabs in North African clothing, sworn enemies of the Jews, grew even more pervasive among those working to preserve Jewish life.[163] The failure of the initial Evian conferences further convinced Jews that they would soon become hostages of the Algerian government, since "in Arab countries, political and economic difficulties always translate into coercive measures against Jewish communities." As local French officials reported, "[T]he fear of later finding themselves in a tête-à-tête with the Muslims in an independent Algeria, in which all cohabitation was impossible" circulated widely.[164]

In addition, regional events continued to stoke fears of the dangers lurking in North African independence. Most notably, just as French/FLN negotiations were collapsing in summer 1961, Tunisia clashed violently with the French over the latter's ongoing presence at the Bizerte naval base. Subsequently, the nationalist press accused Jews of supporting the French as departures for Israel and France increased substantially again.[165] As one Joint observer commented on Algerian Jewish reactions to these events: "If even in moderate Tunisia, ruled by Western oriented Premier Habib Bourguiba, such things can happen, then there is no future for us anywhere in Moslem North Africa."[166] Or according to the AJC, "Jews particularly feel that there is no place for them in an independent Moslem state, citing Tunisia and Morocco as examples of what can happen to Jews in Moslem lands. They add that the situation will be much worse in Algeria where passions have been aroused to a pitch never felt in the neighboring countries."[167]

Many of these tensions came to a head in Oran in September 1961—on the morning of Rosh Hashanah—when a father en route to synagogue with his daughter was killed with another man. Jewish self-defense units retaliated, burning cars and shops and murdering local Muslim residents.[168] While the FLN warned Oran's Muslims not to be diverted into a war against the Jews, and the CJAES called for calm, anger and fear were palpable throughout the city.[169] A boycott of Jewish businesses followed, while commentators reported that "feelings between Jews and Moslems is even worse than between Moslems and the rest of the European population."[170] One angry depiction thus described Jews as "shouting slogans borrowed from the racist Europeans, and taking part in actions analogous to those of the ultra imperialists when they organized demonstrations and *ratonades.*" By imitating "the blinding racial hatred of imperialist criminals and [throwing] themselves onto a suicidal path," local Jews had committed a kind of treason: "We deeply regret this disease that has infected the Jews, driving them to shout sordid and hostile slogans likely to cause hatred and provoke reactions contrary to their interests and to the peaceful coexistence of Algeria's communities. Furthermore, in acting this way, the Jews risk seriously compromising their future in our country."[171] While the murder was very likely carried out by the Organisation de l'armée secrète (OAS), the counterrevolutionary paramilitary group formed in February 1961 to protect French Algeria, such discourse contributed to the sense of a growing Jewish-Muslim polarization.[172]

For some Jews who found themselves in a "state of bewilderment and chaos" in fall 1961, previous ambivalence around migration dissolved.[173] In September alone, departures for France more than doubled.[174] As one official reporting on Jewish choices made clear: "fears over the attacks and aggravated relations between communities has transformed into panic in certain regions. Emigration seems the least harmful solution to many."[175] While many pieds noirs made a similar decision, this commonality masked the particular contours of the Jewish exodus.[176] Initial migrations thus brought out a greater percentage of Jews and reflected particularistic concerns.[177] As the chief rabbi noted to an American reporter, "[Y]ou Americans still believe Algeria should be independent because that's democracy! Your democracy—see what it does to us—the holy Torah in the mud, the house of God defiled."[178] In Constantine, where the 1956 violence and the destruction of the synagogue had left notable scars, street confrontations and assassinations of Jewish targets forced most families to remain indoors. By January 1962 only 8,000 of the city's 18,000 Jews remained. Life in Algiers and Oran seemed equally bleak; by January 1962 at least some were predicting, "Oran's 28,000 Jews will not be able to remain."[179]

Among those who stayed, sympathy for the OAS spiked considerably, although scholars disagree over the depth of Jewish support for the movement.[180] While most agree that Jews—like many in the "European" population—hoped the OAS would prevail, few, it is argued, openly supported the OAS due to its antisemitic leanings.[181] Thus if Jewish support was evident in Oran where Jewish commandos assassinated opponents and organized self-defense units,[182] generally speaking Jews were not enthusiastic supporters.[183] More recently, Todd Shepard has dissented, arguing that there was significant Jewish support for the OAS by early 1962 when press accounts and military officials took note of increasing anti-Muslim vigilantism among Jews and when government sources reported that those in Algiers and Oran in particular were abandoning their previously moderate politics.[184] Moreover, Jewish departures slowed down—evidence to Shepard of renewed hopes for French Algeria—while *Paris Match* charged the Israeli Irgun with training OAS commandos.[185]

Shepard's argument, and particularly his position on Jewish departures, challenges work that has emphasized Jewish panic and dislocation.[186] However, a variety of Jewish sources confirm his assessment. The American Jewish Committee (AJC), for example, reported in January that "the mass of the Jews are overwhelmingly pro-OAS or Algérie-Française or at the least for French presence in Algeria. Even those who are not pro OAS believe that such gains as have been wrenched from the FLN are due to the OAS intransigence."[187] Local Joint employees concurred, noting significant Jewish arrests for their OAS participation.[188] In addition, the French Jewish organization, CRIF, debated the risks of condemning OAS activities given their belief that the "vast majority of our Algerian co-religionnaires" supported the organization.[189]

Shepard errs, however, when he links the drop in departures too fully with support for the OAS. Intimidation may have had as much to do with this shift as OAS appeal, since the diminution in exit visa requests directly followed increased threats against emigration.[190] OAS posters announcing the murder of Moise Choukroun, vice president of the Cultuelle de Maison-Carée, for "desertion," thus provoked significant consternation among Jews planning to leave.[191] Another factor contributing to the reduced Jewish departures included the migration of most communal leaders by late 1961 due to fears of targeted assassination, leaving those remaining "without advisors."[192] This flight of visible leadership, it should be noted, was another sign of the particularity of Jewish migration at this stage, since among non-Jewish Europeans there was no similar loss of spokesmen.[193] By February, rumors of substantial assistance for those leaving Algeria for France and a belief that the French government was winning concessions during negotiations provided those remaining with hope that they still had time.[194] According to the Joint's M. Jordan in March, Algerian Jews believed they would have an extended period to adjust their affairs and were putting off immediate departure.[195]

As such evidence suggests, the diminution in Jewish departures in early 1962 was the result of a complex landscape. While support for the OAS grew and many hoped that France would hold on to Algeria, other factors, including lack of resources, loss of most communal leadership, and fear of reprisals also contributed.[196] Shepard is thus right to argue that in these months "departures . . . became *pied noir*, and no longer 'Israelite' 'Spanish' or of 'French origin.'" I would argue, however, that as departures became fully linked to the pied noirs destiny, they rendered invisible the Jewishness that was still shaping perceptions of future possibilities in an Algerian state.[197] As the AJC summarized, "The Jews in Algeria are today beset by the same passions and conflicts as all others in Algeria, with an additional set of difficulties arising out of conditions special to them."[198]

Arguments that suggest that repatriation pushed Algerian Jewish identity into the background, while magnifying allegiances to France, downplay the way departures reinforced notions of Jewish particularism.[199] This paradox was on full display in a meeting between Jean Morin (France's délégate général in Algeria), Jacques Lazarus, and Andre Narboni in February 1962 where the question of migrations was discussed. During the meeting, Morin offered the two men positions on a provisional body charged with carrying out the transition of power from French to Algerian hands. Both refused on the grounds that Algerian Jews did not need a representative, since they did not make up a political entity. And yet, if Jews had no "special status," they still had particularistic concerns. Thus as Lazarus and Narboni argued for the importance of facilitating migration to France for all citizens, they emphasized "the fundamental problem of relations between Israel and the Arab States with all that implies for Jews living in independent Arab countries," as a way of making clear that Jews could not remain in Algeria.[200] Here, then, claims of universal citizenship masked particularistic concerns that were also at play.

Moreover, a sense that Jews were still being negatively singled out, despite FLN concessions to treat Jews as Europeans, continued to influence Jewish political discourse.[201] In late spring 1962, for example, when FLN spokesman Abdelkader Chanderli threatened reprisals against Jews who participated in the OAS's "indiscriminate killing of Muslims," the Joint's Abe Karlikow remarked that "the FLN harbors *particular resentment* that Jews should thus have identified with the rest of the Europeans in Algeria, with some few exceptions, in support of the OAS." He pointed to a rise of kidnappings and executions in spring 1962 as well as to an FLN letter to Jewish leaders in Oran demanding 400,000,000 old francs (approximately $800,000) as evidence that anti-Jewish sentiment was intensifying.[202]

"Repatriation" reached its zenith in summer 1962 between the signing of the Evian accords in March and the declaration of Algerian independence in July with over half a million "Europeans" departing despite extensive protections promised to them. Jews, like others, fled in fear of reprisals, ongoing violence, economic upheaval, and uncertainty.[203]

Yet if their departure marked a "symbolic step in establishing their Frenchness," it also reconfirmed newly solidified "lessons" about the place of Jews in Muslim lands. As Jean Bensimon, a French soldier turned FLN supporter, noted, "When it was my turn to be threatened, I went to find refuge among my Algerian friends in the city's outskirts. I well understood from their cold welcome how futile it was to be between two sides [*entre deux bords*] and how impossible to reconcile the irreconcilable. I also knew that there was nothing else for me here.[204] Likewise, one Jewish communist who joined the FLN early in the war was infuriated to discover that he would not automatically attain Algerian citizenship: "For Jews there was a particular problem; the Jews were in Algeria before the Arabs! And now they would be asked to fill out forms to become Algerian citizens! That was unbearable because even Arabs or Muslims who had betrayed the cause or their country or their brothers were automatically

Algerians. And [Jews] had to fill out forms because . . ." When he complained, a fellow Algerian Muslim communist accused him of Zionist affiliations.[205]

Such comments remind us of the distinct dilemmas facing Jews as the Algerian crisis came to a head, and particularly as the more virulently anti-Israel Ahmed Ben Bella began to assert control within the FLN. As Bensimon asked,

> When Ben Bella says that he is "an Arab, an Arab and again an Arab," how can the other not detect a threat and why can I not write "I am a French Jew, a French Jew, and again a French Jew"? They would object that if the Jews were identified with an Algerian Algeria, Arabism would not frighten them any more than French Christianity. Perhaps, but didn't Tunisian Jews, for example, equally colonized and identified with Tunisian nationalism, feel like outsiders when the first article of the Tunisian constitution announced that the republic was Muslim and Islamic?

The position of Jews elsewhere in North Africa as well as fears over Algeria's deteriorating relationship with Israel—as more moderate GPRA members lost out to their opponents—reinforced fears that Jews could never be Algerians like all others.[206] Ben Bella's denunciation of Israel and his threat in April 1962 to send troops to fight the Jewish state exacerbated such fears.[207] "When Ben Bella promised to send one hundred thousand Algerian soldiers against Israel," continued Bensimon, "I wondered what Ben Bella and I, born on the same land, under the same sky, had in common."[208]

Such concerns merged with wider fears of retribution and upheaval to push four-fifths of Algerian Jews out of the country by October. Their decision to embrace their French citizenship led to what Benjamin Stora has called a "a double erasure of Algerian history, as if the war of independence and the departure of the 1960s had slowly but surely eroded all of Algeria's ancient Jewish heritage. In Jewish memories, Muslims seem to embody the negative representation of the 'other,' while the hostility of the Europeans has been minimized."[209] If such narratives were not the only way that departing Algerian Jews remembered the war, images of Muslim-Jewish discord remained prevalent. As Bensimon described, "Algerian nationalism seemed to threaten their Jewish selves as much as their French selves," a view that was perpetuated in communal discourse as subsequent migrations emptied North Africa of its Jewish populations.[210] These "lessons" coupled with those learned in 1948 about the way French policies in the Middle East indexed unequal power relations in the metropole created the discursive terrain on which Muslim and Jewish immigrants met in France.

Encounters in the Metropole

The Impact of Decolonization on Muslim-Jewish Life in France in the 1950s and 1960s

The lessons learned in North Africa from 1948 to 1962 had significant repercussions in France. First, for many French Jewish leaders preoccupied with rebuilding from the recent Nazi and Vichy persecutions, the Jewish meanings in French decolonization were all too clear. While those on the left expressed empathy for Muslim victims of French racism and called for Muslim-Jewish cooperation throughout the Algerian crisis, many of those representing major Jewish institutions or publications echoed fears that the "Arab world" had turned on its Jewish residents. As a result, distrust and animosity rather than commonalities and cooperation tended to dominate mainstream institutional representations of the "Arab world," a broad designation that often collapsed Muslim North Africans uncritically within it.

A comparison with Muslim institutions and periodicals in France in the same period is impossible given the far more developed Jewish communal structures in these decades and the greater number of sources they have left behind. However, this very imbalance points to the second major consequence of the decolonization process on Muslim-Jewish relations in France–the importation to the metropole of the profound juridical and social inequities embedded in colonial North Africa. As noted in the Introduction, thousands of Muslim and Jewish migrants came to France throughout the decolonization process. Importing similar cultural, linguistic, and even religious practices from Algeria, Tunisia, and Morocco, Muslim and Jewish migrants often shared a sense of displacement and common origins that facilitated bonds between them. However, differing relationships to the French state—many resulting from the legacy of French colonialism—were equally powerful in shaping mutual perceptions in the 1950s and early 1960s. Early encounters in the metropole must be understood, therefore, as intimately connected to the North African past and France's violent departure from the region.

An examination of migration and settlement in Marseille in the 1950s and early 1960s illustrates the impact of colonial legacies in shaping the contours of Muslim-Jewish relations in the metropole. While Paris remained the main pole of attraction for both, Marseille's close proximity to North Africa, its Mediterranean climate, and its expanding economy meant that the city attracted thousands of repatriates and immigrants in the 1950s and 1960s. Shared cultural frameworks and the common experiences of migration and displacement meant that Muslim and Jewish newcomers often had much in common, creating the basis for convivial exchange in the mixed immigrant neighborhoods where many initially settled.

Such commonalities did not, however, ensure similar processes of incorporation into French urban life. Differing relationships to the French state and levels of communal development meant that incoming Jews often not only had more resources available to them than Muslims arriving in the same period but also benefited from a local administration sympathetic to their concerns. Governed by socialist mayor Gaston Defferre—a vocal advocate of Israel with deep ties to the Jewish community—Marseille's political establishment embraced its Jewish minorities in ways that emphasized the inequities between Jews and Muslims evident in the colonial structure. Colonial legacies, then, had long-term consequences in the metropole.

French Jews and North African Decolonization

Given the diversity of French Jewish life, there was no unified communal perspective on French decolonization, North African nationalism, or the Algerian war. As the Algerian conflict intensified, conscriptions increased, and violence spread to the metropole, opposition to the war began to grow throughout many sectors of French society. French Jews, like other citizens, responded with the variety typical of a heterogeneous population. Nevertheless, the recent anti-Jewish persecution in Europe coupled with the birth of Israel and its complex relations with its Arab neighbors meant that French Jews, like the international Jewish agencies discussed in chapter 2, often saw Jewish meaning in France's disentanglement from its North African territories, meaning that was debated extensively in communal organizations and media outlets. While some called for dialogue and cooperation based on a shared Muslim-Jewish commitment to national self-determination and anti-racist struggles, others focused on Jewish victimization at the hands of "Arabs" and dismissed dialogue as impossible due to rising antisemitism in the Arab world. It was the latter perspective that came to dominate most mainstream communal discourse by the mid-1960s.

French Jewish interest in the "Jews of Arab lands" increased after World War II as part of the wider American and European Jewish focus on the issue. While the CRIF continued to rely on the AIU to take the lead on all North African projects, focusing primarily on European antisemitism and war restitutions, delegates nevertheless took interest in the region beginning in 1948.[1] Moroccan Zionist Paul Calamaro was thus invited to speak at a January meeting, and in

April, CRIF president Léon Meiss visited Morocco for an AIU school inauguration.[2] Following the riots in Oujda and Djérada, CRIF delegates protested
to French authorities and called for restitution.[3] Likewise, the Fédération des
sociétés juifs de France, the umbrella organization representing East European
Jewish immigrants, introduced a new charge in November 1948 that called,
among other things, for French Jewish aid to North Africa.[4] Both the FSJF and
the CRIF also joined other organizations in protesting the persecution of Iraqi
Jews from 1949 to 1951,[5] often comparing Iraq's policies to Hitler's.[6] Egyptian
Jews similarly captured attention, first in 1948 when two hundred families
sought asylum in France, and more consistently after "Operation Susannah"
in July 1954, when a small network of Egyptian Jewish and Israeli spies fire-
bombed several sites in Alexandria and Cairo.[7] It was following the Suez crisis,
however, when thousands of Egyptian Jews fled, five thousand of whom sought
shelter in France, that French Jewish organizations took greatest notice.[8] If the
presence of these new Jewish refugees strained aid institutions still working to
rebuild from the Holocaust, they also inspired empathy from those who shared
a recent past of persecution.[9]

In response, anti-Arab discourse mounted, as audiences at pro-Israel rallies
were warned to "remain on their guard before the Arab world" so that "the
Arab cannot practice the verse in the Koran: 'If you cannot convince, extermi-
nate.'"[10] Jewish publications were also saturated with comparisons of Nasser to
Hitler.[11] According to the secretary general of the Association indépendante des
anciens deportés et internés juifs: "Barely twelve years have elapsed since the
destruction of the last barbed wire fences around the Nazi concentration camps
stopped the tragic deportations in which six million of our own perished, when
once again the nightmare of Nasser's deportations and concentration camps
confronts our Egyptian brothers." Or as one speaker proclaimed at a December
1956 rally, thousands of Egyptian Jews were being "thrown into prisons, new
Auschwitzes, now with Arab names."[12] While some commentators downplayed
widespread Egyptian antisemitism, emphasizing instead the government's role
in requisitions, arrests, and expulsions, headlines in the Jewish press, such as
"The New Cairo, Mecca of Anti-Semitism," blurred such distinctions.[13] Baron
Alain de Rothschild, president of the Consistoire, similarly drew parallels between the Holocaust and the persecution of Egyptian Jews: "We would betray
the memory [of the six million martyrs massacred under Hitler] if, at this crucial moment, we did not declare our total solidarity with the members of a
community threatened with complete and brutal annihilation."[14] Rhetorically
linking European antisemitism with Arab nationalism, such pronouncements
placed Jews in a politically antagonistic relationship with "Arabs," a perspective
that solidified as the North African crisis accelerated.

Prior to the mid-1950s, French Jewish spokesmen had relatively little to
say about their nation's policies in Morocco, Tunisia, and Algeria. In January
1948, for example, Léon Meiss echoed the CRIF's perennial discomfort with

criticizing the government when he reminded delegates to be prudent in pronouncements on Maghrebian Jews.[15] While that organization did protest the
1948 riots in Morocco and while the AIU encouraged the French government
to better conditions for Jews in the protectorate, such efforts were rare. In 1954,
however, as Moroccan and Tunisian Jews began departing for the metropole,
questions over how to respond became more acute.[16] On one side stood those
who believed that North African Jewish life was in peril. As one CRIF member
remarked in November, "As long as France remains, the situation for North
African Jews will be bearable, but make no mistake about the meaning and
import of current developments."[17] Many French Zionists also expressed skepti-
cism over the Jewish future in an independent North Africa, with some underscoring the antisemitism of all Arab states—thereby asserting the "Arabness"
of the region—and others warning that the anti-Israeli stance of North African
nationalist leaders made migration to Israel essential.[18] On the other side stood
the Zionist left, which rejected such analyses, as did a range of non-Zionist
intellectuals and activists.[19] In August 1954, the Bund's French chapter thus
argued that Zionists were exploiting the situation to encourage migration to
Israel.[20] While in favor of helping Jews who desired to emigrate, Bund members
also called for faith in Muslim promises of security, arguing that many indigenous Jews supported the independence struggle.[21]

This debate—between those arguing that Jews qua Jews were the target of
Muslim animosity and those arguing that Muslims and Jews shared common
aspirations—intensified in tandem with the Algerian conflict.[22] In fall 1955,
for example, as demonstrators in several French cities protested an increase of
troop contingents, the Union des étudiants juifs de France (UEJF)—the main
body representing Jewish high school and university students—publicly condemned collective repression in Algeria and insisted that all French youth, and
Jewish youth in particular, be spared participating in military occupations.[23]
Their stance infuriated CRIF officials who had adopted a predictably cau-
tious position on growing militarization in Algeria.[24] In their condemnation
of French colonial policies, however, the Bund and the UEJF joined various
prominent Jewish thinkers and leftist activists who criticized the army for its
violent tactics and argued that it was unethical and hypocritical to support Israeli independence while rejecting the same for Morocco, Tunisia, and Algeria. Well-known Jewish intellectuals such as Jean Daniel, Pierre Vidal-Naquet,
Claude Lanzman, and Wladimir Rabi wrote in favor of Algerian independence,
condemned French torture tactics, and defended those unwilling to serve in
the army. While not all rooted their political positions in their Jewishness, others very consciously made such links.[25] Rabi, for example, argued that FLN
terrorism rarely targeted Jews and called for Jewish protests against Algerian
Muslim mistreatment: "Others may allow themselves to be derelict. We do not
have the right."[26] For Alain Geismar, the founder later of the Maoist, Gauche
Prolétarienne, and eighteen at the time of the Algerian conflict, activism was

very much a response to prior Jewish persecution. Stopped often by police due to his dark skin, Geismar recalled their excuses once realizing he was French: "Pardon us, we thought you were Algerian. Excuse us, we thought you were an Arab." Such racism, Geismar insisted, "is intolerable and can only remind us of Jews who were arrested fifteen years before."[27] Other French Jews signed petitions, worked as "suitcase carriers" transporting documents and funds for the FLN, or defended imprisoned Algerian militants in court. According to Janine Cahen, a twenty-nine-year-old Mulhouse teacher who worked as a suitcase carrier, "It is because I am Jewish that I aid the FLN; it must be made known that those who proclaim 'Algérie française' are the same as those who scrawl out 'Death to Jews.'"[28] Or as one Jewish activist declared somewhat hyperbolically, "Ninety percent of those who made up the underground network were Jews . . . maybe not ninety percent, but eighty-five percent."[29]

Even those most convinced of the righteousness of the Algerian cause, however, at times had trouble reconciling their Jewish commitments with their progressive politics. Such difficulties emerged clearly in the UEJF's efforts at interethnic dialogue, which while pursued with great enthusiasm in the late 1950s and early 1960s, also reflected significant ambivalence.[30] The organization, founded in Paris in 1945, sought to bring together Jewish students of all political, religious, and cultural orientations. With fifteen chapters in universities throughout France as well as several subsections in Paris, the UEJF attracted approximately 10 percent of the most highly engaged Jewish students (or about 2,500 people), many of whom believed deeply in pluralism and cross-cultural dialogue.[31] In March–April 1957, for example, the UEJF's organ, *Kadimah*, featured the essay, "Plea for a Certain Metropolitan Dialogue."[32] Written by René Kochmann, a frequent contributor, the article argued for improved communication between Jewish and Muslim students in France. Even this initial call for dialogue, however, was marked by a certain ambivalence, as Kochmann reflected on the naïveté of asking North African Muslim students to accept the independence of a Jewish state without asking the same for Algeria. Here, then, a desire for exchange was quickly shadowed by awareness that to engage in dialogue required putting Algerian Muslim needs ahead of French or Jewish national priorities.

According to Henri Atlan, an Algerian Jew who had come to Paris in 1949 to pursue his studies, and one of the movement's leaders, UEJF members in fact worried that dialogue with North African nationalists might conflict with their Jewish commitments. By defending "the values that seemed to be essential to our history and traditions . . . we appeared to be allying ourselves with Arab nationalism, which we had from the outset every reason to suspect of anti-Israelism and therefore of anti-Semitism." For Atlan such fears were unwarranted, since the UEJF was not seeking "to give up our identity in the name of a utopian universalism as those on the left are occasionally tempted to do, but to establish a dialogue based on a mutual comprehension of our hopes, differences, and needs."[33] *Kadimah* seemed to reflect this perspective. The June–July 1957 issue, for example, featured an article by the Algerian Muslim nationalist writer, Yacine Kateb, a proponent of Muslim-Jewish cooperation in Palestine, in addition to a transcript of a heated discussion following his presentation to *Kadimah*'s editors and students.[34] The exchange excited the journal's editors, who commented: "Usually, student conferences are raucous, violent, and impassioned [but] we all had the feeling that . . . something at once positive and intangible was created here."[35] And yet Kateb was the only prominent author in *Kadimah*'s pages to receive a lengthy explanatory note and rebuttal, which narrowed the scope of the dialogue by imposing an interpretation on his analysis.

Likewise, several attempts to bring together Jewish and Muslim students in France failed due to mutual distrust. As Albert Memmi, the Tunisian Jewish author, described of his participation in one such group in Paris: "Must I acknowledge that reticence was almost equal on both sides? That the non-Jews and the non-Arabs who were with us were full of goodwill but skeptical. In brief, we failed; we must acknowledge it because nobody expected it."[36] Such failures came, in part, because progressive politics was often directly at odds with group affiliations. Lionel Cohn captured this dilemma in winter 1960 in *Kadimah* when asserting that Jews were caught between the impossible choice of "their love for their Jewish brothers [and] their passion for justice." Drawing on Camus, he noted, "If I had to choose between my mother and justice, I would choose my mother."[37] In the interest of dialogue, *Kadimah* published a response by Mohammed Ben Bachir, an Algerian Muslim student in France, who argued that Algerian Jews were African and more welcome there than in France.[38] And yet UEJF editors published Ben Bachir's piece with numerous disclaimers, cutting out sections they believed to be inflammatory and insisting that his arguments were "baseline invalid." The UEJF commitment to dialogue was thus highly circumscribed despite its criticisms of French policies in Algeria and its commitment to the ideal of national self-determination and Muslim-Jewish exchange.

Given the difficulties of establishing dialogue among those most committed to the endeavor, it is not surprising that others proved even more skeptical. In a special edition of the popular Jewish monthly *L'Arche* entitled, "Is Israeli-Arab Peace Possible?," the editors seemingly committed themselves to such a good-faith exchange. The decision to devote an entire issue to the question, the editors explained, emerged from growing pressure from the Left " 'to open a dialogue,' 'to stretch out a hand,' " so as "not to avoid an objective confrontation with opposing theses." With this goal in mind, the editors posed a set of questions to specialists on North Africa and the Middle East about the possibility of peace between Israel and its neighbors. The questions reveal much about the framework from which certain mainstream French Jewish institutions approached the issue. Although ostensibly about peace in the Middle East, the first question focused on "Muslim anti-Semitism," asking if "such anti-Semitism was a constant of the historical tradition of Islam." While the subsequent questions returned to "Arabs" and the conflict in the Middle East, the issue had been firmly contextualized as part of a deeply rooted Muslim rejection of Jews.[39]

Despite the biased questions, *L'Arche* editors expressed shock and dismay that only the Parisian delegate of the Bureau arabe de presse et de publications responded to the dozens of requests sent to North African and Middle Eastern spokesmen. Lamenting the more than fifty unanswered letters, the editors denounced the refusal to discuss "a problem that presents so many analogies with their own." Those student activists who demurred on the grounds that they had nothing to add to the Arab League's pronouncements or because they were focused on their own independence struggles were condemned for their unwillingness "to be seen in the columns of a Jewish journal." The editors concluded darkly that Muslim-Jewish dialogue was impossible due to a "lack of viable interlocutors." "Make no mistake," they warned.

> This is not a "small matter" around the Israeli-Arab conflict, this is not a phenomenon on the "margins" of the major challenges that Islam faces today as it adapts to the modern world. This is, to the contrary, what the Anglo-Saxons call a "test case," a prime example. The way in which the Arabs learn to overcome their resentment towards the Jews will determine their aptitude for re-shaping their old Islamic societies and for adapting to the standards that govern the contemporary behavior of States and individuals."[40]

Here, then, "Arabs," whether Middle Eastern or North African—overtaken with an essentialist rejection of the Jew embedded in Islam—were presented as an existential threat to the Western world. Dialogue, framed as the debate between two equivalent "sides," failed because of one side's backwardness and bigotry. Of course, not all commentators described Muslim-Jewish relations this starkly. The same magazine published pieces that emphasized good relations between North African Muslim and Jewish residents or that downplayed anti-Jewish conspiracies.[41] More dire assessments, however, continued to gather steam.[42] By summer 1961, as Bizerte and the Algerian crisis pushed ever larger numbers of Tunisian and Algerian Jews to the metropole, depictions increasingly stressed anti-Jewish biases. One article, for example, cited a Tunisian Jewish man saying, "We no longer have any future in Tunisia; we do not dare to go out or to speak. It is as it was under Hitler."[43] Other articles, collected and circulated by the CRIF, also emphasized Muslim antisemitism. One story in the CRIF's "Note d'information," told of Dr. Ovadia who had fled Oran "threatened with death as a Jew." In his words, "If we do not immediately take appropriate action, we will see in Oran in the coming days the bloodiest pogrom in all of Jewish history."[44] Another editorialized that "only the willful or the partisan would ignore the anti-Semitism that has filtered down from the top to the bottom in the Arab nationalist world."[45] Still another spoke of Muslim students in Tlemcen who carved swastikas on school walls and forced Jewish students to kiss them.[46]

Such perceptions of increasing antisemitism spreading from the Middle East to North Africa were accompanied by a growing belief that many Algerian Jews supported French victory and even the OAS. Rumors of a Jewish chapter of the OAS began circulating in March 1961, leading to vigorous debates within the CRIF over whether to condemn OAS violence.[47] To do so, one member remarked, would cut off the CRIF from "our Algerian co-religionists, whose sympathies are leaning mostly toward the OAS." Or as another commented: "The large majority of Algerian Jews have adopted a position contrary to the official policies of the metropole. They very actively support a movement that symbolizes the Resistance."[48] While the left-leaning member associations rejected such assertions, arguing that Algerian Jewish opinion was diverse and that most opposed the OAS, and still others criticized the stoking of anti-Arab panic,[49] their opponents saw diminishing common ground between Jewish and Muslim North Africans.[50]

Such debates also circulated following the brutal police repression of Algerian anti-war demonstrators on 17 October 1961.[51] In the aftermath, several Jewish organizations held protests, making comparisons with antisemitic persecution in the 1940s. In this instance, however, parallels between Nazi/Vichy oppression and contemporary events were used to underscore solidarities between Muslims and Jews. The UEJF, for example, declared itself unable to remain silent before "measures recalling those taken against us Jews by the Nazis under occupation." Its protest on 21 November condemned all forms of racism; called for the prosecution of those responsible; and demanded the reestablishment of peace in Algeria.[52] Likewise, the FSJF condemned silence, "as some did during the period when we were forced to wear the yellow star" and expressed its solidarity with the victims. The Jewish communist organization, Mouvement contre le racisme, l'antémitisme, et pour la paix (MRAP), formed after World War II to fight inequity in France, was equally vocal in its criticisms. As Rabbi Sirat, France's Jewish youth chaplain, commented during the MRAP's demonstration, "the poor treatment that the Algerians suffered touched me personally." Recalling the recent persecution of French Jews, he insisted, "We must do something so that it does not begin again."[53] The president of the Union des engagés volontaires et anciens combattants juifs, Isi Blum, urged the CRIF to speak out as representative of a people that had also suffered racial persecution.[54]

The CRIF's response to this appeal, however, points to diverging Jewish perspectives on the Algerian war and to difficulties in forging Muslim-Jewish alliances around areas of common concern. While the governing board condemned violence against Muslim Algerians, it expressly refused to compare recent events with antisemitism in the 1940s.[55] While in part reflecting the CRIF's traditional commitment to republican universalism, this decision also reflected pressure from the wider Jewish population, such as a November article by Algerian Jewish repatriates who insisted that Muslim immigrants deserved *no*

Jewish support having never taken a stand against antisemitic violence.[56] Thus while a progressive Jewish wing urged greater support for Algerian Muslims based on profound commonalities, the most prominent Jewish institutions refused to make such links, often presenting a far more dire perspective on Muslim-Jewish relations throughout North Africa.

Such debates persisted throughout the last year of the Algerian war. While those on the left continued to insist that "in an era when all men must choose only one loyalty," Algerian Jews had a moral duty to side with the FLN— culminating in a June 1962 collective appeal to Algerian Jews to remain in their country—for many others, the emptying out of North Africa's Jewish population provided evidence of the Jews' particular fate.[57] As M. Moch of CRIF remarked in January 1963, Algerian Jews had left for "for distinctive reasons," citing their flight in percentages larger than other Europeans as evidence.[58] Or as Gérard Israel asserted in L'Arche, "Algerian Jewish repatriates in France find themselves in a situation a bit different [than other repatriates] because they were rejected by an Algerian society of which they were, in some ways, the integral part."[59]

Such perspectives became a central trope in French Jewish discourse throughout the late 1950s and early 1960s as Jewish departures increased, seemingly confirming the dire predictions of those who had warned against mounting antisemitism. While calls for dialogue and cooperation were never fully extinguished, mainstream Jewish institutions increasingly portrayed Jews and Muslims as antagonists in a polarized political crisis in which the latter had been infected with the Arab League's propaganda.[60]

For most French Jews, however, "Arabs" remained an abstraction associated with the Middle East and North Africa, and few Jewish publications or organizations expressed any opinion about what, if anything, the growing Muslim population in France meant for Jewish life.[61] In the late 1960s, however, when events both at home and abroad finally drew Jewish attention to the local Muslim population, frameworks forged during decolonization established the parameters of communal discourse around the Muslim question. While those who had fought hard for Algerian independence continued to defend interethnic dialogue, their perspective was increasingly marginalized in mainstream Jewish circles.

Early Encounters in the Metropole

If the Jewish establishment proved largely oblivious to the potential communal implications of surging Muslim migration to France, arriving Moroccan, Tunisian, and Algerian Jews proved far more cognizant of this development. Sharing a sense of displacement and an overlapping cultural and linguistic heritage with Muslim North Africans, many Jews found comfort in the familiarity of the other. One Tunisian Jew, for example, capturing his sense of discomfort after arriving in France, described "Arabs, whose path I cross only by chance in certain neighborhoods of Paris and who, like me, have become immigrants," with a sense of having undergone a similar experience of displacement.[62] Moreover, France's postwar housing crisis meant that incoming Muslims and Jews sometimes settled in similar neighborhoods where common origins and similar challenges served as a social bridge. Within relatively short order, however, differing relationships to the French state and levels of communal development rooted in the colonial past highlighted stark contrasts.

Housing shortages sometimes led Muslims and Jews to settle in similar neighborhoods on the outskirts of large French cities. Although the government sought to distribute repatriates throughout the country so as to avoid overwhelming any one area, most Jews gravitated toward France's largest cities.[63] There, housing shortages and high prices sent many to newly constructed apartment projects on the urban periphery, some of which were initially reserved for repatriates, including in Sarcelles, Aulnay-sous-Bois, Bondy, and Créteil in the northern and eastern Parisian suburbs and Saint-Marguerite (9th), Saint-Tronc (10th), La Rose (13th), and Pont de Vivaux (10th) in Marseille. While few Moroccan and Tunisian Jews benefited from government subsidies, many moved to similar areas or to inexpensive neighborhoods within city limits, such as the traditionally East European Jewish neighborhoods of the 4th (Marais) and the 20th (Belleville) as well as the 12th, 18th, and 19th arrondissements in Paris or to the 1st and 2nd arrondissements in Marseille. These residential patterns meant that newly arriving Jews at times shared city spaces with North African Muslims who settled in similar areas, although economic differences and the repatriates' political status as citizens often gave them access to neighborhoods unavailable to Muslim migrants.[64]

The cafés, groceries, restaurants, schools, and streets in mixed neighborhoods became meeting spots for those with shared culinary, cultural, and linguistic practices. In the 1960s and 1970s, most Algerian, Moroccan, and Tunisian Jewish adults spoke Arabic, helping to forge bonds with other Arabic-speaking North Africans.[65] As one transplanted Algerian Jew made clear: "We are Berbers. We are from there and France is elsewhere [c'est un ailleurs]. We always lived there; my grandmother did not even know how to speak French. My parents' maternal language is Arabic. Me, I speak Arabic. I love Arab music. I am from there."[66] Neighborhood grocers sold to a mixed clientele raised on couscous, olive oil, and North African alcohol. Muslim and Jewish men played cards and smoked together in local cafés. Interactions in these neighborhoods were often friendly, rarely reflecting the wider political struggles taking place in the Maghreb or Middle East.[67]

If common origins and similar settlement patterns helped establish new forms of sociability, however, they could not mask divisions that influenced the integration of both into the French state.[68] In the 1950s, Muslims and Jews from Algeria came with French citizenship, as did some Jews from Morocco and Tunisia and Egypt. Equality on paper did not translate into equivalent access to French society, however, where distrust and fear of Muslims surged in response to a brutal war of decolonization.[69] Subsequently the decision to recognize the French citizenship of Jewish Algerians in the final war negotiations provided legal justification for excluding Muslims while opening the door to Jewish integration.[70] Algerian Jews thus benefited from the extensive housing subsidies, working papers, professional *reclassement* and medical and social security available to repatriating citizens.[71] In contrast, Moroccan, Tunisian, and particularly Algerian Muslims faced administrative structures that distinguished them even from other incoming migrants, including Jews from the same countries whose integration was often made easier by sympathetic French administrators.[72]

A focus on Marseille underscores the way in which shared cultural connections and a postwar housing crisis initially pushed Muslim and Jewish migrants together, while colonial legacies and differing relationships to the French state pulled them apart. Some aspects of Marseille's story are, of course, unique. The 40 percent increase in the city's population in the 1950s and 1960s as it welcomed French citizens expelled from Egypt, European settlers and functionaries from Tunisia and Morocco, North African laborers, and Algerian "repatriates," meant that at least statistically, Marseille was more affected by France's loss of its North African territories than other French cities.[73] Moreover, the leadership over several decades of Mayor Gaston Defferre gave the city unmatched political stability in which some groups fared better than others. Despite Marseille's particularities, however, the processes that pushed Muslims and Jews together and eventually pulled them apart mirrored those at work in other large French cities.

As in other cities, Marseille's Muslim and Jewish populations increased substantially. In 1951 alone, 195,000 Algerian Muslims passed through Marseille's port and airport, a number that grew to 210,000 the following year. While most did not remain due to the city's depressed economy, by 1953, approximately 15,000 Algerian Muslims had settled in the Bouches-du-Rhône, primarily in Marseille, a number that reached 24,000 by 1959.[74] This migration, largely male until 1950, was distinctive for the relatively large number of women and children that soon followed. Although Marseille housed 8–9 percent of France's North African population in the early 1950s, it sheltered 17 percent of all families. These relatively large numbers gave rise to particularly acute problems regarding housing, education, and social services but also provided more permanence to the migrant population.[75]

Like Muslims, Jews poured into Marseille in the 1950s primarily en route from Morocco and Tunisia to Israel.[76] At the peak of the decade's migration in October 1956, more than 35,000 Moroccan Jews passed through Grand Arénas, which continued to be controlled by the Jewish Agency and had become the major transit camp for those en route to Israel. Egyptian Jews fleeing the Suez crisis also passed through Marseille.[77] While most migrants only stayed a few days or weeks and left few traces of their presence, others remained, bringing Marseille's Jewish population to between 12,000 and 15,000 by 1955.[78]

France's postwar housing crisis, particularly acute in Marseille, meant that new arrivals often settled in mixed neighborhoods where similar backgrounds, overlapping struggles, and shared public spaces facilitated neighborly relations. Ironically, Grand Arénas itself became such a site, as those unable to depart rapidly due to medical or other concerns settled in for a longer sojourn. If, in 1948, the transit camp had served as a space to act out colonial political struggles for those passing through, by the 1950s, the camp and its surroundings had become a site of integration *into* the metropole. No longer transients, its permanent residents—whether Muslim or Jewish—sought to make a home for themselves in France, providing space for their cultural similarities rather than their political differences to emerge.

Such contacts were initially limited due to the Jewish Agency's efforts to isolate camp residents from the wider metropolitan area. Organizing Grand Arénas as a world unto itself, the Jewish Agency maintained its own staff, educational system, medical team, hospital, religious facility, and eating space. A clearly defined boundary marked its Jewish sections from the parts still populated primarily by Algerian Muslim workers. The latter faced dire conditions in the early 1950s. While often receiving aid from several private agencies, most notably the Association d'aide aux travailleurs d'outre-mer (ATOM), which received government subventions to ease the migrants' transition, needs surpassed resources.[79] "One word characterizes the material and moral condition in which the majority of North Africans in France reside," noted a 1952 report, "turmoil."[80] Living without electricity or plumbing in shantytowns known as bidonvilles or in hotels or worker hostels, most of the 36,000 families in Marseille that lacked adequate shelter in 1951 were Muslim laborers. According to estimates in 1953, 8,600 Muslim workers lived in insufficient housing, including overpopulated rooms, cellars, attics, and sheds.[81] The Algerian Muslims who lived in temporary barracks in and surrounding Grand Arénas thus resided alongside their Jewish neighbors without the resources available to the latter. According to one Jewish resident, "There was a camp for Jews and a camp—really a shantytown—in the other part of the barracks in which French generally of Muslim origin lived. In between was barbed wire. They were absolutely separate."[82]

Complete isolation, however, proved illusive as those Jewish residents who remained in the camp began establishing commercial relationships in the surrounding neighborhood, attending local cafés and cinemas, playing soccer in parks with neighborhood residents, and sometimes establishing friendships. Once Jewish migration through Grand Arénas began to diminish in the early 1960s, poor squatters—often Muslim laborers from Algeria—began moving into its blocks and barracks, increasing their numbers and the camp's diversity. Given that Marseille's housing crisis was not fully addressed until the 1970s, many lived in what became a kind of shantytown for years.

Despite the poverty and poor living conditions, residents remember the neighborhood as one in which people from contrasting backgrounds lived together in harmony. As one Algerian Muslim recalled, Jews and Muslims from the Maghreb connected around common origins: "We didn't know much about the Maghreb. . . . [A]nd we learned about our country through these people who were North African before they were Jews." For him, neighborhood relations were strong: "We never had communal or relational problems between us. . . . There was a solidarity that continues to this day. Me, I often get together with people from that epoch, Jews who did not leave for Israel."[83] Others stressed the neighborhood cafés, cinemas, and bars as sites of interaction and convivial exchanges. "When there was a party—a baptism in the small chapel on rue Vaucanson, a circumcision—everyone took advantage, both Jews and Arabs. . . . When there was an Arab wedding, a gypsy wedding, everyone went."[84]

While Grand Arénas may have been atypical, it was not unique thanks to a housing crisis that pushed poor Jews—and even those with considerably more resources—into the same urban areas as North African Muslims. Such settlement patterns were particularly notable in the traditional immigrant neighborhoods of the city center. On the rue Sainte-Barbe (1st and 2nd arrondissements), for example, Jews, Armenians, Greeks, Italians, Spanish, Algerians, and Moroccans lived together, and on the perpendicular, rue Puvis de Chavannes, "the determining characteristic" was the "lack of spatial segregation," with a Jewish fabric store, for example, next to a Tunisian restaurant. The adjacent rue des Chapeliers, held thirty-two North African Muslim businesses and twenty-seven Jewish, Armenian, Greek, and "European" shops.[85] According to one Muslim resident, "My mother and all the other women bought cloth at the fabric stores, Arab or not (Jewish or Armenian), but they all spoke Arabic."[86]

Here, then, shared linguistic and cultural heritages bridged other divisions and were even built into the cityscape in the immigrant commercial districts surrounding the Old Port and the train station, where those with North African roots could find food and goods from home. Indeed, unlike other large French cities, Marseille's visibly "North African" downtown, which cut the city's northern industrial sectors from its middle- and upper-middle-class neighborhoods to the south, created a centrally located space in which residents of all educational, economic, national, ethnic, and religious background could interact, providing those with North African roots a means through which to connect with their past and one another.[87]

Such interactions, as we saw above, were not unique to Marseille. Shared city spaces, such as Belleville or the Marais in Paris or in Sarcelles, just to the north, allowed Muslim and Jewish neighbors to interact regularly. Jewish entrepreneurs at times also employed Muslim workers. As one assessment of these encounters argued, "In these neighborhoods as in these small businesses, these small shops, these restaurants, relations between Jews and Muslims are mostly good: they are marked by a certain collusion [*connivence*] that comes from the 'land of the sun' that both left."[88]

As the class implications of Jewish bosses hiring Muslim employees suggests, however, common origins and a shared newcomer status could not erase all differences among those arriving in the 1950s. Thus while only 3 percent of incoming Jews lacked a primary education, most Muslims were not formally educated.[89] And while North African Jewish arrivals tended to represent a lower socioeconomic level than their largely middle-class French co-religionists, often dropping in economic status due to the migration itself, they nevertheless experienced rapid social mobility as they moved from artisanal, industrial, and commercial employment into salaried positions, the civil service, and the liberal professions, such as law or medicine.[90] Muslim migrants, in contrast, were most often employed in the most dangerous, difficult, and poorly paid sectors of the French economy, including the building trades, public works projects, industrial labor, mines, and cleaning services.[91] Moreover, observers comparing them in 1953 noted that while North African Jewish and Muslim communities had similar social structures, Jews as the "longer anchored element" were more "rooted and assimilated" and had "less difficulty" than Muslim workers.[92] Emile Touati, for example, writing in the French Jewish magazine, *L'Arche*, differentiated between Muslim and Jewish arrivals by noting Jews' greater knowledge of the French language and culture; their inclination to migrate as families; their plans to settle permanently in France; and their urban middle-class status versus the poor agricultural backgrounds of most Muslim immigrants.[93] Such differences, while varying among Jewish migrants from Tunisia, Morocco, and Algeria, and modifying as larger numbers of Muslim families established permanent roots, influenced initial opportunities.[94]

Incoming Muslim and Jewish migrants also encountered vastly different communal structures that influenced their social and economic integration. French Jews, scarred by the Holocaust and seeing in the new arrivals the hope for a more vibrant future, relied on AJDC aid to establish a network of old-age homes; child care and medical facilities; youth programs; scholarship funds; employment agencies; professional retraining bodies; cultural, religious, and educational programs; and financial assistance bodies.[95] Through these efforts, Jewish agencies aided fifty thousand new arrivals between 1954 and 1959 alone, primarily from Morocco, Tunisia, and Egypt.[96] Although facilities were often stretched to the breaking point and communal leaders bemoaned their inability to prevent newcomers "[from] living in truly terrible and degrading conditions,"[97] such aid provided a crucial safety net.[98] Other arriving Jews—primarily from Egypt and Algeria—held French citizenship, giving them access to national welfare programs, or came with sufficient resources to care for themselves. According to Marseille's chief rabbi, "the new arrivals generally do not show up at [the] same reception centers as Muslims."[99]

The very way Rabbi Salzer framed the issue points to the distinction between incoming Jews and Muslims in the 1950s. While impoverished Jewish refugees often required aid, others could fend for themselves, and those who *did* need help could take advantage of an institutional structure determined to help, guide, and support them. Muslims, in contrast, faced a more precarious situation. With nothing like the established communal infrastructure of France's Jewish population, the largely Algerian population that made up the Muslim labor force after World War II was constituted primarily of young, single, and highly mobile workers whose primary base remained in North Africa. Although technically French citizens, they lacked the philanthropic, religious, or social network that French Jews had built since World War II. In the words of one Jewish aid worker, "There is no Arab set up in French life to welcome a co-religionist."[100]

The 1950s surge in North African nationalism made the settlement of Muslim laborers even more fraught as they became trapped in the struggle between French authorities and the FLN. Marseille's Algerian Muslim population was too disorganized and transitory to engage in much political activism. Police nevertheless saw a mounting threat as early as 1951, insisting that the Kabyle population, the majority of the city's Algerian migrants, were "almost all anti-French nationalists" and had won over many of those previously believed to be pro-French, encouraging Algerian, Tunisian, and Moroccan Muslims—who had "previously formed distinct clans"—to unite around common aims.[101]

In 1954 such concerns intensified following the FLN's initial insurrection. By 1956, as troops and supplies began moving unceasingly through Marseille's port, travel restrictions cut Algerian Muslim workers off from their families. Meanwhile, the FLN, having established itself in the city through the networks that had supported Messali Hadj, sought supporters in cafés and lodging houses, particularly in the city center (Belsunce-Porte d'Aix).[102] While FLN activities were limited and police repression intense, the nationalist organization was able to carry out several strikes against the French and internal opponents, making police more nervous about a citywide insurrection.[103]

In this environment, surveillance of Muslim workers intensified, a shift evident in new urban development projects that allowed for more efficient policing. Although the postwar housing crisis had allowed some mixed Muslim-Jewish neighborhoods to emerge, these new policies encouraged greater social and economic segregation. In 1958, city officials thus began systematically demolishing migrant slums and moving residents to cités de transit as part of a larger process of improving urban hygiene and policing suspect populations. Constructed on vacant lots in the urban periphery and often lacking basic infrastructure or resources, these structures were meant to last for a year or two after which immigrants would move into the more permanent Habitations à loyer modéré (HLM), the public apartment blocks that made up the central component of the national housing plan. In practice, however, many cités de transit remained in place for two decades, allowing authorities to police Muslim workers during the Algerian conflict and beyond. The result was their structural isolation, including from incoming "repatriates" who had privileged access to the HLM structures.[104]

The contrasting living conditions of Muslims with incoming Jews, many of whom took advantage of housing for repatriated "Europeans," did not go unnoticed by the former. One Algerian Muslim in France since the early 1940s complained to the mayor of his many co-nationals waiting without adequate housing for years, "while the families of how many French Jews and other people departed from Egypt and elsewhere since 1957" were already lodged. "This practice is not only revolting for its injustice but particularly for its separatism and for all the hatreds it creates." As his comments suggest, at least some Muslims viewed the relative ease of Jewish settlement as a stinging reminder of their own second-class status and of ongoing French willingness to favor some citizens over others: "I believe that it is the obligation of a politician doubling as an administrator," he continued, "to ensure equality between all citizens . . . so that public services are really used by all and do not favor one fraction of the privileged."[105]

If by 1960 when this letter was written, the uneven settlement patterns facing Muslim and Jewish arrivals were already apparent to some, such distinctions became even sharper over the next few years as the Algerian crisis stripped citizenship from Muslim Algerians while re-affirming the Frenchness of Jewish Algerians. Given the initial chaos of such a large migration, the impact of this shift was not always evident. With time, however, the imprint of France's colonial legacy and the violent war that ended it became clear, shaping Muslim and Jewish economic and political fortunes in the metropole and their evolving relations with each other.

Algerian Independence, Repatriation, and City Politics

The "repatriation" crisis of 1961 and 1962 brought tens of thousands of former Algerian residents to Marseille. As part of this migration, the Jewish population surged, reaching approximately sixty-five thousand by the early 1970s. With twenty synagogues and over sixty rabbis or preachers, Marseille's Jewish community became the second largest in France.[106] Nor did North African independence do anything to stem the tide of Muslim arrivals fleeing political unrest and economic turmoil.[107] As Marseille's industrial and construction sectors developed, the population of primarily Algerian Muslim laborers rose to more than fifty thousand by 1974.[108] The enormous growth of both populations, however, did little to flatten the differences between them with regard to access to city resources. Rather such differences were exacerbated as thousands of Algerian Jews—all bearing French citizenship—arrived in Marseille.

The speed and intensity of the massive migration, particularly in June and July 1962, initially overwhelmed all municipal services, masking distinctions among those arriving in city ports. On 25 June alone, seven boats brought nine thousand "repatriates" to the city. "Marseille is asphyxiated," reported *Le Figaro* on 7 July, "and can no longer cope with the massive arrivals such as those of last week."[109] The series of building projects to replace housing destroyed during the war were still under construction in 1962.[110] Hotels were inundated quickly. In June, Marseille was so saturated that incoming families were being sent fifty miles away for one night's lodging.[111]

In this context, Algerian Jews—like all newcomers—faced significant challenges. Although receiving extensive aid from Jewish agencies, no institution could fully address the problems accompanying such a large and rapid migration.[112] Primarily civil servants, shopkeepers, and craftsmen, the new arrivals were often unprepared to work in France's industrial labor force. Government subsidies and job retraining aided some while civil servants were often reclassified, but it took several years for the dust to settle. Those who remained in Marseille were generally less well off than those who went to Lyon, Paris, Nice, or Strasbourg, making the initial years more challenging. As one noted, "We do not have enough money to consolidate communal structures as we should."[113] While most had found an economic foothold by the mid-1970s, as late as 1968, commentators were noting significant numbers of "idlers" [*oisifs*] among Marseille's Algerian Jewish population.[114]

Moreover, just because the organized Jewish community coordinated aid for incoming Algerian, Moroccan, and Tunisian Jews, their landing was not always soft. Indeed, Marseille's Jewish population, which was extremely diverse, was riddled with strife.[115] As one FSJU representative noted, it would be impossible to talk of Marseille as "*a* community." Rather, the city's Jewish population was made up of a "conglomerate of groups of various ethnical [*sic*] origins, scattered all over an area larger than the city of Paris."[116] This heterogeneity was reflected in congregational terms.[117] Thus, the previously settled largely Ashkenazi population controlled the main synagogue on rue Breteuil, while three small synagogues on the rue de la Dragon housed those from Turkey, Poland, and Constantine, respectively. Jews from Oran prayed primarily on the rue Saint Dominique while those from Tunisia and Morocco attended synagogue on the rue Montgrand. Such divisions dominated commercial life as well, and power struggles among the groups could be intense.[118] Not only did Marseille's Jewish population increase by 400 percent, but also North African Jews—with their own practices, levels of religiosity, and cultural traditions—quickly became the majority.[119] Although the settled Jewish population was smaller, it had little intention of turning over communal institutions to the newcomers.[120] As a result, tensions and personal animosities dominated communal politics for years, and commentators made dire predictions about Marseille's Jewish future given the name-calling and ugly rifts, such as when one Consistoire member accused his North African co-religionists of having "the mentality of Arabs."[121]

This "slur" is suggestive at multiple levels. Clearly pointing to the divisions and cultural conflicts that encumbered Marseille's Jewish population as it adjusted to its growth, the angry remark challenged the "Europeanness" of arriving North African Jews. While legal categories may have allowed the latter to assert their "Frenchness," the established Jewish leadership was not convinced, suggesting that juridical categories could not fully capture the reality of such a heterogeneous population.[122] In addition, and perhaps more relevant to this analysis, the remark reflected the negative associations with the term "Arab," which, as we have seen, circulated in communal discourse during and after the Algerian crisis.

Yet whatever divisions prevented the easy integration of Marseille's Jewish community, their position was far more assured than that of incoming Muslims, 140,000 of whom were so-called *harkis* and their families, the auxiliaries in the French army and others who had supported the French presence and who had fled with departing troops.[123] Rejected by the established Algerian Muslim population, harkis were often viewed as traitors.[124] Thus although 26,000 harkis arrived in Marseille in summer 1962 (6,000–9,000 of whom remained in the Bouches-du-Rhône), no representative "introduced himself to them at the port of arrival to welcome, guide, or advise them. They were alone before the administration that repatriated them."[125] For those arriving in Marseille's port, the difference was immediately apparent. As one Jewish representative working at the docks to direct arriving co-religionists to communal welfare agencies reported: "Our placard attracted many looks. Two young Tunisian Muslims, noting the blue Star of David [*Magen David bleu*], shrugged their shoulders."[126] Or as one Algerian Jewish author described the scene at Orly airport in Paris:

[I]n a quarter of the airport, someone installs a small counter with stools. The seats are cramped and the signs touch each other. "Catholic Relief Services," "Jewish Social Services [FSJU]," "Students," "Algerian Gas and Electric," and others with more mysterious signs. Each comes to find his own. Only the Arabs have no right to any sign in particular. Having disengaged, they are part of our past, and as such we abandon them to the good heart of the Red Cross."[127]

As such comments suggest the French administration did little to welcome their former supplemental military forces. Initially opposed to their "repatriation" and worried that the harkis would transport subversive political affiliations to France and/or create conflict within the Algerian Muslim migrant population, French settlement policies isolated them, preventing them from living in apartments set aside for "European" repatriates, and placing them instead in military transit camps before moving them to cités de transit, *hameaux de forestage*, or subsidized housing units constructed for them on the urban periphery.[128]

Harkis were not, however, the only incoming Muslims to live isolated from other North African arrivals. The settlement patterns of most Muslims when compared to Jewish repatriates clearly demonstrates how different relationships with the French state influenced residential options. While many Jews settled into temporary housing wherever it was available, within relatively short order, they—like other pieds noirs—were able to relocate to new HLM housing projects, 30 percent of which were reserved for repatriates over five years.[129] Certain developments became magnets for pieds-noirs, and particularly Jews, including Roy d'Espagne, La Cravache (around Boulevard Michelet), La Rouvière, and Frais-Vallon. While Jews also settled in St. Marguerite (9th arrondissement), St. Tronc, Pont de Vivaux (10th arrondissement), La Rose (13th arrondissement), and streets around the main synagogue on rue Breteuil (6th arrondissement), as well as in the working class and commercial neighborhoods of the city center, few moved into the 14th, 15th and 16th arrondissements or the quartier des Baumettes in the 9th arrondissement where North African laborers were generally located.[130]

Settlement patterns for the latter became increasingly concentrated in the city's industrial periphery. In the 1960s and early 1970s, an expanding labor market combined with growing investment in the industrial and construction sectors led to property speculation in the city's outlying areas (90 percent of housing developments were built at least 5 km outside central Marseille in these years). At the same time, urban renewal programs sought to restore large areas of the city (such as the area around the train station), demolishing the poorest and most unsanitary residential sectors and pushing their populations to the large *cités*. Given that many of those in the demolished areas were Muslim North Africans, the program of Marseille's urban renovation became intimately linked to the problem of housing immigrants. The long-term impact was the socioeconomic division of Marseille between a poorly equipped northern industrial sector with a high concentration of immigrants and a well-equipped middle- and upper-class southern sector.[131]

The fate of Grand Arénas residents points to these shifts. Constructed as a temporary structure to deal with housing shortages and population overflow, the camp had fulfilled its purpose by the late 1960s. As Jewish migration diminished, the Jewish Agency removed its remaining population to the former military hospital in Montolivet. In 1973, as part of a wider urban development plan, Grand Arénas was razed and the remaining population moved elsewhere. If the friendly relations that emerged in this transitional space capture the way the city's infrastructure—so unprepared for the massive arrivals of the 1950s and early 1960s—created opportunities for interethnic contact, its demise points to the different opportunities available to Muslim and Jewish newcomers over time. Divided at arrival between "Europeans" and "Muslims," Jews were absorbed into the former, while Muslims became immigrants of a lower order.[132] These differences shaped more than housing, ultimately influencing schooling, economic opportunities, and levels of integration.

One area where such inequities were particularly visible was in the arena of city politics. Under the supervision of Mayor Gaston Defferre, Marseille's political establishment embraced its Jewish minority with remarkable intensity. Indeed, according to municipal records, beginning in the early 1960s, Mayor Defferre fostered "strong ties, almost emotional" with many of those representing communal life,[133] including Rolland Amsellem, a lawyer who held leadership positions in many local Jewish institutions, and Robert Safrani, a businessman, both of whom served as town councilors on Defferre's list.[134] In addition, Defferre went out of his way to support organized communal life, providing municipal space for religious activities when synagogues proved too cramped and supporting Jewish political activities. Whether his solicitousness was—as some suspected—a simple calculation that Jews represented "a non-negligible potential electorate" or a particular affinity for the community, his outreach was a source of commentary in the city.[135]

With regard to international affairs, Defferre also consistently sided with his Jewish constituents on matters about which they cared. Most importantly, he was a vocal supporter of Israel, lending his voice to the young state's struggle on numerous occasions. In June 1961, for example, Defferre called for the GPRA to distance itself from the Arab League's anti-Israel politics and to establish formal ties between the two countries, warning that a more aggressive course would diminish French and Jewish support for Algerian independence. Linking Algeria's ability to succeed as a "modern enterprising nation directed toward the future" with its willingness to let go of antagonisms toward Israel, Defferre expressed wariness at Algeria's readiness to govern, and unadulterated respect for the Jewish state.[136] In fact, Defferre's support for Algerian independence had solidified only late in the conflict due to his concern for the pieds noirs.[137] This stance coupled with his pro-Israeli politics won him friends among incoming Jews who found the city a comfortable space in which to express their Zionist affiliations.

Indeed, one of the notable political developments among Marseille's Jews in the 1960s was their vocal support for Israel.[138] If, in the 1950s, Zionist activists regularly complained that Marseille's Jews donated too little to pro-Israel causes and while only one thousand turned out for a May 1950 celebration of Israel's anniversary, the May 1962 celebrations drew thousands, making the southern port city one of France's most active Zionist centers in the early 1960s.[139] Defferre's public support for the Jewish state facilitated this development. After visiting in spring 1962, for example, Defferre published a three-part article entitled, "Impressions of Israel" in his newspaper, Le Provençal, calling the Jewish state "a future solution for the free world" and an example of "efficiency and democracy."[140] Establishing Marseille as a sister city of Haifa that year, Defferre also created numerous cultural connections between the two countries.[141] In August 1962, for example, he welcomed a leading Israeli folk group to the Hôtel de Ville.[142] Only one of numerous ongoing links between the municipality and the Jewish state, such efforts provided a politically sanctioned space in which Marseille's Jews could express their affections for Israel without fearing accusations of dual loyalty.[143]

Causing few evident tensions with Marseille's Muslim population prior to 1967, thereafter the combination of the outbreak of another war in the Middle East, vocal support for Israel, and the municipality's repeated willingness to take sides on a distant conflict, once again created tensions. As we will see in the next chapter, in 1967 as in 1948, the struggles between Israelis and Palestinians became an opportunity to express the local resentments that had been building since even before French decolonization.[144]

Even in the early 1960s, however, colonial legacies left their mark. In January 1962, the French Jewish commentator Rabi thus reported that Marseille's Jewish population "feels endangered in a majority Muslim milieu."[145] While a vast exaggeration of the city's demographics—Muslims were little more than half the city's foreign population that was itself less than 10 percent of its total population—Rabi's comment captures the powerful way in which the previous decade's focus on Jewish victimization at the hand of North African "Arabs" had begun to frame understandings of Muslim-Jewish relations in the new context even though relations on the ground were often cordial.[146] Indeed, whatever the daily reality, colonial legacies—both in the story of Jewish victimization at the hands of Muslims and in the inequities built into the colonial structure and transferred to the metropole—created the context in which Muslim-Jewish relations would evolve in France.

4

The 1967 War and the Forging of Political Community

This chapter investigates how the 1967 war between Israel and its Arab neighbors influenced Muslim-Jewish relations in France. As will become clear, this conflict—which ended with Israel's occupation of significant Arab lands including the Gaza Strip and the West Bank—had little impact on daily interactions more fundamentally shaped by the colonial North African past and the French present than the Middle East. Nevertheless, the unprecedented mobilization of Jewish organizational life around Israel and efforts to create parallel affinities in the Muslim North African population around Palestine continued to shape political discourse in binary terms. The result was that while conflict between France's large Muslim and Jewish populations was rare, the story of two polarized ethno-religious political units hardened as new political actors, particularly university students, began to use French campuses as spaces in which to engage in discussions of foreign policy.

It is a truism of modern Jewish history that 1967 transformed Jewish identity throughout the Western world. France was no exception as Jews became politically visible in unprecedented ways, raising enormous sums, participating in vocal demonstrations, and even volunteering for Israeli military service. Our grasp of the "Zionization of French Jewry" is not matched, however, by an equally clear picture of Muslim political affiliations in France during the Middle East conflict.[1] This chapter will address this gap by tracing early efforts of FLN representatives, the Arab league, and Muslim student activists to encourage North African Muslim immigrant identification with the Palestinians. Such efforts, while less successful than Jewish efforts to assert the same with regard to Israel, increasingly made disagreements over outcomes in the Middle East relevant to minority politics in France.

In 1967, however, these disagreements rarely influenced life on the ground in French cities. In other words, although French Jewish political rhetoric continued to demonize Israel's Arab enemies, and those seeking to mobilize Muslim immigrants around the Palestinian cause harshly criticized Israel, such criticisms were generally directed at the Middle East rather than at each other. Indeed, France experienced little conflict during that summer's brief war, and in the rare examples in which discord did break out, once again mostly in

Marseille, the anger seemed, as in 1948, to reflect frustration at evident inequities in city politics since decolonization–this time expressed in the municipality's dramatically vocal pro-Zionist stance and ongoing willingness to favor one minority over another.

If, however, such tensions point to the way the colonial past continued to shape ethno-religious relations in contemporary France, clashes on French campuses indicate the way political struggles over the Middle East began to pit Jewish and Muslim activists against one another in new ways. Foreshadowing the significance of campus politics in shaping Muslim-Jewish encounters in the decade to come, summer 1967 saw new political actors come of age who began creating political coalitions around Israel and Palestine. These new alliances would have far-reaching consequences in 1968 and beyond.

The Impact of 1967 on Jewish Political Mobilization

With the Arab-Israeli war in 1967, Jewish commitment to Israel burst onto the public stage, as French Jews, traditionally reluctant to link their heritage with a visible ethnic politics, began "display[ing] a political activism which at times took prominent leaders of the Parisian community by surprise."[2] This transformation emerged for three key reasons. First was the shift in French policy away from its unambiguously pro-Israeli stance of the early 1960s.[3] Due to France's departure from North Africa and its evolving interests in the Middle East, by 1967 de Gaulle was cultivating alliances in the Arab world. These efforts coupled with a belief that Israeli actions in the weeks preceding the conflict were unnecessarily aggressive led de Gaulle to declare French neutrality and to impose an arms embargo on Israel.

Frightening French Jewish leaders who saw de Gaulle's move as a national repudiation of the Jewish state, many also accused the French media, traditionally supportive of Israel, of adopting a more critical tone and the French left of fostering anti-Israeli sentiment.[4] Given that national polls in June showed 56 percent of the French public supporting Israel as opposed to 2 percent supporting the Arab states, such fears were overstated. Indeed, by September, pro-Israel sentiment had surged to 68 percent versus 6 percent for their opponents.[5] Moreover, support for and criticisms of Israel during the 1967 war cannot be divided neatly into left and right.[6] Jewish organizations worked assiduously to represent all political affiliations at pro-Israel rallies to demonstrate cross-party support.[7] Nevertheless, both the French Communist and Socialist parties, which had both enthusiastically supported Israel following 1948, readjusted these positions somewhat after the 1967 war.[8] And even earlier, numerous Jewish leaders expressed fears that the "French left"—influenced by Soviet pressures and anti-colonialist struggles—was hostile to Israel and Jews.[9] Thus despite the overwhelming pro-Israel sentiment expressed at all levels of society, French Jewish representatives feared a growing ambivalence in governing circles.[10] The impact of this perception should not be underestimated when thinking about the significance of 1967 on communal galvanization.[11] Indeed, the "Zionization" of French Jewry was less a newfound expression of pro-Israeli sentiment, which was already well entrenched by the mid-1950s, than a new willingness to pursue an ethnically infused Jewish politics even when it conflicted with France's international agenda.[12]

A second factor fueling this vocal politicization was the influx of North African Jews to France. These new arrivals were less self-conscious about expressing an ethnic politics than their French co-religionists. Having fought in their native lands to preserve their rights as newly independent Muslim states threw off French rule, they arrived in the metropole more politically militant than the local French Jewish communities and more viscerally connected to Israel.[13] Moreover, anti-Jewish hostility in Tunisia and Morocco in summer 1967 led several thousand more Jews to seek refuge in France despite government efforts in both countries to protect and reassure their Jewish minorities. Arriving with fresh stories of Muslim aggression, the newcomers provoked strong responses from those who had departed in previous waves, fueling agitation in France.[14] As the president of the CRIF described their impact on communal life: "North African Jews made us less inhibited. They pushed us to shout, to cry, to sing, to pour into the streets. They have no inferiority complex [*aucun complexe*]. And France watched this extroverted Judaism with curiosity."[15]

Thirdly, as Joan Wolf has demonstrated, French Jews perceived the 1967 war as an immediate threat to Jewish survival, reading events through the prism of World War II. As the Egyptian president Gamal Abdel Nasser repeatedly called for the annihilation of Israel, French Jews became consumed with "the threat to survival—of Israel, the Jewish people, and Judaism." Although the majority of France's Jewish population was North African and therefore distanced from the Holocaust's most extreme brutality, the postwar conflation of Muslim antisemitism with previous violence against Jews made such distinctions less meaningful. Communal discourse was thus saturated with Holocaust imagery, as the Jewish community, and particularly those who had come of age after World War II, sought to come to terms with their past.[16] Blurring the boundaries between Europe during World War II and Israel in 1967, for example, the newly formed Comité democrate socialiste pour le droit d'Israël warned, "The brothers and sons of the martyrs of the arrests in Paris, the Warsaw Ghetto, and the camps of Auschwitz and Treblinka are once again threatened by hate and death."[17] Or as Claude Lanzman proclaimed at a rally on 31 May, "If Israel was destroyed, it would be more serious than the Nazi Holocaust. For Israel is my freedom."[18] One man proposed that all Jews don a yellow star—the symbol of their oppression under the Nazis—as a sign of solidarity with the Jewish state.[19] For these Jews, Israel's war was their own.

The combination of the new political context, enlarged numbers, and fears of Israel's destruction, provided French Jews with new confidence to speak publicly as Jews.[20] By late May, mounting tensions between Israel and Egypt brought thousands of people—both Jewish and not—to meetings dedicated to alerting public opinion to the "grave situation facing Israel's frontier."[21] Thirty thousand Parisians, for example, demonstrated in front of the Israeli embassy on 31 May while another twenty thousand attended a rally at the Cirque d'Hiver the same day.[22] Similar demonstrations took place in many major provincial cities, including in Marseille, Lyon, and Toulouse.[23] All synagogues affiliated with the centralized consistorial system conducted prayers for Israel on 26 and 27 May.[24]

Jewish organizations also leaped into action in unprecedented ways, establishing, for instance, a Comité national de coordination on 26 May under the presidency of Guy de Rothschild (president of the two largest French Jewish philanthropic bodies) to express their "total solidarity" with Israel and to convey their "determination to participate with all the means at their disposal in Israel's struggle for existence."[25] This new body coordinated all aid for Israel, including rallying support among religious leaders, professors, and journalists; organizing demonstrations; intervening with elected officials at all levels of government; raising and centralizing funds; surveying press coverage; gathering medical supplies; and organizing volunteers for civil service in Israel.[26] Concern that too many demonstrations and financial appeals would wear out goodwill, the Comité de coordination also sought to prevent other organizations from taking their own initiatives, intervening, for example, in efforts to send packages to Israel outside their own control.[27] Such efforts, if somewhat heavy-handed, led to unprecedented coordination.[28]

By 4 June, when 1,200 delegates came together representing sixty Jewish communities and all French Jewish organizations, local committees had been established in five Parisian neighborhoods and in 39 towns and cities (a number that eventually grew to 130).[29] Speeches focused heavily on Israeli and French Jewish solidarity. Chief Rabbi Jacob Kaplan, for example, reminded attendees that, "Israel's crisis is our test,"[30] while André Neher declared, "Even yesterday, I confess, I regret, only a fraction of my being struggled for Israel. Today my entire being is with Israel. . . ." For Théo Klein, a lawyer and CRIF delegate, "French Jews had maintained a vague friendship for Israel. Brutally, their Jewish identity now leaps into their faces. They have learned that *their* freedom is at risk [*en cause*] in Akaba." Put even more starkly by Jacques Dreyfus, representative of Lyon's Comité de coordination: "Those who do not help Israel do not have the right to call themselves Jews."[31]

Such proclamations defined French Jews and Israelis as one—linked by religion and culture but also by *politics*. Critiquing their birth nation in unprecedented ways, Jewish leaders spoke against France's policies in the Middle East. Chief Rabbi Kaplan, for example, who had remained virtually silent throughout the Algerian crisis, publicly criticized the arms embargo.[32] Guy de Rothschild described French policies as "making us uncomfortable in our skin,"[33] while André Neher urged his co-religionists to challenge their government: "[T]his is the time to remember that in certain cases the sacred obligation of all citizens in a free country is to disagree with their nation's policies and to protest and to act based on that disagreement."[34] While mainstream French Jewish institutions had long worked to influence government policies behind the scenes, Jewish leaders had also parroted the republican ideal that Jews had no political identity qua Jews. The 1967 war challenged such perspectives. As Claude Kelman, vice president of the Comité de coordination, argued "[T]he steps that we are taking are the product of the adoption of a clear-cut position with no ambiguity or prevarication; we are acting as *Jews*, our reactions are Jewish reactions."[35]

This shift was more than symbolic. Indeed, an "irresistible need, an urge . . . to do something" penetrated Jewish communities.[36] As Adam Loss, the director of the Fonds social juif unifié described the sentiment: "I have never experienced anything as wrenching. Old women rushed to my office and begged me to take their last remaining jewels to send to Israel. All French Jews were desperate."[37] Fund-raising for Israel was particularly successful in this environment. Tapping into mounting fears for Israel's security, philanthropic outreach built on the widely circulating themes of Israel/Diaspora unity. According to one appeal, it was an obligation to aid a "state that struggles heroically for its own freedom that is also our own."[38] Or as another insisted, "the first thing that you can do and that you must do for yourself is to contribute financially to this sacred and vital struggle."[39] Such appeals stressed the value of symbolic sacrifice, urging potential donors to give up a month's salary, sell a piece of property, or transform vacation time into labor for Israel.[40] Pressure to donate was so intense that those who refused could face social ostracism or even more severe repercussions.[41]

Such efforts were enormously successful. By uniting all fund-raising under the Comité de coordination, halting all other philanthropic projects, and framing donations as a tax on those in the Diaspora "so that Israel can live," contributions reached fifteen million francs within one week of the campaign's launch.[42] Even when the war had ended, solicitations continued;[43] by July, more than fifty million francs had been raised from sixty thousand donations, a 50 percent increase in the numbers of individual contributors to pro-Israel causes and a sum greater than French Jews had ever raised for Israel.[44] According to one community official in Marseille, "The phenomenon of an awakening of consciousness has even moved peripheral Jewish populations, those whose numbers, means, and ways of expressing (or not) their Jewishness is unknown to us."[45]

Particularly affected by the pro-Israel campaign were Jewish youth born after World War II, who, coming of age in the late 1960s, found in Israel's struggle an answer to the Holocaust's legacy and a means of exploring their Jewish identities. In the preceding year, a survey of Jewish university students in Paris indicated that 90 percent considered their ethno-religious identity meaning-ful.[46] With the 1967 conflict, this identification became newly visible. As *L'Arche* declared triumphantly in a June headline, "Our Youth Rediscovers Its Soul."[47] Journalist Anne Sinclair documented the moment in the following terms: "I was nineteen and I affirmed my Jewishness at that precise moment because Israel's solitude seemed unbearable to me."[48] Similarly, Françoise Tenenbaum, seventeen years old in 1967, reported sneaking radios into school to follow war news: "It was my dream to go to Israel even though I didn't speak Hebrew."[49] As another young French Jewish woman remembers: "The war in 1967 was when I started to want to meet other Jews. I didn't know much about Israel, but the Six Day War had a very important impact on my life. My mother supported Israel, and in Paris I had friends who didn't talk to me at the time because I was Jewish. I was shocked. I realized then that I needed to start meeting more Jewish people."[50]

Drawing on such sentiments, the Comité de coordination established sections for university students and youth that encouraged them to "be among the thousands of young Jewish boys and girls who are going to help Israel during its difficult hours."[51] Likewise, pro-Israel youth movements challenged young Jews to prove their new loyalties with migration: As one opined: "After the public demonstrations and the slogans must come action."[52] Such appeals resonated to such a degree that the Israeli government created a civil service program to place volunteers in the hospitals, factories, and administrative positions previously occupied by soldiers, a program that brought 675 young French Jewish volunteers to Israel by 16 June.[53] While the end of the brief war brought this migration stream to a halt, many young Jews still left for Israel.[54] Thirty to forty departures a month in the early 1960s thus grew to 500 by 1969,[55] and between 1965 and 1971, 6,852 Jews made a similar move, substantially increasing the post–World War II numbers.[56] While many of the migrants were of North African origin, French Jewish spokesmen understood 1967 to be a turning point.[57] As Simon Sibony, a rabbi from Dijon, reflected: "In the past the community was indifferent to Israel. That changed after the Six Day war. It was an important moment for all the communities in France."[58] Government analysts concurred, asserting that the 1967 war had established a "new phenomenon: almost all French Jews are concerned by Israel's fate. Sensitivity toward Israel has become one of the components of French Judaism."[59]

The depth of this transformation is difficult to gauge. Many clearly believed that "French Judaism, which we previously deplored for its passivity, has come out of its lethargy."[60] In the words of one communal leader in Marseille, the Jewish population had "suddenly discovered unity—a dignity and a depth that only yesterday we were wondering how long it would take to achieve (if indeed we ever could)."[61] Certainly many were elated with Israel's victory, and the Comité de coordination sought to transform the momentum into a broad pro-Israel movement.[62] As another Jewish organization declared, "The Eternal miraculously saved us, and now that we have been freed from the terrible threat are we going to take up our daily routines as if nothing happened?"[63] The FSJF likewise insisted that many of its members, "traumatized by June events . . . have realized their obligations to Israel and the Jewish community as a whole."[64]

Such assessments overstated the unity around Israel in June 1967. A vocal minority—particularly those affiliated with the Communist party—criticized Israel as the aggressor and for its occupation of newly conquered territories. Holding demonstrations or writing in the leftist press, they made clear that their Jewishness was irrelevant when assessing the crimes of an imperialist state.[65] Eastern European Jewish immigrant communities, long divided over Communism, were particularly polarized in summer 1967, as is clear from a perusal of the Parisian Yiddish dailies.[66] The Communist *Naye Presse*, mirroring Soviet pronouncements, adopted a critical stance toward Israel and accused its Zionist and Bundist rivals of working with neo-Nazis to create a second Auschwitz. For their part, the newspapers of the non-Communist Jewish left demanded that Jewish organizations remove all Communists from their rosters.[67] Other Jewish leftists reacted with shock to the vocal nationalism from their co-religionists. Daniel Cohn-Bendit, the soon-to-be-infamous student radical who led the May 1968 uprisings, described his shock that summer: "It was awful, all these nationalist and chauvinistic Jews. This was the first time that I experienced Jewish racism: exactly the same comments that the Germans make about the Turks today or the French about the North Africans. When I tried to explain that national unity in Israel would resolve nothing, I almost got beaten up. Nobody could open a discussion. My Jewish identity was broken."[68] Some of these Jewish leftists—many of whom had been actively engaged in the struggle to free Algeria—reached out to Muslim activists on the left. Representatives from the Jewish Communist group, MRAP, thus used the June crisis as an opportunity to connect with Arab workers and to assert their commitment to fighting anti-Arab racism.[69] Several Jewish leftists, notably Tony and Benny Lévy, founded the Comité des étudiants juifs antisionistes, which later established contact with Yasser Arafat.[70] Others published a petition in *Le Monde* on 15 June, proclaiming themselves "entirely in solidarity with the Arab people in their just struggle" and criticizing Israel for its "war of aggression and conquest."[71] These alliances proved essential in the emergence over the next few years of a pro-Palestinian movement in France.

For many Jews, however, the 1967 war had the opposite impact, pushing them away from those on the left with whom they shared years of political struggle. A number of prominent Jewish intellectuals thus made clear that they resented accusations of Israeli aggression and imperialism, while others—uncomfortable with Israeli policies toward Palestinians—sought to differentiate their unconditional support for the state of Israel from its policies.[72] Still others left the Communist party in anger over its criticisms of Israel.[73] Inside the CRIF, some argued that Communist member organizations should sign a statement critiquing the Soviet anti-Israel campaign and acknowledging Arab responsibility for hostilities.[74]

Such divisions over the war meant that pro-Israel energy necessarily dissipated when hostilities ended, leading some analysts to question the long-term impact on French Jewish life.[75] In 1968, for example, sociologist Sylvie Korcaz argued that commitment to Israel varied considerably and that charitable donations and willingness to move to the Jewish state had already decreased significantly.[76] Jewish leaders often agreed, as was clear at a meeting in Marseille that April in which participants questioned the depth of the war's transformation of French Jews.[77] Others disagreed, however, seeing in 1967 the moment that "caused many Jews living in France to find their way back to Judaism."[78] Whatever the extent of the long term transformation, 1967 was clearly a moment when Jews of different origins, political orientation, and level of religious practice came together to support a single issue, and when passive support for the Jewish state was transformed into a visible, combative stance on its behalf.

1967 among Muslim Migrants to France

At the very moment when French Jews found their political voice, Muslims were facing an increasingly hostile environment that made political mobilization far riskier. If the former felt betrayed by the government's neutrality and the arms embargo on Israel, they were nevertheless bolstered by the widespread public perception that Israel was the victim of unprovoked Arab aggression. For Muslims, in contrast, de Gaulle's policies could do little to assuage an increasingly precarious social context in which anti-Arab racism grew and in which media images portrayed Arabs as violent religious fanatics who had provoked the conflict.[79] According to historian Yvan Gastaut, the 1967 war played an important role in liberalizing racist discourse largely silenced since World War II, by refocusing it away from Jews and onto Arabs.[80] In particular, those still angry over French decolonization saw a renewed "Arab threat" in the making and rallied around Israel. Readers of the newspaper *Minute* or of *Aspects de la France*, for example read, "Arabs love war," or "with Arabs only one policy is possible that of the rod and kicks in the ass because [Arabs] only understand and respect force."[81] Such rhetoric was accompanied by physical attacks against several Muslim North Africans in Nice on 7 June and the harassment of others in Paris and the Midi.

Moreover, as we have seen, French Jews took advantage of a highly developed institutional structure put in place after World War II to create a centralized and efficient fund-raising and political apparatus. This infrastructure provided space for unprecedented political mobilization and collective ethnic expression. For incoming North African Muslims, the majority of France's Muslim population in 1967, few similar structures existed. While the Arab League, which had established an office in Paris in 1965, and the Union générale des étudiants palestiniens (UGEP), an outgrowth of the Palestinian Liberation Organization (PLO) founded the previous year, sought to bring attention to the Palestinian issue, Muslim activism around the issue remained relatively muted throughout May and June 1967 particularly when compared to the pro-Israel activities among French Jews.[82]

One key exception was the Amicale des Algériens en France, a social welfare organization for Algerian Muslim immigrants that worked tirelessly to inspire pro-Palestinian sentiment among its constituents.[83] If its failures underscore the divergent paths of Muslim and Jewish communal politics in 1960s France, the effort nevertheless initiated the use of the Palestinian issue as a tool for forging political cohesiveness among France's North African laboring population, a strategy that gathered significant steam over the next decade.

Created in November 1962, the Amicale took shape after the FLN's political bureau closed its local chapters and "comités de soutien," transforming them into a social welfare organization for Algerian Muslim nationals in France.[84] Financed by the FLN and charged with enforcing its policies in Europe, by 1967, the organization, now called the Amicale des Algériens en Europe (ADAE),[85] aspired to educate and unite Algerian Muslims abroad.[86] Boasting youth groups, sporting clubs, publications, religious institutions, and clubs throughout Europe, the ADAE claimed to have one-fifth of the Algerian Muslim migrant population in its ranks (French authorities called the number highly inflated; in their estimation, only 4,000 out of the approximately 500,000 Algerian Muslims in France had joined).[87]

French laws on foreign associations limited the ADAE's activities to the educational and cultural realm. Moreover, because officials feared the Amicale would spread FLN propaganda, the Ministries of Interior and Foreign Affairs denied it formal recognition, only "tolerating" its existence unofficially. Such a status compelled the Amicale to refrain from all political activism. Most ADAE campaigns thus focused on issues such as literacy, housing aid for large families, defense of Algerian Muslims threatened with expulsion, hospital visitations, religious and Arabic instruction, and efforts to solidify Franco-Algerian relations.[88]

With the mounting crisis of summer 1967, however, the ADAE changed course, manifesting ardent support for Arab nationalist movements and becoming a vocal supporter of the Palestinian cause. Adopting similar rhetorical strategies as Zionist activists who blurred distinctions between French Jews and Israeli citizens, the ADAE asserted direct links between French Algerian Muslims and the wider Arab world:

> Events in the Middle East have bereaved the entire Arab nation. From the Atlantic to the Persian Gulf, Arabs feel their flesh wounded. . . . The distance that separates us from the Orient does not alleviate the feelings of indignation that each one of us suffers in light of these sly maneuvers. Our

determination will tolerate no equivocation and no momentary setback will weaken it. *Each Algerian must feel Palestinian* and provide concrete support to the Arab cause.[89]

This solidarity, the ADAE insisted, should lead Algerian Muslim migrants to demonstrate, raise relief funds, mobilize military recruits, and boycott Israeli products.[90] The ADAE itself worked to promote such solidarity by circulating pamphlets and holding meetings to raise awareness of the ongoing struggle.[91] Moreover, the organization's journal, *L'Algérien en Europe*, devoted its June issues to the Middle East conflict. The cover of the 15 June edition, for example, pictured a determined soldier, masses of troops, and a tank captioned: "The National People's Army against Imperialist Aggression." Articles addressed Algerian support for the Palestinians, the history of "Zionist aggression," and support for Arab nationalism.[92] Future editions were concerned with similar matters.[93] Indeed, a survey of *L'Algérien en Europe* over several years makes clear that the Palestinian issue had become one of the ADAE's central concerns.

Moreover, like Zionist activists, ADAE officials, working with the Algerian consulate, encouraged their constituents to volunteer for military duty in Palestine. In Marseille, for example, 150 recruits signed up on 5 June due to Amicale urging.[94] Similar efforts took place in Paris, while the Prefect of Essone reported the recruitment of approximately thirty Algerian Muslims from that region.[95]

Why did the ADAE focus so heavily on the Palestinian issue? Most simply, as a representative of the Algerian political establishment, the ADAE reflected national priorities.[96] Algerian officials were early supporters of the Palestinian liberation movement. Yasser Arafat's older brother headed the Arab Maghreb Bureau at the Arab Higher Committee office in Cairo through which he met most of the FLN's leading members. Fatah delegates attended the Algerian independence ceremony in 1962, during which they gained permission to establish a Palestine Office in Algiers. Soon after, 400 Palestinian teachers were recruited for the expanding Algerian education system (a number that rapidly grew to 1000), and 150 Palestinians enrolled in Algerian universities. In summer 1964, the Algerian army also trained 100–200 Palestinians in guerrilla warfare, and President Ben Bella publicly railed against Palestinian suffering.[97] Likewise, in May the Union générale des travailleurs algériens (UGTA) announced a day of solidarity with Palestinians.[98] The coup in September 1965 that brought Houari Boumediene to power did little to minimize this support. In 1966 the Algerian military academy ran an advanced course for twenty Fatah trainees, and in March 1967, the FLN organ, *El Moudjahid*, began a ten-day special series that showcased the PLO and the Palestinian cause.[99] In June 1967, the Algerian president pledged to aid in the war against "Israel and imperialism."[100] Huge pro-Palestinian demonstrations were coupled with fund-raising efforts, blood banks, and military recruitments.[101] By 1968 Algeria had emerged as the second largest supplier of arms to Fatah, over China.

Such policies were rooted in Algeria's recent war against French domination and the country's anti-imperial philosophy. When the ADAE argued that "the enemy is still on Arab land," it recalled this long history of revolutionary struggle. Echoing the Algerian government's wider anti-colonial agenda, the ADAE insisted that "Israel is only the lowly executor; the secular arm is imperialism. Without the aid, protection and encouragement of imperialist and colonialist authorities, the Zionists would never have dared attack the Arab world."[102] Articles in *L'Algérien en Europe* similarly proclaimed, "Israel is not a state but an imperialist base planted in the heart of the Arab world."[103] The anti-imperialism that was deeply entrenched in FLN culture provided an obvious justification for supporting Palestinian self-rule; for the ADAE, linking anti-Zionism with the Algerian independence struggle was self-evident.[104]

Yet if the ADAE's pro-Palestinian stance reflected the Algerian government's priorities, such appeals also served a broader agenda—uniting Algerian Muslim nationals in France. In numerous calls to support Arab unity and protest racism, the ADAE presented itself as *the* voice of Algerian Muslims in France. *Algérien en Europe* was replete with calls not only to fight imperialism and Zionism but also to foster Arab unity in the face of Western hostility.[105] The adoption of the Palestinian cause was central to this endeavor. In summer 1967, as part of calls to support the Palestinians, for example, Algerian Muslim migrants were instructed to refrain from listening to Western radio programs and reading Western newspapers, considered arms of Zionist propaganda. Rather Radio Alger and particularly "our own news organ *L'Algérien en Europe*" should be their news source. As such directives suggest, the ADAE's work for Palestinians, while ideologically rooted, also reflected a larger effort to influence Muslim migrants' political allegiances. As its own writings made explicit: "For the Algerian émigré to mobilize at this juncture [summer 1967], means above all, to join the activities of the Amicale and to pay subscription fees regularly. Those who have not yet done so are obliged to do so; it is their duty to join our organization under fear of betraying the unity that must cement our struggle."[106] Here support for Palestine and membership in the ADAE were directly linked; to remain aloof, a form of betrayal.

Not surprisingly, French officials, traditionally averse to any immigrant activism, and particularly distrustful of the ADAE due to its ongoing links to the FLN, warned it and the Algerian embassy to cease all political activities.[107] By December, ADAE officials had agreed to limit their efforts to social and cultural work once again, and pro-Palestinian efforts diminished.[108] Governmental concern may, however, have been misplaced, since most evidence suggests that the pro-Palestinian campaign launched in summer 1967 enjoyed limited success among France's North African Muslim population. While *L'Algérien en Europe* asserted an overwhelming response to the 15 June 1967 edition with dozens of respondents asking how they could help the Palestinian cause, such responses were atypical.[109] The French Ministry of Interior thus reported in July that the

ADAE's fund-raising efforts only raised about 120,000 francs, a small sum when compared to the 5,000,000 French Jews raised during the same period. While police informants undoubtedly had an incomplete picture of the migrant community's financial contributions and while the vastly inferior capabilities of the Algerian Muslim working population cannot be easily compared to the middle-class and wealthier French Jewish population, it is still clear that many Algerian Muslim migrants did not find appeals for Palestine attractive enough to turn over hard-earned wages. Indeed, support for Palestine stands in stark contrast to the large sums such migrant communities contributed to Algerian independence efforts earlier in the decade.[110] While many of these "donations" had been made under pressure, similar processes were clearly at work in 1967. Furthermore, military recruitment efforts remained paltry. The thirty volunteers from Essone, for example, did not comply after receiving mobilization orders.[111] In fact, if anything, ADAE efforts to recruit supporters seem to have fostered resentment, as some Algerian Muslim merchants complained of feeling pressured to aid the war effort despite their own disinclination.[112]

As such evidence suggests, the ADAE's decision to use the Palestinian issue as a means of creating political solidarity among Algerian Muslim migrants remained limited. The ADAE never managed to attract most Algerian Muslims to its ranks precisely because the organization was perceived as too heavy-handed and because most of the new immigrants were, in fact, disinclined to take part in activist politics regardless of the cause.[113] As one police report noted: "Such efforts have failed to mobilize the Algerian masses in France to aid and support the Palestinian resistance. . . . [T]he Algerians, for the most part, are not concerned with the Palestinian matter."[114] While such assessments may overlook the degree to which the Palestinian issue surfaced around café tables or markets in Muslim neighborhoods, they accurately reflect the differing levels of political mobilization of French Muslim and Jewish populations during the 1967 war.

The Impact of 1967 on Muslim-Jewish Relations in France

Whatever the degree of political mobilization among Jews and Muslims, the 1967 war had few immediate repercussions for interethnic relations on the ground. Indeed, insofar as pro-Palestinian efforts took hold among Muslims, they generally focused on the conflict abroad without much consideration of Jewish efforts in France to influence public opinion. To the contrary, at the end of June, the *Algérien en Europe* underscored the problems with conflating an ethnic/racial category, Jews, with a political category, Israel.[115] Similarly, French Jewish activists directed their efforts overwhelmingly toward the Middle East and French international policy, rarely expressing interest in or even awareness of their Muslim neighbors. And insofar as they did speak of the surrounding Muslim population it was often to divide events in the Middle East from a wider condemnation of the Arab people. For example, Gerard Bismuth, representing Marseille's Comité de coordination de la jeunesse juive, underscored that his organization's quarrel was with Arab governments, "and not the Arab people, who without doubt desire peace like the Israelis."[116] Or, as a flyer from the mixed Muslim-Jewish neighborhood of Sarcelles reminds us, after calling on Jewish residents to attend a demonstration on 7 June 1967 to "stop genocide," their quarrel had no impact on the "friendship" and "esteem" they felt for "the Arab people." While condemning Israel's enemies for instigating a second Holocaust, meeting organizers also called for a rapid, peaceful, and constructive solution to the problem of Arab refugees "instead of nursing a hateful and negative attitude against them."[117]

It would nevertheless be a mistake to dismiss the impact of the 1967 war in negatively shaping interethnic relations. As this section will argue, if intercommunal relations in France remained generally calm, tensions mounted in two specific arenas. First, while Paris and other large cities experienced no unrest, Marseille showed signs of strain. These tensions, many believed, were the result of the city's ethnic mix, its proximity to the conflict, and its port, which brought the Middle Eastern conflict home. As *Le Monde* later reported, "Eighty-thousand Jews (the third largest population in Europe after London and Paris), thirty thousand Arab workers, longstanding links with the Middle East and Mediterranean countries, French bombs and tanks leaving from its port for Tripoli and Djedda: Marseille cannot help but feel more strongly than most the Israeli-Arab conflict."[118] However accurate, this analysis overlooked the way the Middle Eastern conflict brought already simmering postcolonial tensions to the fore as Mayor Defferre used Israel's war to link Jews evermore tightly with the municipality, highlighting their integration and Muslim marginality. Second, conflict between student activists began to increase as highly politicized sectors of the student body seized the Middle East crisis as a way to promote group belonging and cement loyalties. While still rare in 1967, these encounters laid the groundwork for greater interethnic strife the next year, after student radicals broadened the boundaries of French political discourse even further.

On 25 May 1967, Jewish political integration reached new heights in Marseille when Mayor Defferre and other local political figures joined Jewish leaders in establishing the Comité unifié de soutien à Israël. A silent demonstration on 31 May brought out 4,500 supporters (Jewish and non-Jewish) to "protest the Arab threat against Israel" and to demand French support.[119] Two days later, Defferre accepted the presidency of the Comité, stating his allegiances with no equivocation: "We at the Federation have chosen our camp. We are with Israel."[120] Subsequently, he campaigned actively in Paris and Marseille to raise funds for Israel's defense,[121] and under his leadership, the city sent large quantities of blood and medical supplies to Jewish soldiers.[122] Nor was Defferre Marseille's only public official backing Israel. As elsewhere in France, support came from a diverse range of political, intellectual, and cultural figures, many of whom participated in the demonstration on 31 May.[123] Both daily papers, *Le Provençal* (Defferre's socialist paper), and *Le Méridional–La France* (the center-right paper), insisted in similar terms on this wide-ranging support for the Jewish state.[124] As one headline read, "A Magnificent Display of Solidarity for Israel Animates Marseille's Population."[125] Only the Communist paper, *La Marseillaise*, refrained from discussing the pro-Israel rally on 25 May, instead publishing an editorial by René Andrieu criticizing Israel's Arab policies.[126] In response, numerous local Jews cut their affiliation with the Communist party.[127]

With their city and its leadership strongly behind them, then, Marseille's Jewish community felt less alienated by de Gaulle's declaration of French neutrality than their co-religionists elsewhere, particularly since Defferre's socialist and center-left coalition used its ardent support of Israel as a way to distance themselves from their Gaullist rivals.[128] As Defferre remarked, "if a broad public movement occurs in the country in the same frank way that I am arguing, the government will be compelled to reconsider its position as has been the case in other circumstances."[129] For local Jews, Defferre's stance reinforced the lines between them and their city. According to Charles Haddad, president of the local Zionist federation, "If the starting point for the government's policy reversal comes from Marseille, we would have another reason to be proud of the city that has adopted us."[130] And the Comité de soutien sought to do just that. Meeting on 3 June at the Hôtel de Ville, it adopted a highly critical motion against French neutrality, drawing local political lines around the Middle Eastern issue. While signatories included a handful of centrist politicians who opposed de Gaulle, the overwhelming majority were members of Defferre's Fédération de la gauche démocrate et socialiste (FGDS).[131]

Local Gaullists responded by arguing that the Comité soutien français Israël had become an offshoot of Defferre's party and was inciting war to attract Jewish voters.[132] Even a local Jewish organizer noted that while Defferre's adoption of such a clear pro-Israel position had been helpful, it "had the corollary of tying the Comité de solidarité français à Israel to [Defferre's] parliamentary agenda, making it a sort of Socialist subsection."[133] This link helped reinforce the alliance between Marseille and its Jewish population. On 7 June, for example, a gathering of young FGDS adherents met at the Cinéma Chavé under the aegis of the Comité de soutien pour Israel.[134] While attendees were primarily young Jews, the support of local political figures was evident.[135] Also vocally supporting Israel was the Section Marseille Provence du mouvement démocratique féminin, the president of which was also on the local FGDS executive committee. When the Centre de liaison et d'information, a club affiliated with the FGDS, declared its support for Israel, it did so on the basis of the "bonds of friendship that tie us to Marseille's Jewish community."[136] On 13 June, the Comité de soutien sponsored yet another pro-Israel demonstration at which more than two thousand attendees wildly applauded Defferre and during which a delegate from Haifa thanked Marseille's mayor for his tireless support.[137]

Over several weeks, such widespread and enthusiastic support for Israel began making the city's Muslim residents uncomfortable. In May and early June, neither tensions in the Middle East nor in the city's first pro-Israel demonstrations moved the North African Muslim population to action.[138] Recruitment efforts in the city's North African quarters, for example, largely failed. While rumors that the Algerian consulate was registering volunteers that brought in thirty men, the ADAE did not participate, and most North African migrants manifested little interest.[139] Once war broke out, however, the growing number of pro-Israel demonstrations began to "worry the Algerians a bit." In response, ADAE recruitment activities increased, and on 5 June, approximately 150 volunteered, while several others returned to Algeria. According to police, Muslims were "sensitized to Jewish reactions, particularly in Marseille where the demonstrations of solidarity for Israel preoccupy the Algerian masses. They seem to fear that the young element of the Jewish community might provoke incidents which, according to their gravity, could lead to a clash between Arabs and Jews."[140]

Such fears were undoubtedly fueled by Zionist propaganda that collapsed all Muslims into singular political categories. Betar, for example, printed tracts that accused "all Arab countries of one goal—exterminating the Jews in good and due form. . . . No Hitler is not dead, because he lives through these wretched creatures that he made."[141] While not all Jewish pronouncements were as extreme, others also blurred the boundaries between North African and Palestinian Arabs. In a strongly worded proclamation supporting Israel, for example, the Association des Juifs originaires d'Algérie (AJOA), founded in 1963 under the guidance of Jacques Lazarus to provide welfare and cultural services to incoming Jews, made striking parallels between the fate of Palestinians and Jews in Algeria.[142] Reminding readers that its membership was "almost entirely . . . Jewish refugees from an Arab country," it stressed their forced departure from a land where "they had lived for centuries," having to abandon property "of considerable value of which they were completely pillaged." While Algerian Jews had responded "neither with hate nor resentment toward Arabs," Palestinian refugees, in contrast, had "spent twenty years in idleness and vengeful excitement serving as an excuse for an imperialist and fundamentally racist expansionism leading to a new attempt at genocide."[143] Here then, a mere five years after Lazarus had stressed the "Frenchness" of Algerian Jewish departures, the "Jewish story" had emerged in full. Jews had fled Algeria not as French repatriates but as Jews fleeing Arab persecution—part of an even exchange for Palestinian refugees leaving Israel.

The political posturing of Marseille's Jews worried Muslim residents to such a degree that in certain bidonvilles, the latter organized surveillance teams to protect themselves against malevolent attacks they feared would be directed against them by their Jewish neighbors. The destruction of two small dwellings [*cabanons*] in Calade was thus attributed to Jews. Aggression, however, went in both directions. A Jewish welfare worker thus opted to leave her post after repeated harassment by Algerian Muslim militants, and Consistoire officials went so far as to request police protection for the synagogue on rue Breteuil. By month's end, Marseille's Muslim residents were purportedly suffering from a "deplorable" state of mind, "traumatized by the failures suffered by their brothers in the Middle East" and constantly listening to anti-Western diatribes on Radio-Alger; they "see enemies everywhere and are "easily provoked; their nationalism has been exacerbated."[144]

By the end of June, then, postcolonial tensions, simmering in the city since the early 1960s, had been reignited thanks to the municipality's investment in the Middle East conflict and seeming embrace of its Jewish minority, a process that continued long after the war had ended. If anything, Defferre's pro-Israel advocacy and support for Marseille's Jewish community increased in subsequent years.[145] Publicly condemning antisemitism in *Le Provençal*, he continued to use support for Jews as a way to differentiate himself from the Gaullist regime. Following de Gaulle's much criticized press conference in November 1967, for example, in which he labeled Jews an "elite people, sure of themselves and domineering," Defferre accused the French president of legitimizing discriminatory campaigns: "and we remember how those ended under Hitler's regime and during the second world war: in the death camps." While stopping short of accusing de Gaulle himself of antisemitism, Defferre used his own support for Jews and against antisemitism as a cudgel with which to beat the president; the hero of the Liberation had opened the door to the return of Nazi horrors.[146] For Marseille's Jews, who like their co-religionists throughout the country expressed profound dismay that such a long revered figure could abandon them, Defferre's public support was deeply reassuring.[147]

Defferre's support for Israel also remained steadfast. In spring 1968, for example, newspaper headlines celebrated Marseille as "Israel's door to Europe" after Defferre sought to increase Israeli exports to Marseille.[148] More interestingly, that February the Fédération sud de français rapatrié (FSFR) and the Comité de soutien à Israel organized a 1,000-person-strong protest of France's arms embargo against Israel at which Defferre spoke. This mix of pieds noirs and Jewish concerns reflected Marseille's post-1962 landscape in which former supporters of *Algérie française*, socialists, and Jews used the Arab-Israeli issue as a basis for creating local solidarities. For Defferre, peace with the pieds noirs was of ongoing importance given early missteps. In summer 1962, as thousands had poured into the city, and police worried about urban instability, Defferre told *Paris-Presse* that the repatriates must "leave Marseille quickly" and "readjust elsewhere."[149] Not forgiven five years later, he used the pro-Israel rally to announce the decision to erect a monument commemorating the departure of French colonial subjects.[150] A rally critiquing French Middle Eastern policy thus became a moment to forge local alliances between pieds noirs and Jews. The FSFR's general secretary, for example, commented that pieds noirs were not surprised by the anti-Israeli embargo having also been abandoned by de Gaulle, while another called for "a veritable union" between repatriates and Jews.[151]

How can we understand a political coupling criticized by the local Communist paper for bringing together "supporters of French Algeria, forgers incidentally of racism and anti-Semitism" with Socialists and Jews?[152] The answers are the same as those that brought the city's Muslim and Jewish populations into conflict in 1967, as divisions forged in the waning days of French colonial rule took on salience in the new context. While few Jews joined the many pied-noir associations established in Marseille following decolonization, their similar socioeconomic position, their support for French Algeria, and the difficulties of the initial years in Marseille encouraged political alliances between them.[153] As Wladimir Rabi wrote as early as 1962 of Jewish life in Marseille, "There is a symbiosis between Christian and Jewish repatriates."[154] If not necessarily "anti-Muslim" or "right wing," these alliances continued to prove useful in Marseille as a tool of political integration.[155] Support for Israel, which most pieds noirs and Jews shared with Marseille's political establishment, thus became a way of forging alliances that necessarily marginalized those more critical of Israeli activities.

If Muslim-Jewish tension in Marseille during the 1967 war point to the way the colonial past shaped ethno-religious relations in contemporary France, clashes on campuses foreshadowed the significance of leftist political activism in shaping Muslim-Jewish encounters in the coming decade. The first evidence of such tensions actually predated the 1967 war by a year when on 25 May 1966, the UGEP and the Association des étudiants musulmans nord-africains en France organized the first pro-Palestinian rally since Israel's founding.[156] Given the small size of the gathering—only one hundred people attended—it should be clear that the Palestinian question was hardly a galvanizing issue in the wider North African Muslim population, student or otherwise. Despite its small size, however, the demonstration was covered in the mainstream press (Le Monde published a story about the rally) and elicited angry responses from several Jewish organizations. Attended by, among others, the Middle Eastern historian Maxime Rodinson–the bête noir of the Jewish community due to his Jewish origins and readiness to attack Israeli policies–the event sought to "convince French public opinion of the unjustified and improper link made between the struggle against anti-Semitism and the Arab-Israeli conflict." If all speakers vigorously condemned antisemitism and the genocide of European Jews, they also all underscored the injustice of "repairing evil with evil" by making Palestinians pay for Nazi crimes. Stressing their opposition to Israel, speakers nevertheless insisted that they did not support "throwing the Jewish populations of Palestine into the sea." Rather—to the prolonged ovation of those in attendance—they called for the reestablishment of "age-old friendship of Jews and Arabs" while distinguishing legitimate political conflict from any religious or racial hostility. The Egyptian journalist Aly El Samman, for example, called on Arabs to become active participants in the fight against antisemitism by joining organizations such as MRAP; as such they would not only rebuild alliances with Jews but would weaken Zionism, which was itself an outgrowth of European antisemitism.[157]

Such arguments proved infuriating to Israel's Jewish supporters, who overlooked the demonstration's appeals for interethnic cooperation. In response, on 7 July 1966 various organizations, including the Fédération des sociétés juives de France, the Alliance France-Israël, the Amitiés France-Israël, and the Ligue internationale contre l'antisémitisme, held their own rally expressing their "indignation to see these students abuse French hospitality by publicly uttering extermination threats towards Israel, one of France's allies." By pointing to the students as "abusers of French hospitality" and underscoring the links between France and Israel, the protesters drew a symbolic line between their own citizenship and the foreignness of the students in question. The sin of the Muslim protestors was that they took part in activist politics in the first place, their specific politics being secondary. Protesting students were thus constructed as "outsiders" abusing French hospitality, not as fellow residents working within the polity to influence its direction.

Like much of the rhetoric surrounding the 1967 war a year later, the proclamation also invoked the Holocaust, "urging all true anti-racists, lovers of freedom and justice, not to accept fallacious arguments that classified Jews into categories, a method used by the Nazis with the tragic consequences that we all know."[158] Well before 1967 the Holocaust had become a reference for those on both sides of the Israeli/Palestinian debate.[159] While protestors at the Mutualité evoked the genocide in their self-defense strategies, the Jewish organizations railed against their right to do so. According to Michel Salomon who condemned the pro-Palestinian demonstration in *L'Arche*, it was both scandalous and intellectually and morally dishonest to compare Israelis with Nazis.

Salomon, like the Jewish protestors on 7 July, also focused on the foreignness of the pro-Palestinian demonstrators. Dismissing the demonstration as the first manifestation of the Arab League's efforts to win over the French population now that the Algerian war was over, Salomon accused the organization of establishing "a phantom Union générale des étudiants palestiniens en France, of which nobody has heard anything before." In this view, not only was a foreign power—the Arab League—promoting hatred in France, but also Middle Eastern and North African intellectuals were following suit. In Salomon's telling, then, the rally had been an ugly event: "For an observer mixed into the shouting crowd . . . there was a singular feeling of nausea that predominated, a nausea that overwhelmed even the disappointment at once again seeing the dimming of the possibility of a true dialogue between Jews and Arabs beyond demagoguery or hatred." Here, as during discussions of the Algerian war, Muslim participants—and particularly those from the Maghreb—were denounced for their unwillingness to engage in a good faith dialogue and for succumbing to the worst forms of bigotry. "Outsiders" from a "phantom" organization were manipulating minds and hearts. Calls to join the MRAP, rather than a sincere appeal to unite to fight bigotry, were a clever ploy manipulated by politically astute racists.[160] Such assertions meant that Salomon and other Jewish critics could withdraw from dialogue while claiming that the "other side" was to blame.

The MRAP, it should be noted, did not accept this characterization. In the association's view, Jews "firmly attached to Israel" and Arabs "whose patriotism cannot be doubted" had proven capable of joining forces in anti-racist struggles. According to Charles Palant, the secretary general, such encounters demonstrated that divisions created by the Middle Eastern conflict were surmountable. Indeed, the MRAP had held a symposium on the Middle Eastern conflict the year before during which "Jews and Arabs held an open dialogue with a remarkable spirit of truth and justice."[161] According to observers, the many hours of discussion were carried out "in a spirit of fraternity and mutual tolerance" and compromise prevailed.[162]

For others, however, the intermingling at universities of young people from different ethnic and religious backgrounds provided an opportunity to promote group solidarity. In November 1965, six months after the MRAP's celebration of Muslim-Jewish cooperation, the Israeli embassy in Paris hosted a meeting of the Union mondiale des étudiants juifs (UMEJ), which brought together eighty students from across Western Europe to discuss historical sources of opposition between Jews and Arabs; recent growth in Israel's Arab population; surveys on the number of Jewish students who had participated in conferences with Arabs; and methods with which to combat Arab propaganda.[163] Far from promoting the "spirit of fraternity and mutual tolerance" that dominated the MRAP's discussions, the UMEJ meeting focused on conflict and polarization. Speakers—including many representatives of the Israeli government—provided students with Israel's perspective on the conflict. While encouraging Jewish students to establish contact with Arab peers in European universities, these efforts were directed toward countering their propaganda.[164] Jewish attendees were thus trained to defend Israel in the emerging hotbed of university politics. As Michel Solomon wrote the subsequent July indicating communal concern with these spaces: "We have certainly had time these last years to accustom ourselves . . . to the aggressive positions adopted by Arab students on the subject of Israel."[165]

As tensions increased in spring 1967, student activists became evermore politicized. In early May 1967 at the Cité Universitaire—a set of dormitories in southern Paris designed to bring foreign students together to promote international harmony—Syrian students circulated anti-Zionist tracts to protest the planned showing of the film *Exodus*, leading the Minister of Education to cancel the film.[166] Either way, campaigns on university campuses to influence student opinion were beginning to spread. Then, on 20 May, the UGEP and the Association des étudiants musulmans nord-africains—which had brought together Palestinian and North African students a year earlier—organized a day of international solidarity with Palestinians against "Zionist imperialism."[167]

As one Algerian Muslim student noted later, "The Six Day War in 1967 was a turning point for us."[168] By June, Jewish sources were reporting worriedly about the intensification of "Arab student propaganda in diverse universities" that "endeavor to spread the myth of Israeli imperialism." The Comité étudiant inter-arabe, which united thirteen student groups, for example, denounced "Anglo-American collusion" with the Zionists and called for the Arab people's triumph over imperialism and Zionism."[169] Meanwhile in Aix a debate between an Arab and Israeli on the Middle East problem was canceled due to fears of mounting hostility among students.[170]

Muslim groups, it should be noted, were often careful about blurring the lines between Judaism and Zionism. In the inflammatory environment of campus politics, however, such nuances could be lost. At the University of Strasbourg, Arab students in the Comité anti-colonialiste, for example, contrasted Judaism and Zionism while insinuating that the latter was in the process of irreparably harming the former. In response, students from Union des étudiants juifs distributed their own tract, which argued that the circulation of such "base propaganda" was inappropriate in a university dedicated to dialogue.[171] Such statements overlooked the fact that Jewish propaganda was also pervasive. Universities in Marseille, for example, were papered with tracts comparing Nasser to Hitler and calling on Jewish students to prevent a second genocide.[172]

Indeed, despite calls for dialogue, Jewish youth organizations made it clear that they too had taken sides. The Comité de coordination de la jeunesse juive de France, for example, insisted that although French Jewish youth had sought to establish dialogue, they now had to stand with Israel: "Without renouncing the desire for such an opening, French Jewish youth, completely taken up with the current situation, want to leave no doubt about their obligation to participate in Israel's struggle and to safeguard its existence."[173] Similarly the UEJF stressed Jewish loyalty to Israel. Still maintaining its leftist leanings and its hopes for Muslim-Jewish dialogue, UEJF members distributed tracts decrying anti-Arab racism in France.[174] Nevertheless, at a UEJF demonstration at the Maison de la Mutualité on 20 May speakers insisted, "we will not tolerate an ambiguous attitude towards Israel among our friends" and promised that all Jewish youth, no matter what their affiliation, would "unite to fight for Israel."[175]

In emphasizing loyalty to Israel while rejecting racism at home, the UEJF was one of several youth organizations that began reconceptualizing the parameters of Muslim-Jewish relations in France, a process that linked developments in the Middle East evermore closely with the inequities in France. It would take the upheaval to French political culture in 1968, however, to raise these developments to a fever pitch, as radical activists—many of them Jewish—brought the Palestinian cause to a wider French audience and moved the Middle East from the margins to the center of Muslim-Jewish relations in France.

5

Palestine in France

Radical Politics and Hardening Ethnic Allegiances,
1968–72

In June 1968, almost one year to the day after the 1967 war, a riot in the Parisian immigrant neighborhood of Belleville between Muslim and Jewish residents took France by surprise. Capturing widespread media attention, many commentators feared the violence was evidence that transnational ethno-religious allegiances had inevitably begun to pit Muslims and Jews against each other. And yet the riot's origins were more complex than such assertions suggested coming, as they did, in the midst of the *événements* of May/June 1968. During those weeks, Anarchist, Trotskyist, and Maoist student groups initiated uprisings that led to the largest general strike in French history. This tumultuous environment not only created the riot's immediate context but also pushed the Israeli-Palestinian issue from the margins to the center of Muslim-Jewish relations in France. Indeed, few commentators at the time or subsequently have traced the powerful impact of late 1960s youth radicalism in making Middle Eastern conflict relevant to local Muslim-Jewish political discourse.[1] This context is crucial, however, for understanding how distant political struggles took on local meaning.

Protests and strikes in late 1960s France brought to mainstream attention issues previously on the social margins, including feminism, sexual freedom, gay rights, and anti-racism.[2] Anti-imperialism and third-worldism, both ideologically central to the New Left in France and elsewhere, also won wider public hearing as campus radicals gained national attention. France's "discovery" of the Palestinian problem was linked to these developments.

Ten months earlier, French campuses had emerged as sites of conflict for Muslims and Jews around this issue. For much of 1968, however, pro-Palestinian activities remained muted.[3] Radicals on the far left—particularly Trotskyists and Maoists on university campuses—began to change that dynamic. Differing in their strategies and ideological aims and distrustful of "bourgeois" national liberation struggles, various radical groups shared a blend of Marxism and third-worldism that translated into broad sympathy for anti-imperial struggles.[4] During 1968, support for Palestinians became fused with this anti-colonialism. Already in June 1967, the Maoist organization, Union des jeunesses communistes marxistes leninistes, held the only pro-Palestinian demonstration in Paris (driven largely by Egyptian exiles Adel Rifaat—an Islamic convert of Jewish origin—and Bahgat El-Nadi, known by pen name Mahmoud Hussein). Interest intensified in March 1968 when Chinese and Vietnamese leftists threw their support behind the Palestine Liberation Organization and the Jordanian army in their battle against the Israel Defense Forces (IDF) in Karameh, Jordan. For French radicals, who drew inspiration from Chinese and Vietnamese revolutionaries, and particularly for Maoists who linked armed struggle and revolution, the Palestinian cause took on profound symbolic resonance. In the words of one Maoist poster that linked Palestinian, Algerian, and other revolutionary struggles: "Vietnam, Palestine, FLN, El Fatah: The same combat."[5]

University campuses, hotbeds of French radical culture, soon became key arenas for attacking the so-called American-Zionist imperial axis. In July 1967, the largest student union, the Union nationale des étudiants français (UNEF), condemned Israeli aggression and recognized Palestinian national rights.[6] During the 1968 uprisings, Arab nationalist and Zionist students constructed competing stands at the entrance of the occupied Sorbonne. Although the Occupation Committee removed both due to resulting tensions, the Palestinian issue had become linked to the anti-racism and anti-colonialism undergirding university discourse.[7]

External developments also facilitated interest in the Palestinian cause. Arab losses in the 1967 conflict pushed Palestinian nationalists to seek new allies. In particular, Yasser Arafat's, nascent organization Fatah, weakened by limited organizational abilities, the power of Israeli countermeasures, insufficient participation of the Palestinian masses, and the failures of Nasserism and the wider Arab world to defeat Israel, was soon forced into exile.[8] Turning abroad in a search for new supporters, Fatah focused on France where it was hoped that pro-Arab policies and a growing Muslim population would help foster sympathy.[9]

This chapter traces how French radicals, North African Muslim students, and Palestinian representatives created alliances that brought the Palestinian issue to French public attention and the way these alliances shaped Muslim-Jewish relations. Although Muslim immigrants were only marginally engaged with pro-Palestinian politics, the period beginning in 1968 with the student uprisings and ending in the early 1970s with the decline of radical politics had a decisive impact on Muslim-Jewish relations, particularly among students. The publicly visible and, at times, violent confrontations between Muslim and Jewish youth resulted in increasing polarization around Middle Eastern politics, as the Jewish community—already galvanized by the 1967 war—took notice, and as larger numbers of Muslim immigrants came to see themselves as having a stake in France's domestic and international affairs.

Yet for all its divisiveness, the tumultuous environment also created unexpected Muslim-Jewish alliances. Indeed, the very radicals who promoted

Palestinian interests and who worked with Muslim activists to fight racism were often Jewish. While rhetorically rejecting identity politics in favor of universal humanism, many understood their leftist commitments in particularistic terms, that is as a direct response to the history of anti-Jewish persecution. Many were in fact children of Holocaust survivors seeking to come to terms with their parents' past.[10] Their participation in pro-Palestinian struggles created bridges between Muslims and Jews at the very moment conflict between them was becoming more visible.

This cooperation reminds us that Jewish-Muslim polarization around the Middle East was not a predetermined outcome of ethnic transnational allegiances. Rather, when "polarization" did emerge, it did so as a product of the political space created by late 1960s French radical culture, which both made room for a new generation of Muslim activists who infused their pro-immigrant politics with the Palestinian issue and pushed politically active members of France's Jewish population—and particularly high school and university students—away from traditional affiliations on the left and toward a more combative politics. The result was a growing number of highly visible Muslim-Jewish conflicts that linked Jews with Israel and North African Muslims with Palestinians in increasingly rigid ways.

The Belleville Riots and the Changing Terrain of Muslim-Jewish Relations in France

On Sunday, 2 June 1968, three days before the anniversary of the outbreak of the 1967 Arab-Israeli war, two Tunisian immigrants, one Jewish and one Muslim, fought over a card game at a local café.[11] The fight soon escalated. Some blamed Jewish observers for breaking the café's windows when the Muslim loser refused to pay his debt. Others asserted that Muslim residents chased Jews with bottles and clubs. The result, however, was that over the next two days, forty to fifty Jewish- and Muslim-owned stores were ransacked and several people injured.[12] Before police finally quelled the unrest, Muslim participants had launched Molotov cocktails at the synagogue on rue Julien-Lacroix, where Jews had congregated for the holiday of Shavuot, and a self-defense squad of Jewish youth had set up barricades in the courtyard.[13]

What explains such violence in the previously harmonious neighborhood?[14] As the game preceding the riot suggests, convivial relations were the norm in Belleville as in other mixed immigrant neighborhoods.[15] The largely Tunisian Jewish and Algerian Muslim residents shared not only their North African origins and many cultural practices but also the struggles of all newcomers.[16] While congregating on differing streets, a vibrant market culture and some mixed apartment buildings brought residents together. Jewish employers, somewhat better off than local Muslim immigrants, hired the latter, sometimes creating class tensions but also establishing neighborhood ties; cafés and groceries served a mixed clientele, and religious festivals saw the sharing of holiday foods, a practice imported from North Africa. As one Jewish café owner asserted after the riot, "We are all brothers. We knew each other in Tunis and we live together." Published in the magazine *Le Jeune Afrique* with a photograph of two boys captioned, "Which is Jewish, which is Muslim," the article stressed the common background and experiences of local residents.[17] Indeed, if ethnic and religious practices distinguished the two populations, there was little in the quarter's daily life to foreshadow the violence.

For many, the riot's proximity to the anniversary of the 1967 war was all the explanation necessary. Local press reports, sensationalizing the violence, referred to the "Six Hour War."[18] As Ethan Katz has shown, while some communal leaders downplayed the Middle East's impact on local Jewish-Muslim relations, many were "ready to embrace the largely mythical view of the Belleville riots as the signal of new Jewish-Muslim tensions that extended directly from those in Israel-Palestine."[19] Although Muslim and Jewish political and religious leaders worked tirelessly to restore calm to the neighborhood,[20] both the Algerian paper *El Moudjahid* and ADAE representatives blamed Zionist provocateurs, while some Jewish spokesmen faulted Fatah and a circulating Arabic tract calling for "holy war."[21] After the riot, Albert Memmi declared that Arab colleagues had warned him of an Arab League plan to provoke conflict, while Jean Simon, vice president of a Zionist youth group, insisted that "Belleville resulted from intensive Arab propaganda."[22] A resulting schisim in the UEJF ensued, as some members broke away to found the Front des étudiants juifs (FEJ), a far-right group dedicated to self-defense and fighting anti-Zionism.[23]

A monocausal focus on war in the Middle East, however, overlooked the generally nonconflictual interethnic terrain in Belleville a year previously and important international and domestic transformations in the ensuing months that had changed the environment. Anti-Jewish riots in Tunisia in June 1967 had increased Belleville's Jewish population by several thousand, bringing to the neighborhood new resentments against the "Arabs" who had destroyed the Grande Synagogue in Tunis and ransacked the Jewish quarter. Although the Tunisian government condemned the violence, departures to France and Israel, which had slowed since the early 1960s, increased substantially; of 23,000 Jews in Tunisia on the eve of the 1967 War, only 7,000–8,000 remained one year later.[24] Those who settled in Belleville joined earlier migrants who saw in the newcomers' arrival affirmation of their own decision to leave and a reminder of lessons learned about "Arabs" during decolonization.[25] Such wounds were still fresh a year later when the French environment became explosive. The UEJF president, in Belleville during the riot, likened the ambience to a Jewish quarter in Algeria, "a wave of panic mixed with some aggression and a general tendency to entertain any kind of bunk [*bobard*] such as, 'there are 500 Arabs in Barbès headed this way with machine guns.'"[26]

The riot also unfolded in the context of the political radicalism of May 1968. The massive protests and worker walkouts, in which many foreign students and laborers participated, transported radical politics from the universities to the streets.[27] Moreover, strikes that month left much of Belleville's working population aimless, as did the Jewish holiday that kept Jewish stores and cafés closed for two days. Even those disconnected from the student struggle were swept up in the surging radicalism. "An effervescence reigned," noted one Jewish student who helped establish a UEJF medical response unit. "Among the group in place were youth who felt somewhat marginal to the events of May 1968. They had a suppressed activism that they set off, believing it was permanent. It lasted from the 5th to the 15th of June. We believed we were living in highly revolutionary times. In hindsight, it seems a bit absurd."[28] The combustible combination of leftist radicalism, massive strikes, postcolonial politics, *and* Middle Eastern tensions explains tensions in Belleville in June 1968.

Whatever the link between the riot and Middle Eastern tensions, however, the former's impact was certainly to increase communal sensitivity to such a linkage. Indeed, two years later, when new disturbances in Belleville and the neighboring district left a sixty-year-old Algerian Jew dead (of a heart attack), several policemen wounded, twenty-eight mostly Jewish businesses vandalized, and thirty-three mostly North African Muslims arrested for defacing the rue de Tourtille synagogue, such linkages were assumed.[29] As in 1968, Jewish and Muslim leaders—such as Rabbi Couchena and the Algerian consul in Paris, Amor Benghezal—patrolled the neighborhood to stem the violence and called for calm. By 1970, however, the Middle East conflict played an even greater role in shaping perspectives on events. Rioters shouted "Vive Israël" and "Vive Palestine," respectively. The ADAE blamed "Jewish residents" and "Zionist provocateurs" and called for justice.[30] A letter from one reader to the *Algérien en Europe* blamed the riot on "Zionist merchants" and the "young Nazis of Betar," the far-right Zionist youth movement, and asserted that police had unfairly punished only Muslims.[31] Muslim student organizations argued that "Zionist propaganda" had been the riot's primary beneficiary and warned that anti-Arab racism and antisemitism would intensify as a result.[32]

Jewish organizations underscored Fatah's role in the violence.[33] While a CRIF statement to *Le Monde* on 21/22 June spoke somewhat vaguely of Jewish victimization at the hands of "provocateurs" (noting that only Jewish stores were attacked and only Muslims arrested),[34] internal CRIF disucssions noted police "certainty" that the incidents were "the work of certain Arab elements" working with Fatah's support. A pro-Palestinian rally held at the entrance to Belleville two days later, which, according to CRIF sources, was attended by a mix of French leftists and "Arab students," confirmed such fears.[35] The FEJ likewise condemned "Palestinian progressives and their leftist and Nazi allies," while Jean-Pierre Bloch, president of the Ligue internationale contre le racisme et l'antisémitisme blamed "provocateurs."[36]

Such accounts reflected growing fears that the Israeli-Palestinian crisis was destabilizing intercommunal relations in France. To understand these concerns, we must move away from Belleville to wider political developments in France after the 1968 student riots. While communal leaders were right to recognize the Palestinian-Israeli conflict as increasingly relevant to Muslim-Jewish relations in France, this development also had local origins.

Building Alliances: Pro-Palestinian Mobilization, 1968–70

This section will explore how Palestinians, largely invisible in France in 1967, became a subject of public concern and how Muslim student activists seized the Palestinian cause as their own. An alliance among three distinct groups of political actors allowed this dynamic to unfold: (1) Palestinian nationalists searching for new allies following Arab losses in 1967; (2) French far leftists seeking to win adherents among Muslim laborers in France via the Palestinian issue; and (3) North African Muslim student activists—already highly politicized in response to developments in their home nations and the radical environment on French campuses—who saw in the Palestinian issue a rallying cry for oppressed Muslims in France.[37] On campuses where these students were increasingly visible and where some Jewish students expressed a more vocal pro-Israel politics in response to the 1968 foment, conflict grew. Interestingly, however, it was often Jewish leftists, well represented in the *gauchistes* movement, who vocally supported Palestinian nationalism, reminding us that at the very moment when many commentators were coming to see Jewish-Muslim political polarization around the Middle East as an essential dividing line, it remained far from automatic.

In January 1969, Fatah representative Muhammad Abou Mayer arrived in Paris to foster international support for Palestinian nationalism. As part of his mission, Mayer and his subsequent replacement, Mahmoud Hamchari, a well-known Palestinian activist and Arafat's close collaborator, were charged with challenging Israel's hold on French sympathies. Establishing themselves as the primary Palestinian representatives among those organizing Muslim political life in France, such as the Arab League and the ADAE, Mayer and Hamchari produced numerous bulletins and tracts, organized public meetings, launched a French language newspaper, *Fedayin*, and forged alliances within the wider anti-colonial movement. Hamchari also established contact with the foreign ministry, regularizing his status, and introducing Palestinian diplomacy to France.[38]

Fatah focused on winning supporters within two overlapping arenas: universities and radical left-wing political organizations. Universities—already sites of pro-Palestinian activism during the student uprisings—remained a welcoming space thereafter.[39] In November 1968, for example, the Comité de liaison des étudiants arabes organized a week of meetings and lectures about Palestine at the university in the western Parisian suburb of Antony, and the next month, the Union générale des étudiants libanais de France held pro-Palestinian meetings on campuses in several large cities.[40] Once Fatah had established a Parisian office, it supported such efforts through the Union générale des étudiants de Palestine.[41] By February 1969, Fatah's student delegates had established alliances with various revolutionary groups known to support the Palestinian cause, such as the Jeunesse communiste révolutionnaire and the Fédération des étudiants révolutionnaires. Together, they established Comités d'action Palestine on many French campuses, including in Marseille and Paris (particularly Censier). These groups held demonstrations, teach-ins, and expositions, and collected funds, medical supplies, clothes, blood, and sometimes volunteers for Palestine.[42]

Creating such institutions was doubly useful to Fatah. First, the Comités d'action Palestine gave Fatah access to a wider audience. As police noted, "El Fatah relies on the zealousness of the 'friends of Palestine' to provide the Arab cause with openings to the general public as well as with a means of eventually putting pressure on the French government."[43] Second, the Comités gave Fatah access to leftist circles where they sought support from those who had backed Algerian independence. Indeed, gauchiste interest in the Palestinians was an early indication to Fatah representatives that the role Jews had historically played in French revolutionary circles would not necessarily be an obstacle.[44] In fact, as we will see, many Jewish leftists supported the Palestinian cause.

For gauchistes, Fatah's appeal was a complex blend of the ideological and the pragmatic. Ideologically, Fatah's arguments invoked long-standing commitments to anti-imperialism and third-worldism. In the various organizations committed to Palestinian liberation, such as the Comité de soutien aux luttes anti-impérialistes des peuples arabes, presided over by the Trotskyist journalist Daniel Guérin, or the Section française du mouvement contre le racisme anti-arabe (MCRA), anti-imperialism was the motivating concern.[45] As the Comité de soutien's journal, *Résistance populaire*, asserted in May 1968, the Palestinian struggle was a battle against imperialism, not the so-called Jewish nation.[46] Likewise, a January 1969 MCRA flyer called followers to "support the liberation struggle of the Palestinian people, victims—like the Vietnamese—of imperialism."[47]

Ideology worked in tandem, however, with pragmatic hopes among leftists that the Palestinian issue could serve as a bridge between North African immigrant workers and the gauchistes. Largely invisible to French media and social commentators since the end of the Algerian crisis, North African laborers attracted significant attention during the 1968 uprisings.[48] The riots, which broke out at the University of Nanterre, were adjacent to France's largest immigrant slum. Striking students visited the area, and various Maoist, anarchist, and Trotskyist groups, hoping to distinguish themselves from large leftist political parties that had little to say on immigrant rights, denounced the deplorable conditions. Seeking to promote proletarian solidarity and internationalism, they argued the West could not reverse bourgeois society alone; third-world radicalism—embodied in immigrant labor—would help spark the coming revolution. Slogans such as "French workers–immigrant workers, same combat," sought to initiate the necessary alliance.

To win supporters in the relatively closed world of France's foreign workforce, however, required new tactics. A wide range of Basque separatists, Spanish anarchists, American pacifists, and student nationalists, thus moved into the immigrant slums, signing up for Arabic classes, offering French literacy courses, encouraging strikes, and distributing tracts.[49] The focus on Palestinian nationalism was central to these efforts, as French radicals linked the struggle for immigrant rights to wider anti-imperial and anti-capitalist campaigns.[50] MCRA activists, for example, positioned themselves against three adversaries: (1) Zionism, (2) Gaullism, and (3) anti-Arab racism, which—in their view— had surpassed contemporary antisemitism in scope.[51] While devoting most columns to the Palestinian issue, *Résistance populaire* thus also condemned the treatment of Arab workers and called for solidarity between French and Arab laborers.[52] Such links were often explicit, such as at a 1971 rally to protest racism that ended with a slide show on Palestine or in posters that read, "Workers, the *fédayins* are also fighting for you."[53]

Maoist militants, particularly those associated with La Gauche prolétarienne (GP), a pro-Chinese revolutionary movement, were the most ardent backers of the Palestinian issue.[54] Of particular significance for our purposes, a number of GP members, including its two leaders, Alain Geismar and Pierre Victor (Benny Lévy), were Jewish. Indeed, gauchisme in general was marked by a small but highly visible Jewish presence. Three of the four most outspoken student leaders, Daniel Cohn-Bendit, Alain Krivine, and Alain Geismar were Jewish. Eleven of twelve of the Ligue communiste revolutionnaire's governing body were Jewish as was a similar proportion of those making up the Lutte ouvrière. Cohn-Bendit later commented that the French gauchiste leadership could have communicated in Yiddish.[55]

Jewish origins did not translate into specifically Jewish agendas, at least in ethnic terms. As descendants of Holocaust survivors or escapees, many radicals had dedicated themselves to fighting fascism, but for them, the war's lessons were universal. Neither hiding nor celebrating their ethno-religious origins, they believed that the answer to fascism and racism was social revolution.[56] Moreover, for many Jewish radicals, nationalism was an anathema, particularly after 1967 when images of occupying soldiers clashed with long-standing images of Jewish victims and resistors.[57] Maxime Rodinson, for example, a Middle Eastern scholar of Jewish origin, emerged as a vocal, leading critic of Zionism.[58] Emmanuel Lévyne, a rabbi whose father was killed in Auschwitz, condemned the "Israelization of the Parisian Jewish community," and authored *Judaïsme contre Sionisme.*[59] Journalist Ania Francos, whose family was also murdered during the Holocaust, maintained close relations with representatives of El Fatah. Supporting leftist causes in Cuba, South Africa, and Algeria, she wrote against Zionism and Israeli occupation. Professors with Trotskyite and Maoist leanings, like sociologist Catherine Lévy, joined the Comités Palestine asserting that to be a revolutionary meant fighting for the Palestinians, while Trotskyist Jean-Louis Weissberg visited a refugee camp affiliated with the Popular Democratic Front for the Liberation of Palestine (PDFLP) in December 1969 and proclaimed it an honor to be a Jew at the side of Palestinians.[60] Nor were all those on the anti-Zionist Jewish left intellectuals. Patrick Rabiaz, a French worker of Jewish origins, for example, justified his hunger strike in sympathy with North African Muslim protestors by comparing Zionist oppression against Palestinians with his own family's suffering in Nazi concentration camps.[61]

As these last two examples suggest, some Jewish radicals did link their politics to their Jewish origins or history while others proved reluctant to criticize Israel too aggressively. According to Yair Auron, the Palestinian cause received relatively muted support in France when compared to support for other leftist causes in part because of Jewish participation in radical groups. For example, in 1971 Toulouse, Maoists in the Comité permanent d'action pour la Palestine pushed out Trotskyists ostensibly over ideological clashes; local observers, however, believed it was the Jewish presence in the Trotskyist organization that had caused the rift.[62] For many Jewish radicals, however, anti-Zionism was a central component of their ideological makeup, and their support was used to prove the righteousness of the cause. One Maoist poster, for example, ended with, "Long live Fatah's Jewish combatants."[63]

Nowhere was the Jewish presence more visible than in the Gauche prolétarienne under Geismar and Levy. Benny Lévy (half brother of Muslim convert and leftist Adel Rifaat) had fled Egypt after the 1956 Suez crisis. As a university student in France, he entered the Union des étudiants communistes and then, in 1966, co-founded the Maoist Union des jeunesses communistes marxistes-léninistes. In response to the 1967 war, he and his brother Tony established the Comité des étudiants juifs antisionistes.[64] Alain Geismar, born in 1939 into a nonpracticing Alsatian Jewish family, faced racist violence at an early age. When the Algerian crisis broke out, Geismar experienced profound guilt over French atrocities, seeing in them parallels to Nazi tactics. He reached out to the FLN, launching his career in radical leftist struggles, a path that took him later to Maoism and anti-Zionism.[65]

Under Lévy and Geismar, the GP became infamous for its pro-Palestinian politics.[66] Establishing ties with Fatah's Parisian office, Geismar and Léo Lévy (Benny's wife) spent August 1969 in Jordan visiting Fatah's military branch, al-Assifa. Symbolically distancing the Maoist organization from links to the French Jewish establishment, in September, three hundred GP demonstrators scrawled anti-Zionist slogans on a Rothschild mansion and bank. This link between Jewish capital and Israeli imperialism was echoed a year later after "Black September" when Jordan's King Hussein responded to an attempted coup by killing and expelling thousands of Palestinians. Posters advertising a subsequent GP demonstration read, "The capitalist Rothschild oppresses the French people; the Zionist Rothschild oppresses the Palestinian people; the imperialist Rothschild oppresses the Jews world over." By linking capitalism, Zionism, and imperialism through the symbol of Rothschild and familiar anti-semitic stereotypes, Maoists made clear that Jewish participation did not influence the movement's allegiances.[67]

The GP's most significant contribution to pro-Palestinian politics in France, however, came in 1970 when it worked with Algerian, Tunisian, Moroccan, Syrian, and Lebanese Muslim students to found the Comité Palestine ouvrier Nanterre. Drawn to Maoist circles because of their commitment to social justice, their criticisms of their home governments, and their interest in pro-Arab causes, these Muslim student activists used the Comité Palestine to fuse the problems facing immigrant laborers in France with a pro-Palestinian agenda.[68]

As already noted, Muslim student interest in the Palestinian issue pre-dated Maoist encouragement. These sympathies intensified in 1968 as various student organizations, including the Union nationale des étudiants algériens, the Association des étudiants musulmans nord-africains, the Union générale des étudiants tunisiens, and the Union nationale des étudiants marocains, expressed increasingly progressive, pro-Arab, and anti-Zionist stances.[69] By 1970 the UGEP and the Parisian branch of the Croissant-rouge had moved into the Foyer des étudiants musulmans nord-africains and the Maison du Maroc at the Cité Universitaire.[70] Indeed, residents temporarily renamed it the Pavillon de la Palestine libre when Moroccan rebels who had sided with the Palestinians against Jordan during Black September escaped there.[71]

The Palestinian issue thus came to play a determinative role in the political evolution of a generation of North African student activists in France.[72] For many, this commitment found expression in the new Maoist Comités Palestine.[73] Linking the Palestinian revolution to the struggle "of all Arab peoples to liberate themselves from all forms of exploitation and imperial oppression," the Comités Palestine connected Algerian nationalists and Palestinians fighting Israel to immigrants in Paris. "In the working districts [of France] . . ." read one pamphlet, "we have organized meetings where for the first time since Algerian independence, 800 immigrant and French workers have come together to support the Palestinian revolution."[74] According to the tract's authors, Algerian Muslims should care about the Palestinian plight both because it mirrors their own struggle and because it is part of Arab efforts to free themselves from Western domination. In this way, the Palestinian cause was linked to anti-racist campaigns in France and to efforts to better working conditions.[75] As one Ministry of the Interior report noted, "As the committee mixes the very real complaints of the people in the neighborhood with those concerning the Palestinian issue, they make it necessary to accept or reject both issues in one block."[76]

The linking of these issues ultimately created tensions between gauchistes and their pro-Palestinian allies in France. Having relied on radicals to promote Palestinian interests, Fatah representatives and their allies in the ADAE soon worried that subversive politics could endanger the cause.[77] Hoping to build alliances with the French government and on record for praising de Gaulle's pro-Arab policies, the wider Palestinian political leadership began working "to neutralize the anti-Gaullism of their French friends."[78] Fatah representatives thus asked the UGEP to refrain from activities that could be perceived as antisemitic or too leftist and insisted in early 1969 that the Comités d'action Palestine remain focused on the Palestinian struggle and promoting Arab self-reliance.[79] Efforts to use North African immigrants for purely Marxist or revolutionary ends should be curtailed.[80] Such views corresponded with Fatah's ideological efforts to build a popular liberation movement based more closely on Algeria's anti-colonial nationalism than on the Chinese and Vietnamese "people's war," but they also reflected pragmatic concerns that the very people who had brought the Palestinian cause to a wider French public would alienate potential supporters.[81] UGEP leaders agreed, fearing French officials would reduce grants to Palestinian students.[82] At a November 1972 rally, the UGEP thus discouraged leftist participation so as to downplay links between Palestinian and gauchiste politics. Rather than calling for a Palestinian "revolution," they opted for the term "resistance" in the hopes of drawing more support.[83]

Fatah's rejection of gauchiste efforts to use the Palestinian conflict as an entrée into the Muslim émigré population suggests that "Arab unity," while a useful clarion call in the propaganda efforts described above, was as much a construct as "Jewish unity" in late 1960s France. Recognizing such divisions does not, however, undermine the significance of the initial relationship forged between Palestinian nationalists, French gauchistes, and Muslim student activists. This relationship not only brought the Palestinian question to France, but also opened the door to the particular blend of Maoism and Palestinian nationalism that drove the Comités Palestine into France's North African immigrant neighborhoods. For French leftists attracted to the movement, the move into North African immigrant neighborhoods was a major appeal. One Jewish student, for example, explained her attraction to the GP because its outreach was to "neither intellectuals nor students but primarily Arab laborers and Palestinians."[84] Ironically, the Maoist Comités Palestine may have been one of the few arenas where Muslims and Jews interacted outside of mixed immigrant neighborhoods like Belleville. While atypical, these collaborations make clear that disagreements around the Palestinian-Israeli issue were not the only option available to Muslims and Jews in late 1960s France. Yet in helping to legitimize the pro-Palestinian movement, these alliances paradoxically helped create the political landscape that was increasingly pushing Muslim and Jewish activists into opposing corners. Indeed, as we will soon see, although the Jews who joined these efforts typically did so on universalist terms that incorporated the Palestinian issue into wider leftist goals, they could not control the way those supporting Palestinian nationalism or Zionism began drawing ethnic boundaries around these political movements.

North African Muslim Immigrants and the
Pro-Palestinian Movement

Before tracing the impact of pro-Palestinian activism on Muslim-Jewish relations, it is important to consider how deeply the pro-Palestinian agenda penetrated into France's Muslim immigrant populations. Did North African Muslim laborers rally around the issue? The short answer is that most did not; in the late 1960s and early 1970s, the period when leftist radicalism was at its peak, Muslim immigrant communities displayed little interest in the Palestinian cause despite the propaganda targeting them. If falling short of their primary goals, however, the efforts of French, Muslim, and Jewish radicals had long-term consequences forever fusing the Palestinian issue with the most important Muslim political body in the 1970s, the Mouvement des travailleurs arabes (MTA), and thereby institutionalizing an ethnically grounded connection between North African Muslims in France and the Palestinian issue.

North African Muslim immigrants became actively engaged with French domestic politics for the first time in the early 1970s. Growing numbers, particularly of women and children, made their permanence irrefutable, while heightened immigration restrictions, police repression, high unemployment, and expulsions increased tensions between immigrants and authorities.[85] The 1971 nationalization of Algerian oil/gas companies put stress on the Franco-Algerian relationship, leading to debates over immigration numbers and a spike in anti-Muslim aggression, including the murder of eight Algerian Muslims and the wounding of forty more in the first trimester of that year. In October, the concierge of a Parisian building argued with and then killed resident Djellali Ben Ali, an Algerian Muslim teenager, claiming simply that he "didn't like Arabs." In autumn 1973, another wave of racism broke out, exacerbated by the war in the Middle East and the oil crisis, after an Algerian Muslim immigrant stabbed a Marseille tram conductor.[86] The poor conditions and increasing hostility spawned large immigrant protests. Housing demonstrations, factory occupations, hunger strikes, and worker walkouts increased over the early 1970s and particularly in 1973.[87]

This new immigrant political mobilization continued to be infused with the Palestine issue, even after June 1972, when its most highly developed body, the Mouvement des travailleurs arabes, broke away from the Comités Palestine and the GP, arguing that even sympathetic French intellectuals could not fully understand the problems facing Muslim immigrants or their attachment to the Arab world.[88] While links to French gauchistes and the GP never fully dissipated, the Comités Palestines were disbanded as the MTA took form.[89]

The Palestinian issue nevertheless remained central to the MTA's agenda.[90] According to one founder, Mimoun Hallouss, "In the 1970s, the Palestinian struggle defined our activism. For us, there was a direct line between the Palestinian struggle and the Arab workers' struggle."[91] *Fedai*, the publication of the Comités Palestines, served as the MTA's organ, and militants continued to raise money and promote the Palestinian issue in neighborhoods and cafés, reflecting the organization's commitment to "Arabness" as the basis for its activism.[92] Despite such efforts, however, MTA militants shifted the *primary* focus elsewhere, reflecting Muslim immigrants' sensitization to political struggles in France proper. Improving housing, regularizing the status of illegal immigrants, increasing wages, improving factory conditions, and fighting racism were now of central concern. According to one MTA militant, Muslim immigrants often criticized the Palestine focus: "You speak to us only of Palestine, us who live in shit. Who is going to defend us?"[93]

Such comments reflect the limitations of the pro-Palestine campaign to reach France's Muslim laboring population. In July 1969, a half year after Fatah launched its campaign, the Ministry of the Interior reported that most Algerian Muslims workers were not all that concerned.[94] By April, the general assessment had not changed.[95] In Marseille, where one might have expected greater support given events in 1967, patterns were similar. Although the local GP became active in 1969, gauchistes had little success winning over North African Muslim adherents despite regular visits to slums, factories, and campuses.[96] In 1970, police reported, Algerian Muslims in Marseille "remained unmoved by Maoist propaganda" and were "impervious to all European political influences."[97]

Following Black September, interest in Palestinians increased as evidenced by larger sales of *Fedai* and attendance at public meetings. In October 1970, for example, six hundred North African Muslim workers and one hundred French and foreign workers attended a pro-Palestinian meeting in Paris. Elsewhere North African Muslims raised two thousand francs for a local Comité Palestine. Some even volunteered to fight with the *fedayin*. Activists in the Comités Palestine reported that if ten demonstrators marched with a Palestine flag in Barbès, residents would emerge in large numbers carrying their own flags.[98] Nevertheless, if in March 1971 French police worried that calls for revolution in Arab countries and particularly the Palestinian revolution "reinforced ideas of combat among Arab workers," by June they reported that the combined propaganda of all the pro-Palestinian organizations had not mobilized Algerian Muslims in France.[99]

In October 1970 new GP leadership came to Marseille from Paris, combining forces with politically energized immigrant organizations and giving new life to the pro-Palestinian movement.[100] March 1972 thus saw 200 demonstrators—primarily Tunisian and Algerian Muslims—protest Jordanian and Israel policies toward Palestinians.[101] That December, another 250 demonstrators—80 of whom were of North African or Middle Eastern origin—marched through Marseille with signs reading, "Halt to Zionist terrorism and anti-Arab racism" and "Long live the Palestinian revolution of workers and Arab students."[102] The formation of Marseille's MTA in summer 1972 undoubtedly influenced this process. According to police, however, "the appeal did not resonate, even in the largest North African quarters."[103]

French police, it should be noted, often portrayed foreign laborers as passive.[104] One 1971 report, for example, described Algerian Muslims as apolitical and isolated from their self-appointed representatives.[105] Likewise, the majority of Moroccan and Tunisian Muslims "were illiterate, without political ideas, and abstained from activism," displaying "evident neutrality" with regard to Arab/Palestinian nationalism.[106] The next month, the consensus was the same: "The majority of North African immigrants are virtually apolitical. They are uninterested even in events as spectacular as the Arab-Israeli conflict and the clashes of May 1968." Only students were sometimes vocal, police felt, and even they were fairly discreet.[107]

Such assessments ignored the way French neutrality on the Middle East conflict and aggressive policing of immigrant activism prevented North African Muslim laborers from supporting Palestinians publicly even if they felt so moved.[108] One pro-Palestinian meeting in October 1970, for example, was interrupted when police arrested fifty-one attendees.[109] In addition, Muslim immigrants must have been all too aware that Palestinians did not enjoy widespread public support. One example makes the point: In May 1971, Fatah and the UGEP worked with several French political figures to organize a week of pro-Palestinian activities.[110] Organizers were disappointed, however, with the low level of public interest. In contrast, a pro-Israel event in December was tremendously successful thanks to larger sums of money available to fund the event and the greater number of politicians and intellectuals who lent their support. According to the Ministry of the Interior, "this Week for Israel demonstrated the feeble impact of Palestinian organizations in France under Zionist influence."[111]

It is impossible to determine if the broader silence around the Palestinian cause among North African Muslim immigrants was a product of fear, self-protection, lack of affinity, or lack of interest in political activism more generally. Certainly militants in the Comités Palestine and MTA continued to claim significant support. The newspaper Fedai, for example, reported that foreign workers in a factory in Suresnes greeted one another daily with, "Palestine will vanquish."[112] Police, however, remained skeptical due in part to the complaints they received from Muslim informants about pro-Palestinian activities in their communities.[113] When the PFLP distributed tracts about its exploits against the

Israeli airline El Al, for example, some Muslims, particularly those employed by or with connections to Jews, gave copies to French police.[114] Others complained over Algerian militants' efforts to use financial incentives to enlist resistance soldiers.[115] Nevertheless, the combined efforts of North African, Middle Eastern, and gauchiste activists forever linked the Palestinian issue with local Muslim political development. The consequence was increasing confrontation with the most militant sectors of the Jewish population, themselves also radicalized by 1968 political upheaval.

Muslim-Jewish Conflict after 1968

Muslim student politicization around the Israeli-Palestinian issue was mirrored in France's Jewish student population. In 1970 there were approximately 170,000 Jewish youth in France, 5,000–6,000 of whom were enrolled in Parisian universities. While only 10 percent were affiliated with Jewish organizations, since 1967 many had begun displaying a greater interest in their Jewishness.[116] The year 1968 proved important in this process. As noted, many of those who took to the streets had families who had suffered during the Holocaust, and their engagement with the student movement often politicized these memories. While for some this process led to the embrace of radical leftist ideologies, for others it led to a newfound militancy around Israel.[117] Given the growing anti-Zionism on French campuses, conflict could be explosive. The growing animosity coupled with the 1968 Belleville riot—which as noted earlier brought out Jewish student activists—meant that what recently had seemed like a Middle Eastern problem now had local saliency.

While Jewish leftists numbered among the most vocal critics of Israel on French campuses, others—having become Israel's ardent supporters in June 1967—felt their post-1968 political radicalism challenged by their love for Israel.[118] The result was often a distancing from those further to the left. After the UNEF declared allegiance with the Palestinians, for example, one Jewish member tore up his membership card, telling writers for L'Arche, "Now it's finished. The UNEF has become a branch of the Arab League and Kuwait."[119] Or as another put it, "Pro-Israeli Jews found themselves rejected from the leftist paradise."[120]

For some young Jews, such as those who stayed affiliated with the UEJF, the late 1960s saw a complicated balancing act between Zionist engagement and a measured criticism of Israeli policies. Despite its stated pluralism, UEJF members were often to the left on the Algerian crisis and other issues. In 1968, however, the UEJF broke away from the anti-Zionist left, asserting Israel's right to exist and moving from "the search for dialogue . . . to the search for authenticity."[121] While acknowledging the Palestinians' right to national self-determination, the UEJF also declared Israel's occupation of its 1967 war gains legitimate, pending its Arab neighbors' formal recognition. According to one UEJF leader, the anti-Zionist climate on French campuses drove this vocal pro-Israel stance.[122] UEJF members thus challenged pro-Palestinian meetings on their campuses even as they opposed certain Israeli actions.[123] In May 1972, for example, Marseille's UEJF chapter publicly criticized Israel's Palestinian policies while warning of a "deep fracture in the student movement" over blurring anti-Zionism and antisemitism.[124] Such positions won them no friends. According to Marseille's UEJF president: his organization was "challenged by the *gauchistes* while also being rejected by the Jewish community."[125] Indeed, for the Front des étudiants juifs, the UEJF had not distanced itself sufficiently from the anti-Zionist left. Having broken away during the height of the 1968 Belleville crisis, FEJ leaders defined their group as *the* pro-Israel organization on French campuses. Criticizing the UEJF for cosigning petitions with the Comités Palestine, the FEJ became vocal supporters of Jews in the USSR and Arab lands and provided "protection" for Jewish university students under attack from political opponents.[126]

In casting French campuses as "dangerous" for Jews, the FEJ struck a chord. Many young Jews were, in fact, feeling singled out in the tense environment. Françoise Tenenbaum, a student at Paris's Jussieu campus, for example, described taking down anti-Israel posters in 1968.[127] Others felt greater unease. One student from Nice, for example, ripped down pro-Palestinian posters attacking Rothschild. Such words "of typically Nazi inspiration," she wrote, made "my heart miss a beat."[128] Propaganda of this nature often linked Israel, Jews, and the United States in a deadly bond. One PFLP poster, for example, depicted Uncle Sam's skull with Israeli defense minister Moshe Dayan in one eye (recognizable by his tell-tale eye-patch over one eye), two dead Arabs in his mouth, and four Jewish stars emblazoned across the blue stripe of his hat. This mix of anti-American, anti-Israeli, and antisemitic iconography implicated all Jews in the murder of Palestinians.[129] Likewise, ADAE spokesmen blamed "the Jews" for a December 1968 shooting that left two dead and three wounded in a Muslim-owned café in Aubervilliers, while the newspaper *El Moudjahid* accused "Zionist henchmen" and racist groups "nostalgic for the OAS" of several attacks against Algerian stores, cafés, and bars, including a brawl in a Parisian bar between Jewish and Muslim customers.[130] The FEJ vowed to protect young Jews against "the sudden virulence of a certain 'anti-Zionism'" and "increasingly violent attacks" by training members in paramilitary techniques.[131]

By 1969, then, many French campuses had small groups of Muslim, Jewish, and gauchiste militants committed to confrontational politics around the Middle East conflict. Their presence meant that no discussion of the Palestinian-Israeli conflict could go uncontested. In Marseille that May, for example, Jewish and Muslim leftists faced off at a pro-Palestinian event at the Faculté des Sciences. That June, the Comité pour la paix negocié au Moyen-Orient called off a Cité Universitaire debate on the Middle East in response to Maoist anti-Zionist threats.[132] The same month, Algerian and Moroccan Muslim gauchistes requested police protection for a pro-Palestinian event in response to threats of "Zionist sabotage."[133] On 4 December 1969 at "Sciences Po" in Paris, students and gauchistes had a brief but violent scuffle, and days later, four people were wounded when thirty Jewish students came armed with sticks to a screening of *La Palestine vaincra* at Censier.[134] When the FEJ protested anti-Jewish activities at Censier the next month, passions erupted once again. According to FEJ president Jacques Kupfer, some two hundred Maoists and Jewish leftists arrived with anti-Zionist tracts. Fistfights ensued to cries of "Palestine will overcome" and "Death to the Jews."[135] The FEJ responded to these "pogrom attempts" by threatening "to crush anti-Semitic vermin."[136] Such rhetoric had repercussions. In early June 1970, vandals ransacked the headquarters of the Union nationale des étudiants algériens and the Association des étudiants musulmans nord-africains, scrawling, "Israel will overcome" on the walls.[137] While no evidence tied the FEJ to this attack, the charged atmosphere was palpable.[138]

The diversity of Jewish responses to campus politics and the Israeli-Palestinian conflict is evident in these events. Indeed, university political culture cannot be understood as a dichotomous split between Jewish and Muslim "sides." While Jewish students often supported Israel, many supported the Palestinians, and neither "side" was united. Thus not only were Jewish leftists among those pitted *against* the FEJ, but also various organizations, including the UEJF, condemned FEJ violence.[139] Similarly, Mischmar—representing the Zionist left—denounced the aggression of both the pro-Palestinian movement and ultra-nationalist Jews.[140] In contrast, the student chapter of the Alliance France–Israël blamed events on "the anti-Semitic psychosis created at the heart of the university."[141] More moderately, the Comité d'entente de la jeunesse juive asked supporters of Israel's struggle for peace "to organize to defend their ideas and their right to speak in French universities."[142] As such rhetoric suggests, late 1960s campus life created and challenged alliances that ran counter to ethnic claims of solidarity. In a telling example, in March 1970, the UEJF complained that to counter Jewish student support for Palestinians on several campuses, the UEJF had established pro-Israel stands only to be thwarted by Jewish elements on the far right who had destroyed their propaganda![143] Jewish students clearly did not all stand on one "side" of the Israel issue nor did they agree on tactics.

A similar diversity was evident in the CRIF's responses to events at Censier. Whereas some sought to distance their organization from "a group of 'fascist' Jews that clashed with Palestinians," others countered that Jewish students had been "ambushed" in the anti-Israel campus environment. According to one, in a university steeped in pro-Fatah propaganda, "Jewish students are molested, terrorized and unable to express themselves. . . . That Jewish students wanted to react for once is essentially normal." Agreeing, another delegate remarked, "If Jews defended themselves, were they wrong?" Worried about taking sides in a divisive matter, CRIF delegates decided that the president, in his own name, should condemn all violence regardless of the source. Even this relatively bland option, however, was soon discarded.[144]

Notwithstanding the CRIF's indecisive response, the debate over Censier reveals the emerging focus on campuses as dangerous for Jews. As *L'Arche* reported, "It is certain that most young Jews are subjected to permanent aggression, sometimes surpassing the purely verbal."[145] For some CRIF representatives, the environment showcased a distinct new danger in French political culture. As one commented, "We are threatened by an anti-Semitic campaign coming from diverse Arab milieus. We must create defense committees ready to respond rapidly."[146] Such comments reflected the dramatic change in both Muslim political activism and Jewish communal perceptions since 1967, at which time "Arabs" had been a distant threat for French Jews worrying about Israel's future; by 1969, the threat had come home.

Significantly, however, CRIF officials did not collapse France's Muslim immigrant population into this equation. As one delegate noted after the second Belleville riot, "North African workers in Paris do not support the Palestinians; El Fatah's outreach has failed to touch them." Rather, they feared that antisemitism in the guise of anti-Zionism was infecting French campuses and that their *own* co-religionists were helping to *create* tensions: "[I]f young Jews allow themselves to be provoked, Arab elements could change their attitude and there will be, alas, a confrontation. We must warn young Jews of this danger."[147] As such comments suggest, at least some CRIF officials worried that growing radicalism around the Palestinian issue would infect intercommunal relations and that Jewish radicalism could prove as dangerous to social relations as its Arab/Palestinian counterpart.

CRIF caution, however, could not stem the dramatic gestures of young radicals. In April 1971, for example, during a reception celebrating Syrian independence, a Jewish militant protested the oppression of Syrian Jews by releasing twenty mice and frogs among the three hundred attending dignitaries. An accompanying pamphlet sought to reclaim leftist politics for the Zionist movement: "Arab comrades . . . Do not allow your leaders to tarnish the name of Socialism; Do not allow them to make you believe that your enemy is the pacific Jewish people and their liberation movement, Zionism. Do not let them divert you from anti-capitalist and anti-imperialist struggles. Down with reactionary Arab leaders; For the immediate cessation of anti-Jewish persecutions. Long live the Socialist revolution in the Middle East!" Such efforts to unify Muslims and Jews around a reclaimed leftism gained little traction in the heated environment. Shortly thereafter, Louis Terrenoire, president of the Association de solidarité Franco-Arabe, the organization that had convened the celebration, received an anonymous death threat.[148] Angry Syrian students called for revenge at an upcoming pro-Israel rally. Conflict was forestalled only due to the UGEP's plea that sympathizers avoid giving their opponents more fodder. ADAE officials similarly instructed Algerians to avoid conflict while recommending that those living near large Jewish populations travel in groups and be prepared to respond to provocation. Such warnings show the degree to which passions had mounted, an observation that police informants and sporadic violence confirmed.[149] In January 1972, for example, ten Jewish teenagers burst into a pro-Palestinian event organized by the Comité d'action contre la guerre mondiale wounding a forty-year-old Algerian Muslim man in the ensuing skirmish.[150] That June, other young activists threatened the Syrian ambassador with the execution of three hundred diplomatic employees and their families if Jews remained trapped in his country.[151]

If such threats never materialized, the environment remained tense, particularly after the September 1972 Palestinian commando attack against Israeli athletes at the Munich Olympics. While a handful of far-left organizations defended the action on the grounds that Israelis were the "real terrorists," images of Jews murdered in Germany were widely condemned in France.[152] Unsurprisingly, Jewish organizations of all stripes denounced the violence.[153] The FEJ, however, launched a counterthreat, declaring it would "take the necessary steps" to ensure communal security.[154] Shortly thereafter, the organization began photographing visitors to the Syrian embassy.[155] After German officials freed three Palestinians who had participated in the killings, the UGEP complained of threats and called on adherents "to prevent themselves from being drawn into a conflict with no relevance on the European scene."[156]

By 1972, however, the Middle Eastern conflict *had* come to Europe, largely in the form of several dramatic Palestinian and Israeli commando attacks. In France, these included explosions at the Librairie Palestine and Hamchari's apartment, the murder of a Syrian journalist, a letter bomb to the former director of the UGEP, the violent disruption of the Conférence des jeunes d'Europe et des pays arabes, threatening letters to several North African and Middle Eastern dignitaries, and fourteen attacks from September through December against Jewish targets, including an explosion at the main synagogue in Marseille.[157]

Local Jewish and Muslim leaders understood the violence to come from outside France.[158] Thanks to years of radical politics around the Israeli-Palestinian struggle, however, distinctions between the "here" and the "there" were breaking down. In early 1973, for example, *L'Arche* speculated whether anger over Hamchari's murder and an impending visit of Israeli Prime Minister Golda Meir would instigate new anti-Zionist campaigns among leftists seeking to recruit North African Muslim immigrants.[159] The explosion of a bomb outside the Jewish Agency the night before Meir's arrival only added to a growing "psychosis" in the Jewish community.[160] Likewise, Jewish and Muslim spokesmen were increasingly blurring the lines between Israeli/Zionist/Jew and Muslim/Palestinian/Arab/North African when referring to one another. The magazine *L'Arche* thus defined the bomb at the Jewish Agency as an act of "Arab terrorism," marking all "Arabs" (the common term in the 1970s for Muslims from the

Middle East and North Africa) as potential aggressors.[161] At a UGEP rally after the Hamchari attack, one speaker denounced the intermingling of Jews in pro-Arab organizations, a particularly caustic remark given that Alain Geismar was one of the speakers. Others criticized the reception Zionists received within public agencies and their participation in police actions against Muslims.[162] The *Algérien en Europe* meanwhile, while rarely referring to Jews qua Jews and indeed often making positive mention of anti-Zionist Jews, blamed French Zionists for bolstering "anti-Arab hysteria" after the Munich affair and of creating a climate of insecurity around Muslims.[163] Such depictions angered French Jews, who, in turn, labeled the pro-Palestinian faction racist.[164]

By early 1973, then, well before the Arab-Israeli war that October, the Middle East conflict was being felt in France in ways unimaginable in 1967.[165] In February, when ten FEJ members attacked the offices of Iraqi and Syrian Arab Airways, throwing a bucket of animal blood and tracts demanding liberty for Jews at the frightened staff, they once again embodied this process. "We will not permit new imitators of Hitler to indulge in their murderous barbarism," read tracts agitators glued to the windows.[166] As we have seen, such linking of the Holocaust to the oppression of Jews in Arab lands echoed developments in Jewish politics from 1948 forward, intensifying in 1967. By 1973, however, radical youth culture in France provided space for a more confrontational politics. While marginal to the Jewish establishment, their mirroring in the Maoist-influenced North African student population created new divisions around the Israeli-Palestinian question.

Nowhere was this more evident than in Marseille, where the postcolonial tensions traced previously became entangled with the new politics around Israel in 1973. That August, a violent racist campaign broke out following the stabbing of a French tramcar driver, Emile Gerlache, by an unstable Algerian Muslim immigrant. Then, on 6 October, Israel went to war against a coalition of Arab states. In Marseille, these issues quickly became fused, as a more radicalized Muslim population drew parallels between the Palestinian situation and their own marginalization. While Jewish and Muslim leaders sought to avoid confrontations, the Israeli/Palestinian conflict began playing a bigger role in shaping dynamics between the two populations.

The Gerlache incident coincided with a period of recession and unemployment that undermined Marseille's already fragile economy and stoked xenophobic resentment.[167] "We have had enough," proclaimed a much-cited editorial in the right-wing newspaper *Le Méridional* after the murder. "Enough of Algerian thieves, enough of Algerian thugs, enough of Algerian troublemakers, enough of Algerian syphilitics, enough of Algerian rapists, enough of Algerian drug dealers, enough of Algerian crazies, enough of Algerian murderers."[168] Five thousand outraged demonstrators attended Gerlache's funeral, and right-wing extremists attacked immigrant shantytowns with rifle fire, killing eight North African Muslims over the next several weeks.[169]

Fearing for their lives, Muslim immigrants stayed inside when they could. The assassination on 28 August of Lounès Ladj by passing gunmen, however, launched a collective rebellion. Two thousand mourners attended the procession carrying his body to the port on 1 September. Two days later, an MTA call for a twenty-four-hour strike to protest racism brought out thousands more.[170] New organizations, such as the Comité des travailleurs algériens, were formed to take on the problems plaguing immigrant life.[171] A massive anti-racism rally on 7 September drew another two thousand to Marseille's streets, and on 14 September, the MTA sponsored the largest nationwide strike by North African Muslim workers to date.[172] Six days later, Algeria suspended migration to France.

Interestingly, neither the mounting racism nor the MTA's anti-racist campaign attracted much attention from France's established Jewish community. L'Arche never mentioned events in Marseille, and the CRIF's public statement notably distanced French Jews from the North African Muslim immigrant population: "Having experienced throughout its history the terrible effects of racism and hatred of the stranger, French Judaism recalls the fundamental biblical principles: 'Thou shall love thy neighbor as thyself and thou shall love the stranger.'"[173] This generic call for brotherhood, simultaneously underscoring the victim's foreignness and drawing no parallels to antisemitism, is particularly notable, since, by the 1980s, the joint struggle against racism served as one of the few bridges between two populations that had begun to see each other as adversaries. In 1973, however, these bridges had not yet been built. Insofar as French Jews took note of the Muslims around them, they focused on anti-Zionism or antisemitic tracts in Arabic.[174] As the president of the French chapter of Keren Kayemet LeIsrael insisted at a CRIF meeting in October while urging a boycott of Arab businesses in France, "You can no longer treat the people you have before you as those you must persuade but rather as those you must combat."[175] Such statements mark the distance that had been traveled since 1967 when French Jews saw "Arabs" as a threat to Israel and to Jews in the Middle East but paid scant attention to those around them.

It was in this charged environment that the October 1973 Arab-Israeli war broke out. As in 1967, France's organized Jewish community publicly defended Israel, raising even more money than had been true six years previously.[176] In Marseille, the Appel unifié juif de France collected nearly 2,500,000 francs, a million more than was raised for Jewish causes the previous year. On 8 October, two days after the outbreak of hostilities, five thousand paraded silently on the city's major thoroughfare, la Canebière, under the banner of the Comité de soutien à Israel. Mayor Defferre was once again in the lead, alongside elected officials from most municipalities and all the major Jewish organizations. As in 1967, only the Communist left remained silent.[177]

In 1973, however, Defferre's unadulterated support for the Jewish community—already an irritant six years previously—was all too evident to a politically energized Muslim population that felt marginalized by their city's surging racism. Already practiced at using the Palestinian issue to motivate the foreign workforce, local Muslim activists responded to events in the Middle East by organizing numerous demonstrations around both issues.[178] The municipality, however, refused them equal access to city streets. During the pro-Israel rally on 8 October, for example, police established a barrier around the immigrant quarter in Belsunce (which abutted the thoroughfare on which Jews were marching). Even though police had registered "no effervescence" in immigrant neighborhoods in response to pro-Israel demonstrations, local law enforcement sought to contain Muslim activism.[179] MTA representatives complained over this biased access to city space, particulary after authorities refused them the same thoroughfare for a pro-Palestinian demonstration on 13 October, instead restricting participants to the area around the Porte d'Aix.[180]

As in other cases of Muslim-Jewish conflict in France, the October 1973 tensions were largely confined to highly politicized groups. While police reported that the MTA's pro-Palestinian rhetoric was finding "a certain echo in the immigrant community,"[181] others pointed to the city's calm interethnic landscape. According to one article, Marseille's Muslim quarters "did not appear to have a different physiognomy than other days." The shared neighborhoods around rue d'Aix "where the jewelers, notably of Jewish origin, are numerous or in the neighboring souks on the rue Sainte Barbe," showed no perceptible change, "other than a few transistor radios stuck to the ears and tuned in to Radio-Alger."[182] The MTA carefully avoided turning attacks against Israel into broad denunciations of Jews, while Jewish leaders encouraged young activists to refrain from provocations.[183] Although Jewish youth handed out tracts, demonstrated, and recruited volunteers for Israel, they followed communal directives to avoid racist and anti-Muslim overtones.[184]

Activists nevertheless continued to make the Middle East a visible part of Marseille's ethno-religious landscape in 1973 and thereafter. In late October 1974, when the French foreign minister met with Yasser Arafat in Lebanon, French Jews were distraught.[185] In Marseille, Jewish organizations declared themselves "ready to do all in their power" to prevent the opening of a promised PLO liaison office in Paris.[186] Muslim activists were likewise highly mobilized to defend Palestinian interests, and on 7 November, both groups manifested their politics on city streets. Three hundred and fifty members of diverse Jewish organizations thus processed down la Canebière shouting, "Arafat assassin; Giscard accomplice,"[187] while the Comité Palestine held a counterdemonstration for North African Muslim laborers.[188] Although the small numbers indicate that Marseille's Muslim and Jewish populations had little interest in the Middle East, spotty evidence suggests tensions had deepened. On 5 November, for example, the vice president of Marseille's Consistoire complained to the prefect over France's rapprochement with the PLO, pointing to "a notable degradation in relations between Muslim immigrants and their Jewish employers" and warning that "clashes" could follow.[189]

While a single source does not provide enough evidence on which to base significant conclusions, it points to the way Marseille's ethno-political landscape had begun to fuse divisions over the Israeli-Palestinian issue with the already embedded postcolonial divisions that had shaped city life since the 1950s. As incoming Jews solidified and often bettered their economic position, Muslim immigrants became trapped in a cycle of poverty. These distinctions took on new political meaning by the early 1970s as the city that had embraced its Jewish residents and their pro-Israel agenda seemingly rejected its Muslim residents, many of whom had begun to see parallels between their own struggles and those of the Palestinians.

Conclusion

In 1975, renowned author Romain Gary published the prize-winning novel, *La Vie devant soi* under the pseudonym Émile Ajar. The novel, soon made into a movie starring Simone Signoret, depicts the relationship between an orphaned Muslim boy, Momo, and a dying Holocaust survivor and former prostitute, Madame Rosa, who runs a boardinghouse for the children of sex workers. Set in Belleville, the story unfolds in the multiethnic neighborhood so recently marked by violence. In Gary's Belleville, however, shared adversity unites those of diverse backgrounds. A former Senegalese boxing champion now working as a transvestite prostitute, a Jewish doctor, an aging Algerian Muslim carpet salesman, a Cameroonian fire-eater, and a Catholic French neighbor are among the many downtrodden who console or help Madame Rosa and Momo throughout the story.

At the novel's climax, when Momo's father, Youssef Kadir, unexpectedly arrives to claim his son, Madame Rosa offers him a Jewish boy instead, claiming the two had been unintentionally swapped. To Kadir, the shock is deadly. As his desperation mounts, he explodes, "I gave you an Arab son in due and proper form and I expect you to give me back an Arab son. I absolutely don't want a Jewish son, Madame. . . . I have nothing against the Jews, Madame, God forgive them. But I'm an Arab, a good Moslem, and I had a son of the same faith. Mohammed, Arab, Muslim. I entrusted him to you in good condition, and I expect you to give him back in the same condition." Madame Rosa's retort captures the novel's central thematic: "Oh well, he was an Arab, now he's slightly Jewish, but he's still your boy," and later, "Arab and Jew are all the same to us here."[190] When Madame Rosa finally dies, Momo hides her corpse, claiming to have sent her to live in Israel. Her Jewish doctor responds in amazement, "It's the first time an Arab has ever sent a Jew to Israel."[191]

Gary's heartwarming if macabre portrayal of the bond between the Jewish woman and the Muslim boy celebrates the humanity linking diverse peoples and, in many ways, serves as a call for such ends. Yet the novel also provides ample evidence of the tensions that had marked France's interethnic terrain. Momo's father's insistence on the return of his Arab son and Dr. Katz's shock at Momo's support for Madame Rosa's departure to Israel serve as crucial reminders of this history as do Momo's numerous references to Jewish and Arab terrorists, Algerian self-determination struggles, and Jewish experiences under the Nazis. While Momo and Madame Rosa transcend this history, their very insistence that "all men were equal when steeped in misery and shit, and if the Jews and Arabs clobber each other it's because whatever you may say to the contrary the Jews and the Arabs are no different from anybody else," reminds us that by 1975, few saw it that way.[192]

To read Gary in this way is to acknowledge how profoundly French public consciousness had come to see Muslim-Jewish divisions as the norm by the 1970s. If traditional chronologies have emphasized the Arab-Israeli wars of 1967 and 1973 as touchstone moments in this increasing ethnic polarization, they have overlooked the way political culture at the local and national level helped shape the ethnic landscape. On the one hand, the unpredictable alliance between radical leftists—many of them Jewish—Muslim students, and Palestinian representatives, bridged core ideological disagreements to bring the Palestinian plight to French public attention and to link the issue to immigrant politics. On the other hand, late 1960s radicalism pushed France's Jewish population—and particularly its high school and university students—away from traditional affiliations on the left and toward a more combative politics. The combustible result was a confrontational communal politics that linked Jews with Israel and North African Muslims with Palestinians in increasingly rigid ways.

The immediate impact of these events was limited. Most Jews and Muslims never came into direct conflict. Belleville's residents, for the most part, laid low during the riots. Membership in radical Jewish and Muslim student organizations was small. North African immigrants—if increasingly sympathetic to Palestinians—saw their own struggles as more pressing. Jewish and Muslim leaders urged moderation to ensure collective safety and prosperity. Moreover, the Jewish leadership continued to see the Muslim immigrant population as distinct from their spokesmen, asserting as late as 1976 that Fatah's impact on the immigrant milieu was limited.[193]

The radical energies of the late 1960s also soon dissipated due to the French government's ban of the Gauche prolétarienne in 1970 and the Ligue Communiste in 1973, the economic crisis that year, disagreements among different leftist currents, and the failures of various internationalist efforts. The MTA lost steam in response to opposition from the ADAE and other North African immigrant associations and the Ministry of the Interior, which imprisoned or expelled the organization's most active militants.[194] While it continued to pursue the Palestinian issue throughout its existence, by 1976 the MTA had dissolved.[195] Jewish gauchistes likewise began backing away from their most radical positions regarding Israel during the 1973 war, frustrated with the emotional and intellectual contradictions in their politics.[196] Jewish student reactionaries, always a small group, continued their activities but remained marginal to wider communal life.[197]

The brief life-span of these developments, however, does not diminish their decisive impact on Muslim-Jewish relations. First, as Gary's novel makes clear, the period's radicalism brought the story of Muslim-Jewish polarization into France's national conversation. While earlier developments had introduced a discourse of polarization in particular circles, 1968 and its aftermath made that story mainstream. Second, if the fusion between gauchisme, immigrant politicization, and Jewish radicalism was brief, the decade's themes were enduring. Ethnic tensions around the Middle East were henceforth presumed. Third, by the mid-1970s, Muslims and Jews had begun to see each other as competitors in the French public square. In the words of one Jewish commentator, "[O]ur only weapon is public opinion in this country where we number hardly 1% (less numerous than the Arabs, who do not have the right to vote, but ballots, alas, count for little, and they can strike, which we cannot)."[198] Although these remarks underscored the Jews' insider position as "citizens" against Arab foreignness, it portrayed them as pitted against each other in the court of public opinion. By the 1980s, as a new generation of French-born Muslim citizens came of age, such distinctions were increasingly meaningless. Yet as a new generation of Muslim activists strove to assert their place in the polity, equal access to all the benefits of French citizenship became a new domain of Muslim-Jewish contestation.

6

Particularism versus Pluriculturalism

The Birth and Death of the Anti-Racist Coalition

This chapter traces the rise and fall of a Muslim-Jewish alliance to fight racism in 1980s France. Two political shifts early in the decade allowed the joint anti-racist campaign to emerge. First was the coming of age of a new generation of French-born Muslim activists who began, often in religious or ethnic terms, to articulate a politics of resistance to their political and social exclusion. Reaching out to the isolated, economically excluded, and socially contained youth of the French *banlieue*, the so-called Beur Movement created momentum around a new identity politics.[1] The second development evolved from experiments in multiculturalism that followed François Mitterrand's victory in the 1981 presidential election on a platform that included calls for greater immigrant rights and decentralization. For the first time, the French political establishment recognized in law the nation's cultural and linguistic diversity, a shift that led to new forms of ethno-religious organization. For young Muslim and Jewish activists who took advantage of this legal recognition of difference, the public square was now open to unprecedented expressions of communal politics.

This shift in French political culture created two overlapping but ultimately competing approaches to ethno-religious participation in the French state, both with implications for Muslim-Jewish relations. The first was a particularistic vision that encouraged intergroup solidarity as a way of fighting for the individual community's needs. Evident in the Beur Movement's anti-racist demonstrations and in increasing Jewish political mobilization, the early 1980s saw a heightened focus on the specific needs of particular communities as distinct from the national collective. In the case of Muslim-Jewish relations, such identity politics could split, as representatives of both articulated priorities that at times placed them on opposite sides of domestic, or more often, international policy debates.

Yet if "particularistism" created opportunities for ethnic polarization, a second response to the legitimization of France's diverse landscape was a new "pluricultural" model of ethno-religious cooperation. The term "pluricultural"—as opposed to the more commonly deployed, "multicultural"—refers specifically to bridging differences in order to create a democratic and just public sphere. Most evident in the anti-racist movement that surged in the middle of the decade, "pluriculturalists" argued that whatever differences marked French citizens, they could work together to create a tolerant and just society. Driven by widespread media attention, the socialist machine, and the electoral growth of the far-right party, the Front nationale (FN), several organizations, including the newly established SOS racisme and the UEJF, worked together to ensure equal rights for all.[2] One highly celebrated aspect of this campaign was the effort to unite Muslim and Jewish citizens in a common struggle. Epitomized by SOS racisme's slogan, "We cannot solve the Israel-Palestinian problem on the banks of the Seine," activists sought to contain differences by stressing similar struggles.

These two approaches to ethno-politics, "particularist" and "pluricultural," both broke with French assimilatory traditions that subsumed ethnic and religious differences in the wider national culture, and in this sense shared a basic commitment to Mitterrand's "right to be different" policies. Such policies, however, never fully broke with republican assimilationist traditions or fully embraced a politics of multiculturalism, a reality that became starkly clear by decade's end when growing support for the FN led officials across the political spectrum to return to more conservative policies toward religious and cultural difference. "Integration" rather than the "right to be different" again became the watchword of the day, as officials and media outlets focused on Beur criminality, the "threat" of Islam, and "Arab" fanatacism as threats to civic life.[3] This mounting conservatism, while mostly directed at France's Muslim population, affected all religious minorities, particularly in 1989 when three girls were expelled from school for wearing the Islamic head scarf, launching a heated debate on religion in the public sphere.[4] While some Jewish figures defended particulalrism in the schools, others backed away from public connection to Muslims, asserting the fusion of Jewishness and Frenchness in contradistinction to Muslim foreignness.[5] Meanwhile, Muslim activists who had seen value in underscoring a common anti-racist agenda began reasserting the particularist nature of their own struggles. By decade's end, pluricultural cooperation had collapsed.

This chapter will argue that widespread excitement over the joint anti-racist campaign in the mid-1980s overlooked ongoing tensions between "particularistic" and "pluricultural" approaches to ethno-religious participation in the French state. Divisions over the Palestinian-Israeli conflict both prior to and during the 1991 Gulf War made these tensions evident as, once again, debates over the Middle East became a means of making sense of politics at home. Although calls for joint anti-racist campaigns never disappeared, by the end of the 1980s, those who articulated such appeals had backed away from a "pluricultural" model. While Muslims and Jews should work together, they argued, their perspectives and goals were necessarily divergent.

Identity Politics in the Early 1980s

Nineteen-eighties France saw an unprecedented rise of identity politics in a nation that had long subsumed cultural, linguistic, and religious diversity in the wider national project. Giving voice to many who had previously been excluded—particularly the so-called Beur generation— this shift provided opportunities for Muslims *and* Jews to articulate "unabashedly public forms of . . . political and religious engagement," an activism that encouraged communal representatives to debate domestic and international issues from the perspective of their "group."[6] Yet the establishment of a multicultural France also provided opportunities for joint endeavors. The spike in antisemitism and Islamophobia early in the decade provided one arena in which the tensions between "particularism" and "pluriculturalism" played out, raising questions over what linked different forms of exclusion. While early 1980s identity politics stressed their unique characteristics, a counterdiscourse emphasized commonalities.[7]

Racism against Muslims began surging in the mid-1970s after the 1973 oil crisis and the U.S. decision to untie the dollar from gold created stresses on the French economy.[8] By 1974, unemployment was widespread. Although France's immigrant populations were hit hardest—introducing a cycle of poverty that was often pushed onto their children—anger at decreasing opportunities and fear for the nation's prosperity led to a rise in xenophobic attacks and a tightening of national immigration policies beginning with the *circulaire Fontanet* in 1972, limiting immigrant mobility, and culminating with the 1974 decision to close national borders to new immigrants (although family reunification policies still allowed newcomers to migrate to France).[9] With attention deflected from new immigrants, however, public interest soon shifted to the residentially, culturally, and politically isolated "second generation," particularly as the latter began expressing their frustrations in clashes with local police. Most notably, the Lyons "rodeos" in July and August 1981—during which 250 cars were burned, seven policemen wounded, and over twenty young Muslims arrested—received widespread media coverage. In these portrayals, North African (read "foreign") "delinquents" were seen as pitted against the forces of order. After the Iranian Revolution, fears of spreading Islamic fundamentalism exacerbated such concerns, as media outlets speculated whether aimless banlieu youth would join global jihad movements.[10] Over these years, then, fears that immigrants were taking jobs evolved into broader concerns that "Muslims" were failing to integrate into the nation or even threatening it with violence.

The spectacular rise of the FN, the far-right nationalist party founded in 1972 by Jean-Marie Le Pen, emerged in response to these developments, obtaining its first victories in the muncipal elections of spring 1983.[11] The June 1984 European elections, which brought Le Pen's group 11 percent of the vote, increased the party's visibility. FN candidates then won 9 percent and 10 percent during cantonal, legislative, and regional elections in 1985 and 1986. While the party's appeal was not limited to its xenophobia, Le Pen and his followers adopted the defense of French national identity as a central motif, arguing that non-European immigration endangered the nation's Christian values and its national community.[12] Although this rhetoric positioned Le Pen against both Jewish and Islamic minorities, the FN's longer trajectory indicated a move away from earlier antisemitic outbursts toward an increasing focus on Muslims as its primary target.[13]

Racism surged in this environment. From 1980 until 1994, 26 Muslims were killed and another 351 injured in racist incidents, while anti-Muslim tracts and graffiti increased significantly.[14] Antisemitic graffiti and violence increased as well, suggesting a wider anti-minority animosity, as several synagogues and cemeteries were desecrated and as bombs targeted the chief rabbi's home, a kosher cafeteria, and the rue Copernic synagogue.[15]

The spike in violence raised new questions about the place of ethno-religious minorities in France. For some, what seemed most striking was their shared marginalization. Already in the mid-1970s, groups that had long taken note of shared aspects of racism—such as the pre–World War II organizations established to fight antisemitism, the Mouvement contre le racisme, l'antisémitisme et pour la paix (MRAP), the Ligue international contre le racisme et l'antisémitisme (LICA), and the Ligue des droits de l'homme—placed a new focus on these commonalities.[16] As one Jewish representative in Marseille noted in the mid-1970s, "[W]hen we see anti-Arab campaigns developing, we must condemn them for we know that racism is never directed against only one minority. . . . Anti-Arab racism can very easily be transformed into anti-Jewish racism."[17] In February 1978, the magazine L'Arche published a screed against contemporary racism that drew direct links with prewar antisemitism.[18] That December, Roger Ascot also warned that anti-Arabism was only one step removed from antisemitism.[19] Most notably, in 1979 the CRIF condemned the murder of two African workers following a series of synagogue fires and Jewish cemetery desecrations by declaring itself "in solidarity with all immigrant workers no matter their origin."[20] By placing synagogue desecrations in the same context as xenophobia, the CRIF went a long way to bridging the distance that had appeared in its earlier anti-racist proclamations. Some French Muslims also drew parallels between the way Jews and Muslims had been targeted in French society. As Houria, an Algerian-born resident from Lyons explained, "we are the Jews of immigration, and I'm afraid yes, afraid that some day the French will do to us what they did to the Jews during the last war."[21]

In the late 1970s, however, there was little infrastructure to promote Muslim-Jewish cooperation around fighting racism or much else. New organizations, such as Identité et Dialogue, founded in 1976 by André Azoulay, a Moroccan-born Jewish newspaper editor and public relations professional, emphasized cultural connections between Muslims and Jews.[22] Seeking to unite North African migrants regardless of their religious beliefs, Azoulay and fellow travelers hoped to highlight a common heritage "at a moment when political discourse is infective."[23] Such efforts remained marginal, however, with identity politics on the ascendancy.

Indeed, despite a flurry of interest in the commonalities among all forms of racism, by 1980 both Jewish and Muslim activists were most interested in their own struggles. Among Jews, the rise in antisemitic attacks raised the specter of their own dark history in Europe.[24] Articles in the Jewish press focused heavily on foreign terrorists (Palestinians or Arabs) and neo-Nazis, thereby highlighting the particularity of anti-Jewish aggression and even portraying Arabs as perpetrators rather than as fellow victims of violence.[25] Even those calling for joint anti-racist activism tended to emphasize differences. In 1980, for example, Jacquot Grunewald urged readers of *Tribune juive* to fight anti-Arab racism as follows:

> I know that most immigrant workers . . . are Arab citizens from North Africa; they support the Arab *ummah* and have a perspective on Israel that is intolerable from our perspective. But, would it not be possible, with men, women, and children who suffer from so many difficulties, for us, the Jews of France, who identify with the Jews of Israel, to open a dialogue that is artificially forbidden by the leaders of the Arab world?[26]

Moreover, while the CRIF continued to express "solidarity and sympathy" with victims of racism, its appeals called on Jewish citizens to aid immigrant foreigners and hence downplayed similarities between French-born Muslims and Jews.[27] CRIF officials were also quick to note that racism had crystallized around "Arabs" while far smaller numbers expressed dislike for Jews.[28] Countering such formulations, the philosopher and political sociologist Shmuel Trigano warned Jews not to believe that anti-Muslim racism could shield them from what was, in fact, indirect racism toward Jews. Hardly calling for a joint anti-racist struggle, however, Trigano warned that "in the worsening crisis, the Arabs are more powerful than the Jews" as a way to push the latter to mobilize on their own.[29]

The emerging Muslim anti-racist movement was also inwardly directed.[30] Originating from the "Beur generation," anti-racism came in two forms that both underscored the distinctive exclusion facing Muslims.[31] The first were peaceful demonstrations that called for greater inclusion in French society, most famously the October–November 1983 Marche pour l'égalité et contre le racisme (and two follow-up marches in 1984 and 1985). Second were retributive protests aimed at police and symbols of economic exclusion, including approximately 250 "rodeos" such as those described above.

Articulated in the context of Mitterrand's presidential victory, the Beur Movement helped usher in recognition of a multicultural French public sphere. Having campaigned on the right to be different (*droit à la différence*) as a fundamental human right, Mitterrand quickly implemented policies that supported minority cultural development and linguistic diversity, such as the option of teaching local languages in public schools. This opening of the public space to a broader range of cultural practices had an impact on all ethnic and religious minorities. For example, in summer 1981, when Mitterrand overturned the 1938 legislation prohibiting immigrant associations and increased funding for local rehabilitation programs and education reform, hundreds of "second-generation" cultural, political, and social associations emerged.

This context also created space for unprecedented Jewish organizational and political development.[32] The Jewish response to the October 1980 bombing of the rue Copernic synagogue illustrated well the shift, as large numbers of Jews poured into the streets to protest. While the 1960s and 1970s had seen large pro-Israel demonstrations, the fight against antisemitism had been largely an institutional affair.[33] In addition, changes in laws on state funding of private schools sent increasing numbers of Jewish students to these institutions, while the 1980s embrace of multicultural politics saw efforts to channel a Jewish vote in a nation where special-interest lobbies and ethnic political organization had been an anathema.[34]

The 1982 Israeli invasion of Lebanon, which like prior Middle Eastern wars exacerbated political divisions between France's Muslim and Jewish populations, took place in this context of heightened identity politics. While French Jews were uncharacteristically divided over Israeli actions, support for Palestinians increased substantially among Beur activists,[35] and anti-war rallies saw some donning keffiahs and crying, "Jewish assassins," particularly after the Sabra and Shatila massacre, when Israeli soldiers were accused of enabling Christian Phalangist militia massacres of two Palestinian refugee camps.[36] As one Algerian-born Muslim commented when dismissing her connection to her home country, "I feel much more involved over the Palestinian problem."[37] Following earlier patterns, Algerian, Moroccan, and Tunisian organizations worked with the Comité Palestine de France to organize protests, fund-raise, and collect medical supplies.[38] In Strasbourg, for example, the Union nationale des étudiants marocains raised 35,000 francs from the city's North African, Iranian, and Turkish populations as well as from those on the far left.[39]

This visible pro-Palestinian sentiment among Muslim youth frightened Jewish residents who accused demonstrators of chanting "death to Jews" at pro-Palestinian rallies.[40] Indeed, if in the early 1970s, Jewish communal leaders feared that Muslims *might* turn against their Jewish neighbors, in 1982, various Jewish representatives asserted that this eventuality had come to pass, and some Jewish communities even organized internal security measures to protect against retributive attacks.[41] According to one Tunisian Jewish communist working in Marseille's banlieues, antisemitism among Beurs was commonly expressed: "[T]he *yids* [*youpins*] have the power and the money. It's the Jews who are in charge, dirty *yids*."[42] In a moment of high scandal, the left-leaning *Libération* published a letter to the editor by a J. P. Kapel threatening vengeance against all Jews for Middle East bloodshed: "The Arabs of France and our friends will not stand with arms crossed. The blood of martyrs calls for vengeance. There will be no quarter. To us Belleville and Sentier, to us Montmartre and Saint-Paul and even Sarcelles."[43] *Le Monde*'s report on a letter denying the Holocaust in the Moroccan newspaper, *L'Opinion* (organ of Istiqlal), added to fears that Muslim antisemitism was coming closer to home.[44]

For young Muslims (identified with Palestinians as symbols of their own struggle) and young Jews (trying to balance support for Israel with a growing criticism of Israel at home) the Lebanese invasion had local meaning. As one Beur told *Le Matin* the next winter, linking murders of French Muslim youth to the Palestinian plight: "We are going through a quiet Sabra and [S]hatila."[45] Such formulations left little room for cross-ethnic cooperation, particularly when many Jews were feeling singled out. In the words of one French Jewish youth, "Someone or something always reminds you that you're Jewish, a spit in the face that in the world's eyes you are a dirty Jew. . . . And you do nothing primarily because you are alone."[46] This construction of Jewish isolation in the face of mounting hostility underscored concerns—bolstered during the 1982 invasion of Lebanon—that Muslim immigrants were themselves antisemitic.[47] However, the new identity politics also created opportunities for cooperation. Three responses in *L'Arche* to the first Marche pour l'égalité point to these contradictions. Highly critical of various aspects of the march, Annie Kriegel expressed dismay that Beur activists wore kaffiyehs in solidarity with Palestinians.[48] An editorial in the same edition titled, "Pluricultural France?" stressed the difficulties of peaceful cohabitation within a diverse nation while nevertheless calling for respect for all.[49] Seven months later, an article titled, "We are all Maghrebins" underscored the dangers Jean-Marie Le Pen posed for all minorities.[50] Such constructions became the basis of SOS racisme's pluricultural anti-racist agenda, which both built on and challenged the particularistic focus of the previous few years.

SOS Racisme and the Invention of Pluriculturalism

SOS racisme was born in fall 1984 to celebrate and defend interethnic France. The Socialist party, eager to capitalize on the energy of the Beur Movement, encouraged the creation of associations that would connect with its own bodies and attract potential voters. Under its tutelage, former Trotskyist activists Julien Dray, Didier François, and Harlem Désir created SOS racisme to extend "second-generation" youth politics to a wider public around the notion of an all-embracing and enlightened France.[51] Like all anti-racist groups, SOS racisme denounced racist crimes and called for open policies toward immigrants and their children, but it did so by distancing itself from the Beur Movement by embracing a multicultural perspective. According to one of its organizers, "it was necessary for the anti-racist movement not to be linked directly to any one community, which had been the Beur movement's weakness."[52] Known best for its hand-shaped yellow badge that read "*Touche pas à mon pote*" (Hands off my friend), SOS racisme was quickly a media sensation. Selling 1.5 million badges in 1985 alone, the term "pote" symbolized a new figure that was neither entirely French nor foreign. Désir, the offspring of an Antillesian father and an Alsatian mother, seemed emblematic of this emerging multiracial society. Engaging in highly symbolic actions, SOS racisme invested its energies in huge concerts, poster campaigns, and television appearances, seeking to win adherents among celebrities, intellectuals, and youth. With 500,000 attendees at the first concert on 15 June 1985 at the Place de la Concorde, SOS racisme surged on the energy of a generation of young voters attracted to multiculturalism and leftist politics.[53] As one of its more prominent supporters noted, "This is a youth movement, foreign to prior political cleavages and based on positive values."[54] Or as another supporter asserted, "SOS Racisme is radically different: it does not represent the desires of immigrants but of the majority of French citizens."[55]

Key, then, to SOS racisme's struggle was the assertion that a truly multicultural France could transcend ethno-religious divisions to constitute a united civil society. As evidence, the organizers pointed to the numerous Jews and Muslims who worked together in its activities. While Désir was president, and many "second-generation" Muslims helped run the organization, Dray—an Algerian Jew from Oran—was one of the its primary animators, and Eric Ghébali, president of the Union des étudiants juifs de France [UEJF], was its secretary general. Moreover, in February 1985, SOS racisme won the sponsorship of prominent Jewish intellectuals Bernard-Henri Lévy and Marek Halter, who created a news agency to disseminate information on its activities. Their appearance in a UEJF-sponsored anti-racist demonstration in Paris on the theme, " 'I am not a racist but . . . ' There is no 'but'!" provided SOS racisme with its initial media prominence.[56] Thus while Muslim-Jewish cooperation was only one aspect of the association's activities, interethnic alliance quickly became linked with its central mission.

In order to justify the alliance, supporters made a range of arguments that stressed profound similarities between Muslim and Jewish experiences in France. As one speaker at the UEJF event argued, "I protest against absurd assertions that say that two million unemployed are two million immigrants too many. That reminds me of another assertion that 600,000 Jews were 600,000 unemployed."[57] Eric Ghébali similarly pointed to the shared immigrant past: "Our history has taught us to be wary of hatred of the stranger, we who, as the Bible tells us, were strangers in Egypt, we who today are almost all children or grandchildren of immigrants."[58] In another interview, he went further, arguing that young Jews had to participate in a struggle that "affects all *basanes* [slang for dark-skinned people]."[59] Such racial linkages expressly connected the two minorities in contradistinction to white European society. For Marc Bitton, another leader of the student organization, Jewish participation in the anti-racist movement was justified by a shared commitment to French society—"each and everyone's business" and "NECESSARILY pluricommunal." Jewish participation would thus broaden anti-racist activities that had been driven by the Beur movement's particularistic concerns.[60]

The UEJF's visible connection to SOS racisme defined the student organization's identity for the next several years. Having entered a period of dormancy in the mid-1970s due to divisions between those favoring an aggressive pro-Israeli migration policy and those favoring stabilization of local structures, membership dropped from 15,000 to 1,500 by 1980.[61] The bombing at rue Copernic, coupled with a rise in Holocaust denial, early calls for multiculturalism, and the increasing youth-centered political culture, however, energized Jewish students—called *feujs* in the *verlan* of the day—as it had their Beur peers.[62] By 1982, two thousand students had joined its ranks, and by 1985, membership had risen to ten thousand.[63] Three years later, fifteen sections throughout Paris and the provinces had fifteen thousand members.[64]

Support for Israel remained central to the UEJF's agenda.[65] The pro-Zionist position, however, coexisted with a commitment to a vibrant Diaspora and a critical stance toward the French government.[66] The three hundred attendees at the 1980 national congress, for example, condemned France's reception of PLO representatives and called on all Jewish citizens "to express their disapproval of national policies by all democratic means" even at the risk of alienating Jewish communal bodies.[67] This readiness to criticize a range of domestic and international policies opened the door to the UEJF's participation in the anti-racist movement.

The primary force driving the UEJF's affiliation with SOS racisme was Eric Ghébali, its president from January 1983 until May 1986. Ghébali, a former member of the Strasbourg chapter and a student of economics in Paris, used the early years of his presidency to rebuild the UEJF's membership and strengthen its Zionism.[68] In his initial election, however, Ghébali also made "Judeo-Arab reconciliation" part of his agenda.[69] This interest in reaching across ethno-religious lines combined with a commitment to fighting antisemitism encouraged Ghébali—and the UEJF with him—to help build SOS racisme.

It was only in March 1985, however, that the UEJF/SOS racisme alliance took center stage. On 21 March, two men murdered a twenty-eight-year-old Moroccan immigrant in Menton explaining, "We don't like Arabs." The following Friday, a bomb exploded at a Parisian Jewish film festival wounding twenty-six, and the next day, eighteen-year-old Noureddine Daouadji was killed on the outskirts of Marseille. An SOS racisme demonstration on 6 April and another the next day in front of the bombed theater saw protesters cry, "Arabs in Menton, Jews in Paris, they are killing our friends [potes]." According to news reports this was "the first time representatives of Jewish movements and Arab immigrant organizations find themselves shoulder to shoulder." Désir was quick to underscore the importance of this development: "Usually when Jews and Arabs share common cause, it's in political corridors [*salons politiques*]. . . . This is the first time it's on the streets of Paris." While the minister of justice, Robert Badinter, blamed the theater bombing on international terrorism, SOS racisme and many of the reporters who covered its activities saw more local origins.[70] In the words of one Jewish representative from SOS racisme, "In terms of racist threats, we are second in line, just behind the Arabs."[71] Jacquot Gruenwald wrote in the *Tribune juive*, "[T]he development in France of an often murderous racism, even if it does not directly target the Jewish community, is intolerable. Racism cannot be divided. Jews who only yesterday were its privileged victims feel directly attacked."[72] Writing in *Le Monde*, Daniel Schneidermann asserted that the two murders and the bombing had "in the course of one weekend begun to weaken the substantial mental barriers between Arabs and Jews in France."[73] Still other reports focused on several Algerian Jews who "had rallied behind Arab immigrants."[74] Even Serge July's 1 April editorial in *Libération*, which argued that diminishing antisemitism could not be compared to the daily rejection of North African immigrants, celebrated new cooperative efforts, noting, "[F]or the first time Arab intellectuals in France also signed a petition denouncing the attack against the cinema Rivioli."[75]

As July's statement suggested, Muslim and Jewish intellectuals encouraged new cooperative endeavors. The writers Marek Halter and Tahar Ben Jelloun, for example, were interviewed together for *Libération* in a story subtitled "Arabs and Jews side by side." In the piece, Ben Jelloun underscored that "racism is not selective. One cannot be anti-Jewish and like Arabs or anti-Black and like Jews." For both, SOS racisme marked a new stage in interethnic exchange.[76]

This new cooperation was most evident in May when a group of prominent Muslim intellectuals publically criticized President Regan's visit to Bitburg, Germany, to lay a wreath at the graves of German soldiers, including forty-nine SS troops. Protesting the "insult to the memory of the victims," the signatories, which included the editorial team of the Beur newspaper, *Sans frontières*, activists such as Souad Bennani and Saliha Amara, the sociologist Adil Jazouli, members of the Association des Marocains en France, and writers Tahar Ben Jelloun and Leïla Sebbar, argued that victims of racism must unite.[77] SOS racisme similarly took part in a UEJF-sponsored protest at Bitburg. As SOS racisme's Dahmane Abderrahmane commented on the Beur presence, "We have put our political differences aside: the Middle East is one thing, the struggle against racism another. We came to demonstrate at the side of our Jewish friends. I hope they will do the same for us when it's necessary."[78]

As Abderrahmane hoped, such cooperative activities occurred several more times over the next few months. When Gorbachev went to Paris, for example, SOS racisme helped organize rallies on behalf of Soviet Jews, and Marek Halter used SOS racisme's banner to declare, "Hey Gorbachev, Soviet Jews are also our friends [*potes*]!"[79] In June 1985, two Muslim members of SOS racisme's governing board participated in a UEJF-sponsored trip to Majdanek and Auschwitz, and in October, the UEJF joined SOS racisme in commemorating Algerians killed in Paris in 1961.[80] Moreover, other groups embraced the new cooperative spirit. In June 1985 the École Central, for example, held a Jewish-Muslim cultural evening in which speakers addressed the need to fight racism together by first combating racism *between* them.[81] In addition, the Jeunes Arabes de Lyon et banlieue (JALB) criticized the Organisation nationale maghrebine for initiating a boycott against Jewish businesses in response to the Israeli bombing of PLO headquarters in Tunis. Rejecting calls for solidarity with Palestinians, one member remarked, "being anti-racist means, of course, not being antisemitic."[82]

These much-fêted cross-ethnic endeavors were, however, always shadowed by the decade's particularistic politics, creating challenges that required Jewish and Beur leaders to test the parameters of their alliance.[83] As one young Muslim told a reporter, SOS racisme was "for the *feujs*, not for us."[84] One dramatic example of such criticism came in December 1984 when the UEJF organized a panel on Middle East peace at Jussieu campus. When the 250 students arrived to hear presentations from Marek Halter and the cultural attaché for the Israeli embassy, they were greeted by 200–300 protestors from different Tunisian, Lebanese, and Moroccan associations screaming, "Zionists, fascists, out of Jussieu." "For us," said one protestor, "this is a racist meeting," and the UEJF, "which walks hand in hand with SOS racisme," is a Zionist front.[85] Similarly, the organization "Palestine vaincra" distributed brochures at metro stations claiming that Zionists had infiltrated anti-racist movements.[86] Marche des Beurs organizers also expressed doubts over SOS racisme's links to the UEJF. Most notably, Christian Delorme, the Protestant minister from Lyons who helped organize the 1983 march, wrote to Harlem Désir in April 1985 criticizing the UEJF's predominance and SOS racisme's efforts to supplant Beur anti-racist associations.[87]

Meanwhile, Jewish critics also expressed doubts about pluriculturalism. While left-leaning organizations, such as Judaïsme et socialisme, Association des Juifs de gauche, and the Cercle Bernard Lazare, publicly supported SOS racisme as did the two Jewish publications *Tribune juive* and *L'Arche* (the latter of which published SOS racisme's small yellow badge on its April 1985 cover), many spokesmen proved suspicious.[88] Remembering cries of "death to the Jews" in summer 1982, Jewish leaders felt no affection for the Beur Movement and its kaffiyeh-wearing demonstrators.[89] As Jean-Pierre Bloch, president of the Ligue internationale contre le racisme et l'antisémitisme (LICRA) remarked, "it would be interesting to know the position of the youth of 'Hands off my friend' toward the abominable UN resolution: Zionism = Racism."[90] Others criticized the UEJF/Beur alliance for ignoring clashing views on Israel.[91] While "a natural link exists between us and we face the same danger," penned Richard Liscia in *L'Arche*, "the Middle East crisis separates us." Skeptical of the optimism around

SOS racisme he noted, "not only do few Arabs feel concerned by the attack against the Jewish cinema, but even fewer would be ready to condemn Islamic Jihad if they confirmed that it originated the attack." Muslims, in his view, unlike Jews, were not yet willing to divide their perspectives on the Middle East from a universalist anti-racism: "I do not even ask them to accept Israel, only to be capable of separating things. To know that there is a struggle that we can carry out together despite all who oppose us."[92] Others embraced SOS racisme's anti-racist charge while questioning its ability to bridge real differences. CRIF president, Théo Klein, for example, displayed the SOS racisme badge on his desk and celebrated the fact that "Jewish and Arab intellectuals are working hand in hand," but explained its popularity as a fad.[93] Jean-Paul Elkan, president of the Consistoire de France, embraced SOS racisme's anti-racist charge while undermining its pluricultural message. When speaking to the Consistoire's Assemblée Générale in June, he reminded his audience that racism against North African immigrants was on the rise and insisted that a history of suffering led Jews to fight for human rights for all. His focus on racism, however, quickly brought him to Zionism since Israel served as the "best line of defense against anti-Semitism in the world."[94]

In light of such particularistic challenges, SOS racisme continued to sharpen its pluricultural approach. Meetings in spring 1985 between the UEJF and prominent members of the Beur Movement tackled thorny questions such as, "Racism and anti-Semitism in France: Is Solidarity Possible between Jews and Arabs?"[95] At one such "cards on the table" meeting, Jewish and Muslim participants tackled their differences around the Middle East. While UEJF representatives unapologetically asserted their Zionism, they agreed with Beur representatives that the Middle Eastern conflict was irrelevant to forging a cohesive anti-racist movement. Attendees left the meeting citing the slogan, "We cannot solve the Israel/Palestinian problem on the banks of the Seine" and agreeing that they shared more than divided them. As Ghébali underscored, "[W]e now have a common cultural heritage between us, we are beginning to get to know each other better."[96] Marek Halter summarized the meeting's significance as follows: "There was someone during the discussion who said: 'If they touch Israel, it's as if they have torn out a piece of my flesh, but in France, if they touch an immigrant—an Arab, a Portuguese—it's the same thing, they tear out a piece of my flesh. That is why I'm committed to SOS Racisme.' Much has changed. Such a speech would have been impossible ten years ago and would had been rejected by young Moroccans, Tunisians, Algerians."[97]

If the vow of silence regarding the Middle East conflict preserved alliances within SOS racisme, supporters of particularistic and pluricultural approaches to the anti-racist struggle still clashed.[98] The following autumn, for example, two anti-racist marches left Bordeaux for Paris after negotiations to unite them failed, the first sponsored by Beur associations and the second by SOS racisme. While the former emphasized the necessity of giving Beurs a political voice,[99]

SOS racisme sought to demonstrate that "French citizens of Jewish origin, Arab origin, etc. constitute a piece of the pluricultural Europe of the future."[100]

Such tensions were likewise evident in a December 1985 *Libération* interview with Julien Dray and Mejid Daboussi Ammar, a Tunisian-born French journalist and founder of *Sans frontières*. While both remained committed to Muslim-Jewish cooperation and both denounced Reagan's visit to Bittburg, Ammar repeatedly stressed the differences facing the two populations. Dray, in contrast, emphasized how theirs was a generation "of mixtures [*mélanges*]" all facing the same question: how to create a society where communities with different histories but with some commonalities can coexist. "Ammar and I have things in common. Our pasts are different but we share a common future." Ammar rejected such formulations, or rather, he noted that French Muslims could not yet embrace "mixture" while still fighting for basic rights: "You, Julien, assert that you are more at ease with 'mixture' and I would like to be able to say the same thing. Except I come from a devestated community that has never had the floor. I cannot afford that luxury. You can have it because you have an organized community that can defend itself." "Before calling for mixture or pluri-culturalism," Ammar continued, "we must establish a certain equality between communities."[101]

Ammar's insistence on his own community's needs was echoed by certain Jewish spokemen who worried about the impact of comparing Muslims and Jews in French society. André Wormser, for example, director of the Centre d'études et de recherches sur l'antisémitisme contemporain (CERAC), wrote to CRIF president, Théo Klein, on the one hand of the "useful" new contacts that young Jews had established with Muslims, while on the other hand warning that some of their initiatives "are inopportune and could take the community down a dangerous path." What exactly was the danger for Wormser? Given Jewish visibility in the anti-racist movement, the press and public opinion were beginning to see Jews as outsiders:

> It is often with the best of intentions that newspapers, *Le Monde* in particular, links all the victims of ordinary racism (immigrants, Jews, Arabs, or blacks), xenophobia, and anti-Semitism, making it seem as if Jews are foreigners to the French nation. We stand in solidarity with and are fraternally concerned by the attacks perpetrated against immigrants. I agree with all of our declarations in this sense and my own commitment to Muslims speaks for itself. However, in these linkages there is, on the one hand, historical error and, on the other, the enclosure of the community in a category where it does not belong. These are distinctions on which we must insist.[102]

Wormser's distinctions between Muslim "immigrants" and Jewish "citizens" was an implicit rejection of pluriculturalism (and a blatant if popular distortion of Beur national status). Given that elsewhere Wormser had argued that Muslims shared a "collective sense of belonging to France," his perspective is particularly revealing of how even sympathetic fellow travelers within the Jewish establishment remained wary of pluriculturalism.[103]

One of the most vociferous opponents of linking Muslims and Jews was Annie Kriegel. In several articles in *L'Arche* she lambasted efforts to create such parallels, arguing that the two groups differed in terms of their history, size, transnational affiliations, leadership, and integrative possibilities. While Jews, she argued, constituted a *community*, which is to say, a voluntary and religiously based group, Muslims constituted a *minority*, and thus the two were incomparable.[104] Dismissing those who emphasized the threat of the FN to Muslims and Jews alike, Kriegel stressed successful Jewish integration and insisted that the real danger came from conflating the Muslim and Jewish experience.[105] Many Jews are "ready to renounce their civic status in order to better share the status and torments of the immigrant condition." Instead, Jews should reflect alongside all citizens on how France could preserve its cohesion and educate newcomers on their rights and duties.[106] Such formulations insisted on profound distinctions between Muslims and Jews, linking Jews fully with the French nation and casting Muslims as perennial outsiders.

Other depictions went further in underscoring Muslim foreignness while also highlighting significant polarization between Muslims and Jews. In a long piece entitled, *"L'Islam contemporain et les juifs"* published by the Comité d'initiative pour Israël, Michel Gurfinkiel argued that although antisemitism had diminished in the West, Muslim immigrants were importing a Koran-based anti-Jewish propaganda with them. Gurfinkiel particularly highlighted anti-Jewish sentiment among Muslims in France:

> In fact, it is 'because of the Jews' that many Muslims refuse to integrate into the French nation where they believe that their efforts are doomed to fail. The presence in France of what [the Muslims] perceive to be a powerful and well organized Jewish community, with positions in politics, business, and even the Church, seems to them an almost insurmountable obstacle in their ambiguous desires for integration. . . . If the effort to enter into a secularized Christian system leads to the de facto submission to a social authority exercised by Jews, the effort is judged impossible. Such responses are found in all Muslim immigrant circles, even the most peripheral or the most integrated to French culture.[107]

Bolstering such fears, in February 1987, LICRA accused an Islamic bookstore in Belleville of selling the *Protocols of the Elders of Zion*, the fraudulent text describing a Jewish plan to achieve global domination.[108] Likewise, the bulletin of the association Décider agir avec vigilance pour Israël et la diaspora (DAVID) warned against antisemitic diatribes on Islamic radio stations seeking to "turn French 'Beurs' against the Jews."[109]

Certainly, not all French Jews accepted such a stark representation of Muslim-Jewish relations, with some even defending SOS racisme as a sign of

Beur integration.[110] Nevertheless, debates between particularlistic and pluricultural approaches to ethno-religious cooperation continued to plague the anti-racist movement throughout the mid-1980s. They gathered steam as France's evolving political landscape shifted the agenda to those emphasizing particularistic priorities.

Cohabitation, Integration, and the End of Pluriculturalism

The 1986 parliamentary elections proved a repudiation of Mitterrand's socialist hold over the French political establishment, ushering in a period with a president from one party (Mitterrand) and a prime minister from another (Jacques Chirac). While Mitterrand won reelection in 1988, bringing back a leftist majority, from 1986 to 1988 the balance of power had shifted. Moreover, the FN continued to win electoral victories, earning 9.7 percent of the vote or thirty-five seats in the 1986 parliamentary elections and, more shocking to many, 14 percent, or nearly 4.5 million of those cast in the first round of the May 1988 presidential elections.[111] In response, Chirac's government ushered in a period of stricter controls on immigration—a touchstone issue for FN voters—reviving financial inducements for immigrants to return home, tightening entry restrictions, and launching debates over the nationality code. The latter, in particular, created widespread debate as conservatives proposed to modify citizenship laws for the children of foreigners.[112] Although the proposal foundered due in part to widespread opposition by anti-racist organizations, by 1988 all parties were emphasizing cultural amalgam over multiculturalism as a means to ensure social stability. If the Right focused on threats to French security and the Left on integration, both saw "immigration" as a "problem" to be solved.[113] For the Socialists, such shifts led to efforts to isolate the Beur Movement from the larger immigrant community. Fearing the movement's collective strength and the development of sectarian religious and ethnic groupings, officials sought to define the boundaries of Beur activism by co-opting the leadership and limiting funding and logistical support to programs that supported the state's integrative interests. Such efforts succeeded in weakening the Beur Movement considerably.[114]

It was in the midst of these shifts that the first intifada broke out in Israel in December 1987. The eruption of yet another Middle Eastern conflict created new tensions within the French anti-racist movement as Beur and Jewish representatives split along pro-Israel or pro-Palestinian lines. To understand debates around the intifada as purely the transplantation of the Middle East conflict to France, however, overlooks the way national conversations on immigration and diversity shaped the outlook of Beurs, Jews, and the wider anti-racist movement. As France's political establishment and media began reemphasizing integration, divisions were exacerbated within and among these groups that

undermined pluricultural experiments. Such shifts did not immediately interfere with cooperative Muslim-Jewish anti-racist campaigns, but the nature of
those campaigns became transformed. Rather than focusing on the formation
of a pluricultural public sphere, Muslim and Jewish activists began stressing
"dialogue." Although a subtle shift, this new framework highlighted divisions
rather than shared struggles.

In this context, a second anti-racist organization, France plus, founded in
1985 by Arezki Dahmani, played a significant role. France plus brought together children of harkis and "second-generation" French Muslims with the
goal of encouraging integration through the exercise of civic rights and respon-
sibilities. The organization thus emphasized voter registration and the election
of Muslim candidates.[115] Like SOS racisme, France plus promoted a multiracial and multi-ethnic society. Unlike SOS racisme, however, France plus, the
considerably smaller of the two organizations, placed far greater emphasis on
Beur politics.[116] If SOS racisme was dedicated to creating minority unity, France
plus was founded on the principle of ethnic political organization.[117] Dahmani
was thus less interested in working *with* Jews than in mirroring their political
strategies. After the outbreak of the first intifada, however, it was France plus—
rather than SOS racisme—that forged a successful alliance with the UEJF, an
alliance that stressed dialogue as the only means of sustaining a unified anti-
racist struggle.

Israel's response to the Palestinian uprising in December 1987 sparked
strong reactions across France's left-leaning Beur organizations.[118] Protesters,
including Hayet Boudjemaa (SOS racisme), Nacer Kettane (Radio Beur), and
Arezki Dahmani (France plus) visited the Israeli embassy, and pro-Palestinian
empathy increased "on the ground."[119] As one Muslim student told a reporter,
"The guys fighting the Zionists are the same age as us. They were born in camps;
we have known the *cités de transit* and the bidonvilles. We put ourselves in their
place." Others articulated an intensifying Arab unity: "North Africans, Egyp-
tians, Palestinians, we all have the same blood."[120]

Such reactions did not, however, fully capture the range of responses to
events in the Middle East. As the president of Sans frontières, Farid Aïchoune,
editorialized in *Le Monde*, if many Beurs identified with the Palestinians, most
did *not* imagine themselves as part of a wider Arab political struggle but as
French: "We *Beurs* do not dream of an I-don't-know-what Arab Revolution
that the Palestinians would spearhead. Myths of this kind are finished for us.
Beurs do not want to scream 'Death to Israel,' even if sometimes we are angered
by certain images."[121] Likewise, according to Khaled Melhaa, secretary general
of Radio Beur, while the station had received some angry calls from listeners,
few expressed the passions of 1973. As one Beur told a reporter, "Frankly, Palestine is kind of far away. . . . What I want first is to find a job. After, we'll see."
Or according to another, "We live in France not in Palestine or another Arab
country. . . . For us, what is happening now is primarily a problem of justice

and human rights." If the Beurs identified with the Palestinians, he continued, it was based on a shared experience of marginalization: "Of course Palestinians are my brothers, I am completely in solidarity with them, and at the same time, we are not 100% Arab."[122]

If Beurs articulated a range of views on the intifada, Jews were equally divided. Media representations portrayed the Jewish population as "in disarray" and "traumatized" over aggressive Israeli responses to the violence.[123] As one reporter noted, "throughout the French Jewish community we find a malaise, an internal rupture between a visceral fidelity to Israel and these painful images."[124] Some well-known Jewish figures—echoing Jewish leftists of past decades—publically criticized Israeli actions, while others were silent, and still others remained loyal to Israel despite mounting discomfort.[125] This diversity of responses created space for Muslims and Jews to issue joint appeals for Middle Eastern peace that echoed the decade's pluricultural themes.[126]

In a context that repeatedly underscored the difficulties of immigrant and Beur integration, however, pluriculturalism was beginning to founder. According to Kaïssa Titous, a member of SOS racisme's steering committee and a Beur activist, "For many Beurs, there has been a rupture with the Jewish community which, in their eyes, does not sufficiently support the anti-racist struggle even if it has taken steps in that direction."[127] As Titous's remarks make clear, while Jews and Muslims sometimes clashed over Middle Eastern policy, domestic issues were also a source of tension. As one young Beur told a reporter, he had distanced himself from his best friend (Jewish) because he refused to admit the "ideological imperialism" that the "Jewish lobby exercised in all areas of society."[128]

This conflation of the international and French identity politics led in the words of the UEJF's Arié Bensemhoun to "a sort of explosion inside the [antiracist] movement."[129] In March 1988, the UEJF announced it was considering dissolving ties with SOS racisme in response to "anti-Israel initiatives" taken by some provincial committees and, in particular, the distribution of anti-UEJF tracts.[130] Harlem Désir's call for direct Israeli negotiations with the PLO, which most Jewish organizations considered a terrorist organization, also angered those who insisted that SOS racisme remain neutral on Israel/Palestine. "We are first and foremost Zionist activists," declared the new UEJF president, Marc Bitton. "We must take into account the concerns of our community."[131] The shift from pluricultural to particularistic politics was clear.

At SOS racisme's congress the following April, Jewish and Muslim members spent hours trying to bridge the impasse. On the one hand, Eric Ghebali demanded that the organization recognize *both* Israeli and Palestinian rights, while, on the other, Kaïssa Titous called for a condemnation of the repression, insistence on Israeli military retreat, and recognition of Palestinian national rights. The three hundred delegates finally settled on a compromise that affirmed their "solidarity with the victims of repression in the occupied territories," while also stating the necessity for Palestinians and Israelis to recognize the other's legitimate existence. Ten members nevertheless abstained because the declaration did not go far enough.[132]

The declaration allowed the UEJF and the SOS racisme to reconfirm their link, a timely move given Le Pen's strong showing in the May presidential elections.[133] In its June-July newsletter, the UEJF thus re-embraced its pluriculturalism, stating that, "racism, xenophobia, and anti-Semitism cannot be fought from a ghetto." Yet, the same article set limits on Beur activism: "It might seem natural for a young Beur to feel close to a young Palestinian, but to fight for the integration of *immigrants* while brandishing the Palestinian flag is nonsensical." Without acknowledging the double standard, the UEJF, which was vocally pro-Israel, criticized double allegiances among the Beurs and highlighted their foreign origins (by definition Beurs were not immigrants), implicitly underscoring differences from their *French* Jewish peers.[134]

The UEJF's reemphasis of particularism while holding firm to its anti-racism was mirrored by France plus, which called for dialogue across ethno-religious lines as a means of strengthening the anti-racist coalition. The call for "dialogue," while seemingly overlapping with SOS racisme's pluriculturalism, differed in significant ways. Like the leaders of SOS racisme, Dahmani understood that certain commonalities linked Muslims and Jews. For him, however, political differences were paramount and he stressed "dialogue" as a way to surmount them. As such, unlike SOS racisme, which had remained neutral on the Middle East, France plus actively supported the Palestinians *while* formally recognizing Israel (becoming the first "Franco-Maghrebin" organization to do so), and in February 1988, launched a committee "Shalom-Salem" for all "French of Maghrebian origin." During a press conference announcing the new organization, Dahmani underscored the importance of dialogue.[135] While disagreeing about the Middle East, Muslims and Jews agreed on a minimum program of past (shared North African heritage), present (anti-racism and inclusion for all in French society), and future (Middle East peace).[136] According to Dahmani: "If in our collective memory, these two youth—'Beurs and Feujs'—are linked, one thing separates them: the Israeli-Palestinian conflict. For France plus, the construction of a democratic anti-racist front necessarily must pass through the settlement of the conflict."[137]

Dahmani took part in numerous public "dialogues" to facilitate this end.[138] In July 1988, for example, Arié Bensemhoun, the UEJF's new president, and Arezki Dahmani published a debate on the Middle East facilitated by historian Benjamin Stora. All three of North African origin (Bensemhoun born in Morocco, Dahmani and Stora in Algeria) and all three highly educated—Bensemhoun was a doctoral dental surgeon, Dahmani and Stora assistant professors—they came to the Middle Eastern conflict with similar investments in intercommunal cooperation but also cognizant of deep divisions. As Bensemhoun said later, "While we were inevitably brought together in the anti-racist struggle, events in the Middle East caused a deep rift to develop between young Jews and young Arabs."[139] A close look at the discussion, however, shows the way disagreements over Israel-Palestine underscored other divisions. Dahmani, for example, distinguished between the racism facing Muslims and Jews even if both shared a common enemy in Le Pen: "For French-Maghrebians, racism is experienced daily, linked to their disadvantaged social status. They face the racism of the 'ground floor.'" For Jews, he argued, whose social status was considerably higher, racism was largely encountered in history and memory. For Bensemhoun, the problem was not structural. Rather he focused on the conflation of anti-Zionism and antisemitism among French Muslims: "There were demonstrations in France because of events in the territories. In the streets, I saw people with whom we have typically fought racism. They were screaming: 'Zionists, fascists, assassins!' and other slogans that sounded more like antisemitism than simple support for the Palestinian cause." Thus while Dahmani accused the anti-racist movement of crumbling around Jews' unwillingness to challenge Israeli racism (versus Beurs who condemned racism everywhere), Bensemhoun accused Beurs of their own form of racism. When asked if Jewish-Arab cooperation was over, Bensemhoun remarked, "Quite. Too often we spout off about Jewish-Arab dialogue. We say: 'Oh! If we could just have dialogue that would fix all the problems in France and the Middle East.' This is insufficient. We have always had dialogue. Jews and Arabs have lived together for centuries. This is not new."[140]

While Bensemhoun was correct that Muslims and Jews had been interacting for centuries, the commitment to "dialogue" as a political strategy *was* new, and both the UEJF and France plus asserted the importance of confronting differences as a way to find common ground. Most notably, on 11 October 1988, five hundred participants came together in what was billed as the "first encounter between Arabs and Jews in France." Organized by the Jewish monthly *Passages*, the event brought the UEJF and France plus together with other activists to discuss "Is Jewish-Arab dialogue possible for tomorrow's France?"[141] Notably absent was SOS racisme, whose pluricultural approach was losing ground in the strident French identity politics of the late 1980s.[142] As Eric Ghébali—still secretary general of SOS racisme but long since replaced as UEJF president—responded to the event,[143] "We obviously favor anything that encourages Israeli-Arab dialogue. But we want to address a whole generation without distinctions. The identity stance taken by l'UEJF and France plus seems like a regression to us. Why emphasize differences and position themselves against each other?"[144]

Ghébali was not the only detractor.[145] Hamadi Essid, head of the Arab League's mission in Paris, criticized the event for leaving out Middle Eastern representatives in what was really a "Franco-French" debate. Here, Essid was right. Held in the National Assembly, symbolic site of political inclusion, the event moved well beyond the Middle East to a range of minority issues. According to Rabeh Touïsi, vice president of France plus, "We will stay in strictly

Franco-French terrain. We are young Jews and Arabs in France. We were born here. We have grown up together, attended the same schools, confronted the same problems. But, alas, too often there are tensions. I have seen them enough myself to speak of them. These are the tensions we must eliminate, and for that, we must begin by speaking frankly together."[146]

Despite such hopes, divisions surfaced throughout the day. While the audience was mixed, Jews and Muslims each sat with their own.[147] Panels were also highly charged, particularly one on the Middle East in which Arié Bensemhoun's passionate pro-Israel presentation led some to yell angrily, "We are not in the Knesset!" Although one Jewish leftist reminded all, "You are no more Palestinian than I am an Israeli citizen," the angry tone permeated other panels as well.[148] In one session, for example, a Muslim attendee circulated a document that read, "What should we think of the *Protocols of the Elders of Zion*—slander or truth—when we see how much of the world finances are concentrated in the hands of the American Jewish lobby and its Judeo-Nazi comportment in Israel, the occupied territories, Lebanon and elsewhere." In the session on racism, UEJF representatives cautioned Beur attendees not to compare the Holocaust to murders in Algeria, while the latter reminded Jewish peers, "In colonial Algeria, the Jewish community chose the occupier over the occupied!" Not to be outdone, their interlocutors retorted, "Jewish blood ran in the synagogues; I don't think that it ran in the mosques." Here, references to colonial Algeria were quickly entangled with the particularist politics of contemporary France. As one Beur complained, "We are the primary victims of racism in France. Maghrebians provide a barrier for the Jews." While Bitton countered, "We are all in the same sack!" another responded, "The Jews are often overvalued: they do everything better. In contrast, Arabs are undervalued: nothing."[149] By the end of the day, Jewish participants were complaining that no Muslims had denounced anti-Jewish activities in Egypt, Syria, and Iraq, while Muslims were attacking the pro-French attitude of the Jews during decolonization, and the lack of recognition of Muslim aid to French Jews during the Holocaust. This reference to decolonization and World War II underscored the multiple layers to identity politics in late 1980s France. Ostensibly a fight about Israelis and Palestinians, the exchange was very much a "Franco-French" debate in which tensions around history, memory, and immigration politics were paramount.[150]

Subsequent debates between Dahmani and Bensemhoun continued to emphasize differences between Muslims and Jews. For Dahmani, the primary challenge facing Muslims was integration into French society. Rather than pursuing the "right to be different," so significant at the beginning of the decade, Beurs required the "right to indifference."[151] Bensemhoun, in contrast, underscored that "Jews have no problem with integration. Jews were in France even before France was France! Even if antisemitism is on the increase, it is difficult to compare the situation of the Jews and the Beurs. The Beurs are still working for their integration." On this Dahmani agreed, "We can not really compare ourselves with the Jewish community."[152] Elsewhere, Bensemhoun went further, "We must differentiate the Jewish community in France from that of the Arab community. While the former has successfully integrated, if not without difficulties, the latter is seeking its place." Here too Dahmani agreed: "[T]he Jewish community is better integrated than the Arab community. . . . What I ask of our Jewish friends is that they draw on their experience to help us succeed with our integration."[153]

In such depictions particularistic concerns overwhelmed pluricultural celebrations, a perspective the UEJF's Marc Rochman emphasized when explaining his organization's relationship with France plus. While the UEJF had co-founded SOS racisme in 1985, the latter's turn to Beur integration had taken it in a different direction, which "if commendable is not our own." The response of certain leaders to the intifada had chilled the collaboration further. Instead, Rochman noted, "we now dialogue with the young Beurs of France plus. Each defends his own ideas on the basis of a fraternal dialogue."[154] What is interesting about this portrayal is that France plus was actually both more openly pro-Palestinian and more vocally committed to Beur integration than SOS racisme.[155] The appeal of France plus was rather its call for "dialogue," which assumed essential differences rather than celebrating similarities, providing the UEJF with the freedom to do the same.

Ironically, this emphasis on difference came at a moment when Jews and Muslims were more the "same" than they had ever been, sharing the status of ethno-religious minority citizens within the French state. Despite this shared "positionality"—or maybe even because of it—Jewish and Muslim activists began to distance themselves from each other. This shift was, necessarily, incomplete, which meant that pluricultural and particularistic approaches to minority integration continued to coexist. Even the CRIF, which had long avoided pluricultural politics, showed greater appreciation for shared minority struggle under its new president Jean Kahn. In fall 1989, for example, Kahn increased contacts with Muslim authorities, arguing, "We must not forget that we live side by side with 3,000,000 Muslims in France, of whom 800,000 are citizens like us who face common problems."[156]

As French political culture took a turn to the right, attempting to solve the "immigration problem" with more forceful calls for integration, however, Jewish links to Muslims appeared increasingly dangerous. In response, some communal leaders stressed fundamental differences between Jews and Muslims.[157] The latter similarly backed away from alliances with a group that seemed to represent all they hoped to achieve but also the limitations on their own integration. For both, it was the particular and not the pluricultural that resonated. Three episodes—two domestic and one international—at the end of the decade cemented this shift.

The Head Scarf, Carpentras, the Gulf War and the End of Pluriculturalism

Three seemingly unconnected social crises at the end of the 1980s rang the death knell on pluriculturalism. The Islamic head-scarf controversy in October 1989, the desecration of the Jewish cemetery in Carpentras in May 1990, and the outbreak of the first Gulf War in January 1991 each in their own way underscored the particular struggles facing Muslim and Jewish French citizens. While each theoretically provided an opportunity for joint activism, the late 1980s shift to an intensified identity politics meant that few such appeals resonated. With the new decade, the UEJF dissolved its ties with SOS racisme, symbolically closing the door both organizations helped open in 1984.

On 3 October 1989 three Muslim girls were expelled from a middle school in Creil (thirty miles from Paris) for refusing to remove their head scarves, expulsions the principal justified on the grounds that the girls were breaking one of the central pillars of republican universalism—*laïcité* or French secularism—by violating the law on the separation of church and state and making religious difference a public rather than private matter. The media frenzy that followed (echoed in similar controversies in 1994 and 2003) can be understood as a response to fears that the public school—the central institution of French republicanism—was under assault and as an indication of the country's increasing discomfort with Islam.[158] Despite the decade's vocal anti-racist campaigns, the end of the 1980s saw mounting fears over terrorism, international Islam, and Arab militancy in response to terrorist attacks in France in 1986, the intifiada, and the 1989 Iranian fatwa against Salman Rushdie. In particular, fears focused on "second generation" French Muslims whose marginalization made them seem ripe for fundamentalist outreach.[159] The seemingly insignificant expulsion of two girls from high school thus soon evolved into a national debate on Islam and minority integration. The debates around *l'affaire foulard*, when coupled with those around the Jewish cemetery desecration in 1990 in Carpentras and the 1991 Gulf War, continued to emphasize Muslim and Jewish difference in ways that brought SOS racisme's pluricultural model to a breaking point.

For Jews, *l'affaire foulard* proved disconcerting, since discussions of the Muslim head scarf seemed to lend themselves to easy comparisons with the Jewish yarmulke.[160] If Islam posed a fundamental challenge to the French public sphere, could the same be said of Judaism? And if so, would the comparisons raise the same kinds of questions about Jewish integration that plagued French Muslims? The answers to these questions reflected the range of pluricultural and particularistic agendas that had coexisted uneasily for much of the decade. The UEJF, for example, criticized "fundamentalist secularism" and stressed the importance of protecting universities, at the very least, as open to all particularistic expressions.[161] Likewise, Chief Rabbi Sitruk joined a group of Catholic and Protestant clerics in arguing for religious tolerance in schools. For him, defending the head scarf was equivalent to defending the yarmulke (although no Jews were forced to remove head coverings during the head-scarf affair). While hardly a "pluriculturalist" (Sitruk's position grew out of deeply particularistic perspectives), his call for religious tolerance necessarily stressed shared concerns between France's two largest religious minorities. More moderate rabbis disagreed. Gilles Bernheim, for example, argued that because Jews had successfully integrated into French society, they "should serve as models for the Muslim community" in remaining faithful to French republicanism. Since very few Muslim women actually wore head scarves (14 percent), Bernheim's position can be understood as stressing differences as a way to legitimize Jewish "Frenchness."[162] Likewise, the CRIF, while never taking a strong stand, promoted state secularism as a way of celebrating Jewish integration, while certain Jewish intellectuals such as Alain Finkielkraut denounced the "holy alliance of clergies" for their attack on public schools.[163] Others adopted a more strident position, drawing decisive lines between Jews and Muslims in response to troubling conflations that seemed to raise doubts about Jewish integration. Richard Liscia, for example, wrote in L'Arche that donning the head scarf was a fundamentalist provocation that differed profoundly from the yarmulke, which only sought to distinguish Jews from other people, and the cross, which served as a national unifying symbol.[164] Such rhetoric, which emphasized Jewish Frenchness in contradistinction to Muslim foreignness, built on the discourse of difference that had emerged over previous years, with some even blaming SOS racisme for the blurring of such distinctions.[165] Shmuel Trigano thus argued that "the brainless policies of certain Jewish institutions like the UEJF" drew equivalencies between Jewish and Muslim assimilation, "giving birth to SOS racisme," and raising new questions about the Jewish community's place in French society.[166]

This emphasis on difference gathered steam in May 1990 when a body was exhumed from a Jewish cemetery in Carpentras. While there had been many desecrations in the preceding period, the impalement of Félix Germont's body on an umbrella created unprecedented public outrage. A huge CRIF-sponsored protest in Paris on 14 May brought out hundreds of thousands, including President Mitterrand and representatives from across the political spectrum. The collective support nevertheless reaffirmed Jewish distinctiveness since the media and official representations generally framed the attack as directed against a unified "community."[167] Moreover, a concerted journalistic and political focus on the "return of antisemitism" had the effect of distinguishing it from other forms of racism.[168]

The massive support for Jews highlighted for many Muslims the differences facing the two populations. In response, France plus made another effort to protect the anti-racist alliance, this time organizing a symposium with the CRIF on Muslim-Jewish dialogue.[169] CRIF president Jean Kahn likewise told Prime Minister Rocard that the Jewish community hoped to increase discussions with

SOS racisme and France plus.[170] His address six months later to SOS racisme's annual congress stressed pluricultural themes: "We feel each attack against a North African as an attack against ourselves, it makes us ache and anxious. . . . Alone you cannot fight racism. Alone we cannot fight anti-Semitism. . . . All is linked."[171] Nevertheless, the very distinction between "racism" and "antisemitism" was itself a kind of particularistic discourse that revealed the limits of the speaker's pluriculturalist vision. Marc Rochman's speech at the same event similarly paid lip service to collective anti-racist struggles while focusing primarily on the particularlistic issues of Holocaust education and antisemitism in France and Eastern Europe.[172]

The first Gulf War dealt the final blow to pluriculturalism. Iraq's August 1990 invasion of Kuwait touched off a storm of controversy, as discussions over the nation's engagements in the Middle East and the prospect of war created fears that Muslims would reject French positions in favor of "Arab" solidarity.[173] Indeed, although French Muslims took diverse positions on the Gulf conflict, mirroring disagreements throughout the Arab world, media outlets and public commentators assumed the worst.[174] According to Charles Rebois in the *Figaro*, "If war breaks out, what side will they be on? . . . No matter what one does or says, the Beur from Seine-Saint-Denis will always feel close to his brothers who jeer France in the streets of Algiers and Tunis." Three national polls from the end of January 1991 showed over 80 percent of the French believing that terrorism would increase, and over 70 percent claiming that war would provoke "serious incidents" within France's Muslim population.[175] International events, such as massive anti-French, pro-Iraqi demonstrations in North Africa, Saddam Hussein's call for jihad, and the Iraqi leader's decision to fire missiles at Israel once war broke out, exacerbated such fears. According to one Marseille resident, "We buy sugar, the Arabs buy bullets." Or, in the words of another, "if [war] explodes, the police and army won't be able to do anything here."[176] In fact, the racist attacks went in the other direction; from Christmas 1990 to the beginning of 1991, anti-immigrant incidents were recorded in the Midi, Béziers, Nimes, Martigues, Istres, Paris, and the Haut-Rhin probably due to the rising heated rhetoric around "Arabs" in France.

Responding to mounting concerns, the Ministry of the Interior implemented the "Plan Vigipirate" in early January, increasing surveillance of airports, official buildings, public gathering places, mosques, and immigrant neighborhoods.[177] Systematic identity checks of North African Muslims facilitated greater connections in the public eye between Beurs and Saddam Hussein. Pro-Iraqi newspapers were banned, several suspected immigrant sympathizers were expelled, and three North African workers were removed from areas around Ain's nuclear power station to prevent sabotage. While President Mitterrand and other officials insisted that law-abiding Muslim residents had nothing to fear, such measures continued to draw negative attention to France's Muslim population.[178]

In this atmosphere, media outlets began predicting a clash between Jewish and Muslim communities, often portrayed as two well-organized bodies preparing to mobilize.[179] According to Marseille's chief rabbi, "an army of journalists invaded the city. . . . expect[ing] a violent confrontation between Arabs and Jews," while in Lyons, *L'Autre journal* told of "an abyss . . . widening between communities."[180] Muslim and Jewish religious leaders echoed these concerns, holding several ecumenical prayer services to stave off interethnic conflict,[181] while the UEJF augmented security in all chapters, and Marseille's Consistoire requested permission to arm key communal figures.[182] Meanwhile, imams used the last Friday before the UN withdrawal deadline of 15 January to call for calm, as did the Conseil national des français d'origine arabe.[183] "All our work to bring the communities together risks being wasted," lamented the French Algerian comedian Smaïn.[184]

The greatest casualty of the tense environment was the joint anti-racist coalition. Despite disagreements, SOS racisme and the UEJF had remained linked throughout the decade.[185] In 1991, however, the UEJF accused SOS racisme of breaking its "neutrality" agreement on the Middle East when the latter began participating in the anti-war movement.[186] In response, several Jewish patrons of the organization quit, including Bernard-Henri Lévy.[187] The UEJF, which had spent the late 1980s defending Israel on college campuses, formally resigned from SOS racisme after Iraq's scud attack on Israel.[188] While both organizations condemned the attack, SOS racisme stressed the importance of avoiding escalation, while the UEJF harshly criticized nations that compelled Israel to remain passive before an evident threat. In addition, the UEJF accused SOS racisme of "facilitating the identification of young French citizens of Maghrebian origin with Saddam Hussein," creating "major risks for intercommunal co-habitation and integration into French society."[189] As the UEJF president replied when asked if he believed that SOS racisme was responsible for the Beurs' attachment to Hussein: "They are not the only ones responsible, but they contributed." Noting that, "young French citizens of Arabic origins are mature and fully enough part of the French democratic universe to resist falling for the incitement of a dictator," he simultaneously implied that those who supported Hussein were not real democrats and hence not fully French.[190] By February, the UEJF was heavily engaged in a pro-Israel campaign, the publicity for which read, "We love Israel like we love liberty, democracy, courage, peace, or even France."[191] Here French citizenship and love for Israel were entangled, an implicit suggestion that to be pro-Arab and fully French was impossible.

The Gulf War, then, sounded the death knell of pluriculturalism. Following the head-scarf affair and the Carpentras cemetery desecration, Gulf War political posturing emphasized the distinctive paths of Muslims and Jews in French society. With SOS racisme and the UEJF having backed into opposing corners and with assertions of interethnic conflict dominating the media, cooperative anti-racist campaigns gave way to the decade's particularistic politics.

A similar process was evident "on the ground" as Muslim citizens were re-minded that despite the decade's lip service to pluriculturalism, they faced dis-tinctive challenges not shared by their Jewish neighbors. Once again, Marseille provides an excellent example of this wider phenomenon. The weeks around the Gulf War witnessed increasingly widespread fears of intercommunal vio-lence and intermittent aggression by some Muslim and Jewish residents, in-cluding one imam's threat that it was necessary to "persecute [Jews] until they disappear," and an unknown Zionist organization's claim to have detonated an explosion at an immigrant workers' hostel. Yet, as I have argued elsewhere, numerous communal spokesmen reminded their co-religionists that such ac-tions were marginal provocations in an otherwise peaceful city.[192] To under-score the point, the chief rabbi and several Islamic leaders took an active role in Marseille-Espérance, a multiconfessional and multiethnic body created in 1990 by Mayor Robert Vigouroux (elected after Defferre's death in 1986).[193] This organization's appeals for calm symbolically demonstrated that peaceful coex-istence was possible even in the most trying times, while the affiliation with the mayor's office opened lines of communication from the municipality to a wide range of religious and ethnic leaders, a distinct change from Defferre's one-sided wooing of Marseille's Jewish community.

Yet if such appeals contributed to the lack of violence in Marseille in winter 1991, they could not prevent Muslim residents' sense of betrayal during the Gulf War, often felt through direct comparison of their own experiences with those of their Jewish neighbors. Indeed, although Marseille's Jews expressed deep pain when Iraq dropped scud missiles on Tel Aviv, widespread Western support and France's decision to join the coalition and condemn the attack sug-gested that French and Jewish concerns were coinciding, easing fears among Jews who had long criticized France's "pro-Arab" policies.[194] Muslims felt no such sense of security. A poll in late January thus reported 58 percent voicing fears for their future and 73 percent fearing a rise in racism.[195] In Marseille, this insecurity manifested itself by a marked decrease in street life, a 60 percent drop in market activity, and low attendance at religious gatherings. Several ex-pulsions of Iraqi, Moroccan, Algerian, and Lebanese activists increased fears, as did the ongoing Vigipirate regulations. As police noted, "the expulsions' psy-chological impact are much greater than one might have imagined. . . . [I]t is thus a sense of fear and an attitude of discretion that dominates."[196]

Thus if in the months prior to the war both Muslims and Jews feared the war's potential ramifications in France, by March, Jewish fears had diminished. For Muslims, in contrast, increased surveillance raised fears that their future was in peril. For many, the 1980s had seen rapid political integration;[197] the sense of rejection that came with 1991 was thus all the more profound. As a prominent Muslim spokesman commented bitterly in a February interview in *Le Méridional*, there was a gap between the inclusive message being promoted by national leaders and its "every day transcription, lived poorly by Muslims."[198] Likewise police reported that Muslims in Marseille were "disappointed" with authorities, believing they had earned greater trust and "the official removal of all ambiguity regarding their citizenship."[199]

While the sense of insecurity engendered by the war explains the root of this alienation, comparisons with their Jewish neighbors played a part. By early March, police thus reported bitterness among Marseille's Muslims at having been considered "citizens of a second order . . . sacrificed to the Jewish community that had the benefit of a reassuring public discourse."[200] Indeed, during the war, Jewish connections to Israel were rarely questioned as authorities seemingly embraced the nation's Jewish minority.[201] For Muslims, in contrast, accusations of double loyalties emerged in force. These differences underscored the different positions of Muslims and Jews in contemporary France, further undermining the assertions of "sameness" that undergirded pluriculturalism.

Conclusion

The high-profile split between SOS racisme and the UEJF, and the erosion of Muslim-Jewish relations during the Gulf War meant that by the end of 1991 particularism had triumphed over pluriculturalism.[202] Among Beur activists, the pluricultural vision—insofar as it had ever been attractive—had become untenable. Due to the machinations of socialist politics, the Beur Movement was in crisis as associations disappeared and as the leadership retreated into professional careers away from the urban enclaves of their youth.[203] For the generation that followed, the urban landscape eroded even further. More disconnected from their countries of origin, this new generation—which adopted the verlan appellation of *rabeus* (an inversion of Beurs)—proved more politically apathetic and disenchanted with collective organization. In their eyes, the politics of pluriculturalism had failed. In its place, the rabeus turned to local affiliations around housing projects or joined transnational ethnic and religious social movements based in Berberist or Islamist politics, both of which rejected calls for integration.[204]

Jews also ended the decade disillusioned with pluriculturalism. Like the "rabeus," many children of North African Jewish immigrants drew into themselves, distancing themselves both from French and Muslim peers.[205] The UEJF, as we have seen, rejected pluricultural formulations. Its 1992 campaign, "I have two loves," featured posters of a baguette holding up an Israeli and French flag, proudly embracing the "dual loyalty" label for which Jews had so often been criticized. While making the mainstream Jewish leadership uncomfortable, the campaign shows how dramatically the student organization had moved away from pluricultural models.[206] Although the 1993 Oslo Accords brought the

UEJF into discussions with Peace Now, France plus, and even the PLO, leading to a publicity campaign that seemingly returned to pluricultural ideals in its celebration of tolerance and pluralism, the focus was entirely on the Middle East; minority politics in France were no longer part of the discussion.[207] After September 2000, when the UEJF once again allied with SOS racisme in an effort to restore peaceful interethnic relations after the outbreak of the second intifada, the two organizations would find themselves trying to undo a polarized landscape they themselves had helped to create.[208]

Conclusion

We end where we began in October 2000, when six Molotov cocktails thrown at a synagogue in Villepinte unleashed in France the violence some had feared would become a regular feature of interethnic relations following the Belleville riots in 1968. Annual statistics and detailed studies have subsequently confirmed mounting antisemitism among French Muslim youth, particularly in the urban banlieus where stereotypes of powerful and wealthy Jews circulate widely.[1] While analysts disagree as to the cause of this hostility, all agree that the year 2000 marked a turning point of significant consequence in which the forces that had previously kept violence at bay gave way to a new, more aggressive ethno-religious landscape.

For many the cause was self-evident. Increasing links between young French Muslims and their co-religionists in Palestine had brought the Middle Eastern conflict to France. Given that violence has increased significantly during moments of Middle East unrest, such as the outbreak of the second intifada, the battle in Jenin in April 2002, and the second Gulf War, such analyses made some intuitive sense. As we have seen, well before 2000, French Muslim youth had begun identifying with the Palestinian cause as a way to express their own social frustrations.[2] For those who feel marginalized and disenfranchised in France's poor urban neighborhoods, the Palestinian struggle for recognition has taken on symbolic meaning, allowing anger at Israel to become increasingly entangled with anti-Jewish stereotypes.[3] In a setting in which, as Esther Benbassa has argued, transnational identifications have taken on greater significance for *both* Muslims and Jews, interethnic relationships have become increasingly fraught.[4] Indeed, as more recent scholarship reminds us, Muslims and Jews have *both* moved away from republican models of cultural integration. Less interested in transnational affiliations, such work has emphasized the way shifts in French identity politics has led to more vocal and politicized minority expression, challenging republican norms in place since the Revolution.[5]

As the previous pages make clear, however, the origins of recent Muslim-Jewish tensions predate the year 2000 by several decades and are more mutual than a focus on the "new Judophobia" suggests.[6] The arguments here have been threefold. First, I have suggested that to understand fully the way Muslim-Jewish political conversations have evolved in France, we must begin in North

Africa in the decade and a half after World War II as France first tried to hold on to and then extricate itself from the region. Throughout the decolonization period, various political actors, including colonial administrators, international Jewish representatives, and indigenous nationalist leaders began singling out a "Jewish story" that emphasized a growing split from their Muslim neighbors. Given the diversity of the region and of the Muslim and Jewish populations therein, this focus on conflict necessarily oversimplified a landscape in which many Muslims and Jews cohabited with ease and even convivially. The emerging focus on a cross-regional Jewish problem just as independent states were breaking away from French colonial control, however, worked to create the very conflict it purported to describe by directing significant attention to the most highly politicized sectors of both populations and shaping conversations about Muslim-Jewish polarization long into the future. While bitterness over Jewish departures or Muslim aggression were not the *only* memories of ethnic relations to take root in France—nostalgic references to harmonious religious exchanges, cultural and linguistic affinities, and neighborly affections also remained a part of Muslim-Jewish life particularly in shared urban spaces following their initial arrival in France—the sense of rupture was profound. During moments of conflict, activists from both populations were easily drawn to this history with Jewish spokesmen reminding their co-religionists of Muslim aggression and their Muslim counterparts referring to Jewish affection for colonial oppressors.[7]

Moreover—and perhaps more importantly—the inequities of colonial administration in North Africa were replicated on French soil. While Muslim immigrants were trapped in a cycle of poverty passed on to their children, Jewish migrants experienced a much more rapid social ascent aided, in part, by a more favorable welcome by French authorities, such as was evident in Marseille. These differences meant that encounters between French Muslims and Jews never happened on an even playing field, helping to shape political choices thereafter, such as in the 1980s when joint anti-racist efforts collapsed in part over a sense that whatever Muslim and Jewish French citizens shared, their struggles were necessarily divergent.

This reference to French minority politics points to a second argument weaving through this text: disagreements over Middle Eastern war and the Israeli-Palestinian struggle cannot in and of themselves explain the evolution of Muslim-Jewish political conversations in France over the last fifty years. To be sure, the Middle East proved highly divisive. Beginning in 1948, when Zionist and Arab nationalist activists sparred in Marseille or in 1968 when Belleville was torn apart at the anniversary of the 1967 war, or in 1982 when the outbreak of the first Palestinian intifada led demonstrators in France to don kaffiyehs, disagreements over Israel sparked confrontations among highly politicized sectors of France's Muslim and Jewish populations. As I have argued, however, these conflicts were often about more than the Middle East, becoming a way of talking about inequities at home. Moreover, if "transnational diaspora affiliations" helped spur conflict since 2000, they were not the inevitable outcome of Israel's birth in 1948 or a necessary result of the encounter between Muslims and Jews in France. Rather, as the chapters on decolonization, 1968 French radical politics, and the 1980s experiments in multiculturalism make clear, the Arab-Israeli conflict often grew in local significance thanks to shifts in *French* political culture that shaped the choices of a wide range of social actors, including police charged with maintaining the social order; media personnel; self-appointed communal spokesmen; political militants on the French far left; international Jewish representatives; Algerian, Moroccan, and Tunisian nationalists; anti-racist activists; and so on. This diverse cast of characters established the parameters of Muslim-Jewish relations in France over several decades and out of a series of developments that were global but also national and local. Indeed, the continued focus on interethnic relations in Marseille has served to remind us of the local dimensions to an issue that is so often framed in terms of an inevitable sparring between "Arabs" and "Jews" wherever they reside. In Marseille, Muslim-Jewish relations were as much a reflection of political culture in the municipality; urban development programs; the struggle over limited resources; city geography; and entangled interethnic commercial networks as they were a reflection of developments in the Middle East. And when disagreements over Israel took center stage, they often served as a proxy for wider Muslim and Jewish political negotiations with the French state.

Lastly, I have stressed the powerful ways in which binary constructions of Muslim-Jewish interaction have worked to erase the more complex social terrain in which Muslims and Jews have interacted in late twentieth-century France. Here too, a brief return to Marseille helps illustrate this point. As numbers of Jews and Muslims grew in the port city in the 1950s and 1960s, their daily interactions were more diverse than a focus on polarization suggests. Just two years prior to the Gulf War and its widespread predictions of interethnic disturbances, local police described convivial relations between neighbors: "In Marseille, 90% of Jewish merchants are found in a quarter with a large percentage of North African [Muslims] and for many years, there have been good relations between these two communities."[8] One controversy from the period shows just how misleading language of political polarization can be. In 1988 and 1989, at the very moment pluriculturalism was collapsing as a rallying cry, a schism *within* Marseille's Jewish community led two synagogues and three kosher butchers to break away from consistorial control. In response, the consistorial leadership, which under French law controls the granting of kosher status to all vendors, revoked the butchers' certification. To get around the ban, the "dissidents" turned to Muslim slaughterers whose ritual techniques are similar to those of religious Jews and whose authorization was governed by Marseille's prefectorial authorities. A local imam even provided one shohet with a card authorizing him to slaughter and sell ritual meat.[9]

This temporary religious alliance between Muslims and Jews in response to an intercommunal conflict among Jews points to the weaknesses of "polarization" as a model for understanding Muslim-Jewish relations in France. Nevertheless, two years later, media outlets, local police, and communal spokesmen from both Muslim and Jewish organizations were predicting violent conflict if war broke out in the Middle East. In this construct, disagreements over possible outcomes in Kuwait overshadowed a longer history in which settlement patterns, relations to the municipality, economic inequities, colonial histories, religious traditions, and shared anti-racist struggles shaped the way peoples from different origins met and lived together.[10] Repeatedly, then, a reductionist-charged narrative of polarization has hidden a more complex set of social interactions, a phenomenon that helps explain why, despite all of the dire predictions, the city of Marseille never manifested the interethnic conflict that so many social commentators feared.

In tracing the way "Muslim-Jewish" has become shorthand for a rigid opposition politics that has obscured a more complex interethnic landscape, *Muslims and Jews in France* has thus sought to trace both the multifaceted origins of the charged political landscape and to underscore its powerful impact. While language of "conflict" may not accurately describe the daily interactions of most Muslims and Jews throughout the period under study, the emergence of this political landscape shaped the parameters of public discourse and narrowed the range of choices available to those representing communal life. The marked rise in anti-Jewish violence in 2000 emerged from this history of narrowing political categories and also helped solidify them, meaning that whatever the diversity of social life on the ground, Muslim-Jewish conflict is likely to remain a salient feature of French political life for the foreseeable future.

ABBREVIATIONS

Archives

AJDC	American Jewish Joint Distribution Committee
AIU	Alliance israélite universelle
AJC	American Jewish Committee
AN	Archives nationale
APP	Archives du Prefecture de police de Paris
BdR	Archives départementales des Bouches-du-Rhône
CAC	Centre des archives contemporaines
CC	Consistoire centrale
CJDC	Centre de documentation juive contemporaine
MAE	Archives diplomatiques, Ministère des affaires étrangères
UEJF	Union des étudiants juifs de France

Abbreviations in Notes

AE	*Algérien en Europe*
ADAM	Archives de la délégation de l'AIU au Maroc
AL	1944–59 Afrique-Levant, 1944–1959
BIL	*Bulletin d'information et de liaison du Comité de coordination des organisations juives de France*
FJL	Fonds Jacques Lazarus
IPFL 1	944–65 Inventaire provisoire du fonds Levant 1944–1965
GILR	Groupe d'information et de liaison régional, région de Provence-Côte d'Azur
MAMT	Ministre des affaires marocaines et tunisiennes
MI	Ministère de l'intérieur
ME	Ministère des affaires étrangères
Préfet des BdR	Préfet des Bouches-du-Rhône
RG	Renseignements généraux (all references to the Service départemental des renseignements généraux, the Direction des renseignements généraux, or the Direction centrale des renseignements généraux, will be designated RG).
SEAA	Secrétariat d'état aux affaires algériennes
SG/1948	Séries géographiques après 1948

Introduction

1. Although of mixed-ethnic origin, the gang that murdered Halimi was led by Parisian-born Youssouf Fofana and reportedly read Koranic verses while torturing their victim. For a recent study of growing Jewish racism, see Kimberly Arkin, " 'It's the French and the Arabs against the Jews': Identity Politics and the Construction of Adolescent Jewishness in France" (Ph.D. diss., University of Chicago, 2008).

2. Citation is from Raphaël Draï, *Sous le signe de Sion: L'antisémitisme nouveau est arrivé* (Paris: Éditions Michalon, 2001), p. 14.

3. Those who make the case for a new form of antisemitism include, Michael Berenbaum ed. *Not Your Father's Antisemitism: Hatred of the Jews in the Twenty-first Century* (St. Paul, Minn.: Paragon House, 2008); Alain Finkielkraut, *Au nom de l'autre: Réflexions sur l'antisémitisme qui vient* (Paris: Gallimard, 2003); Raphael Israeli, *Muslim Anti-Semitism in Christian Europe* (New Brunswick: Transaction Publishers, 2009); Pierre-André Taguieff, *La nouvelle judéophobie* (Paris: Mille et une nuits, 2002); and Shmuel Trigano, *La démission de la République: Juifs et Musulmans en France* (Paris: Presses universitaires de France, 2003). In contrast are those who question both the "newness" of recent anti-Jewish violence and the level of threat it poses. See, for example, Anthony Lerman, "Sense on Antisemitism," in *A New Antisemitism? Debating Judeophobia in 21st Century Britain*, eds. Paul Iganski and Barry Kosmin (London: Institute for Jewish Policy Research, 2003): 54–67 and Amikam Nachmani, " 'The Triangle': Europeans, Muslims, Jews," in *Muslim Attitudes to Jews and Israel: The Ambivalences of Rejection, Antagonism, Tolerance and Cooperation*, ed., Moshe Ma'oz (Portland: Sussex Academic Press 2010): 264–84. Matti Bunzl, *Anti-Semitism and Islamophobia: Hatreds Old and New in Europe* (Prickly Paradigm Press, 2007), provides a helpful critique of this debate.

4. For the former, see Esther Benbassa, *La République face à ses minorités: Les Juifs hier, les Musulmans aujourd'hui* (Paris: Mille et une nuits, 2004). For the latter, see Jean-Marc Dreyfus and Jonathan Laurence, "Anti-Semitism in France," *U.S.-France Analysis*, 14 May 2002; Jonathan Laurence and Justin Vaisse, *Integrating Islam: Political and Religious Challenges in Contemporary France* (Washington, D.C.: Brookings Institution Press, 2006), pp. 222–43; Denis Sieffert, *Israël-Palestine, une passion française: La France dans le miroir du conflit israélo-palestinien* (Paris: Éditions la Découverte, 2004), pp. 212–30. For Jews, Arkin " 'It's the French and the Arabs against the Jews.' "

5. More nuanced analyses include Michel Wieviorka's, *La tentation antisémite: Haine des Juifs dans la France d'aujourd'hui* (Paris: Robert Laffont, 2005), which debunks the link between Islam and antisemitism and posits that antagonism will recede with the alleviation of socioeconomic inequities, and Ethan Katz, "Jews and Muslims in

the Shadow of Marianne: Conflicting Identities and Republican Culture in France (1914–1975)" (Ph.D. diss., University of Wisconsin–Madison, 2009), which explores the long and rich historical connections between Muslims and Jews in France.

6. French law prohibits census takers from distinguishing among citizens based on religion, meaning estimates of the Jewish and Muslim populations vary widely. In the early 1980s, Doris Bensimon and Sergio Della Pergola, *La population juive de France: Socio-démographie et identité* (Jerusalem, The Institute of Contemporary Jewry, Hebrew University, 1984), p. 25, put the number of Jews at 535,000. Erik H. Cohen, *The Jews of France Today: Identity and Values* (Leiden and Boston: Brill, 2011), pp. 59–63, estimates the number today at 500,000–550,000. For lower estimates on Muslims, see Michèle Tribalat, "Counting France's Numbers—Deflating the Numbers Inflation," *The Social Contract Journal* 14, 2 (Winter 2003–2004), http://www.thesocialcontract.com/artman2/publish/tsc1402/article_1210.shtml (last accessed 2 January 2013). In 2000, the French Ministry of the Interior, *L'Islam dans la République* (Haut conseil à l'intégration, November 2000), p. 26, claimed 4.1 million. Politicians on the far right claim as many as 6–8 million. See Laurence and Vaïsse, *Integrating Islam,* 17–22, who settle on 5 million, for more on this debate.

7. For linguistic and cultural similarities, see Arkin, "'It's the French and the Arabs against the Jews,'" 171. For comparisons of Muslim and Jewish integration into French society, see Martine Cohen, "Juifs et Musulmans en France: Le modèle républicain d'intégration en question," *Sociétés contemporaines* 37 (2000): 89–120; "Laïcité et intégration des vagues migratoires juives et musulmanes en France: Du cadre national à la mondialisation," in *Politiques de la laïcité au XXe siècle,* ed. Patrick Weil (Paris: Presses universitaires de France, 2007): 571–89; "Jews and Muslims in France: Changing Responses to Cultural and Religious Diversity," in *Legal Practice and Cultural Diversity,* ed. Ralph Grillo (London: Ashgate, 2009): 219–36; Rémy Leveau and Dominique Schnapper, *Religion et politique: Juifs et Musulmans maghrébins en France* (Paris: Association française de science politique and the Centre d'études et de recherches internationales, 1987); and William Safran, "Ethnoreligious Politics in France: Jews and Muslims," *West European Politics* 27, 3 (May 2004): 423–51. Shmuel Trigano challenges the legitimacy of such comparisons in "Les logiques perverses de la politique française," *Observatoire du monde juif,* November 2000, pp. 22–28 and elsewhere. For links between antisemitism and other forms of racism in France, see Gérard Noiriel, *Immigration, antisémitisme et racisme en France (XIX–XX siècle): Discours publics, humiliations privées* (Paris: Fayard, 2007). Yvan Gastaut, *L'Immigration et l'opinion en France sous la Ve République* (Paris: Éditions du Seuil, 2000), insists, in contrast, on the singularity of anti-Muslim attitudes in France.

8. As Ethan Katz, "Jews and Muslims," 44–235, has convincingly argued, colonialism, nationalism, and French minority policies began shaping the contours of Muslim-Jewish relations by World War I. My focus on a later period, however, reflects my sense of the seismic impact of decolonization on subsequent Muslim-Jewish politics in the metropole.

9. Joëlle Bahloul, *The Architecture of Memory: A Jewish-Muslim Household in Colonial Algeria, 1936–1962,* trans. Catherine du Peloux Ménagé (Cambridge University Press, 1996), p. 85.

10. A Middle-Eastern focus is common. For example, according to Henry Weinberg, "French Jewry: Trauma and Renewal," *Midstream* (December 1982), p. 12: "In the end, the place of Jews in French society will to a large extent be determined in a region distant from France's boundaries." Doris Bensimon, *Les Juifs de France et leurs relations avec Israël, 1945–1988* (Paris: Éditions l'Harmattan, 1989), p. 237, asserts that Jews and Muslims were "too implicated" in the Israeli-Arab conflict to establish a legitimate dialogue.

11. For the significance of North African history to the postcolonial migrant experience, see Sayad Abdelmalek, *La double absence: Des illusions de l'émigré aux souffrances de l'immigré* (Paris: Seuil, "Liber", 1999), p. 56.

12. Patrick Weil, *La France et ses étrangers: L'aventure d'une politique de l'immigration de 1938 à nos jours*, 1st ed. (Paris: Calmann-Lévy, 1991), pp. 41–128. By 1975, newcomers made up 6.5 percent of the French population. Noiriel, *Immigration, antisémitisme et racisme*, 484.

13. Figures come from Neil MacMaster, *Colonial Migrants and Racism: Algerians in France, 1900–62* (New York: St. Martin's Press, 1997), pp. 3, 189, and Benjamin Stora, *Ils venaient d'Algérie: L'immigration en France (1912–1992)* (Paris: Fayard, 1992), pp. 94, 401. The citation is from Belkacem Hifi, *L'immigration algérienne en France: Origines et perspectives de non-retour* (Paris: l'Harmattan CIEM, 1985), p. 171.

14. Noiriel, *Immigration, antisémitisme et racisme*, 543.

15. Bensimon and Della Pergola, *La population juive de France*, 36. Also see Jacques Taïeb, "Immigrés d'Afrique du Nord: Combien? quand? pourquoi?" in *Terre d'exil terre d'asile: Migrations juives en France aux XIXe et XXe siècles*, ed. Colette Zytnicki (Paris: Éditions de l'Éclat): 149–54.

16. Véronique Poirier, *Ashkénazes et Séfarades: Une étude comparée de leurs relations en France et en Israël* (Paris: Cerf, 1998); Sarah Sussman, "Changing Lands, Changing Identities: The Migration of Algerian Jewry to France, 1954–1967" (Ph.D. diss., Stanford University, 2003), pp. 321–64.

17. Pierre Baillet, "Les rapatriés d'Algérie en France," *Notes et études documentaires*, No. 4275–76 (29 March 1976), pp. 46–57. As Clifford Rosenberg, *Policing Paris: The Origins of Modern Immigration Control Between the Wars* (Ithaca: Cornell University Press 2006), makes clear, if inequities toward Muslims were embedded throughout the colonial project, they were not only "imported" to France but also emerged out of metropolitan efforts to define citizenship and belonging under the Third Republic.

18. For Morocco, see Jonathan Wyrtzen, "Constructing Morocco: Colonial Struggle to Define the Nation, 1912–1956" (PhD. diss., Georgetown University, 2009), pp. 39–83. For Tunisia, see Richard C. Parks, "Hygiene, Regeneration, and Citizenship: Jews in the Tunisian Protectorate" (Ph.D. diss., University of Minnesota, 2012). For the power of French ethnic constructions in Algeria, see Paul Silverstein, *Algeria in France: Transpolitics, Race, and Nation* (Bloomington: Indiana University Press, 2004), pp. 35–67, and Patricia Lorcin, *Imperial Identities: Stereotyping, Prejudice and Race in Colonial Algeria* (London: I. B. Tauris, 1995) and *Kabyles, Arabes, Français: Identités coloniales* (Limoges: Presses universitaires de Limoges, 2005).

19. Joshua Schreier, *Arabs of the Jewish Faith: The Civilizing Mission in Colonial Algeria* (Piscataway, N.J.: Rutgers University Press, 2010) argues that Jewish "worthiness" for emancipation was used to exclude Muslims who were seen as comparatively less able to become French.

20. Arkin, "It's the French and the Arabs," chap. 1, nicely synthesizes this history while underscoring the blocks preventing complete Jewish integration into French colonial society. Pathways to citizenship existed for certain Jews, particularly in Tunisia where several thousand were naturalized primarily in the 1920s and early 1930s despite French colonial administrators' opposition to blanket naturalization. See Parks, "Hygiene, Regeneration, and Citizenship," 34–37, 98–100. Fayçel Cherif, "Jewish-Muslim Relations in Tunisia during World War II: Propaganda, Stereotypes, and Attitudes, 1939–1943," in *Jewish Culture and Society in North Africa*, eds. Emily Benichou Gotreich and Daniel Schroeter (Bloomington: Indiana University Press, 2011), p. 314, reports 7,160 Jewish naturalizations from 1911 to 1940. In Morocco, the rules against naturalization were tighter. André Chouraqui, *Histoire des Juifs en Afrique du Nord: Le retour en orient* (Monaco: Éditions du Rocher, 1998), p. 39.

21. Citation from Noiriel, *Immigration, antisémitisme, et racisme*, 537. For ongoing administrative limitations on Algerians, see Abdelmalek Sayad, Jean-Jacques Jordi, and Émile Témime, *Le Choc de la décolonisation (1945–1990)*, vol. 4 of *Migrance: Histoire des migrations à Marseille*, ed. Émile Témime (Aix-en-Provence: Éditions Jeanne Laffitte, 1991), pp. 48, 187–78, and Emmanuel Blanchard, *La police parisienne et les Algériens (1944–1962)* (Paris: Nouveau monde éditions, 2010). Amelia Lyons, "Invisible Immigrants: Algerian Families and the French Welfare State in the Era of Decolonization (1947–1974)" (Ph.D. diss., University of California–Irvine, 2004), pp. 9, 40–49, argues that prior to 1962, welfare institutions did seek to incorporate Algerian Muslims into French society.

22. Todd Shepard, *The Invention of Decolonization: The Algerian War and the Remaking of France* (Ithaca/London: Cornell University Press, 2006), pp. 39–43, 172–73.

23. For Algerian Jewish settlement, see Sussman, "Changing Lands, Changing Identities," 188–89. Alexis Spire, *Étrangers à la carte: L'administration de l'immigration en France (1945–1975)* (Paris: Grasset, 2005), pp. 189–222, shows how even Muslim repatriates who had fought for the French army were treated as administratively distinct from "European" repatriates. Fatima Besnaci-Lancou and Gilles Manceron eds., *Les harkis: Dans la colonisation et ses suites* (Paris: Les Éditions de l'Atelier, 2008), pp. 30–31, 112. Tom Charbit, *Les harkis* (Paris: La Découverte, 2006), pp. 60–61. For aid to repatriates, see Jean Jacques Jordi, *De l'exode à l'exil: Rapatriés et pieds-noirs en France* (Paris: Éditions l'Harmattan, 1993) and *1962, L'Arrivée des pieds-noirs* (Paris: Autrement, 1995).

24. Robert Lever, "Finding the Promised Land," *Present Tense*, January–February 1989, pp. 33–35. Martin Messika, "L'accueil des Juifs marocains en France," in *Terre d'exil, terre d'asile*, 175–78.

25. Maud Mandel, *In the Aftermath of Genocide: Armenians and Jews in Twentieth-Century France* (Durham: Duke University Press, 2003).

26. Mônica Raisa Schpun, "Les premiers migrants Juifs d'Afrique du Nord dans la France de l'après guerre: Une découverte pour les services sociaux," and Laura Hobson Faure, "Le travail social dans les organisations juives françaises après la Shoah: Création made in France ou importation Américaine," *Archives juives* 42, 1 (2012): 43–73; Colette Zytnicki, "A immigration d'un nouveau type, réponses nouvelles: Les organisations communautaires et l'exodes des Juifs d'Afrique du Nord," in *Terre d'exil, terre d'asile*, 155–70. Conflict between incoming North African Jews and their

French Jewish co-religionists is documented in Poirier, *Ashkénazes et Séfarades*; Sussman, "Changing Lands," 321–64. For organizational efforts to fight antisemitism, see Samuel Ghiles-Meilhac, "From an Unsolvable Dispute to a Unifying Compromise: Zionism at the Heart of the Debates Underlying the Creation of the French Jewish Umbrella Organization, the CRIF," *Bulletin du centre de recherche français à Jérusalem*, 20 (2009), http://bcrfj.revues.org/6196 (last accessed on 26 June 2012).

27. Stora, *Ils venaient d'Algérie*.

28. The inclusion of Arabic sources would likely enhance the picture of how Muslim discourses on Jews shifted over time and place, particularly in chapter 2, which deals with North African decolonization. However, given my focus on discourses of conflict in mainland France (where very few Arabic archival sources were produced), the absence is less significant than it would be for a study rooted in North Africa.

29. For the shifting Jewish economic and professional profile, see Cohen *The Jews of France Today*, 67–72.

30. Noiriel, *Immigration, antisémitisme et racisme en France*, 622–24.

31. Joan Scott, *Politics of the Veil* (Princeton: Princeton University Press, 2007), pp. 1–2.

32. Arkin, "It's the French and the Arabs," 207–17; Pierre Birnbaum, *Jewish Destinies: Citizenship, State and Community in Modern France*, trans. Arthur Goldhammer (New York: Hill and Wang, 2000), pp. 191–213.

33. For divisions before the war, see Nancy Green, *The Pletzl of Paris: Jewish Immigrant Workers in the Belle Époque* (New York: Holmes and Meier, 1986); Paula Hyman, *From Dreyfus to Vichy: The Remaking of French Jewry, 1906–1939* (New York: Columbia University Press, 1979); and David H. Weinberg, *A Community on Trial: The Jews of Paris in the 1930s* (Chicago: University of Chicago Press, 1977). Nadia Malinovich, *French and Jewish: Culture and the Politics of Identity in Early Twentieth-Century France* (Oxford: Littman Library of Jewish Civilization, 2008), pp. 5–6, 109–14, argues that such divisions have been too starkly drawn. As noted, Poirier, *Ashkénazes et Séfarades* and Sussman, "Changing Lands," 321–64, document tensions between Jews settled in France and those incoming in the 1950s–1970s.

34. Laurence and Vaïsse, *Integrating Islam*, 7, 15–48.

35. Silverstein, *Algeria in France*, 130.

36. The majority of initial Algerian migrants were Kabyles, a mountain-dwelling people of Berber descent. When more Algerian Arabs began arriving in the interwar years, tensions emerged between them and their predecessors, as did tensions between Algerians and those from other North African countries. Macmaster, *Colonial Migrants*, passim, and Stora, *Ils venaient d'Algérie*, 13–74.

37. Abdellali Hajjat, "Les usages politiques de l'héritage colonial," in *Immigrances: L'immigration en France au XXème siècle*, ed., Émile Temime (Paris: Hachette littératures, 2007), pp. 198–99.

38. Laurence and Vaïsse, *Integrating Islam*, 16. Benjamin Stora, *Ils venaient d'Algérie*, 117–18, reminds us that Arabic and Islam also created bridges.

39. Dominique Schnapper, Chantal Bordes-Benayoun, and Freddy Raphaël, *Jewish Citizenship in France: The Temptation of Being among One's Own*, trans., Catherine Temerson (New Brunswick and London: Transaction Publishers, 2010), pp. 13–16, 111, argue that although many French Jews still speak of Ashkenazic and Sephardic divisions, modes of identity and political expression do not differ substantially between those identifying with either group.

40. Joyce Dalsheim, "On Demonized Muslims and Vilified Jews: Between Theory and Politics," *Comparative Studies in Society and History* 52, 3 (2010), p. 586, n. 11. Thanks to Ethan Katz for directing me to this article.

41. Naomi Davidson, *Only Muslim: Embodying Islam in Twentieth-Century France* (Ithaca and London: Cornell University Press, 2012), p. 4 and passim.

42. Shepard, *The Invention of Decolonization*, 238. Shepard and Davidson disagree as to the timing of this process, with Davidson emphasizing the interwar and World War II period, and Shepard emphasizing the Algerian war.

43. Mandel, *In the Aftermath of Genocide*, 151–77.

44. Blanchard, *La police parisienne et les Algériens* 36–40.

45. For the stereotypes associated with the label "Arab," see Gastaut, *L'Immigration et l'opinion*, 109. For North African Muslim attraction to Arab political causes, see Rabah Aissaoui, *Immigration and National Identity: North African Political Movements in Colonial and Postcolonial France* (London and New York: Tauris Academic Studies, 2009) and Abdellali Hajjat, "Les Comités Palestine (1970–1972): Aux origines du soutien de la cause palestinienne en France," *Revue d'études palestiniennes*, 98 (Winter 2006): 74–92, and "L'expérience politique du mouvement des travailleurs arabes," *Contretemps* 16 (May 2006): 76–85. For a combined revision of these two articles see "Des Comités Palestine au Mouvement des travailleurs arabes (1970–1976)," in Ahmed Boubeker and Abdellali Hajjat, eds., *Histoire politique des immigrations (post) coloniales: France, 1920–2008* (Paris: Éditions Amsterdam, 2008): 145–56.

46. Silverstein, *Algeria in France*, 106, 108; Noiriel, *Immigration, antisémitisme et racisme,* 611–13; Gastaut, *L'immigration et l'opinion*, 478–512.

47. Demographers, sociologists, and historians have suggested that the saliency of Islam among those of North African Muslim heritage has intensified in recent decades. For a summary of this literature, see "Muslims in the EU: Cities Report, Preliminary Research Report and Literature Survey, France" (Grenoble: Open Society Institute EU Monitoring and Advocacy Program, 2007), pp. 19–27.

48. The first figure comes from Marie Attard-Maraninchi and Émile Témime, *Le cosmopolitisme de l'entre-deux-guerres (1919–1945)*, vol. 3 of *Migrance: Histoire des migrations à Marseille*, ed., Émile Témime (Aix-en-Provence: Édisud, 1990), p. 160. The latter come from Sayad, Jordi, and Témime, *Le Choc*, 8, 61–64, 89–98.

49. Jean-Jacques Jordi, "L'été 62 à Marseille: Tensions et incompréhensions," in *Marseille et le choc des décolonisations: Les rapatriements, 1954–1964*, eds., Jean-Jacques Jordi and Émile Témime (Aix-en-Provence: Édisud, 1996), p. 73. Émile Témime, *Histoire de Marseille de la Révolution à nos jours* (Perrin 1999), p. 330. Algerians made up 30,190 of the 35,860 Muslims in 1968. By 1974, they were still the majority, but the number of Tunisians and Moroccans had grown. Institut national d'études démographiques, Universités de Lyon II et III, Aix-Marseille I et Poitiers, *Immigrés du Maghreb: Études sur l'adaptation en milieu urbain* (Paris: Presses universitaires de France, 1977), pp. 10, 13. Sayad, Jordi, and Témime, *Le Choc*, 121, claim 44,000 Muslims in Marseille in 1975.

50. Statistics from 1945 come from Roland Avitol, "Marseille," *L'Arche* (March/April, 1968): 19–20, and from Donna F. Ryan, *The Holocaust & the Jews of Marseille: The Enforcement of Anti-Semitic Policies in Vichy France* (Urbana and Chicago: University of Illinois Press, 1996), p. 13. The figure of 12,000 comes from the FSJU and is included in Julian Breen to Boris Sapir, 15 February 1963, 309, AJDC. Avitol put the figure at 15,000 as did Jacques Sabbath, "Communauté vivante," *L'Arche*, November

1962, pp. 2–4. The city's Jewish demographics in the late 1950s are documented in an untitled report, November 1964, 346, AJDC.

51. Préfet de la région de Provence to RG, "La communauté juive de Marseille," 17 January 1972, 135W57, BdR, claimed 75,000 Jews in Marseille by the early 1970s. However, Bensimon-Donath, *L'intégration des Juifs*, 55, reports 65,000 in 1966. Some reports put the population as high as 100,000 in 1967, perhaps due to transients. R.G., Mle, "Milieux juifs," 30 May 1967, 137W363, BdR. For Algerian Jewish repatriation, see, Sussman, "Changing Lands," 188–245.

52. Yvan Gastaut, "Marseille cosmopolite après les décolonisations: Un enjeu identitaire," *Cahiers de la Méditerranée* 67 (2003), http://cdlm.revues.org/index134.html#bodyftn17 (last accessed 6 August 2012).

53. For the impact of Marseille's urban development pattern on ethnic collectivities, see Cesari, *Être musulman en France*, 71, and Katharyne Mitchell, "Marseille's Not for Burning: Comparative Networks of Integration and Exclusion in Two French Cities," *Annals of the Association of American Geographers* 101, 2 (2011), p. 414.

54. Témime, *Histoire de Marseille*, 366–67; INED, *Immigrés du Maghreb*, 17–19.

55. Émile Témime, *Marseille transit: Les passagers de Belsunce* (Paris: Éditions Autrement, 1995), p. 19; Mitchell, "Marseille's Not for Burning," 412–13.

56. Jean André Carreno, Alain Hayot, and Francis Lesme, *Le quartier de la porte d'Aix à Marseille: Ethnologie d'un centre urbain* (Aix-en-Provence: Université de Provence, 1974), p. 15, make clear that notwithstanding the large numbers of immigrants in these neighborhoods, the majority were "French." Jocelyne Cesari, Alain Moreau, and Alexandra Schleyer-Lindenmann, *"Plus marseillais que moi, tu meurs!" Migrations, identités et territoires à Marseille* (Paris: L'Harmattan, 2001), pp. 20–21, 121, argue that while economic and social cleavages divide northern sectors to this day, all residents consider themselves part of the city and have spent considerable time in its center.

57. Sayad, Jordi, and Témime, *Le Choc*, 11, 124.

58. Témime, *Marseille transit*, 12. For Belleville, see Patrick Simon and Claude Tapia, *Le Belleville des Juifs tunisiens* (Paris: Éditions Autrement, 1998).

59. Francis Lesme, *Provence, Bulletin de l'association des anciens élèves*, Marseille, n. 4, May 1972, cited in Gastaut, "Marseille cosmopolite après les décolonisations." Gastaut makes clear that despite its image of convivial cosmopolitan intermingling, the city experienced plenty of racist extremism.

60. Mitchell, "Marseille's Not for Burning," links the city's ethnically networked capitalist system with its urban development to help explain the relatively peaceful ethnic landscape.

61. Claire Berlinski, "The Hope of Marseille," *Azure* 19 (Winter 5765/2005), p. 38.

Chapter 1. Colonial Policies, Middle Eastern War, and City Spaces: Marseille in 1948

1. Telegram, Cairo to Département de Levant, 14 June 1948, IPFL 1944–65, 401, MAE. The source in this instance refers to "North African dockworkers" and not "Muslims" as such. See the Introduction for clarification of my use of terminology.

2. RG, Mle, "L'affaire palestinienne," 28 January 1949, 148W185, BdR.

3. Idith Zertal, *From Catastrophe to Power: Holocaust Survivors and the Emergence of Israel* (Berkeley: University of California Press, 1998), pp. 52–53. Émile Témime, *Histoire de Marseille de la Révolution à nos jours* (Perrin 1999), p. 329, puts the number at 15,000.

4. By 1954, Algerian Muslims numbered 210,000 throughout the country, mostly in Paris. Abdelmalek Sayad, Jean-Jacques Jordi, and Émile Témime, *Le choc de la décolonisation (1945–1990)*, vol. 4 of *Migrance: Histoire des migrations à Marseille*, ed. Émile Témime (Aix-en-Provence: Éditions Jeanne Laffitte, 1991), p. 49; Benjamin Stora, *Ils venaient d'Algérie: L'immigration en France (1912–1992)* (Paris: Fayard, 1992), p. 143.

5. Sayad, Jordi, and Témime, *Le Choc,* 40; 48, 187–88, and Todd Shepard, *The Invention of Decolonization: The Algerian War and the Remaking of France* (Ithaca and London: Cornell University Press, 2006), pp. 39–43.

6. RG, Mle, 6 September 1950, 148W191, BdR. As Sayad, Jordi, and Témime, *Le Choc,* 70–71, make clear, Marseille was never the center of Algerian political mobilization in France thanks to the size and transience of its Algerian Muslim population.

7. Although on record for backing Jewish national ambitions after the 1917 Balfour Declaration, French diplomats had, since the 1920s, expressed concern that support for Zionism would alienate their Muslim subjects and promote Arab nationalism. Tsilla Herscho, *Entre Paris et Jérusalem: La France, le Sionisme et la création de l'État d'Israël, 1945–1949,* trans. from Hebrew by Claire Darmon (Paris: Honoré Champion, 2003), p. 16; Catherine Nicault, *La France et le Sionisme, 1897–1948* (Paris: Calmann-Lévy, 1992), pp. 158–72; Denis Sieffert, *Israël-Palestine: Une passion française* (Paris: La Découverte, 2004), pp. 56–57. Jonathan Wyrtzen, "Constructing Morocco: Colonial Struggle to Define the Nation, 1912–1956" (Ph.D. diss., Georgetown University, 2009), pp. 39–83, 224, 231, 234–38, traces these fears in Morocco.

8. Zertal, *From Catastrophe to Power,* 52–92. Herscho, *Entre Paris et Jérusalem,* 31–32 notes that some foreign ministry officials favored moderate migration to Palestine (and elsewhere) to encourage Jewish departures from France.

9. "Le problème palestinien: La fin éventuelle du mandat et les intérêts français" (1947), IPFL 1944–65, 373, L.72.1, MAE.

10. Examples of such concerns include Gabriel Puaux to Monsieur le Général d'armée, "Émigration juive vers la Palestine," 8 November 1944, IPFL 1944–65; "Note sur l'attitude française à l'égard de la Déclaration Balfour et du Sionisme," 13 July 1946, IPFL 1944–65, 373, L.72.1; Note pour le ministre, "Installation en France d'un gouvernement exilé de la Palestine hébraïque," no date, IPFL 1944–65, 23, K.13.7, MAE.

11. "Note pour le ministre," 8 April 1947, 30, G3, MAE.

12. Tsilla Herschco, "France and the Partition Plan: 1947–8," *Israel Affairs,* 14, 3 (July 2008): 486–98.

13. Jacques Dalloz, *Georges Bidault: Biographie politique* (Éditions l'Harmattan, 1992), p. 273.

14. "Question étrangères," and "Entrée clandestine en France de Juifs en provenance de camps de concentration allemands," Direction générale de la sûreté nationale, 13 September 1946, f/1a/3368, AN; RG, Mle, "Activité du service social de la Fédération des sociétés juives de France à Marseille," 13 May 1947, 148W185, BdR; Zertal, *From Catastrophe to Power,* 52–92; Herscho, *Entre Paris et Jerusalem,* 20–44, 59–62, 69–70.

15. Direction d'Afrique-Levant to Direction des conventions administratives et sociales, "Émigration clandestine vers la Palestine et activité en France d'organisations sionistes," no date, IPFL 1944-65, 376, L.72.2, MAE.

16. Ambassadeur de France en Grande Bretagne to Bidault, "Camp d'entraînement pour combattants juifs en France," 5 July 1948, IPFL 1944-65, 401, MAE. As Mônica Raisa Schpun, "Les premières migrants juifs d'Afrique du Nord dans la France de l'après-guerre: Une découverte pour les services sociaux," *Archives juives* 45, 1 (2012): 61–73, makes clear, a significant percentage of North African Jews who went to Israel returned home and some who went were already living in France.

17. Yves Chataigneau to MI, "Sionisme," 2 November 1946, AL 1944-59, 5, K.38.2, MAE; RG, Mle, "Activité des Juifs d'Algérie en faveur des Sionistes," 10 June 1948, 148W185, BdR; E. de Beauverger to ME, "Départs israélites pour la Palestine, via France," 3 February (1948?), IPFL 1944-65, 376, 72.2, MAE.

18. Paula Hyman, *The Jews of Modern France* (Berkeley: University of California Press, 1998), p. 137.

19. Neil MacMaster, *Colonial Migrants and Racism: Algerians in France, 1900-1962* (New York: St. Martin's Press, 1997), p. 223.

20. Esther Benbassa, *Jews of France: A History from Antiquity to the Present*, trans. M. B. DeBevoise (Princeton: Princeton University Press, 1999), p. 149.

21. Ethan Katz, "Tracing the Shadow of Palestine: The Zionist-Arab Conflict and Jewish-Muslim Relations in France, 1914-1945," in *Israeli-Palestinian Conflict in the Francophone World*, ed., Nathalie Debrauwere-Miller (Routledge, 2009): 25–40.

22. Unless otherwise noted, discussion of the period prior to and during World War II is drawn from Ethan Katz, "Jews and Muslims in the Shadow of Marianne: Conflicting Identities and Republican Culture in France, 1914–1975" (Ph.D. diss., University of Wisconsin, 2008), pp. 44–235.

23. For Jewish life after World War II, see Mandel, *In the Aftermath of Genocide*.

24. Blanchard, *La police parisienne*, 17–18.

25. Patrick Weil, *Qu'est-ce qu'un Français? Histoire de la nationalité française depuis la Révolution* (Paris: Bernard Grasset: 2002), p. 243.

26. Sayad, Jordi, and Témime, *Le Choc*, 40, 48, 187–88. Shepard, *The Invention of Decolonization*, 39–43, argues that while the category *citoyens français musulmans d'Algérie* emerges from 1944–46, it was not given a legally binding definition until 1956. Also see Blanchard, *La police parisienne*, 20–27.

27. Accounts of French Zionism vary between those who stress its initial institutional weakness and those who underscore its long-term impact on ethnic cohesion. For the former, see Nicault, *La France et le Sionisme*. For the latter, see Michel Abitbol, *Les deux terres promises: Les Juifs de France et le Sionisme, 1897–1945* (Paris: Orban, 1989); Paula Hyman, *From Dreyfus to Vichy: The Remaking of French Jewry, 1906-1939* (New York: Columbia University Press 1979), chap. 6; Nadia Malinovich, *French and Jewish: Culture and the Politics of Identity in early Twentieth-Century France* (Oxford: Litmann Library of Jewish Civilization, 2007), pp. 57–67; Aron Rodrigue, "Rearticulations of French Jewish Identities after the Dreyfus Affair," *Jewish Social Studies* 2, 3 (1996): 1–24.

28. For French Zionism after World War II, see Mandel, *In the Aftermath of Genocide*, 134–48; Hershco, *Entre Paris et Jérusalem*, pp. 21–22, 57–74; Nicault, *La France et le*

Sionisme, 207–230; Renée Poznanski, "Le Sionisme en France pendant la deuxième guerre mondiale: Développements institutionnels et impact idéologique," in *Les Juifs de France, le sionisme et l'État d'Israël*, eds., Doris Bensimon and Benjamin Pinkus (Paris: Publications Langues'O, 1989), p. 212.

29. Poznanski, "Le Sionisme en France," pp. 212, 265–70; Samuel Ghiles-Meilhac, "From an Unsolvable Dispute to a Unifying Compromise: Zionism at the Heart of the Debates Underlying the Creation of the French Jewish Umbrella Organization, the CRIF," *Bulletin du Centre de recherche français à Jérusalem*, 20 (2009), put online 10 March 2010, consulted on 26 June 2012, URL: http://bcrfj.revues.org/6196. Jewish communists, guided by Soviet instructions, initially supported Israel's establishment. By the late 1950s, however, disenchantment with Soviet antisemitism had raised doubts about communism, and by the Suez crisis, many Jewish communists (and former communists) actively supported Israel. See Jacques Frémontier, *L'étoile rouge de David: Les Juifs communistes en France* (Paris: Fayard, 2002), passim, and Benjamin Pinkus, "La campagne de Suez et son impact sur les Juifs de France," in *Les Juifs de France*, 357–60.

30. "La propagande antibritannique dans les milieux juifs de Paris," 11 July 1946, Palestine—Zionism, f/1a/3368, AN.

31. Minutes, Comité d'études questions juives, 28 April 1945, IPFL 1944–65, 23, K.13.14, MAE.

32. Hershco's assessment in *Entre Paris et Jérusalem* that French Jews went from "opposition to indifference" understates sympathy for the movement, but is correct in that most believed Zionism was a solution for Eastern European Jewish refugees and not applicable to them.

33. Benjamin Stora and Emile Témime, *Immigrances: L'immigration en France au XXe siècle* (Paris: Hachette littératures 2007), p. 37; Abdellali Hajjat, "L'expérience politique du Mouvement des travailleurs arabes," *Contretemps* (16 May 2006), p. 79; Hajjat, "Les Comités Palestine (1970–1972): Aux origines du soutien de la cause palestinienne en France," *Revue d'études palestiniennes*," 98 (Winter 2006), p. 75. For Algerian Muslim migrants' engagment as citizens, see Amelia Lyons, "Invisible Immigrants: Algerian Families and the French Welfare State in the Era of Decolonization (1947–1974)" (Ph.D. diss., University of California–Irvine, 2004), p. 260. According to Catherine Wihtol de Wenden, *Les immigrés et la politique: Cent cinquante ans d'évolution* (Paris: Presses de la Fondation nationale des sciences politiques, 1988), pp. 155–80, France's Muslim population became politically active in domestic affairs in 1968. See also Daniel A. Gordon, *Immigrants and Intellectuals: May '68 and the Rise of Anti-Racism in France* (Merlin Press, 2012).

34. Chef de la brigade du quartier de la bourse to Commissaire central à Marseille, "Population musulmane," 13 June 1949, 148W191, BdR. Gordon, *Immigrants and Intellectuals*, makes clear that French police consistently downplayed immigrant political activities.

35. Stora, *Ils venaient d'Algérie*, 93–119, 163.

36. Rabah Aissaoui, *Immigration and National Identity: North African Political Movements in Colonial and Postcolonial France* (London and New York: Tauris Academic Studies, 2009), pp. 118–21; Katz, "Jews and Muslims," 245–46.

37. Stora, *Ils venaient d'Algérie*, 107–10. See Paul Silverstein, *Algeria in France: Transpolitics, Race, and Nation* (Bloomington and Indianapolis: Indiana University Press,

2004), pp. 68–70, for a challenge to the binaries associated with the so-called Berber crisis. Sieffert, *Israël-Palestine*, 101, suggests with scant evidence that most French Muslim Algerians shared the pro-Palestinian sentiment of certain nationalist leaders in the 1950s.

38. For more on this meeting see Katz, "Tracing the Shadow of Palestine," 25–40.

39. K. Hakki to ME, 30 October 1944, IPFL 1944–65, 373, L.72, MAE.

40. For the re-bonding of French Jews with the republic after World War II, see Mandel, *In the Aftermath of Genocide*, passim.

41. Herscho, *Entre Paris et Jérusalem*, 45–53, 95–99, 113–23; Dalloz, *Georges Bidault*, 269–77. Herscho argues that because Arab representatives were officially recognized state actors, they had an initial advantage, since Jewish Agency representatives lacked similar access to the Quai d'Orsay. She overlooks, however, the way well-placed French Jews—even those not fully convinced of the need for a Jewish state—sought to promote Jewish refugee settlement in Palestine or to defend Jewish interests on the international stage.

42. "La Propagande du Sionisme en France," *Al Afif*, 12 September 1948.

43. Association des amis de la Palestine arabe to ME, 18 February 1947, IPFL 1944–65, 373, L.72.1, MAE; Herscho, *Entre Paris et Jérusalem*, 83–88.

44. AIU officials, for example, protested to the Foreign Ministry that British policies "would encourage already developing tendencies towards unity and autonomy across the Arab world." René Cassin to Bidault, 4 July 1946, IPFL 1944–65, 373, L.72.1, MAE; (René Mayer and Jules Braunschvig to ME), no date, Nᵒ 30 G3, MAE. Nicault, *La France et le Sionisme*, 215, notes that AIU representatives were more comfortable demanding liberal immigration policies in Palestine than asserting long-term political solutions.

45. CRIF meeting, 15 May 1945, MDI 1–55, CDJC.

46. "La propagande du Sionisme en France," *Al afif*, 12 September 1948.

47. "Activité des Sionistes en France," 14 January 1948, BA 2315 Communauté juif, PPA.

48. RG, Afrique du Nord, "Activité du parti du peuple algérien," 2 February 1948, 5 Activités nationalistes, K.38.3, MAE.

49. Clipping from *Franc-Tireur*, 14 April 1948 in CRIF meeting, 27 July 1948, MDI 1–55, CDJC. The paper defined protestors as "Arabs," a catch-all phrase often used by the press to describe North African Muslim laborers. For the conflation of these terms, see Yvan Gastaut, *L'immigration et l'opinion en France sous la Ve République* (Paris: Éditions du Seuil, 2000), p. 109.

50. Nicault, *La France et le Sionisme*, 214, 258; Doris Bensimon, *Les Juifs de France et leurs relations avec Israël, 1945–1988* (Paris: Éditions l'Harmattan, 1989); Bernard Wasserstein, *Vanishing Diaspora: The Jews in Europe since 1945* (Cambridge, Mass.: Harvard University Press, 1996), pp. 85–102. Laura Hobson Faure, "Un 'Plan Marshall juif': La présence juive américaine en France après la Shoah, 1944–54" (Ph.D. diss., École des hautes études en sciences sociales, 2009), p. 361, notes that French Jews raised 200 million francs for Israel in 1948.

51. Flyer, "Grand meeting," LICRA and MNCR, Dossier 43-d, Antisémitisme 1948, CC.

52. Témime, *Histoire de Marseille*, 296; Marie Attard-Maraninchi and Émile Témime, *Le cosmopolitisme de l'entre-deux-guerres (1919–1945)*, vol. 3 of *Migrance: Histoire des migrations à Marseille*, ed. Émile Témime (Aix-en-Provence: Édisud, 1990), pp. 159–60.

53. Émile Témime and Nathalie Deguigné, *Le camp du Grand Arénas Marseille, 1944–1966* (Paris: Éditions Autrement, 2001), pp. 17–19.

54. Sayad, Jordi, and Témime, *Le Choc*, 18–26, note that a weak economy from 1945 through 1954 lowered immigration when compared to elsewhere in France.

55. Témime and Deguigné, *Le camp du Grand Arénas*, 20.

56. The practice of lodging Muslims in camps began during the war, particularly after the Allied invasion of North Africa trapped thousands in France, and grew thereafter. Attard-Maraninchi and Témime, *Le cosmopolitisme*, 150–53; Sayad, Jordi, and Témime, *Le Choc*, 48; Témime, *Histoire de Marseille*, 330; Témime and Deguigné, *Le camp du Grand Arénas*, 21. Minutes, Bureau des affaires musulmanes nord-africaines de Marseille, 24 October 1944, 150W170, BdR.

57. For the immigrant roots of this neighborhood, see Émile Témime, *Marseille transit: Les passagers de Belsunce* (Paris: Éditions Autrement, 1995).

58. MI to Direction Afrique Levant, "Egypte: Émission radiophonique 'En Algérie: Arabophobie et pro-Sionisme de la France,'" 17 September 1947, AL 1944–59, K.38.2, MAE.

59. Attard-Maraninchi and Témime, *Le cosmopolitisme,* 131–60. The actual tally was probably higher due to those in hiding, seeking passage out of the country, or incarcerated in internment camps. Florence Berceot, "Renouvellement socio-démographique des Juifs de Marseille 1901–1937," *Provence historique* 175 (1994), 39–40, 44, and Donna F. Ryan, *The Holocaust & the Jews of Marseille: The Enforcement of Anti-Semitic Policies in Vichy France* (Urbana and Chicago: University of Illinois Press, 1996), p. 13, offer slightly different numbers of Jews from Turkey, Greece, and the Maghreb in the late 1930s.

60. Figure comes from Pascal le Pautremat, *La politique musulmane de la France au XXe siècle: De l'hexagone aux terres d'Islam. Espoirs, réussites, échecs* (Paris: Maisonneuve & Larose, 2003), pp. 302–303, who lists fifteen thousand in Marseille in 1934 and seventeen thousand in the Bouches-du-Rhône and Le Gard in 1938.

61. "État d'esprit de Musulmans algériens de Marseille," 13 December 1941, 76W205, BdR. Thanks to Ethan Katz for sharing this document.

62. Katz, "Jews and Muslims," 181–88, 200, 221–22, 225–30; Charles-Robert Ageron, "Les populations du Maghreb face à la propagande allemande," *Revue d'histoire de la Deuxième Guerre Mondiale,* 114 (April 1979): 1–39.

63. Mandel, *In the Aftermath of Genocide*, 52–85.

64. Roland Avitol, "Marseille," *L'Arche* (March/April, 1968): 19–20; Ryan, *The Holocaust & the Jews of Marseille*, 13.

65. While Jews lived in all areas of the city in 1941, 62 percent lived within 1.5 kilometers of the Old Port. Given that this area was hardest hit during the war, the remaining Jewish population was necessarily dispersed. For this and for the ethnic and class distinctions that marked Jewish life before the war, see Ryan, *The Holocaust*, 13–18, 176–93.

66. Interview with Silvio Benveniste, cited in Sarah Sussman, "Changing Lands, Changing Identities: The Migration of Algerian Jewry to France, 1954–1967" (Ph.D. diss., Stanford University, 2003), p. 350.

67. Frederick Cooper, *Decolonization and African Society: The Labor Question in French and British Africa* (Cambridge: Cambridge University Press, 1996); Eric T. Jennings, *Vichy in the Tropics: Pétain's National Revolution in Madagascar, Guadeloupe, and Indochina, 1940–1944* (Stanford: Stanford University Press, 2001).

68. Shepard, *The Invention of Decolonization*, 39–43.

69. MI to Commissaires de la République and préfets, "Carte d'identité des français Musulmans d'Algérie," 20 February 1946; Préfecture des Bouches-du-Rhône to Chef de service des étrangers, 25 July 1947, 150W170, BdR.

70. Blanchard, *La police parisienne*, 36–40, shows how police consistently ignored Algerian Muslim citizenship even after the 1947 statute formally changed their status.

71. The poverty and difficulties facing Muslim migrants are detailed in Préfet to Ministre du travail et de la sécurité sociale, "Commission consultative pour la main-d'œuvre nord-africain," 13 June 1947, 150W170, BdR. High crime rates testify to the difficulties many faced making ends meet. Chef de la brigade du quartier de la bourse to Commissaire central à Marseille, "Population musulmane," 13 June 1949, 148W191, BdR.

72. Although police noted that Muslim factory workers would not cross picket lines, Sayad, Jordi, and Témime, *Le Choc*, 21, argue otherwise. For CGT efforts to win Muslim adherents, see documents in 148W191, BdR. Statistics on Muslim voters comes from Chef de la brigade du quartier de la bourse to Commissaire central à Marseille, "Population musulmane," 13 June 1949, same file. For North African political engagement, see Jocelyne Cesari, *Être musulman en France: Associations, militants, et mosquées* (Paris: Éditions Karthala et Iremam, 1994), 30–31; Wihtol de Wenden, *Les immigrés et la politique*, passim.

73. Aissaoui, *Immigration and National Identity*, 129.

74. Cabinet du préfet, "Les renseignements généraux communiquent," 10 October 1946; Direction général de la sureté nationale to Préfet des Bouches-du-Rhône (BdR), "Note d'information," 11 October 1946; Direction générale de la sureté nationale to Préfet BdR, "Thèmes essentiels développés dans les divers discours prononcés à l'occasion du passage de Messali Hadj," 10 October 1946; Chef de cabinet to Préfet des BdR, "Réunion tenue à la 'Cassa d'Italia,' par le leader nord africain Messali Hadj," 10 October 1946, 150W170, BdR.

75. Préfet to Commissaire principal, "Activité déployé à Marseille par les nationalistes algériens," 24 October 1947, 150W170; Commissaire de police, "Population musulmane," 13 June 1949, 148W191, BdR.

76. RG, Mle, "Réaction dans les milieux musulmans de Marseille après la réception de leurs représentants par M. le Préfet des Bouches-du-Rhône," 5 January 1950, 148W191, BdR. Michel Renard, "Aperçu sur l'histoire de l'Islam à Marseille, 1813–1962: Pratiques religieuses et encadrements des Nord-Africains," *Revue française d'histoire d'outre-mer* 90 (2003): 269–96.

77. RG, Mle, "Présence des Nord Africains à la manifestation de CGT du 1er Mai à Marseille," 2 May 1950, 148W146, BdR.

78. RG, Mle, "Compte rendu du meeting MTLD de Marseille organisé au cinéma St. Lazare à 10h, le 7.5.1950," 9 May 1950, 148W191, BdR.

79. Inspecteur de la brigade de la bourse to Commissaire de police, 13 May 1950; RG, Mle (Untitled), 6 September 1950, 148W191, BdR. Police were still describing most of Marseille's laboring Muslim population as apolitical at this time and "shocked by the separatists' outrageous tone." Furthermore, it is worth noting a diversity of Algerian Muslim positions on independence. See Ethan Katz "Jews and Muslims," 281–82.

80. *L'Émigré* 2, no date, in Directeur départemental des services de police to Préfet BdR, "A/S Journal du PPA, *L'Émigré*," 19 December 1947, 150W170, BdR.

81. RG, Mle, 6 May 1950, 148W146, BdR.

82. "Note," 6 May 1948, 148W185, BdR.
83. Telegram to MI, "Attitude des milieux musulmans à l'égard des Israélites," 9 June 1948, 148W185, BdR.
84. RG, 9 June 1948, 148W185, BdR.
85. Robert Assaraf, *Une certaine histoire des Juifs du Maroc: 1860-1999* (Paris: Jean-Claude Gawsewitch, 2005), 522-25; Mohammed Kenbib, *Juifs et Musulmans au Maroc, 1859-1948* (Rabat: Publications de la faculté des lettres et des sciences humaines, Université Mohammed V, 1994): 677-87; Michael Laskier, *North African Jewry in the Twentieth Century: The Jews of Morocco, Tunisia, and Algeria* (New York: New York University Press, 1994), pp. 5-19, 94-101, Yaron Tsur, *Ḳehilah ḳeru'ah: Yehude Maroḳo yeha-le'umiyut, 1943-1954* (Tel Aviv: Universiṭat Tel Aviv, ha-'Amutah le-ḥeḳer ma'arkhot ha-ha'palah 'a. sh. Sha'ul Avigur: 'Am 'oved, 2001), pp. 84-91; Wyrtzen, "Constructing Morocco, 271-74.
86. While some have argued the violence was a spontaneous outbreak of war tension, most see the events as preplanned by nationalists. Norman A. Stillman, *Jews of Arab Lands in Modern Times* (Philadelphia: The Jewish Publication Society, 2003), p. 152, for example, calls the riot in Oujda a response to Arab failures to demolish Israel. Tsur, *Kehilah keru'ah*, 87-89, points out the difficulty of knowing whether events were spontaneous or preplanned while stressing anti-Zionist sentiment and nationalist activities. Benbib, *Juifs et Musulmans*, 677-87, places considerable emphasis on the role of the French administration and Israeli agents. For conflicting interpretations, see Laskier *North African Jewry*, 94-101, who emphasizes Moroccan nationalist agitation.
87. Telegram, A. Juin, Rabat, 18 June 1948, SG/1948, 75 (ex 29), MAE. Officials also noted temporary alliances between Communist activists and Moroccan nationalists. Ministre plénipotentiaire to Schuman, "Situation politique intérieure au Maroc: Attitude du parti communiste et du parti nationaliste l'Istiqlal," 29 July 1948; Brunel to Résident général, 19 June 1948, same file.
88. Paroles personnelles par M. Obadia, 12 June 1948, ADAM, 425, AIU.
89. "Extrait d'une lettre de M. Pinhas Eshkénazi, instituteur à Oujda," 7 July 1948, ADAM, 425, AIU.
90. Tajouri to président de l'Alliance israélite, June 1948, ADAM, 425, AIU. In Djérada, he argues, perpetrators were not nationalists but Muslims who worked with Jews in the mines.
91. Tsur, *Kehilah keru'ah*, 87, notes that because many illegal Jewish immigrants collected in the town, all others were viewed as potential migrants.
92. Assaraf, *Une certaine histoire*, 271-72.
93. Juin, in contrast, reported that violence began when a Muslim customer stabbed a Jewish shopkeeper. Telegram from Juin, Rabat, 8 June 1948, SG/ 1948, 75 (ex 29), MAE.
94. Brunel to Résident général, 19 June 1948, SG/1948, 75 (ex 29), MAE.
95. Telegram from Juin, 10 June 1948, SG/1948, 75 (ex 29), MAE. Subsequently, he emphasized the role of the Parti populaire algérien and nationalists more generally. Telegram, A. Juin, 17 and 18 June 1948, same file. Months later, he linked nationalist agitation and clandestine departures again. Juin to Schuman, "Règlement des incidents d'Oujda," 21 October 1948, same file.
96. Circulaire Nº 157-IP, ME, Service d'information et de presse, "Des incidents entre Arabes et Juifs à Oujda et Djérada," 10 June 1948, SG/1948, 75 (ex 29), MAE. By

the early 1950s, Francis Lacoste, the resident general, described clandestine migration as the spark in Oujda. Lacoste to MAMT, 17 December 1954, SG/1948, 96 (ex 22c), MAE.

97. RG du port, "État d'esprit des travailleurs arabes dans le port," 9 June 1948, 148W185, BdR.

98. RG du port, "A/S incidents judéo-arabes," 9 June 1948, 148W185, BdR.

99. Telegram to MI, "Attitude des milieux musulmans à l'égard des Israélites," 9 June 1948; RG du port, "État d'esprit des travailleurs arabes dans le port," 9 June 1948, 148W185, BdR.

100. RG, Mle, "La guerre en Palestine—Projection de films jugés provocateurs par les Arabes de Marseille," 10 June 1948, 148W185, BdR. Police shut down the film in response. Commissaire de police to Commissaire divisionnaire, 12 June 1948, same file.

101. Préfecture BdR, "Note pour monsieur le préfet: Circulation et transit des Musulmans français d'Algérie dans le sens Afrique du Nord, métropole et vice versa," 16 August 1948; "Situation dans le département des Bouches-du-Rhône au regard de la présence de l'accueil et du rapatriement des Nord Africains," 22 July 1948, 148W191, BdR.

102. RG, Mle, "Attitude des divers milieux arabes de Marseille et du département envers les Juifs de Marseille et de la région," 9 June 1948, 148W185, BdR.

103. Unless otherwise noted, the discussion of Zionist activities in Marseille is drawn from Témime and Deguigné, *Le camp du Grand Arénas*, 56–69, and Sayad, Jordi, and Témime, *Le Choc*, 35–37.

104. Témime and Deguigné, *Le camp du Grand Arénas*, 66–68.

105. RG, Mle, "Activité de la Ligue française pour la Palestine libre," 24 May 1947, 148W185, BdR. Arrests of Irgun arms smugglers are recorded in F715292, AN. For the Marseille link, see "Après l'affaire du camion de la rue Marx Dormoy la police opère à Marseille: Onze tonnes d'armes onze arrestations," *Populaires*, 9 March 1948. RG, Mle, "Existence éventuelle d'une filiale de l'Irgun à Marseille," 23 October 1947, 148W185, BdR; Sayad, Jordi, and Témime, *Le Choc*, 35. More information on Irgun activities in France is located in "Terrorisme juif, 1946–1950," IPFL 1944–65, 376, L.72.3, MAE.

106. Foreigners only became a majority in this neighborhood in the 1970s. In the 1980s, Algerian Muslims made up 40 percent of the total. Témime, *Marseille transit*, 38–39, 42–43.

107. Having been shut in November 1942, the postwar Fédération relied on aid from the Joint and the UNRRA. RG, Mle, "État critique de la situation financière de la FSJF," 25 June 1947, 148W185, BdR.

108. Laura Margolis to Henrietta Buchman, 31 December 1948, 316, AJDC.

109. The Zionist youth organization, Hechaloutz, and the religious organization, Bahad, created their own camps housing 3,500–4,000 in 1950, and 35,000 by the middle of the decade. RG, Section frontières, "Le mouvement de transmigration des Israélites: La question israélienne," June 1950, F7/15589, AN.

110. RG, Mle, "Attitude des divers milieux arabes de Marseille et du département envers les Juifs de Marseille et de la région," 9 June 1948; RG, Mle, "Activité de groupements israélites à Marseille," 30 June 1948, 148W185, BdR.

111. Cabinet du Préfet BdR, no date, 148W185, BdR.

112. RG, Mle, "Réaction des milieux arabes de Marseille à la suite de la trêve en Pales-tine," 16 June 1948, 148W185, BdR.

113. RG, Mle, "A.S du navire Altalena amarré à Martigues par l'armement des Juifs," 15 June 1948, 148W185, BdR.

114. 11 June 1948, 148W185, BdR; RG, Mle, "L'ordre de trêve en Palestine," 12 June 1948, 148W185, BdR. According to historian Saul Friedländer, *When Memory Comes*, trans. Helen R. Lane (New York: Farrar, Straus, and Giroux, Inc., 1979), p. 179, who was sailing to Israel on the boat, the French army and many passengers loaded it.

115. RG, Mle, "Attitude des divers milieux arabes de Marseille et du département envers les Juifs de Marseille et de la région," 9 June 1948; RG, Mle, "Activité de groupe-ments israélites à Marseille," 30 June 1948, 148W185, BdR.

116. RG, "Activité de groupements israélites à Marseille," 30 June 1948; RG, Mle, "Pro-pagande du PPA en faveur des armée arabes en Palestine," 16 June 1948; RG, Mle, "L'Office d'immigration de l'État d'Israël," 19 June 1948, 148W185, BdR.

117. RG, Mle, "Incidents entre Juifs et Arabes au centre d'accueil du Grand Arénas à Mazargues," 14 June 1948, 148W185, BdR. While the report is not explicit as to who forced the lost Algerian Muslim laborer to work in the canteen, the implica-tion is that Jewish residents detained him.

118. Commissaire de police du quartier de St. Giniez to Commissaire divisionnaire, Mle, 27 June 1948, 148W185, BdR.

119. This organization, formerly the Congrès musulman algérien de Marseille, was es-tablished in November 1944 to create links between "French Muslims from Algeria and their French brothers in the metropole." Mohamed Seghir Talmoudi to Préfet, 29 November 1944; RG, Mle, "A/S de l'Association des Musulmans algériens de Marseille," 26 March 1945, 150W170, BdR.

120. RG, Mle, "Incidents entre Juifs et Arabes au centre d'accueil du Grand Arénas à Mazargues," 14 Juin 1948; RG, Mle, "Incidents entre Juifs et Musulmans au camp du Grand Arénas à Mazargues," 30 June 1948, 148W185, BdR.

121. Vernet, Directeur départemental du travail et de la main-d'œuvre, to Préfet BdR, "Hébergement de réfugiés israélites au centre de transit du Grand Arénas," 25 Oc-tober 1948, 148W141, BdR.

122. Commissaire divisionnaire to Directeur départemental des services de police-préfecture, "Tension judéo-arabe," 11, 12, and 14 June 1948, 148W185, BdR.

123. Local Muslims nevertheless complained that the truce was partial to Israel. RG, Mle, "A/S de la cessation des combats en Palestine," 21 July 1948. Anger mounted again when a training camp for Jewish pilots was found outside Algiers, forty of whom escaped to Palestine via Marseille. RG, Mle, "Pilotes juifs venant d'Alger, à destination de la Palestine," 8 October 1948, 148W185, BdR.

124. RG, Mle, "La guerre de Palestine jugé par les divers milieux arabes de Marseille," 7 January 1949, 148W185, BdR.

125. RG, Mle, "L'affaire Palestinienne," 28 January 1949; RG, Mle, "A/S de la guerre de Palestine," 4 February 1949, 148W185, BdR.

126. RG, Mle, "La position du gouvernement français vis à vis du nouvel état d'Israël vu par la colonie de Marseille," 21 June 1948, 148W185, BdR.

127. Témime and Deguigné, *Le camp du Grand Arénas*, 68–69.

128. Note for Préfet, 18 October 1948; Note for Préfet, 29 November 1948, 148W185, BdR.

129. Directeur départemental des services de police to Commissaire central (pour éducation), 14 May 1949; Directeur départemental des services de police to M. Thau, 14 May 1949; Commissaire principal to Directeur départemental des services de police, 11 May 1949, 148W141, BdR.

130. Joan Wolf, *Harnessing the Holocaust: The Politics of Memory in France* (Stanford: Stanford University Press, 2004), pp. 28–29, points out that Jewish publications were more devoted to Israel than to any other issue. For institutional support, see Phyllis Albert, "French Jewry and the Centrality of the State of Israel: The Public Debate, 1968–1988," *From Ancient Israel to Modern Judaism: Intellect in Quest of Understanding, Essays in Honor of Marvin Fox*, vol. 4, eds. Ernest Frerichs and Jacob Neusner (Atlanta: Scholars Press, 1989), pp. 207–209.

131. Emile Touati, "Profil d'une jeunesse indécise," *La revue du FSJU*, 13 (1955), pp. 16–17.

132. Raymond Aron, *Mémoires* (Paris: Julliard, 1983), pp. 502–505. For the reticence of Jewish intellectuals to embrace Israel, see Maurice Szafran, *Les Juifs dans la politique française: De 1945 à nos jours* (Paris: Flammarion, 1990), pp. 83–92.

133. Sylvie Korcaz, *Les Juifs de France et l'État d'Israël* (Paris: Éditions Denoël, 1969), p. 78, explains this gap by arguing that American-style fund-raising was less valued in France as a sign of social prestige.

Chapter 2. Decolonization and Migration: Constructing the North African Jew

1. Norman A. Stillman, *Jews of Arab Lands in Modern Times* (Philadelphia: The Jewish Publication Society, 2003), pp. 71–72. Général de corps d'armée de Latour to MDMT, "Émigration des Juifs nord-africains en Israël," 24 January 1955, SG/1948, 96 (ex 22c), MAE; Michael Laskier, *North African Jewry in the Twentieth Century: The Jews of Morocco, Tunisia, and Algeria* (New York: New York University Press, 1994), p. 274.

2. Claude Tapia, *Les Juifs sépharades en France (1965–1985)* (Paris: L'Harmattan, 1986), p. 27. Jacques Taïeb, "Immigrés d'Afrique du Nord: Combien? Quand? Pourquoi?" in *Terre d'exil terre d'asile: Migrations juives en France aux XIXe et XXe siècles,* ed. Collette Zytnicki (Paris: Éditions de l'Éclat): 150, puts the number at a much lower twelve thousand. Jewish departures in the 1950s were statistically proportionate to that of other French citizens. Doris Bensimon and S. Della Pergolla, *La population juive de France: Socio-démographie et identité* (Jerusalem: Hebrew University of Jerusalem and CNRS, 1984), p. 50; Sarah Sussman, "Changing Lands, Changing Identities: The Migration of Algerian Jewry to France, 1954–1967" (Ph.D. diss. Stanford University, 2002), p. 174.

3. Esther Benbassa, *Jews of France: A History from Antiquity to the Present* (Princeton: Princeton University Press, 1999), p. 186. While 90 percent of Moroccan Jews settled in Israel, French citizenship brought a similar percentage of Algerian Jews to the metropole. About half of Tunisian Jews went to France and half to Israel.

4. For a discussion of the complex factors pushing departures, see Taïeb, "Immigrés d'Afrique du Nord," 149–54.

5. According to Jonathan Wyrtzen, "Constructing Morocco: Colonial Struggle to Define the Nation, 1912–1956" (Ph.D. diss. Georgetown University, 2009), pp. 232–38, such concerns dated from early in the century when Zionism first emerged in Morocco.

6. Todd Shepard, *The Invention of Decolonization: The Algerian War and the Remaking of France* (Ithaca and London: Cornell University Press, 2006). Kimberly Arkin, " 'It's the French and the Arabs against the Jews': Identity Politics and the Construction of Adolescent Jewishness in France" (Ph.D. diss., University of Chicago, 2008), chap. 1, and Elizabeth Friedman, *Colonialism and After: An Algerian Jewish Community* (South Hadley, Mass.: Bergin and Garvey Publishers, Inc., 1988), make clear that "Frenchification" was not as successful on the ground as legal categories suggest.

7. Michael M. Laskier, *The Alliance Israélite Universelle and the Jewish Communities of Morocco, 1862–1962* (Albany: State University of New York Press, 1983).

8. Yaron Tsur, "L'AIU et le Judaïsme marocain en 1949: L'émergence d'une nouvelle démarche politique," *Archives juives* 34, 1 (2001): 54–73.

9. For international Jewish aid in Tunisia, see Claude Nataf, "Les mutations du Judaïsme tunisien après la seconde guerre mondiale," *Archives juives* 30, 1 (2006): 125–36.

10. As Tsur, "L'AIU et le Judaïsme marocain en 1949," shows, Jewish organizations pursued both Zionist *and* assimilationist goals.

11. For a useful discussion of how even ostensibly inclusive, universalizing nationalist thought can function to delineate ethnic categories, see Jonathan Glassman, *War of Words, War of Stones: Racial Thought and Violence in Colonial Zanzibar* (Bloomington: Indiana University Press, 2011).

12. For example, Muslims and Jews worked closely together in the Communist party, particularly in Tunisia and Morocco, providing an alternative political vision to the one I am describing here.

13. Recent scholarship has rightly stressed the differences among Moroccan, Algerian, and Tunisian Jews following a wider historiographical move to challenge colonial frameworks that collapsed "North Africa" into one unvarigated analytic construct. My decision to tell a cross-national story seeks not to rehomogenize the North African landscape. However, as the sources traced here make clear, many of the actors under study spoke of Jewish life in cross-regional terms. The goal of this chapter is to understand the political consequences of such homogenization.

14. Martin Thomas, "From French North Africa to Maghreb Independence: Decolonization in Morocco, Tunisia and Algeria from 1945 to 1956," in *Crisis of Empire: Decolonization and Europe's Imperial States, 1918–1975* (London: Hodder Education, Part of Hachette Livre UK), pp. 209–27.

15. Lacoste to MDMT, "Départ pour la Palestine d'Israélites marocaines," 16 December 1954; Lacoste to Embassy in Tel Aviv, 13 May 1955, SG/1948, 96 (ex 22c), MAE.

16. Note pour la Direction des affaires administratives et sociales from Direction générale des affaires politiques (Afrique-Levant), "Émigration des Juifs nord-africains vers Israël" (September 1955), SG/1948, 96 (ex 22c), MAE.

17. Stillman, *Jews of Arab Lands*, 166. Of these 28,781 were from Morocco (about 10 percent of the population). According to Yaron Tsur, *Ḳehilah ḳeru'ah: Yehude Maroḳo*

yeha-le'umiyut, 1943–1954 (Tel Aviv: Universiṭat Tel Aviv, ha-ʿAmutah le-ḥeḳer maʿarkhot ha-haʿpalah ʿa. sh. Shaʾul Avigur: ʿAm ʿoved, 2001), pp. 93–96, although Zionism increased in Morocco after 1948, support actually waned in response to the poor treatment of Moroccan immigrants in Israel. According to Haïm Saadoun, "L'influence du sionisme sur les relations judéo-musulmanes en Tunisie," in *Juifs et Musulmans en Tunisie: Fraternité et déchirements*, ed., Sonia Fellous (Paris: Somogy, 2003), p. 228, in Tunisia, the movement's emphasis was not on migration but on expressing ethnic belonging.

18. MI to ME, Direction Afrique-Levant, "Emigration des Israélites marocains," 28 February 1949, IPFL 1944–65, 376, L.72.2, MAE.

19. Note pour le Ministre from Direction d'Afrique Levant, sous-direction des protectorats, "Emigration à destination de la Palestine d'Israélites originaires de l'Afrique du Nord," 5 March 1949, IPFL 1944–65, 376, L.72.2, MAE.

20. Others objected to migration on the grounds that Morocco and Tunisia would be deprived of loyal Jewish subjects. ME, Direction d'Afrique–Levant to Rabat, Tunis, Tanger, and Tétouan, "Émigration à destination de la Palestine d'Israélites originaires de l'Afrique du Nord," 6 April 1949; Telegram, ME, direction d'Afrique–Levant to Parodi, Clappier, de Sourbon, and Busset, 30 May 1949, IPFL 1944–65, 376, L.72.2, MAE. Some Ministry of Interior officials *did* support Jewish migration based on the principle of self-determination and on hopes it would facilitate relations with Israel. RG, "Le mouvement de transmigration des Israélites: La question israélienne," June 1950, F7/15589, AN.

21. Those claiming refugee status, in this view, were European Zionists who had traveled clandestinely to Algeria to push the issue. AE, Direction des conventions administratives et sociales, "Note: Israélites d'Afrique du Nord," 23 March 1949, SG/1948, 93 (ex 30), MAE. Direction des conventions administratives et sociales to Ministre plénipotentiaire, Tanger, "Émigration juive vers Israël," 11 April 1949, IPFL 1944–65, 376, L.72.2, MAE.

22. Telegram from Juin, 8 April 1949, SG/1948, 93 (ex 30), MAE.

23. The one exception was Tunisia, where resident general, Jean Mons, reported difficulties were receding. Mons to Schuman, "Départs de Juifs tunisiens pour la métropole," 21 December 1948, F716088, AN; Mons to Schuman, "Départ des Israélites de Tunisie pour la Palestine," 29 March 1949, IPFL 1944–65, 376, L.72.2, MAE. Saadoun, "L'influence du Sionisme," 22, confirms little hostility to Jewish migration in Tunisia from Neo-Destour, despite some sensitivity "on the ground."

24. M. Ernst to MI, "Situation d'Israélites marocains arrivés en Algérie," January 1949, F716088, AN.

25. E. de Beauverger, Ministre plénipotentiaire, Tanger, to ME, "Activité pro-Sioniste des milieux israélites tangérois" and "Émigration juive vers Israël," 8 and 19 March 1949, IPFL 1944–65, 376, L.72.2, MAE.

26. Concerns over numbers are recorded in ME to Résident général, Rabat, "Émigration des Juifs marocains à destination d'Israël," 12 January 1953, and Direction général des affaires politiques, "Note pour la direction des affaires administratives et sociales," 17 August 1953, SG/1948, 94 (ex 22a), MAE. Others sought to limit migration because Jews represented a source of social stability who "assimilate to Western customs more easily than the Muslims." Note pour le secrétaire général, "M. Jarblum de l'Agence juive," 20 February 1954, SG/1948, 95 (ex 22b), M.9.3, MAE. By early

1953, Israeli officials were predicting that American Jewish aid, French efforts to stabilize living conditions, and poor economic horizons in Israel would encourage Jews to stay. Yves Debroise, Chargé d'affaires de France A.I. en Israël to Bidault, "L'immigration des Juifs nord-africains," 11 February 1953, SG/1948, 94 (ex 22a), MAE; Consul général de France, Jerusalem, to ME, direction Afrique-Levant, 18 February 1953, same file.

27. ME to MAMT, "Immigration des Juifs nord-africains en Israël," 13 November 1954, SG/1948, 96 (ex 22c), MAE.

28. Résident général Rabat to Martuni, 14 September 1954, SG/1948, 96 (ex 22c), MAE.

29. While many administrators blamed Zionist propaganda for Jewish flight, others, such as Lacoste to MAMT, 17 December 1954, SG/1948, 96 (ex 22c), MAE, faulted widespread poverty.

30. Ironically, the push to *legalize* migration to Israel grew out of such fears, as some argued that regularized policies would alleviate pressures that came from *illegal* migration. Francis Lacoste, Minister Plenipotentiary and delegate to the resident general in Morocco, for example, one of the fiercest opponents of Jewish migration as late as September 1948 made this case. Lacoste to Schuman, "Émigration juive marocaine vers l'État d'Israël," 3 June 1949, IPFL 1944–19, 376, L.72.2, MAE. Numerous documents in the MAE attest that by the 1950s, while French administrators were still worried about their interests in North Africa, they also feared offending Israel.

31. "Après les pogroms de Petitjean (Maroc): La situation des Juifs, noyés dans une masse arabe fanatisée, devient chaque jour plus tragique," *La Terre retrouvée*, 1 October 1954.

32. Board of Deputies of British Jews, "Memorandum: Safeguards for Jews in Morocco and Tunisia," November 1954, SG/1948, 95 (ex 22b), MAE.

33. Jonathan Wyrtzen, "Constructing Morocco: Colonial Struggle to Define the Nation, 1912–1956" (Ph.D. diss., Georgetown University, 2009), p. 268.

34. Telegram from Bonnet, 22 June 1948, SG/1948, 93 (ex 30), MAE.

35. Cited in Robert Assaraf, *Une certaine histoire des Juifs du Maroc: 1860–1999* (Paris: Jean-Claude Gawsewitch, 2005), p. 526.

36. Laskier, *North African Jewry*, 168–69. Henri Bonnet to Schuman, "Attitude du World Jewish Congress concernant les problèmes de l'Afrique du Nord," 8 August 1952, SG/1948, 94 (ex 22a), MAE.

37. Yaron Tsur, "Les dirigeants du Judaïsme marocain et l'indépendance: Le problème de l'intégration et l'influence des organisations juives internationales," in Michel Abibol, ed., *Relations judéo-musulmanes au Maroc: Perceptions et réalités* (Paris: Éditions Stavit, 1997): 225–36.

38. Roger Vaurs, Directeur du service de presse et d'information de l'Ambassade de France to Henri Bonnet, Ambassadeur de France, "World Jewish Council conférence du Dr. Perlzweig sur la politique française en Afrique du Nord," 15 September 1954, SG/1948, 95 (ex 22b), MAE.

39. "Les organisations israélites américaines et l'Istilqlal," 20 June 1955, SG/1948, 95 (ex 22b), MAE.

40. An August 1955 Istiqlal press release insisted that accusations of Muslim antisemitism came from French efforts to discredit the movement. Muslims and Jews had a shared past and a common enemy; independent Morocco would guarantee equality

for all. Ahmed Balafrej, Sec. Gen., Istiqlal Party of Morocco, "Moroccan Jews" 12 August 1955, SG/1948, 95 (ex 22b), MAE.

41. Maurice Couve de Murville, Ambassadeur de France aux États-Unis to Antoine Pinay, ME (Direction d'Afrique–Levant), 22 September 1955; Murville to Pinay, "Contacts entre le Congrès juif mondial et l'Istiqlal," 18 November 1955, SG/1948, 95 (ex 22b), MAE.

42. Murville to Pinay, 22 September 1955, SG/1948, 95 (ex 22b), MAE. For the WJC's efforts to avoid irritating both sides, see Laskier, *North African Jewry*, 169–70.

43. "Meeting of the Administration Committee of the Joint Distribution Committee," 5 April 1955, 55/64 # [45/64#114], AJDC.

44. Benjamin B. Goldman, "Information on North Africa and Other Moslem Lands," 11 October 1949, 45/54 #6, AJDC.

45. "Notes of the New York JDC Staff Meeting No. 2–49," 17 January 1949, 45/54 #6, AJDC. Motivating many Joint officials was the hope that Jews of Arab lands would serve as a "resource for the upbuilding [*sic*] of the Jewish people" after the Holocaust. "Notes of the New York JDC Staff Meeting No. 2–49," 17 January 1949, same file.

46. "Memorandum on visit to North Africa by Rabbi Shapiro from December 7th to December 28th, 1949," 45/54 #5, AJDC.

47. "Minutes of meeting held at 2, rue de Cygne," 19 October 1948, 45/54 #6, AJDC.

48. Hélène Cazes-Benatar, "Report on the Political Situation in North Africa," October 1950, 45/54 #5, AJDC.

49. "Meeting of the Administration Committee of the Joint Distribution Committee," 5 April 1955, 55/64 # [45/64#114], AJDC.

50. Haber's comments on poverty are documented in Samuel L. Haber, "Dir. 593," 30 December 1954, 45/54 #9, AJDC. His call for migration is cited in Laskier, *North African Jewry*, 168.

51. André Blumel to Comité d'action sioniste, 24 August 1955, MDI 69, CDJC.

52. Interestingly, migration was also not obvious to many Moroccan, Tunisian, and Algerian Jewish leaders who expressed exasperation at the "excessive zeal" of American Jewish organizations. Such outsiders, they feared, were *creating* disruption through their visits and calls to action without paying adequate attention to local Jewish concerns. Indeed, in the early 1950s, indigenous Jewish leaders often feared that migration would hurt communal vitality and diminish chances for improving local conditions even if they favored modest migration for Morocco's poorest Jews. "Israélites d'Afrique du Nord," Paris, 8 July 1955, SG/1948, 95 (ex 22b); Lacoste to MAMT, 17 December 1954, SG/1948, 96 (ex 22c), MAE. Algerian Jewish organizations also begged international Jewish agencies not to do anything that could backfire. Jacques Lazarus, "Rapport sur la situation des Juifs en Algérie au début de l'année 1958," Assises du Judaïsme algérien, 12–13 March 1958, republished in *Archives juives: Revue d'histoire des Juifs de France* 29, 1 (1ère semestre 1996), p. 59.

53. Tsur, *Ḳehilah ḳeru'ah*, 112–27; Tsur, "L'AIU et le Judaïsme marocain en 1949," 54–73. Léon Meiss to Olivier Marin, 11 October 1948, SG/1948, 75 (ex 29); S.M. le Sultan, Secrétariat particulier to René Cassin, 18 May 1949, SG/1948, 93 (ex 30), M.9.3, MAE and ADAM, 237, AIU

54. For Morocco, see Wyrtzen, "Constructing Morocco, 264–77; Tsur, "Les dirigeants du Judaïsme marocain et l'indépendance," 225–36; Joseph Levy, "Témoignage d'un militant Juif marocain," in *Juif du Maroc: Identité et dialogue*, Actes du colloque

international sur la communauté juive marocaine (Paris, 1980). For Tunisia, see Nataf, "Les mutations du Judaïsme tunisien," 125–36. For Algeria, see numerous citations in part 3 of this chapter.

55. Jacques Dalloz, *Georges Bidault: Biographie politique* (Éditions l'Harmattan, 1992), p. 273. For Neo Destour on Zionism, see Haïm Saadoun, "L'influence du Sionisme sur les relations judéo-musulmanes en Tunisie," in *Juifs et Musulmans en Tunisie: Fraternité et déchirements,* ed., Sonia Fellous (Paris: Somogy, 2003): 219–29. For Morocco, see Wyrtzen, "Constructing Morocco, 264–77. For Algeria, see part 3 of chapter.

56. For example, in 1955 the Tunisian Resident General only allowed Jews to depart in small groups so they would not stand out from other travelers. Général de corps d'armée de Latour, res. gen. de France en Tunisie to MAMT, "Émigration des Juifs nord-africains en Israël," 24 January 1955, SG/1948, 96 (ex 22c), MAE.

57. For example, in December 1954, the Egyptian radio station, *La voix des Arabes*, protested migrations (not particularly surprising coming from Nasser's international mouthpiece). Lacoste to MAMT, 17 December 1954, SG/1948, 96 (ex 22c); "Traduction d'une émission radiophonique de langue arabe, Radio Damas du 15/2/55," SG/1948, 95 (ex 22b), MAE.

58. Lacoste to MAMT, "Émigration juive vers Israël," 13 May 1955, SG/1948, 96 (ex 22c), MAE.

59. MAMT to ME, "Émigration vers Israël des Juifs nord-africains," 8 July 1955, SG/1948, 96 (ex 22c), MAE.

60. Gilbert to ME, "Immigration marocaine en Israël," 25 September 1955, SG/1948, 96 (ex 22c), MAE.

61. Maurice J. Goldbloom, André Zaoui, and Henry Levy, "Foreign Countries: North Africa," *American Jewish Year Book* 58 (1957), p. 356.

62. Saadoun, "L'influence du Sionisme," 226.

63. More came in the after that point. Taïeb, "Immigrés d'Afrique du Nord," 149–51.

64. Jewish figure is from Sussman, *Changing Lands*, 1 (Taïeb, "Immigrés d'Afrique du Nord," 150, puts the figure of Algerian Jews at 120,000). The wider figure is from Jacques Fremeaux, "Le reflux des Français d'Afrique du Nord 1956–1962," in *Marseille et le choc des décolonisations*, eds., Jean-Jacques Jordi and Emile Temime (Aix-en-Provence: Édisud, 1996), p. 15. The number of harkis includes 85,000 who participated in the military's supplemental units (families included) and 55,000 notables, functionaries or career military men who adopted a pro-French position during the war. Tom Charbit, *Les harkis* (Paris: La Découvert, 2006), pp. 9, 21–23, 62, 71.

65. Shepard, *The Invention of Decolonization*, 182. Sussman, "Changing Lands," 162, argues that Jewish and pieds noirs destinies converged while still asserting that "[Algerian Jews] represent the only Jews in history to migrate en masse not because they suffered discrimination as Jews." Also see, Jacques Frémontier, *L'étoile rouge de David: Les Juifs communistes en France* (Paris: Fayard, 2002), p. 56.

66. Arkin, " 'It's the French and the Arabs against the Jews,' " 129–30; Chantal Benayoun, "Juifs, pieds-noirs, séfarades ou les trois termes d'une citoyenneté," in *Marseille et le choc des décolonisations*, 125–32; Ethan Katz, "Jews and Muslims in the Shadow of Marianne: Conflicting Identities and Republican Culture in France, 1914–1975"

(Ph.D. diss., University of Wisconsin, 2008), pp. 263–66; Albert Memmi, "The Colonized Jew," *Jews and Arabs*, trans. Eleanor Levieux (Chicago: J. Philip O'Hara, Inc., 1975), pp. 38–45; Benjamin Stora, *Les trois exils: Juifs d'Algérie* (Paris: Stock, 2006), p. 144; and Sussman, "Changing Lands," 87–186.

67. Max Lapides, "An Algerian Odyssey," 3 May 1961, 55/64 # [45/64#28], AJDC. For Jewish support for the FLN, see Jean Laloum, "Portrait d'un Juif du FLN," in *Archives juives: Revue d'histoire des Juifs de France* 29, 1 (1ère semestre 1996): 65–71, and Frémontier, *L'étoile rouge de David:* 250–53. For diverse Algerian and French Jewish positions on the war, see Katz, "Jews and Muslims," 263–81. For generational diversity, see David Cohen, "Le Comité juif algérien d'études sociales dans le débat idéologique pendant la guerre d'Algérie (1954–1961)," *Archives juives* 29, 1 (1ère semestre 1996), pp. 37.

68. Ethan Katz, "Between Emancipation and Persecution: Algerian Jewish Memory in the *Longue durée*," *Journal of North African Studies* 17, 5 (November 2012): 793–820, argues convincingly that Algerian Jews began articulating a "violence and vulnerability narrative" following the 1934 Muslim-Jewish riots in Constantine, which served as a powerful counter to long-standing narratives focused on the progress and patriotism of Algerian Jews. This "violence and vulnerability narrative" then fed into a more regional narrative following World War II and at the beginning of the French decolonization process when a wide range of social actors began speaking of Jewish victimization throughout Algeria, Tunisia, and Morocco.

69. Phrase used by Jewish representatives visiting Paul Delouvrier, Délégué général du gouvernement en Algérie, Note d'information de Jacques Lazarus, "Algérie," 23 October 1959, III, FJL, AIU.

70. According to Stillman, *Jews of Arab Lands in Modern Times*, 170–71, Algerian Jews were "caught in the cross fire," unable to "identify with either side." See also Richard Ayoun, "Les Juifs d'Algérie pendant la guerre d'indépendance," *Archives juives* 29, 1 (1996): 15–29; Sussman, *Changing Lands*; Shepard, *The Invention of Decolonization*, 170; Mylène Sultan, "La synthèse impossible, 1954–1962," in Jean Laloun and Jean Luc Allouche eds, *Les Juifs d'Algérie: Textes et images* (Paris 1987) pp. 42–48; Stora, *Les trois exils*, 140, and "L'impossible neutralité des Juifs d'Algérie," in Mohammed Harbi and Benjamin Stora, *La guerre d'Algérie* (Paris: Hachette, 2005), pp. 287–316. Katz, "Jews and Muslims," 236–310, in contrast (and more convincingly), traces a shift in Jewish responses over time.

71. For some, French control was framed as pro-Muslim. Georges Zerapha thus wrote to Jacques Lazarus, 19 May 1960, XVI, FJL, AIU, that the only way "to draw the Arabs from their destitution and duress" was under French rule. Katz, "Jews and Muslims," 265, discusses Jewish sympathy for Muslim political aspirations.

72. Cited in Felix Allouche, "Il y a dix ans: Les Juifs d'Algérie quittèrent ce pays," *Information juive*, 1 August 1972. Also see Henri Chemouilli, "La grande peur des Juifs d'Algérie," *L'Arche*, 8–9 (August–September 1957), pp. 20–22.

73. Procès-Verbal du CJAES, 2 November 1954, FJL, AIU. For the CJAES position, see Cohen, "Comité juif algérien d'études sociales," pp. 30–50.

74. Cited in Lazarus, "Rapport sur la situation des Juifs," 59–60. Published as "Une déclaration du Comité juif algérien d'études sociale," *Information juive* 82 (November 1956).

75. Note d'information de Jacques Lazarus, "Algérie," 23 October 1959, III, FJL, AIU. Sussman, "Changing Lands," 112, and Stora, *Les trois exils*, 147, note that Jewish "neutrality" was often a smoke screen for more partisan views.
76. Hélène Cazes-Benatar, "Report on the Political Situation in North Africa," October 1950, 45/54 #5, AJDC.
77. Congrès juif mondial, Bureau nord-africain, "Note concernant le séjour en Afrique du Nord de M. Emmanuel Celler et le séjour à Tunis de MM. Perlzweig et Lazarus," 25 November 1954, XVI, FJL, AIU.
78. André Chouraqui, Louis D. Horowitz and Hélène Cazes-Benatar, "Foreign Countries: North Africa," *American Jewish Year Book* 54 (1953), p. 372.
79. For "European" reactions to decolonization, see Yann Scioldo-Zürcher, *Devenir métropolitain: Politique d'intégration et parcours de rapatriés d'Algérie en métropole (1954–2005)* (Paris: Éditions de l'École des hautes études en sciences sociales, 2010).
80. Stillman, *Jews of Arab Lands in Modern Times*, 172–75.
81. Claude Martin, *Histoire de l'Algérie française 1830–1962* (Paris: Éditions des Quatre fils Aymon, 1963), p. 467; Cohen, "Le Comité juif," 36.
82. For examples, see, "Rien ne doit altérer les sentiments de fraternité qui existent entre Israélites et Musulmans," and "En marge des événements du Moyen Orient," *Information juive*, November 1956.
83. Stora, *Les Trois Exils*, 151–52; Bahloul's informants in *The Architecture of Memory: A Jewish-Muslim Household in Colonial Algeria, 1937–1962,* trans. Catherine de Peloux Ménagé (Cambridge: Cambridge University Press, 1996), p. 119, claimed first becoming nervous during the Suez crisis.
84. RG, Mle, "Étrangers-Égyptiens. Brimades exercées par le gouvernement égyptien envers les ressortissants égyptiens juifs," 9 February 1952, 148W141, BdR; "La masse musulmane algérienne saura-t-elle toujours distinguer entre Israélites et Israéliens?" *Le Monde*, 2 November 1956, p. 7; "Un article déplacé" *Information juive*, November 1956.
85. Elie Gozlan to Mr. Haber, 9 July 1955, 55/64# [45/74#28, 86], AJDC.
86. Malka to Lazarus, 6 October 1962, I, FJL, AIU.
87. The AJDC's Stanley Abromovitch, touring Algeria that June, blamed French police for paying Jewish informants to expose Algerian nationalists. The Tunisian nationalist paper, *L'Action*, 15 October 1956, also asserted that Jews spied for payment. For alternative explanations, see Gilbert Meynier, *Histoire intérieure du FLN, 1954–1962* (Paris: Fayard, 2002), p. 255, and Laskier, *North African Jewry*, 319–21 who, like, Stora, *Les trois exils*, 152–54, assert that unbeknownst to the French or FLN, Israeli military emissaries aided these efforts.
88. Cited in Moses Leavitt to Charles H. Jordan, 19 April 1957, 55/64# [45/74#28, 86], AJDC.
89. Jacques Attal to Lazarus, 14 April 1957, XVI, FJL, AIU.
90. In Jean-David Attal's interview in Robert I. Weiner and Richard E. Sharpless, eds. *An Uncertain Future: Voices of a French Jewish Community, 1940–2012* (Toronto: University of Toronto Press, 2012), pp. 246–55, for example, he notes that his father, while angered by the Algerian nationalists' extremism, did not feel victimized as a Jew but as a French citizen. For a similar assessment, see "Le FLN algérien menace les Juifs" *Notre drapeau*, 25 October 1956, pp. 1–2. According to Jacques Mosel,

"Parcours algérien," *L'Arche* 2, 15 (March 1958), pp. 14–15, a sense of Jewish specificity differed according to location.

91. S. Cohen to Lazarus, "Rapport sur les attentats terroristes au quartier juif d'Oran les samedi 27 et dimanche 28 juillet 1957," 1 August 1957, I, FJL, AIU. Henri Chemoulli, "Le Judaïsme français change de visage," *Évidences*, September 1962, pp. 2–5, likewise noted that victims were not necessarily killed as Jews.

92. Armand Barmon, Communauté israélite de Boghari, "Note d'information sur la situation locale avant et après l'attentat du 29 septembre 1958," I, FJL, AIU.

93. Samuel Lévis to Sidney Nelson and Marits Souget, 20 December 1960, 55/64# [45/74#28, 86], AJDC. For examples of neighborly outreach, see untitled document accompanying "Photos publiées dans mois de juin 1992," *Information juive*, III, FJL; Sussman, "Changing Lands," 108; Ayoun, "Les Juifs d'Algérie," 25.

94. Henri Chemouilli, "La grande peur des Juifs d'Algérie," *L'Arche*, 8–9 (August–September 1957), pp. 20–22.

95. Sciodo-Zürcher, *Devenir métropolitain*, 55, argues that all "Europeans" fled out of fear.

96. See, for example, Sussman, "Changing Lands," 107–109, and Katz, "Jews and Muslims," 300. For Stora, *Les trois exils*, 135, the crucial moment came with the murder of Jewish musician Raymond Leyris, famous for his mastery of Arabo-Andalusian music and deep connections with all religious communities.

97. Cohen, "Le Comité juif," 40.

98. Stora, *Les trois exils*, 132, argues that in the mid-1950s, Jews—like most Algerian French citizens—believed themselves safe. Katz, "Jews and Muslims," 266, and Sussman, "Changing Lands," 89–105, point to the building of new Jewish institutions throughout the late 1950s as an indication of communal leaders' belief in an Algerian Jewish future. Yves C. Aouate, "Note et observations sur une histoire en construction," *Archives juives: Revue d'histoire des Juifs de France* 29, 1 (1e semestre 1996,) p. 8, concurs while positing a transition from "confidence to fear" from 1954 to 1958.

99. Daniel Timsit, *Algérie, récit anachronique* (Paris: Bouchène, 1999), cited in Stora, *Les trois exils*, 133.

100. Jean Bensimon, "Être juif en Algérie: Une illusion perdue?" *Kadimah*, December 1962.

101. "Moslem Countries," 14 January 1958, 55/64# [45/74#28, 86], AJDC. The Hebrew Immigrant Aid Society (HIAS) initially failed to establish an office to help Jews leave due to lack of interest. AJC, "North African Jews on the Move," January 1962, 55/64 # [45/64 #27], AJDC. Discussions about bringing HIAS to Algeria appear in Réunion du conseil du CJAES, 3 December 1955, XVI, FJL, AIU.

102. Frederick Fried to Louis Horowitz, 28 January 1956, 55/64# [45/74#28, 86], AJDC.

103. Some posited a class dimension to migration in these years, with wealthier Jews preparing for possible migration, while employees, workers, and others waited. Lévis to Nelson and Souget, 20 December 1960, 55/64# [45/74#28, 86], AJDC. Max Lapides made similar observations.

104. Fried to Horowitz, 28 January 1956, 55/64# [45/74#28, 86], AJDC.

105. Abromovitch, "Memorandum: Report on Algeria," 11 June 1956, 55/64# [45/74#28, 86], AJDC.

106. Ibid.

107. Réunion du conseil du CJAES, 19 June 1957, XVI, FJL, AIU.

108. Abromovitch, "Memorandum: Report on Algeria," 11 June 1956, 55/64#, [45/74#28, 86], AJDC.

109. Lazarus, "Rapport sur la situation des Juifs," 54.

110. Jacques Lazarus, "Foreign Countries: North Africa," *American Jewish Year Book* 61 (1960), 332; "Moslem Countries," 6 October 1959, 55/64# [45/74#28, 86], AJDC; Katz, "Jews and Muslims," 267–68.

111. Charles-Robert Ageron, *La décolonisation française* (Paris: Armand Colin, 1991), p. 158. Sciodo-Zürcher, *Devenir métropolitain*, 63, 78, argues French Algerians experienced a "collective catharsis" after de Gaulle's return to power. His declaration to support autodetermination, however, alienated many.

112. Rabbi Abraham Sellem (Bou Sadda) to Lazarus, 16 October 1959, I, FJL, AIU.

113. Henry Levy, "Foreign Countries: North Africa," *American Jewish Year Book* 60 (1959), p. 277.

114. Réunion du conseil du CJAES, 19 June 1957, XVI, FJL, AIU.

115. Lazarus to Nehemiah Robinson, 17 June 1957, III, FJL, AIU.

116. Sussman, "Changing Lands," 95–97.

117. Press clippings are in I, FJL, AIU. Lazarus also asked Léon Elbaz, 23 September 1958, I, FJL, AIU, to be updated on "all incidents affecting our co-religionists in your area particularly with regard to security."

118. Lazarus to Perlzweig, 14 January 1957, III, FJL, AIU.

119. Lazarus, "Rapport sur la situation des Juifs," 52.

120. For Jewish efforts to prove their "Frenchness," see Shepard, *The Invention of Decolonization*, 169–82.

121. Sussman, "Changing Lands," 115; Ayoun, "Les Juifs d'Algérie," 21. This claim was particularly important for the FLN's efforts to win international legitimacy. Mathew Connelly, *A Diplomatic Revolution: Algeria's Fight for Independence and the Origins of the Post–Cold War Era* (Oxford: Oxford University Press, 2002). According to Stora, *Les trois exils*, 160, the FLN's failure to win over Algerian Jews played a role in its "ideological hardening."

122. See Frémontier, *L'étoile rouge de David*, 252, for the story of an FLN request to one Jewish member to establish a group of Jewish supporters for which only five expressed interest.

123. Charbit, *Les harkis*.

124. Scholars disagree on the penetration of Algerian nationalism in the 1950s. Meynier, *Histoire intérieure*, 153–57, posits that by summer 1955 most Algerians had embraced the FLN's struggle. Benjamin Stora, *La gangrène et l'oubli: La mémoire de la guerre d'Algérie* (Paris: Découverte, 1991), pp. 161–71, and Paul Silverstein, *Algeria in France: Transpolitics, Race, and Nation* (Bloomington: Indiana University Press, 2004), 39–40, argue that colonial policies had strengthened ethnic distinctions among Algerian Muslims, limiting nationalist penetration. Katz, "Jews and Muslims," 255–57, makes clear that in the 1950s, many Muslims still believed in French republicanism while Shepard, *The Invention of Decolonization*, passim, shows how decolonization itself created "Algerians."

125. Many scholars have posited, in contrast, that FLN activists did not believe their own rhetoric on Jewish belonging to the nation and have thus deemphasized the

FLN's hardening views *in response* to Jewish politics. See Charles-Robert Ageron, "Une guerre religieuse, "*Archives juives: Revue d'histoire des Juifs de France* 29, 1 (1e semestre 1996): 11–14; Ayoun, "Les Juifs d'Algérie," 24; Sussman, "Changing Lands," 128.

126. "La parole du peuple" in the PPA newspaper *L'Émigré*, for example, called for universal suffrage for all Algerians, no matter their race or confession. Excerpt in Directeur départemental des services de police to Préfet des BdR, "A/S Journal du PPA, *L'Émigré*," 19 December 1947, 150W170, BdR.

127. Cited in Cohen, "Le Comité juif," 31.

128. *Al Istiqlal*, June 1956, cited in Ayoun, "Les Juifs d'Algérie," 21.

129. On the Congress, see Meynier, *Histoire intérieure,* 191–200, who suggests that most Algerians never embraced the idea of a non-Muslim state. For the Congress's implications for Jews, see, Ayoun, "Les Juifs d'Algérie," 22; Cohen, "Le Comité juif," 31–32; Katz, "Jews and Muslims," 258–61; and Stora, *Les trois exils*, 142–43.

130. "Lettre aux Israélites d'Algérie," in *El Moudjahid* 3 (September 1956), p. 52.

131. "Le FLN et les Israélites algériens," *France observatoire*, 18 October 1956.

132. Sussman, "Changing Lands," 123–25, and Ayoun, "Les Juifs d'Algérie," 23, argue that following de Gaulle's September 1959 declaration proclaiming the value of self-determination, nationalist appeals to Jews diminished.

133. "La communauté juive d'Algérie," Twelth Session of the General Assembly of the United Nations, No date, XVI, FJL, AIU.

134. "Executive Meeting," 14 January 1958, 55/64# [45/64#28, 86], AJDC. For rising violence, see Katz, "Jews and Muslims," 262. Meynier, *Histoire intérieure*, 255, notes that blackmail attempts were concentrated in the country's southern regions.

135. "Les Juifs d'Algérie dans le combat pour l'indépendance nationale," *Le Monde*, 19 February 1960. For a discussion of this piece and the original proclamation by the FLN, see Cohen, "Le Comité juif," 32–33.

136. The comment was made in an interview with Guy Mollet, secretary general of the SFIO and member of de Gaulle's cabinet. "Le général de Gaulle m'a dit: Ma solution pour l'Algérie, un état fédéral," *Le Monde*, 18 February 1960.

137. Cohen, "Le Comité juif," 40–45, covers this history from the CJAES's perspective and Shepard, 170–73, from the French government's perspective.

138. Lazarus to Easterman, 13 June 1960, III and IV, FJL, AIU.

139. Maître Benizri, "Mémoire: Inspiré par les préoccupations des Israélites français d'Algérie à la suite de la politique dite des communautés," 1961, SEAA, 121 bis, MAE.

140. Extract from "Jewish Chronicle, Features," 16 March 1960 in "Menaces du FLN contre les Juifs d'Algérie," 17 March 1960, MDI 87, CDJC; "FLN warns Algerian Jewry," *Jewish Telegraphic Agency*, 25 July 1960, Bulletin No. 194, p. 4, in XVI, FJL, AIU.

141. "Le FLN condamne l'antisémitisme," 16 January 1961, MDI 89, CDJC; Ayoun, "Les Juifs d'Algérie," 24. Meynier, *Histoire intérieure*, 255, argues that FLN literature was only rarely antisemitic, and then only in nonmainstream texts from the southern regions.

142. Cited in Cohen, "Le Comité juif," 34. Demonstrations calling for "Muslim Algeria" rather than "Algerian Algeria" during de Gaulle's December 1960 visit suggest that the revolution was changing course.

143. WJC, Information Department, "Antisemitism in Algeria" (excerpts from a letter by A. Chanderli, Permanent representative of the Algerian Front of National Liberation), 7 March 1961, XVI, FJL, AIU.

144. RG Alger, "FLN Documents intitulés 'Les Juifs d'Algérie dans le combat pour l'indépendance nationale,'" 14 March 1961, SEAA, 121 bis, MAE; "Les tentatives du FLN auprès des communautés israélites d'Algérie," *Écho d'Alger*, 16 March 1961, XVI, FJL, AIU.

145. AJC to Moses Leavitt, "Conference with M. Chanderli on March 27," 25 April 1961, 55/64 # [45/64 #28], AJDC.

146. Lazarus to Louis Joxe, "Algérie," March 1961, III, FJL, AIU. Lazarus and the CJAES demanded the same right of autodetermination that Muslim Algerians sought for themselves. "Mémoire sur le Judaïsme algérien, présenté par le Comité juif algérien d'études sociales et la fédération des communautés israélites d'Algérie," Alger, 1 March 1961, II, FJL, AIU. For the CJAES response, see Cohen, "Le Comité juif," 35.

147. Moses A. Leavitt to Mr. Philip Soskie, 30 December 1960, 55/64 # [45/64#28, 86], AJDC. Emphasis mine.

148. AJC, "Memorandum to Foreign Affairs Department," 8 June 1961, 55/64 #, [45/64 #28], AJDC.

149. Lapides, "An Algerian Odyssey," 3 May 1961, 55/64 # [45/64 #28], AJDC, claimed that while most Algerian Jews, stressed the necessity of departure, there was a great deal of "indecision, hesitation and confusion" around the issue. HIAS finally established an Algerian office in March 1961.

150. "Droits égaux en Algérie," *L'Observateur du Moyen Orient*, 13 September 1957. GPRA spokesmen cited in Kalef, "Conversations algériennes," *L'Arche*, August–September 1961, p. 34. Also see Ayoun, "Les Juifs d'Algérie," 24.

151. For Algerian relations with Israel, see Michael Laskier, "Israel and Algeria and French Colonialism and the Arab-Israeli Conflict, 1954–1978," *Israel Studies* 6, 2 (2001): 1–32, and Stora, *Les trois exils*, 154–55.

152. The WJC and Jewish Agency denied encouraging such departures. Jean Morin, Délégué général en Algérie, to Ministre d'état, Chargé des affaires algériennes, "Activité des missions israéliennes en Algérie," 24 March 1961, SEAA, 121 bis, MAE. For Israeli efforts in Algeria, also see Shepard, *The Invention of Decolonization*, 174–77. "Memorandum: Report on Algeria," 11 June 1956, 55/64# [45/64 #28, 86], AJDC, discusses nationalist irritation at Israeli agents' training of Jewish self-defense groups.

153. AJC to Moses Leavitt, "Conference with M. Chanderli on March 27," 25 April 1961, 55/64 # [45/64 #28] AJDC.

154. Henri Chemouilli, "Un an après: Lettres à un ami d'Algérie," *L'Arche* 78 (July 1963): 22–26.

155. Claude Estier, "Les journées de décembre," *Droit et liberté*, January 1961.

156. A French deputy, Chibi actively pushed for peace. "End of War Called For," *Herald Tribune*, 21 July 1959. The written exchange occurred via a Jewish teacher in Bône, Charles Levy, 12 March; 24 March; 6 April 1961; and letter from Lazarus to Chibi, 20 March 1961, II, FJL, AIU.

157. *France soir* and *France observateur* reported Algerian accusations that Jews had instigated the violence, while *Le Monde* and Algerian Jewish sources insisted that

such claims were a pretext for the destruction. Note à l'attention de M. le Grand Rabbin J. Kaplan, "Sac de la synagogue de la Casbah à Alger," 11 December 1960, MDI 87, CDJC.

158. In June 1961, Algerian Jewish personalities met again to reaffirm their French citizenship. RG, Alger, "Communauté juive," 4 July 1961, 121 bis, MAE.

159. Le Monde diplomatique, July 1961, cited in Ayoun, "Les Juifs d'Algérie," 24. See also Sussman, "Changing Lands," 130. The AJC and Lazarus also reported on this shift. "North African Jews on the Move," January 1962, 55/64 # [45/64 #27], AJDC; Note d'information de Jacques Lazarus, "Algérie," 28 February 1962, Entretien entre le Délégué général en Algérie M. Jean Morin et MM. Jaques Lazarus et André Narboni, III, FJL, AIU.

160. Shepard, The Invention of Decolonization, 168–82.

161. Samuel Lévis to Herbert Katzki, 20 October 1961, 55/64 # [45/64 #28], AJDC.

162. Abe Karlikow, Untitled, 19 June 1962, 55/64 # [45/64# 27], AJDC.

163. Katz, "Jews and Muslims," 300, counts over 130 attacks against Jews or Jewish establishments from January 1961 until April 1962.

164. Délégation générale en Algérie, Direction générale des affaires politiques et de l'information, "Note sur les réactions de la communauté israélite d'Algérie face à l'évolution du problème algérien," 24 January 1962, 121 bis, MAE.

165. Paul Sebag, Histoire des Juifs de Tunisie: Des origines à nos jours (Paris: Éditions l'Harmattan, 1991), pp. 296–98; Laskier, North African Jewry, 299–302; Taïeb, "Immigrés d'Afrique du Nord," 151–52.

166. Abe Karlikow, Untitled, 19 June 1962, 55/64# [45/64 #27], AJDC.

167. AJC, "North African Jews on the Move," January 1962, 55/64# [45/64 #27], AJDC.

168. Stora, Les trois exils, 161; "Meeting on Algeria" 9 November 1961, 55/64# [45/64 #28]; AJC, "North African Jews on the Move," January 1962, 55/64# [45/64 #27], AJDC. Léo Palacio, "Violents incidents à Oran entre Musulmans et Israélites," Le Monde, 13 September 1961, p. 3.

169. Gilbert Cohen-Tanugi, Victor Malka, and Arnold Mandel, "Foreign Countries: North Africa, South Africa," American Jewish Year Book 64 (1963) 405–406; RG, "Communauté juive," September 1961, 121 bis, MAE. For FLN efforts to curb interethnic violence, see M. Souget to Charles H. Jordan, "Algeria," 9 January 1962, 55/64 # [45/64 #27], AJDC. CJAES discussions are in Réunion du conseil du Comité juif algérien d'études sociales, 13 September 1961, XVI, FJL, AIU.

170. AJC, "North African Jews on the Move," January 1962, 55/64 #, [45/64 #27], AJDC.

171. "Tunis en Arabe," 11 September 1961, 121 bis, MEA.

172. Cohen, "Le Comité juif," 37 and Henri Chemouilli, Une diaspora méconnue: Les Juifs d'Algérie (Paris: 1976), p. 390, blame the OAS for this attack. Jewish fears are documented in Délégation générale en Algérie, Direction générale des affaires politiques et de l'information, "Note sur les réactions de la communauté israélite d'Algérie face à l'évolution du problème algérien," 24 January 1962, 121 bis, MAE; Eugène Mannoni, "Juifs et Musulmans à leur tour à Oran," Le Monde, 14 September 1961, p. 2.

173. Herbert Katzki to Moses Leavitt, "Situation in Algeria," 15 November 1961, 55/64 # [45/64 #28], AJDC.

174. RG, "État d'esprit de la communauté israélite," 7–10 October 1961, 121 bis, MAE.

175. Délégation générale en Algérie, Direction générale des affaires politiques et de l'information, "Note sur les réactions de la communauté israélite d'Algérie face à l'évolution du problème algérien," 24 January 1962, 121 bis, MAE.

176. RG, "État d'esprit de la communauté israélite," 7–10 October 1961, 121 bis, MAE.

177. James Rice to members of the United HIAS Service Board of Directors and National Council, 13 July 1962, 55/64 # [45/64 #27], AJDC; "La communauté israélite d'Algérie," 19 October 1962, 121 bis, MAE.

178. Joseph Barry, "Algeria: Again the Cruel Dilemma," *The ADL Bulletin*, December 1961.

179. M. Souget to Charles H. Jordan, "Algeria," 9 January 1962; AJC, "North African Jews on the Move," January 1962, 55/64 # [45/64 #27], AJDC; Stora, *Les trois exils*, 166–69.

180. M. Souget to Charles H. Jordan, "Algeria," 9 January 1962, 55/64 # [45/64 #27], AJDC, predicted 40–50 percent would remain.

181. Stora, *Les trois exils*, 164–65, and AJC, "North African Jews on the Move," January 1962, 55/64 # [45/64 #27], AJDC, explain how Jewish OAS members reconciled themselves to their choice.

182. Ayoun, "Les Juifs d'Algérie," 28; Cohen "Le Comité juif," 37.

183. Stora, *Les trois exils*, 165, and Sussman, "Changing Lands," 133, argue that Jewish support for French Algeria could be confused with support for the OAS. For an example of Jewish opposition to the OAS, see Cathie Busidan's testimony in *An Uncertain Future*, 23–33, and Bensimon, "Être juif en Algérie."

184. Délégation générale en Algérie, Direction générale des affaires politiques et de l'information, "Note sur les réactions de la communauté israélite d'Algérie face à l'évolution du problème algérien," 24 January 1962, 121 bis, MAE.

185. Shepard, *The Invention of Decolonization*, 174, 177–80.

186. Stora, *Les trois exils*, 135, describes a wave of panic from December 1961 through June 1962.

187. AJC, "North African Jews on the Move," January 1962, 55/64 # [45/64 #27], AJDC. Those who supported the FLN, according to the AJC, had changed their minds or had found it better to stay silent. "Half of Jews in Algeria Reported to Have Fled," *New York Times*, 26 June 1962, also reported "deep complicity" between Jews and the OAS, while pointing largely to Oran.

188. "Meeting on Algeria" 9 November 1961, 55/64 # [45/64 #28], AJDC.

189. Bureau du 22 décembre 1961, MDI 1–55, CDJC. CRIF debates are from meetings on 18 July 1961, and 18 and 25 January 1962, same microfilm. For OAS outreach to Jews, see Katz, "Jews and Muslims ," 302–305; Shepard, *The Invention of Decolonization*, 178–80; and Sussman, "Changing Lands," 135–36. OAS, "Appel aux Israélites d'Algérie," No date, II, FJL, AIU.

190. AJC, "North African Jews on the Move," January 1962, 55/64 # [45/64 #27], AJDC. M. Souget to Charles H. Jordan, "Algeria," 9 January 1962, same folder, makes the same point. Joint officials were threatened with assassination for helping "deserters" leave the country, and wealthy Jewish businessmen paid large sums to protect themselves against OAS threats. "Moslem Countries: Algeria," 21 November 1961, 55/64 # [45/64 #28], AJDC.

191. JTA Daily News Bulletin, "French Underground in Algiers Warns Jews against Leaving Country," 17 January 1962. For OAS assassinations of Jews, see Ayoun,

"Les Juifs d'Algérie," 27, and Stora, *Les trois exils*, 162–63. Despite its opposition to emigration, the OAS never blocked departures to Israel, which Jewish sources explained by noting that to the OAS, "Israel is something of a 'hero state,' being considered the only country that 'really knows how to deal with Arabs.'" AJC, "North African Jews on the Move," January 1962, 55/64 # [45/64 #27], AJDC.

192. "Memorandum of discussions between Mr. Warburg, Mr. Leavitt, Mr. Jordan," 20–21, November 1961, 55/64 # [45/64 #28], AJDC. Samuel Lévis to Herbert Katzki, 20 October 1961; Herbert Katzki to Moses Leavitt, "Situation in Algeria," 15 November 1961, same file.

193. "La communauté israélite d'Algérie," 19 October 1962, 121 bis, MEA.

194. Souget to AJDC, Geneva—Attn. H. Katzki, 28 February 1962, 55/64 # [45/64 #27], AJDC.

195. Administrative Meeting, 12 March 1962, 55/64 # [45/64 #27], AJDC.

196. Christian Mouly, "L'exode des familles israélites d'Algérie est particulièrement sensible à Constantine," *Le Monde*, 17 February 1962, p. 2, posited that departure rates increased after children got out of school.

197. Shepard, *The Invention of Decolonization*, 180. Juridically Shepard is correct that the Frenchness of Jewish migrants mattered over their ethnic affiliations.

198. AJC, "North African Jews on the Move," January 1962, 55/64 # [45/64 #27], AJDC. Per one reporter: "It is conceivable, the Algerian Jews believe themselves to be too deeply compromised to remain. The chances of a clash with Algerian Arab nationalism seem to them too great for safety." "The Jews of Algeria—Extrait d'un article de Aaron Secal in *The Spectator*, 23 February 1962," MDI 88, CDJC.

199. Sussman "Changing Lands," 144.

200. Note d'information de Jacques Lazarus, "Algérie," 28 February 1962; "Entretien entre le Délégué général en Algérie M. Jean Morin et MM. Jaques Lazarus et André Narboni," III, FJL, AIU.

201. "Appeal to Jews to Remain," *The Jewish Chronicle*, 13 April 1962.

202. Citation and threat from Abe Karlikow, Untitled, 19 June 1962, 55/64 # [45/64 # 27], AJDC.

203. Sussman, "Changing Lands,"185. For departures, see pp. 143–85.

204. Bensimon, "Être juif en Algérie."

205. Cited in Frémontier, *L'étoile rouge de David*, 250.

206. Stora, *Les trois exils*, 154–55, and Laskier, "Israel and Algeria and French Colonialism and the Arab-Israeli Conflict," 16–17. In summer 1961, the WJC ended negotiations with the FLN due to its stance on Israel. "Le Congrès juif mondial parle de l'Algérie," 25 August 1961, in XVI, FJL, AIU.

207. Laskier, "Israel and Algeria and French Colonialism and the Arab-Israeli Conflict," 12.

208. Bensimon, "Être juif en Algérie."

209. Stora, *Les trois exils*, 175. Also see Friedman, *Colonialism and After*, 33; Frémontier, *L'étoile rouge de David*, 37–42; and Denis Sieffert, *Israël-Palestine: Une passion française* (Paris: La Découverte, 2004), pp. 60–61.

210. Bensimon, "Être juif en Algérie."

Chapter 3. Encounters in the Metropole: The Impact of
Decolonization on Muslim-Jewish Life in France in the
1950s and 1960s

1. CRIF meetings, 6 and 20 January 1948, MDI 1–55, CJDC.
2. Delegates asked about basic matters of communal composition and religious practice, demonstrating how little was known about Moroccan Jews. CRIF meeting, 6
January 1948 and 6 April 1948, MDI 1–55, CJDC.
3. CRIF meeting, 8 June and 6 October 1948, Joseph Fischer to Schuman, 30 November 1949, in CRIF meeting, 6 December 1949; MDI 1–55, CJDC; Meiss to
Marin, 11 October 1948, SG/1948, 75 (ex 29), MAE. The CRIF also held periodic
discussions of Moroccan Jewish difficulties migrating to Israel. CRIF meeting, 8
June 1948; Meiss to Olivier Marin, 11 October 1948, in CRIF meeting, 6 October
1948; CRIF meeting, 4 and 26 April 1949; Note d'information, 9 May and 2 June
1949; MDI 1–55, CDJC.
4. "Résolutions votées au 20ème congrès de la FSJF, le 8 novembre 1948," 13 November
1948, BA 2315 Communauté juive, APP.
5. Minutes, CRIF meeting, 20 October 1948, MDI 1–55, CDJC. Fédération des sociétés juives de France, Organisation sioniste de France, Congrès juif mondiale, 9
November 1949, BA 2315 Communauté juive, APP. For Iraqi Jews, see Esther Meir-
Glitzenstein, *Zionism in an Arab Country: Jews in Iraq in the 1940s* (London and
New York: Routledge, 2004).
6. CRIF meeting, 8 November and 6 December 1949, MDI 1–55, CDJC. Representatives disagreed on how publicly to make their case, agreeing finally to a behind-
the-scenes approach. Links between Nazism and Iraqi persecutions are evident in
Joseph Fischer to Robert Schuman, 30 November 1949; CRIF meetings 8 May 1951
and 5 February 1952, same reel.
7. CRIF meetings 20 October 1948 and 8 November 1949, MDI 1–55, CDJC. Joel
Beinin, *The Dispersion of Egyptian Jewry: Culture, Politics, and the Formation of a
Modern Diaspora* (Berkeley: University of California Press, 1998), pp. 19–21.
8. For the problem with migration statistics, see Beinin, *The Dispersion*, 288, note
83. For French Jewish responses, see Alexandre De Aranjo, "L'accueil des réfugiés
d'Egypte en France et leur réinstallation en région parisienne, 1956–1960," in *Terre
d'exil, terre d'asile: Migrations juives en France aux XIXe et XXe siècles*, ed. Colette
Zytnicki (Paris: Éditions de l'Éclat, 2010), p. 133, and Benjamin Pinkus, "La campagne de Suez et son impact sur les Juifs de France," trans. from Hebrew by Jules
Danan, in *Les Juifs de France, le Sionisme et l'État d'Israël*, vol. 2, eds., Doris Bensimon and Benjamin Pinkus (Paris: Publications Langues'O, 1987), pp. 357–60.
9. Mandel, "In the Aftermath of Genocide," chap. 8.
10. Jacques Piette, "Meeting de solidarité avec les combattants et l'État d'Israël, organisé
par l'Association des anciens combattants et engagés volontaires juifs 1939–1945," 20
November 1956, BA 2315 Communauté juive, APP.
11. This linkage was also embedded in the French press. Denis Sieffert, *Israël-Palestine:
Une passion française* (Paris: La Découverte, 2004), p. 106.
12. "Meeting organisé par l'Association indépendante des anciens déportés et internés
de France et le Concours d'organisations juives, le 17/12/1956," 18 December 1956,
MDI 69, CDJC.

13. One Egyptian Jewish lawyer, for example, downplayed public antisemitism and blamed the government. Assemblée plénière du 6 décembre 1956, MDI 1–55, CDJC. Jacques Baulin, "Le Caire nouvelle Mecque de l'antisémitisme," *L'Arche*, January 1960, pp. 23, 59.
14. Allocution de M. le Baron Alain de Rothschild to Conférence inter-organisations juives sur l'Égypte, 21 January 1957, MDI 1–55, CDJC. Conference documentation can be found in CRIF meeting, 25 January 1957; Bureau du CRIF, 8 January 1957, MDI 1–55 CDJC.
15. CRIF meeting, 6 January 1948, MDI 1–55, CDJC. For Jewish reluctance to criticize French policies in Algeria, see Ethan Katz, "Jews and Muslims in the Shadow of Marianne: Conflicting Identities and Republican Culture in France (1914–1975)" (Ph.D. diss., University of Wisconsin–Madison, 2009), pp. 270–71.
16. Most discussions focused on how to manage and pay for Jewish arrivals. See Mandel, "In the Aftermath of Genocide," chap. 8, and Sarah Sussman, "Changing Lands, Changing Identities: The Migration of Algerian Jewry to France, 1954–1967" (Ph.D. diss., Stanford University, 2002), pp. 252–319. The CRIF did protest the Petitjean murders. CRIF meeting, 4 October 1954, MDI 1–55, CDJC.
17. Bureau du CRIF, 4 November 1954, MDI 1–55, CDJC.
18. For the former, see "Après les pogroms de Petitjean (Maroc): La situation des Juifs, noyés dans une masse arabe fanatisée, devient chaque jour plus tragique," *La Terre retrouvée*, 1 October 1954. For the latter, see André Blumel, president, Fédération sioniste de France to Comité d'action sioniste, 24 August 1955, MDI 69, CDJC.
19. Philippe Boukara, "La gauche juive en France et la guerre d'Algérie," *Archives juives: Revue d'histoire des Juifs de France* 29, 1 (1ère semestre 1996): 72–81.
20. "CRIF" in "Press survey du WJC," 15 September 1954, MDI 68, CJDC.
21. Bureau du CRIF, 29 September 1955; CRIF meeting, 13 October 1955, MDI 1–55, CDJC.
22. For an in depth analysis of French Jewish responses to the Algerian war, see Katz, "Jews and Muslims," 269–76. Also see, Doris Bensimon, *Les Juifs de France et leurs relations avec Israël: 1945–1988* (Paris: Éditions l'Harmattan, 1989), pp. 236–37; Boukara, "La gauche juive en France et la guerre d'Algérie," 72–81; Benjamin Stora, *Les trois exils: Juifs d'Algérie* (Paris: Éditions Stock, 2006), pp. 157–60.
23. For mobilization protests, see Benjamin Stora, *Histoire de la guerre d'Algérie, 1954–1962*, 4th ed. (Paris: Éditions La Découverte & Syros, 2006), pp. 18–19.
24. CRIF delegates believed that political circumstances made intervention "inopportune." Bureau du CRIF, 4 November 1955; CRIF meeting, 23 December 1955, MDI 1–55; V. Modiano to l'Union des étudiants juifs de France, 9 December 1955, MDI 57, CDJC. The disagreement was as much over process as politics, since the UEJF had issued its statement without CRIF approval. Nevertheless, a year later CRIF delegates still proved hesitant to express their views on Algeria, arguing that they did not represent Algerian Jews. CRIF meeting, 18 October 1956, MDI 1–55, CDJC.
25. Raymond Aron, "Israël face à la tragédie," *Le Figaro littéraire*, 12–18 June 1967, for example, notoriously distanced his pro-independence position from his Jewish roots.
26. W. Rabi, "Nos frères: Au coeur du drame algérien," *L'Arche*, June 1959, pp. 28, 59.
27. Cited in Yair Auron, *Les Juifs d'extrême gauche en Mai 68: Une génération révolutionnaire marquée par la Shoah*, translated from Hebrew by Katherine Werchowski (Paris: Albin Michel 1998), pp. 62–63.

28. Cited in Lionel Cohn, "Réflexions d'un étudiant juif religieux sur le problème algérien," *Kadimah*, December 1960–January 1961, p. 1.

29. Cited in Auron, *Les Juifs d'extrême gauche*, 64.

30. Benjamin Hyman, " 'The Hospitality of Your Columns': French Jewish and Muslim Student Press and the Rhetorical Construction of 'Dialogue,' 1957–1969," undergraduate paper, Brown University, fall 2010. I would like to thank Ben for allowing me to develop upon his insights in the following pages.

31. Henry Pohoryles, "1940–1955: Résurrection et évolution des mouvements de jeunes," *La Revue FSJU*, October 1955, Bibliothèque, UEJF. Roger Berg, "Studieuse et grave jeunesse," *L'Arche*, February 1957, p. 44, claimed two thousand members. Also see Lucine Lazare, "Student Movements, Jewish-France," *Encyclopaedia Judaica*, eds., Michael Berenbaum and Fred Skolnik, 2nd ed., vol. 19 (Detroit: Macmillan Reference, 2007), pp. 265–69.

32. While the UEJF supported Jewish independence in Palestine, it also favored Muslim-Jewish cooperation. "Union des étudiants juifs de France," F715292, AN.

33. Henri Atlan, "Rapport du conseil d'administration," 9ème congrès de l'UEJF, January 1963, II, FJL, AIU. This position caused a rift between the UEJF and their Algerian counterparts. "A nos camarades d'Algérie," *Kadimah*, December 1962. Atlan, while remaining committed to his prior position, acknowledged later, "it is true that I was not with them on site." Cited in Jean-Luc Allouche, "Algérie: Le vent de l'histoire," *L'Arche* December 1979, p. 36.

34. For more on Kateb, see Katz, "Jews and Muslims," 282–84.

35. Yacine Kateb, "Les rapports judéo-arabes," *Kadimah*, June/July 1957, p. 10ff.

36. "La paix israélo-arabe est-elle possible?" *L'Arche*, March 1958, p. 19. Memmi nevertheless remained committed to dialogue "because it is the only way."

37. Lionel Cohn, "Réflexions d'un étudiant juif religieux sur le problème algérien," *Kadimah*, December 1960–January 1961.

38. "Mohammed Ben Bachir, "Un étudiant musulman nous répond," *Kadimah*, April/May 1961, p. 1ff.

39. "La paix israélo-arabe est-elle possible?" in *L'Arche*, March 1958, p. 18. While acknowledging the inaccuracy of the term "antisemitism," the editors adopted it nonetheless.

40. Interestingly, most questionnaire respondents did not reflect the editorial biases, downplaying anti-Jewish animosity in the Muslim world while agreeing that relations had deteriorated. "Lettre aux lecteurs," *L'Arche*, March 1958, p. 5.

41. Jacques Mosel, "Parcours algérien," *L'Arche*, March 1958, p. 14. For more measured discussions of Muslim-Jewish relations in North Africa, see "Le Judaïsme nord-africain s'interroge sur son avenir," *L'Arche*, February 1957, pp. 10–11; Henri Chemouilli, "La grande peur des Juifs d'Algérie," *L'Arche*, August–September 1957, pp. 20–22; Albert Memmi, "Une tragédie si quotidienne," *L'Arche* February 1961, pp. 18–23. As should be clear from earlier citations, Memmi's views vacillated somewhat.

42. Perhaps unsurprisingly, French Zionist publications remained consistently pessimistic, as in "La chronique politique de J. Ariel: La mise en demeure du FLN," *La Terre retrouvée*, 15 May 1960, which warned that an FLN victory would mean "the end of Algerian Judaism" or "Le FLN algérien menace les Juifs," *Notre drapeau*, 25 October 1956, pp. 1–2.

43. Emile Touati, "Avec un dinar en poche: Après Bizerte, le problème des réfugiés d'Afrique du Nord se pose encore d'une manière plus aiguë. Notre communauté saura-t-elle y faire face?" *L'Arche*, October 1961, p. 34. This depiction can be contrasted to "La communauté juive menacée," *Les Écoutés*, 31 August 1961, in MDI 89, CDJC, that described anti-Jewish sentiment as emerging from the political establishment rather than from the wider population.
44. "Menaces de pogrom à Oran," 1 June 1962, MDI 88, CDJC.
45. While written in English this piece by Joseph Barry, "Algeria: Again the Cruel Dilemma," *The ADL Bulletin*, December 1961, in Notes d'information, 1961, MDI 88, CDJC, was part of the CRIF's clippings collection.
46. Robert Buchard, "Des élèves musulmans passent à tabac des Israélites," *Paris presse*, 20 November 1961, MDI 89, CDJC.
47. "Un tract OAS juive," *Le Figaro*, 13 March 1961, in MDI 89, CDJC.
48. The CRIF's left-leaning member organizations called for a condemnation of OAS violence in May 1961, unleashing a debate over whether the OAS was antisemitic (given FLN attacks against Jews), whether CRIF involvement would harm Algerian Jews, and whether the CRIF should speak out on French political questions. CRIF meetings, 8 May and 8 December 1961; Bureau du CRIF, 22 December 1961, MDI 1–55, CDJC.
49. Marcel Liebman, "Les Juifs devant le problème algérien," *Les Temps modernes*, 18 April 1961, pp. 1328–42.
50. The CRIF's final statement (which passed with several abstentions) was decidedly apolitical, condemning violence and Nazi-inspired tactics with no mention of Jews, Muslims, the OAS, the FLN, or French policy. CRIF meetings, 18 and 25 January 1962, MDI 1–55, CDJC. On Jewish leftists and the Algerian crisis, see Bensimon, *Les Juifs de France*, 236–37; Boukara, "La gauche juive en France, 72–81, and Stora, *Les trois exiles,* 157–60.
51. Jim House and Neil MacMaster, *Paris 1961: Algerians, State Terror, and Memory* (Oxford: Oxford University Press, 2006).
52. Elio Boublil to Vidal Modiano, 6 November 1961, MDI 73B; "Meeting juif contre le racisme musulman," 24 November 1961, MDI 89, CDJC.
53. Boukara, "La gauche juive," 78–79.
54. Isi Blum and Dr. Danovski to Docteur Modiano 25 October 1961, MDI 73B, CDJC.
55. Bureau du 27 novembre 1961; Assemblée plénière du 8 décembre 1961, MDI 1–55, CDJC.
56. *La Terre retrouvée*, 15 November 1961, cited in Boukara, "La gauche juive," 79. For republicanism and Jewish responses to the Algerian war, see Katz, "Jews and Muslims," 269–98.
57. Citation comes from Robert Sommer, Jewish author and founder of Fondation sepher and Bureau du Chabbat, to Jacques Lazarus, 14 March 1961, XVI, FJL, AIU. Lazarus's infuriated response is in the same file. Information on the protest can be found in Raph. Feigelson, Sec Gen. Comité juif d'action anti-fasciste, 25 June 1962, MDI 71, CDJC. Signatories included: Amicale des anciens déportés juifs; Amicale des Juifs anciens résistants; Cercle Bernard Lazare; Cercle Mishmar; Fédération générale et industriels, Artisans et façonniers juifs; Union des engagés volontaires et anciens combattants juifs; Union des Juifs pour la résistance et l'entraide; Union des sociétés juives de France, and the Cercle d'études juives Beth Hakerem.

58. M. Moch à l'attention de M. Jacques Meyer, "Note sur la situation de la communauté juive d'Algérie et l'exode massif de Juifs en France," 4 January 1963, MDI 83, CDJC. For another example, see André Nehar, "Dans le feu de l'épreuve," *L'Arche*, March 1963, p. 29.

59. Gérard Israel, "Éléments pour un portrait-robot du rapatrié," *L'Arche*, March 1963, pp. 52–53.

60. Arab attempts in 1964 to boycott French companies with contracts in Israel exacerbated this view. Relevant CRIF discussions can be found MDI 1–55; MDI 84; MDI 85; MDI 91, and MDI 93, CJDC. Also see Kassir and Mardam-Bey, *Itinéraires de Paris à Jerusalem*, 16–17.

61. One exception was Pierre Vidal-Naquet, "La guerre révolutionnaire et la tragédie des harkis," *Le Monde*, 11–12 November 1962, who condemned the treatment of Muslim immigrants. Most Jewish journalists paid little attention to incoming Muslims. See, for example, T.C. "Le FSJU face au problème social des Juifs nord-africains," *La revue du FSJU*, December 1953, p. 9, which comments that Jewish arrivals were "often submerged in the mass of Muslim immigrants of the same origin," but never again mentioned the latter. Emile Touati's article discussed below is another exception.

62. Chouchana Boukhobza, "Exil, quand tu nous tiens," *Communauté nouvelle*, No. 23, February–March 1985.

63. Paul Hyman, *The Jews of Modern France* (Berkeley: University of California Press, 1998), p. 195. Paris held 175,000 Jews and 126,000 Muslims by the late 1950s. Katz, "Jews and Muslims," 248.

64. Kimberly Arkin, " 'It's the French and the Arabs against the Jews': Identity Politics and the Construction of Adolescent Jewishness in France" (Ph.D. diss., University of Chicago, 2008), pp. 170–71; Doris Bensimon and Sergio Della Pergolla, *La population juive de France: Socio-démographie et identité* (Jerusalem: Institute of Contemporary Jewry of Hebrew University and Centre national de la recherche scientifique, Paris, 1984), pp. 250, 253, 286–87, have shown, traditional Jewish neighborhoods in Paris actually included both Muslims and Jews. For Marseille, see René Duchac, "Facteurs urbains de l'adaptation des immigrés maghrébins: Étude comparative de trois quartiers de Marseille," in *Les immigrés du Maghreb: Études sur l'adaptation en milieu urbain, travaux et documents* 79 (Paris: Presses universitaires de France, 1977), pp. 14–15; Sussman, "Changing Lands," 235–36.

65. Numbers of Arabic speakers differed according to country and region of origin. Doris Bensimon, *L'intégration des Juifs nord-africains en France* (La Haye: Mouton, 1971), p. 22–23.

66. Interview cited in Jacques Frémontier, *L'étoile rouge de David: Les Juifs communiste en France* (Paris: Fayard, 2002), p. 197. The interviewee was a communist and a member of the FLN during the Algerian War.

67. Katz, "Jews and Muslims," 249–54, 287–94.

68. Pierre Baillet, "Les rapatriés d'Algérie en France," *Notes et études documentaires*, No. 4275–76 (29 March 1976), pp. 46–57.

69. Gérard Noiriel, *Immigration, antisémitisme et racisme en France (XIXe–XXe siècle): Discours publics, humiliations privées* (Paris: Fayard, 2007), p. 537. Amelia Lyons, "Invisible Immigrants: Algerian Families and the French Welfare State in the Era of

Decolonization (1947–1974)" (Ph.D. diss., University of California, Irvine 2004), pp. 9, 40–49, argues that prior to 1962, welfare institutions did seek to incorporate Algerian Muslims into French society.

70. Even Jewish refugees often benefited from a welcoming administrative structure. See Aranjo, "L'accueil des réfugiés d'Egypte en France," 141, for example, for governmental attitudes toward arriving Jews.

71. "Sources of Financing for the Principal Relief and Rehabilitation Programs in France in 1962," Julian Breen, 29 July 1963, 309, AJDC; Sussman, "Changing Lands," 188–89.

72. For distinctions between Jewish and Muslim Algerians, see Todd Shepard, *The Invention of Decolonization: The Algerian War and the Remaking of France* (Ithaca/London: Cornell University Press, 2006), pp. 172–73. Alexis Spire, *Étrangers à la carte: L'administration de l'immigration en France (1945–1975)* (Paris: Grasset, 2005), pp. 189–222, shows how even Muslim repatriates who had fought for the French army were treated as administratively distinct from "European" repatriates. Fatima Besnaci-Lancou and Gilles Manceron eds., *Les harkis: Dans la colonisation et ses suites* (Paris: Les Éditions de l'Atelier, 2008), pp. 30–31, 112. Tom Charbit, *Les harkis* (Paris: La Découverte, 2006), pp. 60–61. For aid to repatriates, see Jean Jacques Jordi, *De l'exode à l'exil: Rapatriés et pieds-noirs en France* (Paris: Éditions l'Harmattan, 1993) and *1962, L'arrivée des pieds-noirs* (Paris: Autrement, 1995). For aid to Morrocan Jewish immigrants, see Martin Messika, "L'accueil des Juifs marocains en France," *Terre d'exil terre d'asile: Migrations juives en France aux XIXe et XXe siècles*, ed., Colette Zytnicki (Paris: Éditions de l'Éclat, 2010), pp 175–78.

73. While more immigrants and pieds noirs went to Paris, they made up a smaller percentage of the city's population. Abdelmalek Sayad, Jean-Jacques Jordi, and Émile Témime, *Le choc de la décolonisation (1945–1990)* vol. 4 of *Migrance: Histoire des migrations à Marseille*, ed. Émile Témime (Aix-en-Provence: Éditions Jeanne Laffitte, 1991), pp. 8, 58–59, 61–64.

74. Préfet des Bouches-du-Rhône, "Exposé sur l'état actuel de la question sociale nord-africaine dans le département des Bouches-du-Rhône et la 9e région militaire," 20 July 1953, 148W193, BdR. While another report put the number at 30,000, or nearly 4 percent of Marseille's total population (Commissaire de police de la sureté to Commissaire principal, "Délinquance nord-africaine et délinquance d'ensemble comparées," 2 January 1953, same file), most others reported 11,000 in Marseille with 3,000–4,000 in the surrounding towns. The numbers of Moroccan and Tunisians Muslims numbered 600 and 550, respectively, in October 1953. André Pelabon to Ministre de l'Intérieur, "Enquête sociale sur la situation des Musulmans originaires d'Algérie résidant en métropole, Département des Bouches-du-Rhône," 26 October 1953, same file. The 1959 figure comes from Sayad, Jordi, and Témime, *Le Choc*, 67.

75. Sayad, Jordi, and Témime, *Le Choc*, 10, 51, 68–89; Émile Témime, *Histoire de Marseille de la Révolution à nos jours* (Paris: Perrin, 1999), p. 334. Only in 1974 did family unification become the primary migratory source. Alain Gillette and Abdelmalek Sayad, *L'immigration algérienne en France*, 2nd ed. (Paris: Éditions entente, 1984), p. 61; Lyons, *Invisible Immigrants*; André Michel, *Les travailleurs algériens en France* (Paris: Éditions du CNRS, 1956); Jacques Simon, ed., *L'immigration algérienne en France: De 1962 à nos jours* (Paris: L'Harmattan, 2002), pp. 16–26, 37, 42–44; Benjamin Stora, *Ils venaient d'Algérie: L'immigration en France (1912–1992)* (Paris: Fayard, 1992), p. 400.

76. From 1949 to June 1950, about seventy thousand traveled through the city, although many were from Eastern Europe. RG, Section frontières, "Le mouvement de transmigration des Israélites: La question israélienne," June 1950, F7/15589, AN.

77. For Grand Arénas, see Émile Témime and Nathalie Deguigné, *Le camp du Grand Arénas Marseille, 1944-1966* (Paris: Éditions Autrement, 2001), pp. 76-136. For Egyptian Jews in Marseille, see Aranjo, "L'accueil des réfugiés d'Egypte en France," 142.

78. Roland Avitol, "Marseille," *L'Arche* (March/April, 1968), pp. 19-20; statistics compiled by the FSJU and included in a letter from Julian Breen to Boris Sapir, 15 February 1963, 309, AJDC.

79. Sayad, Jordi, and Témime, *Le Choc*, 69-70.

80. A. H. Boullet, Sec. Gen., Association des foyers nord-africains de Provence to Préfet, 23 August 1952, 148W193, BdR.

81. André Pelabon to MI, "Enquête sociale sur la situation des Musulmans originaires d'Algérie résidant en métropole, Département des Bouches-du-Rhône," 26 October 1953, 148w193, BdR.

82. Cited in Témime and Deguigné, *Le camp du Grand Arénas*, 99.

83. Ibid., 115-16, 117-18.

84. Ibid., 117.

85. Jean André Carreno, Alain Hayot and Francis Lesme, *Le quartier de la porte d'Aix à Marseille: Ethnologie d'un centre urbain* (Aix-en-Provence: Université de Provence, 1974), pp. 39-41.

86. Cited in Sayad, Jordi, and Témime, *Le Choc*, 159-60.

87. Jocelyne Cesari, Alain Moreau, and Alexandra Schleyer-Lindenmann, *"Plus marseillais que moi, tu meurs!" Migrations, identités et territoires à Marseille* (Paris: L'Harmattan, 2001), pp. 20-21, 121.

88. Bensimon, *Les Juifs de France*, 237. Katz, "Jews and Muslims," 250, 253, 286-87.

89. Algerian Jews attended European public schools while Moroccan and Tunisian Jews attended AIU schools. For rates of Jewish immigrant education in France, see Bensimon and Della Pergola, *La population juive de France*, 167. Simon, *Immigration algérienne en France*, 95, notes that by the 1980s, Algerian Muslim families had embraced education as the key to success.

90. North African Jews of varying socioeconomic backgrounds experienced rapid social mobility in France. Bensimon and Della Pergola, *La population juive de France*, 179-220; Hyman, *The Jews of Modern France*, 196-97; Véronique Poirier, *Ashkénazes et Séfarades: Une étude comparée de leurs relations en France et en Israël (années 1950-1990)*, pp. 92-94, 137-401; Claude Tapia, *Les Juifs sépharades en France (1965-1985): Études psychosociologiques et historiques* (Paris: Éditions l'Harmattan, 1986), p. 221.

91. Simon, *L'immigration algérienne en France*, 20. The cultural and scholarly level of the migrants improved over time. Gillette and Sayad, *L'immigration algérienne en France*, 210.

92. M.S. "Témoignages: Les Juifs nord-africains de St-Fons." *L'Arche* (December 1953), p. 121.

93. Émile Touati, "Analyse de l'immigration nord-africaine," *L'Arche* (March 1956), pp. 36-38. Katz, "Jews and Muslims," 273-74, notes that although Touati's portrayal reflected some truth, it also served to highlight differences between Jewish citizens and Muslim "outsiders."

94. Simon, *L'immigration algérienne en France*, 211-12; Gilette and Sayed, *L'immigration algérienne*, 62–63. According to Catherine Wihtol de Wenden, *Les immigrés et la politique: Cent cinquant ans d'évolution* (Paris: Presses de la Fondation nationale des sciences politiques, 1988,) pp. 175-76, Tunisian Muslim migrants were more urban and educated than those from Morocco and Algeria.

95. Mandel, *In the Aftermath of Genocide*, 167–77; "Philanthropy or Cultural Imperialism? The Impact of American Jewish Aid in Post-Holocaust France," *Jewish Social Studies*, 9, 1 (Fall 2002): 53–94; and Laura Hobson Faure, "Un 'Plan Marshall juif': La présence juive américaine en France après la Shoah, 1944–54" (Ph.D. diss., École des hautes études en sciences sociales, Paris, 2009).

96. Aranjo, "L'accueil des réfugiés d'Egypte en France," 142–44; Julien Samuel, "Rapport moral: Regard sur 10 années d'activité du Fonds social juif unifié," in *Assemblée générale du Xe anniversaire du Fonds social juif unifié* (Paris: 1960), p. 5. Mônica Riasa Schpun, "Les premiers migrants juifs d'Afrique du Nord dans la France de l'après-guerre: Une découverte pour les services sociaux," *Archives juives* 45, 1 (2012): 61–73.

97. "Integration of Algerian Jews in France: Report from Paris Office, American Jewish Committee," Meeting of the External Affairs Committee, 13 November 1962, Anglo-Jewish Association Papers, AJ95/1/31, Parkes Library.

98. Encounters between native French Jews and their incoming North African coreligionists could also be conflictual. See Mandel, "In the Aftermath of Genocide," chap. 8; Poirier, *Ashkénazes et Séfarades*, 66–69, 70–74; Sussman, "Changing Lands," chaps. 4 and 5.

99. Israel Salzer to Germaine Haguenau, 28 May 1956, Juifs et Afrique du Nord, Archives Mlle Haguenau, CC.

100. "Table ronde du FSJU: La communauté et l'intégration des Juifs nord-africains," *L'Arche*, 15 (March 1956), p. 34.

101. RG, Mle, "Propagande anti-française dans les milieux NA de Marseille," 13 September 1951, 148W191, BdR. The small numbers of Moroccan and Tunisian Muslim migrants limited their participation in separatist movements. RG, Mle, "Nord Africains: Réactions des N.A. à l'occasion des événements du Moyen-Orient," 2 November 1951, same file. Témime, *Histoire de Marseille*, 331.

102. Émile Témime, *Marseille transit: Les passagers de Belsunce* (Paris: Éditions Autrement, 1995), pp. 70–71.

103. "Place Jules-Guesde: Plastique devant un bar exploité par un Nord-Africain," *Le Méridional*, 12 January 1962; E.R., "A Marseille: Les bandes musulmanes rivales règlent leurs comptes au plastique," *Le Méridional*, 22 January 1962; Sayad, Jordi and Témime, *Le Choc*, 74–77, Témime, *Histoire de Marseille*, 333–34.

104. The cités de transit were designed as way stations to ease "poorly adjusted" immigrants into European society. Residence, however, often became permanent. While not all inhabitants were immigrants, new arrivals and their descendants made up the majority. Marie-Claude Blanc-Chaléard, "Les immigrés et le logement en France depuis le XIXe siècle: Une histoire paradoxale," in Benjamin Stora and Emile Témime, eds., *Immigrances: L'immigration en France au XXe siècle* (Paris: Hachette littératures, 2007), pp. 67–96; Richard Derderian, *North Africans in Contemporary France* (New York: Palgrave Macmillian, 2004), pp. 8–9; Yvan Gastaut, *L'immigration et l'opinion en France sous la Ve république* (Paris: Éditions du Seuil,

2000), pp. 71–72, 77–93, 262–64; Sayad, Jordi and Témime, *Le Choc*, 79, 135–39; Témime, *Histoire de Marseille*, 334–35, 368–72; Simon, *L'immigration algérienne en France*, 81–91, notes that biases against Muslim residents often prevented their settlement in the HLMs.

105. Abed Guendouz to Maire de Marseille, 24 February 1960, 138W73, BdR. Thanks to Ethan Katz for sharing this source.

106. Préfet de la région de Provence to Préfet, "La communauté juive de Marseille," 17 January 1972, 135W57, BdR, counted 75,000 Jews in Marseille by the early 1970s. However, Bensimon-Donath, *L'intégration des Juifs nord-africains*, 55, documents 65,000 in 1966. Reports in 1967 numbered the population as high as 100,000, perhaps due to transients. RG, Mle., "Milieux juifs," 30 May 1967, 137W363, BdR.

107. "A Marseille quand arrive le bateau d'Algérie," *Al Djazaïri*, 4 February 1965, pp. 4–5.

108. INED, *Les immigrés du Maghreb: Études sur l'adaptation en milieu urbain* (Paris: Presses universitaires de France, 1977), pp. 13, 16–17. Sayad, Jordi, and Témime, *Le Choc*, 107–8, 121, claim 44,000 Muslims in Marseille in 1975.

109. Jean-Jacques Jordi, "L'été 62" and Guy Pervillé, "Les conditions de départ: L'Algérie," in *Marseille et le choc des décolonisations: Les rapatriements 1954–1964*, ed., Jean-Jaques Jordi and Emile Temime (Aix-en-Provence: Édisud, 1996), pp. 54–74. Sayad, Jordi, and Témime, *Le Choc*, 89–98. Citation and statistics are from Témime, *Histoire de Marseille*, 338–39.

110. Between 1952 and 1964 more than eighty thousand new housing units were built. Témime, *Histoire de Marseille*, 369.

111. Irving (Dickman) to Moe (Moses Leavitt), 7 June 1962, 328, AJDC.

112. Eighty percent of Jewish repatriates entered through Marseille where Jewish organizations, in particular the FSJU, directed those seeking aid to relevant agencies. Sidney Nelson to Charles Jordan, "Summary Report," 25 April 1963, 309, AJDC. Louis Hackett, "It's 1945 All Over Again," press release, no date, 328, AJDC. Sussman, "Changing Lands," 351–52. "A l'œuvre: Le Fonds social juif unifié," *Le Provençal*, 30 May 1962; "Le Fonds social juif unifié a fait le bilan de l'année écoulée," *Le Méridional*, 1 April 1963. For the FSJU's local efforts, see Avitol, "Marseille," 19–20. For Jewish responses to arriving Algerian Jews more generally, see Colette Zytnicki, "A immigration d'un nouveau type, réponses nouvelles: Les organizations communautaires et l'exodes des Juifs d'Afrique du Nord, in *Terre d'exil, terre d'asile: Migrations juives en France aux XIXe et XXe siècles,* ed. Colette Zytnicki (Paris: Éditions de l'Éclat): 155–70.

113. F. de Muizon, "Les Juifs de Marseille: La 'révolution' des pieds-noirs," *Regard*, no date (1976?), MDI 159, CDJC.

114. Avitol, "Marseille," 19.

115. As Michel Wieviorka, "The Changing French Jewish Identity," in *Contemporary Jewries: Convergence and Divergence*, eds., Eliezer Ben-Rafael, Yosef Gorney, and Yaacov Ro'i (Leiden: Koninklijke: Brill NV, 2003): p. 255, reminds us, although North African Jewish arrivals shared some characteristics, they nowhere constituted a homogeneous community.

116. R. Musnik and L. Cohn, "Visit to Marseilles," 14–15 May 1961, 346, AJDC. While downtown Marseille still held most of the French Jewish population, the newcomers generally lived in HLM structures eight or ten kilometers away. Moreover, unlike Paris and Lyon, Marseille had no communal structure in the city center and

no "Jewish quarter." Deborah Miller, "Visit to Marseilles," 17–19 May 1961; Untitled Report on Marseille, November 1964, 346, AJDC. De Muizon, "Les Juifs de Marseille."

117. Jordi, *De l'exode*, 218–19.

118. Préfet de la région de Provence to Directeur central de RG, "La communauté juive de Marseille," 17 January 1972, 135W57, BdR. Muizon, "Les Juifs de Marseille." W. Rabi, "Le 'boom' de Marseille: La vague des rapatriés d'Afrique du Nord disloquera-t-elle la seconde communauté de France ou lui donnera-t-elle un nouvel essor?" *L'Arche* 60 (January 1962), pp. 41–45, 67, and De Muizon, "Les Juifs de Marseille."

119. Sussman, "Changing Lands," 350; Richard Ayoun and Bernard Cohen, *Les Juifs d'Algérie: Deux mille ans d'histoire* (Paris: Jean-Claude Lattès, 1982), p. 198; Jacques Sabbath, "Communauté vivante," *L'Arche*, November 1962, pp. 2–4.

120. Untitled Report on Marseille, November 1964; R. Musnik and L. Cohn, "Visit to Marseilles," 14–15 May 1961, 346, AJDC.

121. Cited in Rabi, "Le 'boom' de Marseille," 44–45. Deborah Miller, "Visit to Marseilles," 17–19 May 1961, 346, AJDC.

122. Whatever the divisions, as Sussman, "Changing Lands," 350–63, argues the Consistoire worked hard to bridge differences. "Outlook Much Brighter Now," *Jewish Chronicle*, 9 August 1963, in "La situation des réfugies Juifs à Marseille," 4/9/63, MDI 83; "La communauté israélite de Marseille 70,000 membres" (May/June 1967), MDI 159, CJDC.

123. The term "harkis," which comes from the Arabic *harka*, applies strictly to soldiers in auxiliary units who fought with the French army against Algerian nationalists in 1954–62. Once in France, however, the term came to refer to all Algerian Muslims who fought for the French or adopted a pro-French position and hence left quickly after independence. The number 140,000 includes 85,000 who participated in the military's supplemental units (families included) and 55,000 notables, functionaries, or career military. While those with some status (such as the notables and upper level military personnel integrated into French society relatively rapidly, those in the supplemental units struggled to be accepted. Charbit, *Les harkis*, 9, 21–23, 62, 71. For the different types of *Français musulmans rapatriés*, see Mohand Hamoumou, "L'histoire des harkis et Français musulmans: La fin d'un tabou?" in Benjamin Stora and Mohammed Harbi, *La guerre d'Algérie* (Paris: Éditions Robert Laffont, 2004), pp. 317–23.

124. As Charbit, *Les harkis*, 29–35, points out, while often accused of treason, the mostly rural army recruits had little ideological or political affiliation with the French.

125. For numbers, see Sayad, Jordi, and Témime, *Le Choc*, 90, 106, 122, and Katz, "Jews and Muslims," 331. For citation, see Baillet, "Les rapatriés d'Algérie en France," 46, 52. Private associations sometimes stepped in to fill this administrative gap. See Hamoumou, "L'histoire des harkis," 334–35. For more on intra-Algerian Muslim tensions, see Charbit, *Les harkis*, 82–83, and Abderahmen Moumen, "Du camp de transit à la cité d'accueil: Saint-Maurice-l'Ardoise: 1962–1976" in Besnaci-Lancou and Manceron, *Les harkis*, 13–40.

126. Émile Touati, "Avec un dinar en poche: Après Bizerte, le problème des réfugiés d'Afrique du Nord se pose encore d'une manière plus aiguë. Notre communauté saura-t-elle y faire face?" *L'Arche* 57 (October 1961), p. 32.

127. René Sussan, "Les grandes vacances des Juifs d'Algérie: Un témoignage de René Sussan," *L'Arche* 66 (July 1962), p. 16. One thousand Jews, it should be noted, sought aid from the *Service des affaires musulmanes* (SAM). Katz, "Jews and Muslims," 330–31; Sussman, "Changing Lands," 172–73.

128. Charbit, *Les harkis*, 58–59, 75–83; Hamoumou, *L'histoire des harkis*, 337–38. Also see essays by Giulia Fabiano, Abdel Kader Hamadi, Abderahmen Moumen, and the Introduction of Besnaci-Lancou and Manceron, *Les harkis*, 31–32, 118–45. For the move from seeing *harkis* as citizens to refugees, see Todd D. Shepard, "Excluding the *Harkis* from Repatriate Status, Excluding Muslim Algerians from French Identity." *Transnational Spaces and Identities in the Francophone World*, eds., Hafid Gafaïti, Patricia M. E. Lorcin, and David G. Troyansky (Lincoln: University of Nebraska Press, 2009): 94–114.

129. Sayad, Jordi, and Témime, *Le Choc*, 190.

130. Sussman, "Changing Lands," 235–36, 350; INED, *Immigrés du Maghreb*, 13, 16–17; Sayad, Jordi, and Témime, *Le Choc*, 122–25; Duchac, "Facteurs urbains de l'adaptation des immigrés maghrébins," 14–15. According to Sussman, a 1992 FSJU study of Jewish poor in Marseille claimed that 15 percent of the Jewish population remained in the city's poor northern quarters.

131. INED, *Immigrés du Maghreb*, 17–19. By the early 1970s, 8,000–9,000 immigrant laborers lived in bidonvilles; 15,000–18,000 lived in HLM housing units owned and managed by the Société nationale de construction de logements pour les travailleurs (Sonacotra), and about 2,000 lived in four transit camps (cité de transit).

132. Shepard, *The Invention of Decolonization*, chap. 9.

133. Direction générale de la police nationale, "Étude sur la communauté juive des Bouches-du-Rhône," 16 October 1989, 1693W233, BdR.

134. De Muizon, "Les Juifs de Marseille."

135. Préfet de la région de Provence to Directeur central de RG, "La communauté juive de Marseille," 17 January 1972, 135W5; Direction générale de la police nationale, "Étude sur la communauté juive des Bouches-du-Rhône," 16 October 1989, 1693W233, BdR.

136. Gaston Defferre, "Israël et l'Algérie," *Le Monde*, 1 June 1962. Laskier, "Israel and Algeria and French Colonialism and the Arab-Israeli Conflict, 1954–1978," *Israel Studies* 6, 2 (2001), p.15 (Laskier incorrectly cites Defferre's piece as from 31 May).

137. For Defferre's views on Algerian independence, see Isabelle Rambaud, "Le fonds Gaston-Defferre aux archives de Marseille," in Jordi and Temime, *Marseille et le choc*, 184–89.

138. The Israeli consul general and other Jewish organizations held numerous events to support the young state. "Le gala du comité de jumelage Marseille-Haïfa a été une grande réussite," *Le Méridional*, 22 January 1962; "Les conférences: 'Vers le deuxième million d'immigrants en Israël,' " *Le Méridional*, 24 January 1962; "La chanteuse israélienne Rika Zaraï à la nuitée des étudiants juifs," *Le Méridional*, 2 March 1962.

139. "Note," 24 April 1950; "Note" for Préfet des Bouches-du-Rhône, 22 May 1950; RG, Mle., "Étrangers juifs: Campagne d'aide à Israël, 1952," 19 February 1952, 148W141, BdR. "Immense succès des fêtes du 14ème anniversaire de l'indépendance d'Israël," *Le Provençal*, 21 May 1962.

140. Gaston Defferre, "Impressions sur Israël," *Le Provençal*, 29–30 May, 1 June 1962.

141. "Marseille et Haïfa officiellement jumelles," *Le Méridional*, 18 May 1962. Haifa built a cultural center in Defferre's honor after his death. "Posé d'une première pierre à Haïfa: Le ciel, le vent, la mer et Gaston Defferre" and "Coup de cœur pour Jérusalem: Impression du voyage," *Haboné*, January 1989; RG, "Numéro spécial de la revue *Haboné* imprimé par le Consistoire à l'issue du voyage de M. Jean Claude Gaudin en Israël, 20 February 1989, 1693W233, BdR. Message de Théo Klein (December 1988), MDI 188 CJDC.

142. "Inauguration de l'exposition de dessins d'enfants d'Israël et de Marseille," *Le Provençal*, 26 June 1962.

143. "Quarante jeunes Israéliens en visite à Marseille," *Le Méridional*, 30 April 1963; "Une exposition sur Israël au palais de la Bourse," *Le Provençal*, 1 April 1967.

144. A counterexample saw vandals set fire to Jewish Agency offices on 20 March 1960. While police never determined the arsonists, efforts to undermine the Jewish Agency's mission were presumably at work. ME to MI, "Au sujet d'un incendie criminel à l'Agence juive pour Israël," 21 March 1960, 137W236, BdR.

145. Rabi, "Le 'boom' de Marseille," 41.

146. The rare conflicts that did occur, such as on 27 May 1963 when a fight broke out between two dozen Muslim and Jewish youth on the rue Sainte-Antoine in Paris, captured media attention, thereby calling attention to atypical antagonism rather than to daily neighborly exchanges. "A Paris, violente bagarre entre Algériens et Israélites à la sortie d'un bal," *Le Méridional*, 27 May 1963.

Chapter 4. The 1967 War and the Forging of Political Community

1. Citation from Paula Hyman, *The Jews of Modern France* (Berkeley: University of California Press, 1998), p. 203. Abdellali Hajjat's pathbreaking work on Muslim activism around the Palestinian issue has focused primarily on the 1970s. See "Les Comités Palestine (1970–1972): Aux origines du soutien de la cause palestinienne en France," *Revue des études palestinienes* 8 (Winter 2006): 74–92 and "Des comité Palestine au Mouvement des travailleurs arabes (1970–1976)," in Amhed Boubeker and Abdellali Hajjat, eds., *Histoire politique des immigrations (post) coloniales, France, 1920–2008* (Paris: Éditions Amsterdam, 2008): 145–56. Ethan Katz's work has focused more fully on this issue in "Tracing the Shadow of Palestine: The Zionist-Arab Conflict and Jewish-Muslim Relations in France, 1914–1945," in Nathalie Debrauwere-Miller, ed., *Israeli-Palestinian Conflict in the Francophone World* (New York: Routledge, 2010): 25–44, and "Jews and Muslims in the Shadow of Marianne: Conflicting Identities and Republican Culture in France, 1914–1975" (Ph.D. diss., University of Wisconsin, 2008).

2. Dominique Schnapper, *Jewish Identities in France: An Analysis of Contemporary French Jewry*, trans. Arthur Goldhammer (Chicago: University of Chicago Press, 1984), pp. xlvi–lxvii.

3. For an overview, see Michel Winock, *La France et les Juifs: De 1789 à nos jours* (Paris: Éditions du Seuil, 2004), pp. 307–16. Samir Kassir and Farouk Mardam-Bey, *Itinéraires de Paris à Jerusalem: La France et le conflit israélo-arabe*, vol. 2: 1958–91

(Paris: Revue d'études palestiniennes, 1993), pp. 52–90, argue that emphases on a "rupture" in French/Israeli relations in 1967 is exaggerated, since diplomatic relations were never cut off.

4. The Jewish press expressed concerns about changing French Middle Eastern policies as early as 1962. See, for example, Michael Salomon, "Le Judaïsme français à l'heure des révisions déchirantes? Un entretien avec Guy de Rothschild," L'Arche, April 1962, pp. 24–33, 65, and "Renversement des alliances au Moyen Orient? La reprise des relations avec le monde-arabe est-elle compatible avec le maintien de l'amitié franco-israélienne?" May 1962, L'Arche, pp. 28–33, 63. For Jewish reponses to the shifting political terrain in 1967, see Doris Bensimon, Les Juifs de France et leurs relations avec Israël: 1945–1988 (Paris: Éditions l'Harmattan, 1989), pp. 154–62; Hyman, The Jews of Modern France, 200–205. Denis Sieffert, Israël-Palestine: Une passion française (Paris: La Découverte, 2004), p. 117, and Kassir and Mardam-Bey, Itinéraires de Paris à Jerusalem, 11, 127–31, argue that the media remained staunchly behind Israel during the conflict if becoming more critical with the occupation of new territories. Nevertheless, Jewish representatives watched the press closely for "misleading information." Moch to Pierre Kaufmann, 2 June 1967, MDI 65C, CDJC.

5. Kassir and Mardem-Bey, Itinéraires de Paris, 131; Winock, La France et les Juifs, 317; Joan Wolf, Harnessing the Holocaust: The Politics of Memory in France (Stanford: Stanford University Press, 2004), pp. 36–37.

6. Michel Winock, Chronique des années soixante (Paris: Éditions du Seuil, 1987), pp. 200–202.

7. BIL, N° 7, 11 June 1967, MDI 98, CDJC.

8. Sieffert, Israël-Palestine, 151–59.

9. Articles in the Jewish press complained of contradictions in leftist positions toward Israel. See, for example, "La gauche française contre Israël?" L'Arche, February 1957, p. 23; Jean Daniel, "Israël avait épuisé toutes les possibilités de négociation," L'Arche, February 1957, p. 24; Ephraïm Tari, "Une certaine gauche toujours prisonnière des mythes," L'Arche, February 1963, pp. 13–17. Jewish organizations also criticized one another for leftist-inspired anti-Israeli politics. In 1957, for example, the FSJF excluded groups whose attitude toward Israel was questionable. Réunion, Fédération stes. juives de France, 18 March 1957, MDI 69, CDJC.

10. See, for example, H. Smolarski, "Suis-je le gardien de mon frère?" Bulletin de nos communautés, 26 May 1967.

11. Daniel Mayer, "La guerre des six jours a-t-elle modifié la conscience juive en France?" L'Arche, March/April 1968, p. 39.

12. Wolf, Harnessing the Holocaust, 34–35, notes that while some of the traditional Jewish leadership conceded only slight disappointment with de Gaulle and called for restrained communal responses, they were out of step with most French Jews. The massive popular backing for Israel also helps explain why Jewish leaders proved so willing to criticize national policies. As one declared on 4 June to a meeting of fellow activists, "The majority of the French are with us. . . . Judaism (and with it, French opinion) will not weaken, no matter how diplomacy evolves." BIL, N° 5, 7 June 1967, MDI 98, CDJC. Numerous letters to the Consistoire (Moyen Orient/Guerre de 6 jours, 1967–68, FCC) document non-Jewish support for Israel.

13. Joëlle Allouche-Benayoun and Doris Bensimon, Juifs d'Algérie, hier et aujourd'hui, mémoires et identité (Toulouse: Privat, 1989), pp. 173, 216, 228; Doris

Bensimon-Donath, *L'intégration des Juifs nord-africains en France* (Paris: Mouton, 1971), pp. 216–35; Claude Tapia, "Religion et politique: Interférence dans le Judaïsme français après l'immigration judéo-maghrébine," in Lasry and Tapia, eds., *Les Juifs du Maghreb* (1989), pp. 207–23 ; and Michel Wieviorka, "The Changing French Jewish Identity," in *Contemporary Jewries: Convergence and Divergence*, eds., Eliezer Ben-Rafael, Yosef Gorney, and Yaacov Ro'i (Leiden: Koninklijke: Brill NV, 2003), pp. 257.

14. The Jewish establishment followed these developments closely, as is clear in documents found in MDI 1–55, MDI 65C, MDI 98, and MDI 100. For articles in the Jewish press, see Cohen Tanougi, "Les otages: 600,000 Juifs ont fusillé les pays arabes mais 110,000 demeurent encore," *L'Arche*, July 1962, pp. 42–43; "Judas pas mort!" *Carrefour*, 21 June 1967.

15. Cited by Annette Wieviorka, "Les Juifs en France depuis la guerre des Six Jours," in *Les Juifs de France de la Révolution à nos jours*, eds., Jean-Jacques Becker et al. (Paris: L. Levi, 1998), p. 377.

16. Wolf, *Harnessing the Holocaust*, 31. Kassir and Mardam-Bey, *Itinéraires de Paris*, 131–35, note that links between Nasser and Hitler, and concerns about a second genocide saturated the press as a whole.

17. Police report, 7 June 1967, 19980547, art. 13 (Israël), CAC.

18. Cited in *BIL*, N° 3, 4 June 1967, MDI 98, CDJC.

19. Alain Seviram to Jacob Kaplan, 22 May 1967, Moyen Orient/Guerre de 6 jours, 1967–68, CC.

20. Direction des renseignements généraux et des jeux, "La communauté juive dans la région parisienne," 1970, 19900353, Art 10 (liasse 1); Préfecture de police, 21 January 1969, 19990426, art. 15 (liasse 6), CAC.

21. Report, 29 May 1967, BA 2315, Fédération des sociétés juives de France, APP; 26 Congrès national de la LICRA, Banquet de clôture, 28 May (29/5/67), MDI 72, CDJC. H. Smolarski, "Suis-je le gardien de mon frère?"; André Neher, "Comme Israël, comme solidarité," *Bulletin de nos communautés*, 26 May 1967; Motion arrêteé par le Comité de rédaction, désigné par l'assemblée plénière, 26/5/67, MDI 65C; Assemblée plénière du 26 mai 1967-procès-verbal, MDI 1–55, CDJC.

22. Report, 7 June 1967, BA 2315, Fédération des sociétés juives de France, APP; Direction des renseignements généraux et des jeux, "La communauté juive dans la région parisienne," 1970, 19900353, Art 10 (liasse 1); Préfecture de police, 21 January 1969, 19990426, art. 15 (liasse 6), CAC.

23. Report, "La crise du Proche-Orient, réactions d'ensemble en France," 31 May 1967, 19980547, art. 13 (Israël), CAC.

24. "La situation en Israël," *Information rabbiniques*, 25 May 1967, Moyen Orient/Guerre de 6 jours, 1967–68, CC.

25. Déclaration adoptée à l'issue de la réunion constitutive du Comité de coordination des organisations juives de France, "La communauté juive de France solidaire d'Israël en péril," *Journal des communautés*, 18e année, Supplément au N° 395, (2 June 1967); *BIL*, N° 2, 29 May 1967, MDI 98, CDJC. While the Fédération sioniste de France joined forces with this new committee, the impetus was consciously handed to others so as to provide the new body with more legitimacy. Joseph Weinberg, Org. sioniste de France to Grand Rabbin Kaplan, 24 May 1967, Moyen Orient/Guerre de 6 jours, 1967–68, CC.

26. *BIL*, N° 2, 29 May 1967, MDI 98, CDJC.
27. *BIL*, N° 2, 29 May 1967, N° 3, 4 June 1967, and N° 7, 11 June 1967, MDI 98, CDJC. MDI 98, CDJC; Michel Salomon, "Israël vivra!" *L'Arche*, June 1967, p. 3. For examples of individual initiatives, see Gisele Rutman to l'ambassadeur d'Israël, 12 June 1967 and Docteur Paul Kossowski to Monsieur le Rabbin, 26 May 1967, Moyen Orient/Guerre de 6 jours, 1967–68, CC. For an example of the Comité de coordination's attempt to maintain control over pro-Israel efforts, see Alain de Rothschild to Monsieur le Rabin Samuel Cohen, 6 July 1967, Moyen Orient/Guerre de 6 jours, 1967–68, CC.
28. While the community's public face was united, divisions were ongoing. In Marseille, for example, the city's traditional leadership clashed with newcomers over appropriate responses to the war. Numerous documents in MDI 159, CJDC, document the rift.
29. Flyer, Comité de coordination des organisations juives de France, MDI 98, CDJC; *BIL*, N° 3, 4 June 1967, same microfilm; Moch to Jean-Pierre Gerschel, 4 January 1968, MDI 65C, CDJC. For an example of how a local committee formed, see Report, Comité local de la Drôme et de l'Ardèche, Moyen Orient/Guerre de 6 jours, 1967–68, CC.
30. *BIL*, N° 5, 7 June 1967, MDI 98, CDJC.
31. Speeches from the Conférence extraordinaire du Comité de coordination, 4 June 1967, are reprinted in *BIL*, N° 5, 7 June 1967, MDI 98, CDJC.
32. "Après l'application de la décision française d'embargo sur les arme destinées à Israël: Déclaration de M. le Grand Rabbin Kaplan," no date, MDI 1–55, CDJC. The CRIF remained reticent to criticize the government publicly. Bureau du CRIF, 3 July 1967, MDI 1–55, CDJC.
33. "Allocation prononcée par M. Guy de Rothschild, président du Comité de coordination, à l'occasion de la Conférence extraordinaire des communautés et organisations juives de France," 4 June 1967, *BIL*, N° 6, 8 June 1967, MDI 98, CDJC. Reprinted as "Nous nous identifions à Israël pour le droit à la vie," *L'Arche*, June 1967, p. 4.
34. André Neher, "Nous sommes l'arrière: Israël est le front!" reprinted in *BIL*, N° 5, 7 June 1967, MDI 98, CDJC.
35. Emphasis in text. "Le peuple juif premier allié d'Israël: Une interview de Claude Kelman, vice-président du Comité national de coordination," *L'Arche*, June 1967, p. 6. Also see Yair Auron, *Les Juifs d'extrême gauche en Mai 68*, translated from Hebrew by Katherine Werchowski (Paris: Albin Michel, 1998), p. 168. While Wolf, *Harnessing the Holocaust*, 34–36, argues that Rothschild and Kelman represented contrasting responses to the war with Rothschild articulating a more traditional perspective on Franco-Jewish solidarity, even Rothschild was more critical of the government than had been typical.
36. "Allocation prononcée par M. Guy de Rothschild, président du Comité de coordination, à l'occasion de la Conférence extraordinaire des communautés et organisations juives de France," 4 June 1967, *BIL*, N° 6, 8 June 1967, MDI 98, CDJC.
37. Cited in Maurice Szafran, *Les Juifs dans la politique française: De 1945 à nos jours* (Paris: Flammarion, 1990), p. 154.
38. Flyer, Comité de coordination des organisations juives de France (section de Nice), Moyen Orient/Guerre de 6 jours, 1967–68, CC.

39. Appeal from Association cultuelle israélite Dantibes—Juan-les-Pins, "Premier jour de la guerre en Israël," Moyen Orient/Guerre de 6 jours, 1967–68, CC.

40. "Un appel de M. Alain de Rothschild," *Journal des communautés*, 2 June 1967; *BIL*, N° 5, 7 June 1967, MDI 98, CDJC.

41. Jacques Frémontier, *L'étoile rouge de David: Les Juifs communiste en France* (Paris: Fayard, 2002), pp. 150, 282–83.

42. *BIL*, N° 2, 29 May 1967 and N° 3, 4 June 1967, MDI 98, CDJC. According to at least one French Jew, the moment for building synagogues in France was over; all efforts now had to be directed to rebuilding the Temple in Jerusalem. Monique Karsenky to M. le Grand Rabbin de France, June 1967, Moyen Orient/Guerre de 6 jours, 1967–68, CC.

43. *BIL*, N° 8, 16 June 1967, MDI 98, CDJC.

44. Sylvie Korcaz, *Les Juifs de France et l'État d'Israël, essai* (Paris: Denoël, 1969), pp. 78, 146. Numbers dropped the subsequent year. "Le peuple juif premier allié d'Israël: Une interview de Claude Kelman, vice-président du Comité national de coordination," *L'Arche*, June 1967, p. 6.

45. S. Castro to A. Loss, "Évolution de la situation générale," 17 June 1967, MDI 159, CJDC.

46. Arnold Mandel, "France," *American Jewish Yearbook*, 1967, p. 313.

47. Patrick Wajsman, "Notre jeunesse retrouve son âme," *L'Arche*, June 1967, pp. 21–22, cited in Samuel Moyn, *A Holocaust Controversy: The Treblinka Affair in Post-War France* (Waltham, Mass.: Brandeis University Press; Hanover: University Press of New England, 2005), p. 163.

48. Cited in Szafran, *Les Juifs dans les politiques française*, 154.

49. Interview with Françoise Tenenbaum in Robert I. Weiner and Richard E. Sharpless, eds. *An Uncertain Future: Voices of a French Jewish Community, 1940–2012* (Toronto: University of Toronto Press, 2012), p. 67.

50. Interview with Cathie Busidan in *An Uncertain World*, p. 25.

51. Police report, 7 June 1967, 19980547, art. 13 (Israël), CAC.

52. Ibid., 29 June 1967, 19980547, art. 13 (Israël), CAC.

53. Two hundred departed from Marseille's Gare St. Charles on 12 June. Préfet to Ministre de l'intérieur, "Manifestation organisée à Marseille par le Comité de soutien à Israël," 1 June 1967; Commissariat central de Marseille, "Départ de volontaires pour Israël," 12 June 1967, 137W363, BdR. "Plusieurs centaines de Marseillais ont signé leur engagement pour Israël," *Le Méridional*, 6 June 1967. Details of the Comité de coordination's civil service program can be found in *BIL*, N°s 3, 7, and 8, 4, 11, and 16 June 1967, MDI 98, CDJC.

54. Police report, "La crise du Proche-Orient, réactions d'ensemble en France," May 31 1967, 19980547, art. 13 (Israël), CAC.

55. Direction des renseignements généraux et des jeux, "La communauté juive dans la région parisienne," 1970, 19900353, Art 10 (liasse 1), CAC.

56. Bensimon, *Les Juifs de France*, 171.

57. According to Korcaz, *Les Juifs de France*, 85–92, Jewish emigration patterns mirrored that of other citizens. Schnapper, *French Jewish Identities*, 44, notes that North African Jews with strong pro-Israel sensibilities often remained in France.

58. Interview with Rabbi Simon Sibony in *An Uncertain Future*, p. 10.

59. Direction des renseignements généraux et des jeux, "La communauté juive dans la région parisienne," 1970, 19900353, Art 10 (liasse 1), CAC.

60. "Le peuple juif premier allié d'Israël: Une interview de Claude Kelman," *L'Arche*, June 1967, p. 6. "La guerre des six jours a-t-elle modifié la conscience juive en France?" *L'Arche*, March/April 1968, pp. 38–42, argued that pro-Israeli sentiment had been a long-standing if latent force in communal life.

61. S. Castro to A. Loss, "Évolution de la situation générale," 17 June 1967, MDI 159, CJDC.

62. *BIL*, N° 7, 11 June 1967, and N° 8, 16 June 1967, MDI 98; Moch to Jean-Pierre Gerschel, 4 January 1968, MDI 65C, CDJC.

63. Untitled statement by a Jewish organization (summer 1967), Moyen Orient/Guerre de 6 jours, 1967–68, CC.

64. Claude Kelman to Messiers, 22 March 1968, MDI 72, CDJC.

65. For example, a Jewish student protested at a debate in Aix-en-Provence over treatment of Palestinian refugees. Commissariat central d'Aix en Provence, "Un groupe de professeurs a organisé hier soir une réunion sur le problème israélien," 8 June 1967, 135W57, BdR.

66. For previous divisions, see Frémontier, *L'étoile rouge de David*, last chapter, and 279–83; Faure, "Un 'Plan Marshall juif,'" 450–73. Paris housed three Yiddish dailies, which W. Rabinovitch (Rabi), *Anatomie du Judaïsme français* (Paris: Éditions de Minuit, 1962), p. 173, estimated at a circulation of three thousand each.

67. Frémontier, *L'étoile rouge de David*, 150. In March 1968, the immigrant Jewish left formed the Fédération des organisations et des sociétés juives de France, which united the traditionally anti-Communist with those that had cut ties with the party during the 1967 war. Report, 25 March 1968, BA 2315 Communauté juive, APP.

68. Daniel Cohn-Bendit, *Le grand bazar* (Paris: P. Belfond, 1975), p. 11, cited in Auron, *Les Juifs d'extrême gauche*, 173–74.

69. For MRAP, see Frémontier, *L'étoile rouge de David*, 271–72. For an example of MRAP's anti-racism commitment, see "Courrier de l'émigration," *L'Algérien en Europe*, 1 June 1967, p. 2 (hereafter referred to as *AE*). According to Kassir and Mardam-Bey, *Itinéraires de Paris*, 141, the MRAP was the only anti-racist organization to protest intensifying anti-Arab sentiment. The Ligue internationale contre le racisme et l'antisémitisme, which was associated with more centrist political parties, increasingly supported Israel. According to Gérard Noiriel, *Immigration, antisémitisme et racisme en France (XIXe–XXe siècle): Discours publics, humiliations privées* (Paris: Fayard, 2007), pp. 486–89, the League des droits de l'homme ignored anti-Arab racism when Zionists were involved.

70. Yvan Gastaut, *L'immigration et l'opinion en France sous la Ve république* (Paris: Éditions du Seuil, 2000), p. 155; Hervé Hamnon and Patrick Rotman, *Génération*, vol. 2, *Les années de poudre* (Paris: Seuil, 1988), pp. 90–94.

71. "Aucun Arabe se trouvant au-delà du Jourdain ne sera autorisé à venir dans le secteur 'israélien,'" *Le Monde*, 15 June 1967, p. 3, and Gastaut, *L'immigration et l'opinion*, 277–78. Kassir and Mardam-Bey, *Itinéraires de Paris*, 142, nevertheless conclude that most intellectuals were "totally blind" to the excesses of pro-Israeli propaganda.

72. Wolf, *Harnessing the Holocaust*, 33–34, 48–49. For a contemporary overview of Jewish political responses to the war, see Rabi, "Israël: Une passion lucide," *L'Arche*, February/March, 1968, pp. 34–35, 63. For criticism of the Left's treatment of Israel,

see Robert Misrahi, "La gauche irresponsable," *L'Arche*, November–December 1967, p. 31, and Albert Memmi, "La libération du peuple juif tout entier," *L'Arche*, March/April, 1968, p. 40.

73. Frémontier, *L'étoile rouge de David*, 271, 278–83, 99. Frémontier joins Auron, *Les Juifs d'extrême gauche*, 166–77, and Schnapper *Jewish Identities*, 95, 154, in noting that those who distanced themselves from the wider Zionist consensus were also not fully in sync with the communist left on Israel.

74. Bureau du CRIF, 18 September, 6 November, and 21 December 1967, MDI 1–55, CDJC. By January 1968, dissent had diminished and the CRIF tabled the discussion.

75. Rabi, "Israël: Une passion lucide," *L'Arche*, February/March, 1968, p. 34, discusses diverging Jewish opinions following the war. For Raymond Aron, "Pas d'unité politique," *L'Arche*, December/January, 1967–68, pp. 36–37, such diversity made a unified communal politics impossible. Wolf, *Harnessing the Holocaust*, 48–49, analyzes divergence over the nature of Jewish identity in the war's aftermath.

76. Korcaz, *Les Juifs de France*, 77–83, 128, 145–50.

77. Yehouda Cohen to "Chère madame; cher monsieur," 10 April 1968, MDI 159, CJDC. The Préfecture de police drew similar conclusions, noting a "crisis of recruitment" in the major Zionist organizations (while noting the cultural renaissance that Zionism had inspired). Direction des renseignements généraux et des jeux, "La communauté juive dans la région parisienne" (1970?), 19900353, art. 10 (liasse 1, Israël), CAC. In 1971, CRIF officials also bemoaned French Jewish apathy toward Israel. Journées nationales du CRIF, 24 October 1971, MDI 136, CJDC.

78. Schnapper *Jewish Identities*, 95, 154.

79. Kassir and Mardam-Bey, *Itinéraires de Paris*, 131, 135–40.

80. Gastaut, *L'immigration et l'opinion*, 275–82, and Kassir and Mardam-Bey, *Itinéraires de Paris*, 140–41. Auron, *Les Juifs d'extrême gauche*, 168, notes in contrast that others see French neutrality in 1967 and de Gaulle's policies toward Israel as providing entrée for a renewed antisemitism silenced following World War II.

81. Cited in Gastaut, *L'immigration et l'opinion*, 113.

82. Small and underfunded, the UGEP joined other groups, such as the Comité de défense de la révolution arabe, a self-proclaimed representative of the Arab left, in condemning Israeli actions in 1967. Police report, 19 June 1967, 19980547, art. 13 (Israël), CAC.

83. In explaining the origins of the pro-Palestinian movement, Hajjat, "Les Comités Palestine (1970–1972)," overlooks the ADAE's earlier interest.

84. For the Amicale, see Alain Gillette and Abdelmalek Sayad, *L'immigration algérienne en France*, 2nd ed. (Paris: Éditions Entente, 1984), pp. 200–205; Jacques Simon, ed. *L'immigration algérienne en France: De 1962 à nos jours* (Paris: L'Harmattan, 2002), pp. 22–23; Benjamin Stora, *Ils venaient d'Algérie: L'immigration algérienne en France* (Paris: Fayard, 1992), pp. 418–19; Catherine Wihtol de Wenden, *Les immigrés et la politique: Cent cinquante ans d'évolution* (Paris: Presses de la Fondation nationale des sciences politiques, 1988), p. 174.

85. Préfecture de police, "L'Amicale des Algériens en Europe," 21 October 1968, Algériens–Activités politiques: Divers (1966–76), 19960311, art. 4, CAC.

86. Simon, ed., *L'immigration algérienne*, 22–23.

87. "Bilan de l'activité de l'Amicale des Algériens en Europe," 22 November 1967, and Préfecture de police, "L'Amicale des Algériens en Europe," 21 October 1968,

19960311, art. 4, CAC. Katz, "Jews and Muslims," 320, cites fifteen thousand as the French assessment of ADAE membership. The discrepancy undoubtedly reflects the authorities' poor grasp of the ADAE's internal workings.

88. Préfecture de police, "L'Amicale des Algériens en Europe," 21 October 1968, and Préfet de police to Ministre de l'intérieur, 15 October 1968, Algériens—Activités politiques: Divers (1966–76); ME, sous-direction Algérie, to MI, direction de la réglementation, "Activités de l'Amicale des Algériens en Europe," 3 October 1967, 19960311, art. 4, CAC. Gillette and Sayad, *L'immigration algérienne*, 200–201, explore the links between the FLN and the Amicale.

89. Emphasis mine. Police report, 12 July 1967, Amicale des Algériens en Europe, Notes relatives à l'organisation (1966–1969), 19850087, art. 37, CAC.

90. MI to ME, 21 September 1967; "Activités de l'Amicale des Algériens en Europe," Algériens—Activités politiques: Divers (1966–76), 19960311, art. 4, CAC.

91. Police report, Untitled, 12 July 1967, Amicale des Algériens en Europe, Notes relatives à l'organisation (1966–1969), 19850087, art. 37, CAC.

92. *AE*, 15 June 1967.

93. "L'émigration algérienne continue de s'organiser," *AE*, 15 July 1967, p. 6.

94. RG, Mle, "Les milieux algériens et la tension au Moyen-Orient," 6 June 1967, 137W363, BdR.

95. MI to ME, "Activités de l'Amicale des Algériens en Europe," 21 September 1967, 19960311, art. 4, CAC.

96. Yezid Sayigh, *Armed Struggle and the Search for State: The Palestinian National Movement, 1949–1993* (Oxford: Oxford University Press, 1997), pp. 102, 126, 182.

97. "Solidarité avec le peuple palestinien," *Al Djazaïri*, 29 February 1964, p. 4.

98. "Journée de solidarité avec les travailleurs palestiniens," *Al Djazaïri*, 30 May 1964, p. 5.

99. "Les Palestiniens ne pleurent plus," *El Moudjahid*, 9–17 March 1967.

100. "Proche-Orient: Au delà de l'état d'alerte," *AE*, 1 June 1967, p. 18.

101. "A l'occasion du 19 juin réaffirmation de nos principes révolutionnaires," *AE*, 30 June 1967, pp. 4–5; "L'Algérie en état de guerre," *AE*, 15 July 1967, p. 7; Gerard Viratelle, "Des milliers d'Algériens ont manifesté aux cris de 'Nasser, trahison!'"; "Les trois pays du Maghreb se sont diversement engagés dans le conflit," *Le Monde*, 11–12 June 1967, p. 5; "Vaincre or mourir: Des dizaines de milliers d'Algériens manifestent dans les rues de la capitale," *El Moudjahid*, 10 June 1967, p. 1. Dozens of articles in *El Moudjahid* in late May and early June document the FLN's support for the Palestinian resistance.

102. Police report, Untitled, 12 July 1967, Amicale des Algériens en Europe, Notes relatives à l'organisation (1966–69), 19850087, art. 37, CAC.

103. Ahmed Ibrahim, "Une enquête sur le Moyen-Orient," *AE*, 15 May 1968, p. 21.

104. For examples of this link, see "L'impunité de l'agresseur: Un défi à la paix," *AE*, 15 July 1967, p. 3, and "13e anniversaire," *AE*, 1 November 1967, p. 2.

105. Every edition of *AE* devoted space to promoting Arab unity, lambasting Israeli aggression, and protesting anti-Arab racism.

106. Police report, 12 July 1967, 19850087, art. 37, CAC.

107. ME, Direction des affaires politiques (sous-direction Algérie), "Activités de l'Amicale des Algériens en Europe" (Sept. 1967), 19960311, art. 4, CAC.

108. Authorities nevertheless remained suspicious. Préfecture de police to Commissaire principal, Direction des RG, "Pour information," 14 December 1967, 19850087, art. 37, CAC.

109. "Le courrier de l'émigration," *AE*, 30 June 1967, p. 2. Katz, "Jews and Muslims," 353–54; 356–67, reports large numbers of Algerian Muslims in France becoming engaged after Israel's attack on 5 June, but ultimately agrees that most Muslim immigrants were unmoved by the pro-Palestinian campaign.

110. Stora, *Ils venaient d'Algérie*, 163–38.

111. Préfet de l'essonne to MI, "Activité de l'Amicale des Algériens en Europe," 4 September 1967, 19960311, art. 4, CAC.

112. Police report, Untitled, 12 July 1967, 19850087, art. 37, CAC.

113. Préfecture de police, "L'Amicale des Algériens en Europe," 21 October 1968, Algériens—Activités politiques: Divers (1966–76), 19960311, art. 4, CAC. Wihtol de Wenden, *Les immigrés et la politique*, 174, and Gillette and Sayad, *L'immigration algérienne*, 200–205, argue that most Algerian Muslim migrants distrusted the Amicale's links to the Algerian government.

114. RG, "Le rôle d'éléments algériens dans le terrorisme international," Algériens—Activités politiques: Divers (1966–76), 19960311, art. 4, CAC.

115. "Tous les Juifs ne sont pas sionistes," *AE*, 30 June 1967, pp. 12–13, 22–23. For a similar assertion the next year, see A. Zehraoui, "Palestine: L'injustice d'il y a 20 ans," *AE*, 15 May 1968. The ADAE had declared itself anti-racist and anti-antisemitic as reported in, "Aux journées contre le racisme à l'U.N.E.S.C.O, 'Nous sommes par définition contre le racisme,' déclare le porte parole de l'Amicale," *Al Djazaïri*, 30 May 1964, p. 9; and "8 Mai: Journée nationale contre le racisme et l'antisémitisme," *AE*, 20 April to 5 May, 1966, p.6. Such rhetoric did not, however, prevent the ADAE from recirculating antisemitic themes. As one tract argued, Israel's birth and the Suez Crisis had inaugurated a new form of Western imperialism that covered the "dreams of conquest and domination of European Jews." Police report, Untitled, 12 July 1967, Amicale des Algériens en Europe, Notes relatives à l'organisation (1966–69), 19850087, art. 37, CAC.

116. RG, Mle, "Comité de soutien à Israël-rassemblement de la jeunesse," 8 June 1967, 137W363, BdR.

117. Flyer, MDI 98, CDJC. Certain writers and intellectuals also emphasized commonality over discord, such as Raymond Aron who lamented in"Israël face à la tragédie," *Le Figaro littéraire*, 12–18 June 1967: "How much time will it take for Jews and Muslims, Israelis and Arabs, who believe in the same God, to begin to understand each other?"

118. The demographics in the piece were inaccurate. Guy Porte, "La quatrième guerre: En marge du conflit-à Marseille, Juifs et Arabes ont su éviter les pièges du racisme," 25 October 1973, *Le Monde*, p. 4. Porte's portrayal, written several years later, nevertheless downplayed racism.

119. "Important cortège de la Canebière à la Préfecture," *Le Méridional*, 1 June 1967, numbered protestors at eight thousand, while *Le Provençal*, 1 June, reported fifteen thousand. Appel unifié pour Israël and Comité de soutien à Israël à Marseille to Monsieur le Préfet, 27 May 1967; RG, "Milieu juif et israélien," 29 May 1967; Préfet to MI, 31 May 1967; RG, Mle, "Milieux juifs," 1 June 1967, 137W363, BdR. *BIL*, N° 2,

2 June 1967, MDI 159, CJDC. Flyer, Le Comité de coordination de la jeunesse juive de France, 137W363, BdR.

120. The Comité unifié de soutien à Israël later joined forces with the Comité de coordination in Paris. Robert Ifrah to Pres. du Comité de coordination des organisations juives de France, no date; *BIL*, Nº 2, 2 June 1967, MDI 159, CJDC. "Réunion et motion du Comité de soutien à Israël," 1 June 1967, 137W363, BdR.

121. Mandel "France," 450; "Informations du S.F. Israël," *Le Méridional*, 5 June 1967.

122. "Magnifique élan de solidarité de la population en faveur d'Israël: A partir de ce matin, collecte du sang," clipping with no paper or date, MDI 159, CJDC; Commissariat central de Marseille, "Note," 7 June 1967, 137W363, BdR.

123. Préfet, Région Provence to MI, 31 May 1967, 137W363, BdR. "Le conflit israélo-arabe a soulevé une vive émotion à Marseille," *Le Méridional*, 6 June 1967. "Pour une paix et une justice qui ne soient pas aux dépens de l'État d'Israël," *Le Méridional*, 2 June 1967.

124. A survey of *Le Méridional* for May and June 1967 shows a largely pro-Israel Marseille, with three pages of calls for and reports on demonstrations appearing daily in the first week of June. At least one such article follows every day until 21 June.

125. "Magnifique élan de solidarité de la population en faveur d'Israël: A partir de ce matin, collecte du sang," clipping with no paper or date, MDI 159, CJDC.

126. René Andrieu, "Regarde la vérité en face," *Marseillaise*, 31 May 1967. Préfet to MI, "Manifestation organisée à Marseille par le Comité de soutien à Israël," 1 June 1967, 137W363, BdR.

127. Mandel "France," 450. When the editor refused to change his stance, Frédéric Thau threatened the withdrawal of all Jewish advertisements. RG, Mle, "Milieux juifs," 2 June 1967, 137W363, BdR.

128. Since the Socialist Party never held an absolute majority in Marseille, Defferre kept the city's large Communist Party in check by forming a centrist coalition with those on the non-Gaullist right. Émile Témime, *Histoire de Marseille de la Révolution à nos jours* (Perrin, 1999), pp. 354–56; Abdelmalek Sayad, Jean-Jacques Jordi, and Émile Témime, *Le choc de la décolonisation (1945–1990)*, vol. 4 of *Migrance: Histoire des migrations à Marseille*, ed., Émile Témime (Aix-en-Provence: Éditions Jeanne Laffitte, 1991), p. 100.

129. "Crise au Moyen-Orient," Bouches-du-Rhône-Marseille, 3 June 1967, 137W363, BdR.

130. RG, Mle, "Comité de soutien à Israël," 3 June 1967, 137W363, BdR.

131. "Conflit israélo-arabe," 6 June 1967, 137W363, BdR. "Le Comité de soutien à Israël a constitué son bureau et voté une motion condamnant l'agression égyptienne," *Le Provençal*, 4 June 1967.

132. RG, Mle, "Comité de soutien à Israël," 5 June, 1967, 137W363, BdR.

133. S. Castro to A. Loss, "Évolution de la situation générale," 17 June 1967, MDI 159, CJDC.

134. "Conflit israélo-arabe," 6 June 1967; Commissariat central de Marseille, "Affichage sur la voie publique pour la paix au Moyen-Orient," 7 June 1967, 137W363, BdR.

135. RG, Mle, "Comité de soutien à Israël-rassemblement de la jeunesse," 8 June 1967, 137W363, BdR.

136. RG, Mle, "Conflit israélo-arabe: Prise de position en faveur d'Israël," 8 June 1967, 137W363, BdR.

137. Commissariat central de Marseille, "Note," 7 June 1967; "Objet réunion publique pour le soutien à Israël," 12 June 1967; Commissariat central de Marseille, "Réunion publique en faveur du soutien français à Israël," 13 June 1967, 137W363, BdR. "Les orateurs du Comité de soutien à Israël longuement acclamés," 13 June 1967, *Le Provençal*, p. 3.

138. Police were nevertheless out in force on 29 May to ensure the city's interethnic harmony. RG, Mle, "Milieux juifs," 30 May 1967; Commissariat central de police, "Manifestation pour le soutien de la paix en Israël," 31 May 1967; RG, Mle, "Les milieux algériens et la tension au Moyen-Orient," 3 June 1967, 137W363, BdR.

139. Préfet to MI, "Manifestation organisée à Marseille par le Comité de soutien à Israël," 1 June 1967; RG, Mle, "Les milieux algériens et la tension au Moyen Orient," 3 June 1967, 137W363, BdR.

140. RG, Mle, "Les milieux algériens et la tension au Moyen-Orient," 6 June 1967, 137W363, BdR.

141. "J'Accuse," Mouvement d'action politique du Betar, RG, Mle, "Diffusion des tracts juifs en milieux étudiants," 29 May 1967, 137W363, BdR. Police claimed the tract was Betar's first foray into Marseille, although as we saw, during the 1948 war, the Irgun (Betar's parent organization), maintained a local presence.

142. For more on the AJOA, see Sussman, "Changing Lands," 351–52.

143. RG, Mle, "Conflit israélo-arabe: Prise de position en faveur d'Israël," 8 June 1967, 137W363, BdR.

144. The Consistoire request, which paralleled requests from other key synagogues, can be found in Préfecture des Bouches-du-Rhône, Communication téléphoniques, 5 June 1967, 135W57, BdR. The citation is from "État d'esprit des populations d'origine algérienne dans le département des Bouches-du-Rhône," 28 June 1967, 19960311, art. 4, CAC.

145. Jewish voters repaid Defferre for his support. While their electoral patterns mirrored the country's spread in the 1974, 1978, and 1981 national elections, in municipal elections, they stood collectively behind Defferre and his party, breaking away only after his death. Direction générale de la police nationale, "Étude sur la communauté juive des Bouches-du-Rhône," 16 October 1989; RG, "Communauté juive des BDR," 23 September 1986; "L'élection présidentielle et la communauté juive de Marseille," 26 February 1988, 1693W233, BdR.

146. Gaston Defferre, "De Gaulle et l'antisémitisme," *Le Provençal*, 8 January 1968.

147. The Comité de coordination requested a meeting with the regional prefect to express their anger at de Gaulle's pronouncement. The prefect never responded. Robert Ifrah to M. le Préfet régional de Marseille, 6 December 1967; Compte rendu de la réunion de l'exécutif du Comité coordination, 8 January 196(8), MDI 159, CJDC.

148. R.O., "Marseille 'porte israélienne' de l'Europe pour une conquête du marché agricole occidental," *Le Méridional*, 20 April 1968.

149. Cited in Témime, *Histoire de Marseille*, 341.

150. "Solidarité et paix thème du meeting de soutien à Israël," press clipping, no date or title, 135W57, BdR. Defferre reached out to the pieds-noirs, delegating a special adjunct for repatriate issues and supporting the indemnification and amnesty of all repatriates. "Importante réunion consacrée aux problèmes des rapatriés en présence du colonel Battesti, président national de l'ANFANOMA," and "En direct," 20 February and 4 March 1967, *Le Provençal*.

151. Préfet de la région Provence to MI, 7 February 1969, 135W57, BdR. "Solidarité et paix thème du meeting de soutien à Israël," press clipping, no date or title, 135W57, BdR.

152. Lucien Pucciarelli, "Étrange rassemblement," *Le Marseillais*, 7 February 1969, 135W57, BdR.

153. Although integrated relatively quickly into Marseille's economic structure, pieds noirs believed themselves abandoned by French authorities and the settled population. Jean-Jacques Jordi, *De l'exode: Rapatriés et pieds-noirs en France: L'exemple marseillais, 1954–1992* (Paris: L'Éditions l'Harmattan, 1993), pp. 216–17; Témime, *Histoire de Marseille*, 340; Sayad, Jordi, and Témime, *Le Choc*, 97–99, 101–105; Jean-Jacques Jordi, "L'été 62 à Marseille: Tensions et incompréhensions," in Jordi and Émile Témime, eds., *Marseille et le choc des décolonisations: Les rapatriements, 1954–1964* (Aix-en-Provence: Édisud, 1996), pp. 72–73.

154. Rabi, "Le 'boom' de Marseille," 43.

155. Sayad, Jordi, and Témime, *Le Choc*, 108–109, remind that "Manichean simplifications" of interethnic relations in Marseille can overemphasize tensions in often convivial neighborhoods. Moreover, the pieds noirs were not uniformally attracted to the far right, but spread out across the political spectrum.

156. "Débats et réunions," *Le Monde*, 24 May 1966, p. 8.

157. "Au cours d'une réunion à la Mutualité: Des organisations estudiantines arabes dénoncent la confusion entre le problème de l'antisémitisme et celui du conflit palestinien," *Le Monde*, 28 May 1966, p. 4.

158. Eric Rouleau, "Des organisations juives s'élèvent contre une récente réunion d'étudiants arabes à Paris," 13 July 1966, *Le Monde*, p. 4.

159. While Wolf, *Harnessing the Holocaust*, points to 1967 as the origin of such Holocaust imagery, by the mid-1960s, Nazi oppression was a common reference for those on both sides of the Israel-Palestine issue. The article, "Le racisme: Les travailleurs français et émigrés face au fléau," *AE*, 1–15 May 1966, pp. 14–15, for example, addressed the mistreatment of immigrant workers in France with a picture of a swastika captioned, "Nazism is not dead. Hunger and racism. Three million immigrant workers." See Moyn, *A Holocaust Controversy*, 149, for a critique of Wolf's focus on 1967 as a turning point.

160. Michel Salomon, "Opération bonne conscience: La gauche française et la propagande arabe," *L'Arche*, July 1966, pp. 8–9. Solomon focused his ire primarily on Claude Glayman, Maxime Rodinson, and French leftists.

161. "Correspondance: Les Juifs, les Arabes et le MRAP," *Le Monde*, 6 July 1966, p. 4.

162. "Résolution adopté à la journée du MRAP," 16 May 1965, MDI 71, CDJC, and Journée nationale contre le racisme, l'antisémitisme et pour la paix, same file.

163. Un colloque de l'union mondiale des étudiants, 14/10/65, MDI 71, CDJC.

164. MM 23/11/65, MDI 72, CDJC.

165. Michel Salomon, "Opération bonne conscience: La gauche française et la propagande arabe," *L'Arche*, July 1966, pp. 8–9.

166. V. Modiano to Alain Peyrefitte, Ministre de l'éducation nationale, 8 May 1967; Alain Peyrefitte to Modiano, 20 July 1967, MDI 65C, CDJC. The Minister of Education claimed fears over the escalation of a tense environment and not Arab student pressure had driven the decision to cancel.

167. "Journée internationale de la Palestine à Paris," *El Moudjahid*, 20 May 1967, p. 8.

168. Cited in Jocelyne Cesari, *Être musulman en France: Associations, militants, et mosquées* (Paris: Éditions Karthala et Iremam, 1994), p. 174.

169. Les étudiants arabes en France dénoncent la collusion de l'impérialisme anglo-américaine avec les sionistes," *El Moudjahid*, 8 June 1967, p. 5.

170. Commissariat central d'Aix en Provence, "Un groupe de professeurs a organisé hier soir une réunion sur le problème israélien," 8 June 1967, 135W57, BdR.

171. "Dans les universités," *Bulletin de nos communautés*, 26 May 1967.

172. MI to Préfet des Bouches-du-Rhône, 30 May 1967; RG, Mle, "Diffusion des tracts juifs en milieux étudiants," 29 May 1967, 137W363, BdR.

173. Police report, 27 May 1967, 19980547, art. 13 (Israël), CAC.

174. Victor Malka, "Incertitude jeunesse," *L'Arche*, December 1964, reported ongoing UEJF efforts to establish contacts with Arab student organizations in France.

175. *BIL*, N° 3, 4 June 1967 and N° 5, 7 June 1967, MDI 98, CDJC.

Chapter 5. Palestine in France: Radical Politics and Hardening Ethnic Allegiances, 1968–72

1. Most studies of postwar French Jewish life have ignored or brushed over the role of 1968 in shaping Jewish political life. For notable exceptions, see Yair Auron, *Les Juifs d'extrême gauche en Mai 68*, translated from Hebrew by Katherine Werchowski (Paris: Albin Michel 1998); Judith Friedlander, *Vilna on the Seine: Jewish Intellectuals in France since 1968* (New Haven: Yale University Press, 1990); Jonathan Judaken, "'To Be or Not to Be French': *Soixante-Huitard* Reflections on '*La question juive*,'" *Journal of Modern Jewish Studies* 1, 1 (2002): 3–21. For discussion of the impact of 1968 radicalism on North African Muslims in France, see Abdellali Hajjat, "Les Comités Palestine (1970–1972): Aux origines du soutien de la cause palestinienne en France," *Revue d'études palestiniennes*," 98 (Winter 2006): 74–92, and "L'expérience politique du Mouvement des travailleurs arabes," *Contretemps* 16 (May 2006): 76–85. A combined revision of these two articles has been published as "Des Comités Palestine au Mouvement des travailleurs arabes (1970–1976)," in Ahmed Boubeker and Abdellali Hajjat eds., *Histoire politique des immigrations (post) coloniales: France, 1920–2008* (Paris: Éditions Amsterdam, 2008): 145–56. Ethan Katz, "Jews and Muslims in the Shadow of Marianne: Conflicting Identities and Republican Culture in France, 1914–1975" (Ph.D. diss., University of Wisconsin, 2008), pp. 311–82, also addresses this issue.

2. Debates over the transformative power of 1968 emerged immediately thereafter. Michael Seidman's *The Imaginary Revolution: Parisian Students and Workers in 1968* (New York: Berghahn Books, 2004), for example, insists on its limited impact. All agree, however, that various social issues won wider public hearing. For important discussions of May 1968 and its impact, see Kristin Ross, *May '68 and Its Afterlives* (Chicago: University of Chicago Press, 2002) and Julian Jackson, *May 68 : Rethinking France's Last Revolution* (New York: Palgrave Macmillan, 2011).

3. Samir Kassir and Farouk Mardam-Bey, *Itinéraires de Paris à Jérusalem: La France et le conflit israélo-arabe*, vol. 2: 1958–91 (Paris: Revue d'études palestiniennes, 1993), pp. 162–64, mark 1967 as the birth of French awareness of the Palestinian struggle,

despite support for Israel. Subsequently, ADAE and the Parisian office of the Arab League continued to push the issue, as did individual politicians and journalists. See, for example, the April 1968 edition of *L'Algérien en Europe*. Untitled report, Préfecture de police, 2 April 1968, 19960311, art. 4; RG, "Les activités du bureau de la Ligue arabe à Paris," June 1972, 19990260, art. 23, CAC.

4. For differences among Maoists, Trotskyists, Anarchists, and other groups, see Hervé Bourges, *The French Student Revolt: The Leaders Speak* (New York: Hill and Wang, 1968).

5. Poster cited in letter to CRIF, 3 November 1969, MDI 147, CJDC.

6. "Les étudiants français dénoncent l'agression impérialo-sioniste," *El Moudjahid*, 9–10 July 1967, p. 6.

7. Direction de la réglementation, 14 September 1971, 19960311, art. 1, CAC; Kassir and Mardam-Bey, *Itinéraires de Paris à Jérusalem*, 164–65, 167; Auron, *Les Juifs d'extrême gauche*, 139–40; "France," *American Jewish Yearbook* (1969), p. 332.

8. Yezid Sayigh, *Armed Struggle and the Search for a State: The Palestinian National Movement, 1949–1993* (Oxford: Oxford University Press, 1997), p. 173.

9. Kassir and Mardam-Bey, *Itinéraires de Paris à Jérusalem,*105.

10. Auron, *Les Juifs d'extrême gauche*, passim; Maurice Szafran, *Les Juifs dans la politique française: De 1945 à nos jours* (Paris: Flammarion, 1990), pp. 181–88; Joan Wolf, *Harnessing the Holocaust: The Politics of Memory in France* (Stanford: Stanford University Press, 2004), pp. 57–58.

11. For the riot, see Daniel Gordon, "Immigrants and the New Left in France, 1968–1971" (Ph.D. diss., University of Sussex, 2001), pp. 164–91, and "Acteurs transméditerranéens dans un quartier cosmopolite: Juifs et Musulmans, entre tolérance et conflit, à Belleville (Paris XXe)," *Cahiers de la Méditerranée* (December 2003); Katz, "Jews and Muslims" (Ph.D. diss., University of Wisconsin, 2008), pp. 311–12, 360–66; and Patrick Simon and Claude Tapia, *Le Belleville des Juifs tunisiens* (Paris: Éditions Autrement, 1998), pp. 168–73. For the riot's impact, see Yvan Gastaut, *L'immigration et l'opinion sous la Ve république* (Paris: Éditions du Seuil, 2000), pp. 47–51. My discussion also draws and from "Les échauffourées de Belleville," *Le Monde juif: La revue du centre documentation juive contemporaine*, 50 (1968).

12. Tapia and Simon, *Le Belleville des Juifs tunisiens*, 170, note that most residents hid at home.

13. Michel Legris, "Après les vifs incidents de Belleville: Les représentants de la communauté israélite et des diplomates maghrébins interviennent pour obtenir le retour au calme," *Le Monde*, 5 June 1968, p. 18; Untitled report, 14 January 1970, La Fédération des sociétés juives de France, BA 2315, APP; "Après les bagarres des deux derniers jours: A Belleville, un tract arabe appelle à la "guerre sainte" contre les Juifs," *Le Figaro*, 5 June 1968, p. 2. Tensions persisted for weeks. Jean Farkas to Rabbi Chouchena, 21 July 1968, 1967–68, CC.

14. For competing theories on the origins, see Gastaut, *L'immigration et l'opinion*, 37–51. Gordon, "Immigrants," 164–91, convincingly critiques four of the most prevelant explanations without offering a new one.

15. Material on Belleville is from Katz, "Jews and Muslims," 336–40; Simon and Tapia, *Le Belleville des Juifs tunisiens*, 161–67; and Claude Tapia, *Les Juifs sépharades en France (1965–1985): Études psychosociologiques et historiques* (Paris: L'Harmattan, 1986), pp. 109–45.

16. Simon and Tapia, *Le Belleville des Juifs tunisiens*, 89, number 82 percent of Belleville's Jewish population as Tunisian in 1970.

17. *La jeune Afrique*, 1–7 July 1968, p. 25, cited in Gordon, "Immigrants," 171.

18. Simon and Tapia, *Le Belleville des Juifs tunisiens*, 168–69.

19. Katz, "Jews and Muslims," 365.

20. "Une déclaration de l'ambassadeur d'Algérie," *Le Figaro*, 5 June 1968, p. 2; "Après les incidents de Belleville: Appels au calme adressés aux communautés musulmane et israélite," *Le Figaro*, 6 June 1968, p. 2; "Les échauffourées de Belleville"; "Le grand rabbin de France s'adresse aux populations Israélites et Musulmanes du quartier de Belleville," 7 June 1968, 1967–68, CC; Bureau du CRIF, 5 June 1968, MDI 1–55, CDJC.

21. For the ADAE's statement, see Untitled, *AE*, 15 June 1968, p. 2. F. Abdelali, "Violences sionistes à Paris," and "Bagarres à Paris entre Algériens et groupe armés sionistes," *El Moudjahid*, 4 June 1968, p. 1, 3. An example of Jewish efforts to blame anti-Israeli agitators appears in Moch to Monica Blum, Anti-Defamation League of B'nai Brith, 21 June 1968, MDI 65C, CDJC. "Après les bagarres des deux derniers jours," 2, refers to the call for Holy War.

22. "Jeunes Juifs de la révolte," *L'Arche*, June–July 1968, p. 77.

23. Front des étudiants juifs to CRIF, "Le FEJ," 9 August 1974, MDI 146 B, CJDC.

24. Norman Stillman, *Jews of Arab Lands in Modern Times* (Philadelphia: The Jewish Publication Society, 1991), pp. 173–74; Michael M. Laskier, *North African Jewry in the Twentieth Century: The Jews of Morocco, Tunisia, and Algeria* (New York: New York University Press, 1994), pp. 308–9.

25. Simon and Tapia, *Le Belleville des Juifs tunisiens*, 35–41, 168.

26. "Jeunes Juifs de la révolte," 77.

27. Scholars debate the level of foreign participation during May 1968. See, for example, Gastaut, *L'immigration et l'opinion*, 38–39, 43, and Gordon, "Immigrants," passim.

28. Cited in Simon and Tapia, *Le Belleville des Juifs tunisiens*, 168–69, 173.

29. Scholarship has largely overlooked these events. Simon and Tapia, *Le Belleville des Juifs tunisiens*, 172, for example, claim that the 1968 riot, "inconceivable and unexpected . . . did not recur." Katz, "Jews and Muslims," 370–74, is a notable exception. Coverage of the riot included, "A Belleville (20ème): Flambée de violence entre Musulmans et Israélites: Une soixantaine de vitrines brisées," *Le Figaro*, 16 June 1970, p. 11; "Violents affrontements entre Israélites et Musulmans: 33 personnes interpellées," *Le Monde*, 17 June 1970, p. 17; "Après les incidents de Belleville," *Le Monde*, 20 June 1970, p. 13; "France," *American Jewish Yearbook* (1970), p. 344.

30. "Belleville: L'agression d'Israël continue," *AE*, 25 June–9 July 1970, pp. 5, 20.

31. *AE*, 9–23 July 1970, p. 2.

32. "Après les incidents de Belleville," 13.

33. "A Belleville, contre les divisions et la haine," *Droite et liberté*, July–August 1970; "Seize personnes sont toujours en garde à vue après les incidents de Belleville," *Le Monde*, 18 June 1970, p. 12.

34. "CRIF communiqué," *Le Monde*, 21–22 June 1970, p. 14.

35. CRIF responses were drawn from meeting, 2 July 1970, MDI 1–55, CDJC; Bureau du CRIF, 22 June (1970), same reel.

36. "Seize personnes," 12; "Violents affrontements," 17.

37. For relationships between gauchistes and immigrants, see Gastaut, *L'immigration et l'opinion*, 37–51; Gordon, "Immigrants," passim; and Gérard Noiriel, *Immigration*,

antisémitisme et racisme en France, XIXe–XXe siècle: Discours publics, humiliations privées (Paris: Fayard, 2007), pp. 558–64. For Maoist and North African student collaboration, see Hajjat, "Les Comités palestine" and "L'expérience politique du Mouvement des travailleurs arabes." While Hajjat expertly covers the history of these organizations, his account downplays Fatah's role in the establishment of the Comités Palestine. My account seeks to correct this imbalance.

38. RG, "Les Organisations palestiniennes en France," 20 June 1972; RG, "El Fatah et les révolutionnaires français," 25 June 1969; RG, "Présence de la Palestine," June 1972, 19990260, art. 23; RG, "Campagne de l'Amicale des Algériens en faveur des Palestiniens," 17 November 1969, 19960311, art. 4; RG, "Association 'Présence de la Palestine,' " 27 May 1971, 19990426, art 176 (liasse 1 N° 454), CAC. Préfecture de police, 1 May 1971, T9 Terrenoire, APP. Kassir and Mardam-Bey, *Itinéraires de Paris à Jérusalem*, 105, 170.

39. See Gordon, "Immigrants," 175, for a face-off between pro-Palestinian supporters and left-wing Zionists on 4 June at the Sorbonne.

40. Notes d'information, 1968, MDI 95, CDJC; Sayigh, *Armed Struggle*, 190.

41. Police incorectly dated the group's birth to 1969 (as noted, the Union first formed in 1965). Conflicting dates appear in Untitled Reports, Préfecture de police, 19 February 1970 and March 1972, 19870799, art. 20, N° 3383; "L'Union générale des étudiants palestiniens en France," June 1972, 19990260, art. 23, CAC.

42. RG, "Les comités de soutien au peuple palestinien," 29 January 1969, 19990426, art. 15 (liasse 6 N° 122); RG, "El Fatah et les mouvements révolutionnaires en France," 29 April 1969, 19990426, art. 15 (liasse 7 N° 140); RG, "Les activités politiques des Nord-Africains résidant en France," April 1970, 19850087, art. 39; RG, "Les activités du bureau de la Ligue arabe à Paris," June 1972, 19990260, art. 23, CAC. Hajjat, "Les Comités Palestine," 80, 84, claims these bodies were intermittently active in 1969.

43. RG, "El Fatah et les révolutionnaires français," 25 June 1969, 19990260, art. 23, CAC.

44. Préfecture de police, 23 January 1969, 19990426, art. 15 (liasse 6 N° 122), CAC.

45. "Prochaine création d'une association dite 'Section française du Mouvement contre le racisme anti-Arabe (M.R.A.A.),'" 18 November 1968, 19990426, art 15 (liasse 5 N° 74); RG, "El Fatah et les mouvements révolutionnaires en France," 29 April 1969, 19990426, art. 15 (liasse 7 N° 140); "Création à Paris d'un mouvement contre le racisme anti-Arabe," *AE*, 1 December 1968, p. 17.

46. "Rubrique: Antisionisme et anti-impérialisme [*sic*]," *Résistance populaire*, 15 May (1968), pp. 22–25.

47. Préfecture de police, 23 January 1969, 19990426, art. 15 (liasse 6 N° 122), CAC. Ideology could also divide. Fatah's commando actions proved particularly attractive to Maoists who believed that Third World liberation movements had revolutionary potential. Trotskyists were drawn to George Habash's Popular Front for the Liberation of Palestine (PFLP), a guerrilla movement that called for social and economic transformation as part of its nationalist revolution, and to Nayef Hawatmeh's Popular Democratic Front for the Liberation of Palestine (PDFLP), a more extreme left-wing break-away organization. RG, "El Fatah et les révolutionnaires français," 25 June 1969; RG, "Le rôle d'éléments algériens dans le terrorisme international," 26 June 1971; RG, "Les organisations palestiniennes en France," 20 June 1972, 19990260, art. 23; RG, "Nervosité chez les Algériens en France," 3 July 1969, 19960311, art. 4; CAC. According to Sayigh, *Armed Struggle*, 232–33, the PFLP's Marxism was "skin-deep."

Also see Auron, *Les Juifs d'extrême gauche*, 219, and Denis Sieffert, *Israël-Palestine, une passion française: La France dans le miroir du conflit israélo-palestinien* (Paris: Éditions la Découverte, 2004), p. 159.

48. Links between *gauchistes* and immigrant workers is drawn from Noiriel, *Immigration, antisémitisme et racism,* 558–64; Gastaut, *L'immigration et l'opinion,* 37–51, 149–67; Direction de la réglementation, "L'Immigration étrangère en France" (1970), 19960311, art. 1, CAC.

49. Préfecture de police, 6 October 1970, 19960311, art. 4; Note pour Monsieur le Ministre de l'Intérieur, 1 March 1971, 19900353, art. 14 (liasse 1); Direction de la réglementation, 14 September 1971, 19960311, art. 1, CAC.

50. Direction de la réglementation, "L'immigration étrangère en France" (1970), 19960311, art. 1, CAC.

51. "Création à Paris d'un mouvement contre le racisme anti-Arabe," 17; RG, "El Fatah et les mouvements révolutionnaires en France," 29 April 1969, 19990426, art. 15 (liasse 7 N° 140), CAC. It is worth noting that what is called "Islamophobia" in contemporary parlance was called anti-Arab racism in the 1960s, reflecting some of the dictional changes discussed in the Introduction.

52. "Rubrique: Unité des travailleurs arabes et français," *Résistance populaire,* 15 May (1968), pp. 26–28.

53. "Meeting contre le racisme à Paris," *AE,* 30 June–15 July 1971, p. 27; Posters, Semaine de la Palestine, 24–28 March 1969, 8 Fi 791/1, BdR.

54. Gastaut, *L'immigration et l'opinion,* 157, dates this interest to the fusion of numerous pro-Chinese groups around Vive la Révolution! and the Gauche prolétarienne in March 1969.

55. Unless noted, discussion of Jewish leftists is from Auron, *Les Juifs d'extrême gauche.*

56. RG, "El Fatah et les révolutionnaires français," 25 June 1969, 19990260, art. 23, CAC.

57. Dominique Schnapper, *Juifs et Israélites* (Paris: Gallimard, 1980), pp. 171–87. Auron, *Les Juifs d'extrême gauche* 71, 163–213, discusses Jewish leftists who refused radical anti-Zionism. Also see Wolf, *Harnessing the Holocaust,* 55–57.

58. In June 1967, Rodinson helped found the Groupe de recherches et d'action pour le règlement du problème palestinien, which declared itself a "defender of Judaism" and "hostile to Zionism." RG, "Groupe de recherches et d'action pour le règlement du problème palestinien GRAPP," June 1972, 19990260, art. 23, CAC.

59. Emmanuel Lévyne, "L'israélisation d'une communauté juive de la région parisienne," *AE,* 1 January 1970, pp. 26–27; A. Zehraoui, "Meeting sur la Palestine à la Mutualité," *AE,* 15 November 1969, p.4. Emmanuel Lévyne, *Judaïsme contre Sionisme* (Paris: Éditions Cujas, 1969).

60. RG, "El Fatah et les révolutionnaires français," 25 June 1969, 19990260, art. 23, CAC. Auron, *Les Juifs d'extrême gauche,* 191.

61. Rabah Aissaoui, *Immigration and National Identity: North African Political Movements in Colonial and Postcolonial France* (London and New York: Tauris Academic Studies, 2009), p. 214.

62. RG, "Les organisations palestiniennes en France," 20 June 1972, 19990260, art. 23, CAC. According to Auron, *Les Juifs d'extrême gauche,* 184. Jews were particularly drawn to Trotskyist organizations, which held less extreme views on Israel.

63. Poster cited in letter to CRIF, 3 November 1969, MDI 147, CDJC.

64. Szafran, *Les Juifs dans la politique française,* 58.

65. Auron, *Les Juifs d'extrême gauche* 60–63, 192–93. Like many Jewish radicals, both Levy and Geismar eventually backed away from their anti-Zionism.

66. Szafran, *Les Juifs dans la politique française*, 188–90.

67. Poster cited in letter to CRIF, 3 November 1969, MDI 147, CDJC.

68. According to Hajjat, "Les Comités Palestine," 75–81, subsequent Comités Palestine were more autonomous from the GP. Also see Aissaoui, *Immigration and National Identity*, 212–17; "L'expérience politique du Mouvement des travailleurs arabes," 78–79; Kassir and Mardam-Bey, *Itinéraires de Paris*, 105, 170, 173; Sieffert, *Israël-Palestine*, 138.

69. RG, "Les activités politiques des Nord-Africains résidant en France," April 1970; RG, "Les activités politiques des Nord-Africains résidant en France," April 1970, 19850087, art. 39, CAC. Hajjat, "Les Comités Palestine," 75–76. For prior activism among such students, see Guy Pervillé, *Les étudiants algériens de l'université française, 1880–1962* (Paris: Éditions du Centre national de la recherche scientifique, 1984).

70. The Croisssant-rouge palestinian was supported in part by the ADAE funds. Préfecture de police, "La situation actuelle de Jordanie révèle l'hostilité des pays arabes vis-à-vis du gouvernement du roi Hussein et déclenche dans la capitale un vaste mouvement humanitaire," 5 October 1970, T9 Terrenoire, APP. Additional ADAE pro-Palestinian activities are documented in RG, "Campagne de l'Amicale des Algériens en faveur des Palestiniens," 17 November 1969 and MI to ME, "Campagne de l'Amicale des Algériens en Europe en faveur des Palestiniens," 18 December 1969, 19960311, art. 4; RG, "El Fatah et les mouvements révolutionnaires en France," 29 April 1969, 19990426, art. 15 (liasse 7 N° 140); RG, "Les activités politiques des Nord-Africains résidant en France," April 1970, 19850087, art. 39; Préfecture de police, 25 November 1972, 19850087, art. 37, CAC. *L'Algérien en Europe* also regularly criticized Israel.

71. As members of Moroccan opposition groups, they could not return home. Untitled report, Préfecture de police, 30 December 1970, 19960311, art. 5 CAC. The Association des Marocains en France (AMF) also served as a meeting spot for pro-Palestinian Muslim leftists, as did the Association des étudiants musulmans d'Afrique du Nord's headquarters on boulevard Saint Michel. Hajjat, "Les Comités Palestine," 76–78.

72. In June 1971, the Popular Front for the Liberation of Palestine, a break-away guerrilla movement from Fatah, estimated that 80 percent of the group's membership was located in universities. RG, "Le rôle d'éléments algériens dans le terrorisme international," 26 June 1971, 19960311, art. 4, CAC. If, as Hajjat, "Les Comités Palestine," 77, and Aissaoui, *Immigration and National Identity*, 154, claim, Algerian students played a smaller role on the Comités Palestine than Moroccans and Tunisians, the Palestinian issue still made inroads among them. Untitled report, Préfecture de police, 17 September 1971, 19850087, art. 39, CAC.

73. Hajjat, "Les Comités Palestine," 84–86. Both the PFLP and the PDFLP also sought to link the anti-imperialist struggle with the problems facing immigrant workers in France via the Palestinian issue, although Hajjat (p. 80) notes that many North African students avoided Trotskyist organizations, which prioritized socialist revolution over national and anti-colonial struggles. Evidence of some North African participation in the PFLP can nevertheless be found in RG, "Le rôle d'éléments algériens

dans le terrorisme international," 26 June 1971, 19960311, art. 4; RG, "Les organisations palestiniennes en France," 20 June 1972, 19990260, art. 23, CAC.

74. Préfecture de police, "Propagande menée par des Musulmans en milieu ouvrier en faveur de la révolution palestinienne," 3 December 1970, 19900353, art. 14 (liasse 1), CAC.

75. RG, "Le rôle d'éléments algériens dans le terrorisme international," 26 June 1971, 19960311, art. 4, CAC. Aissaoui, *Immigration and National Identity*, 160–66, 174–80.

76. Préfecture de police, 19 November 1969 (1970), 19900353, art. 11 (liasse 1), CAC.

77. The ADAE worked closely with Fatah once the latter established a presence in France, raising money; providing security for pro-Palestinian rallies; distributing pro-Palestinian tracts; and even sending a representative to a PLO training camp. Direction centrale des renseignements généraux, "El Fatah et les mouvements révolutionnaires en France," 29 April 1969, 19990426, art. 15 (liasse 7 N° 140); Direction centrale des renseignements généraux, April 1970, "Les activités politiques des Nord-Africains residant en France," 19850087, art 39, CAC. In 1972, the ADAE dedicated funds raised during Ramadan to Palestinian relief efforts, mimicking FLN policies in Algeria where such donations were mandatory. Prefecture de police, 25 November 1972, 19850087, art. 37, CAC. Hajjat, "Les Comités Palestine," 77, notes that the ADAE often clashed with Muslim leftists.

78. RG, "Les comités de soutien au peuple palestinien," 29 January 1969; RG, "El Fatah et les mouvements révolutionnaires en France," 29 April 1969, 19990426, art. 15 (liasse 7 N° 140), CAC. Articles praising de Gaulle's pro-Arab stance can be found in *AE* on 1 December 1967, 15 February 1968, 15 January 1969, and 15 April 1969, although criticism of covert military aid to Israel appears in "Où en est l'embargo?" *AE*, 16 January 1970, p. 26.

79. Directeur central des RG to Directeur de la règlementation, 6ème bureau, "Renseignements sur l'Union générale des étudiants de Palestine," 18 August 1970, 19870799, art. 20, no. 3383; RG, "Les organisations palestiniennes en France," 20 June 1972, 19990260, art. 23, CAC; Sieffert, *Israël-Palestine*, 138–42.

80. RG, "El Fatah et les révolutionnaires français," 25 June 1969, 19990260, art. 23, CAC.

81. Sayigh, *Armed Struggle*, 196–200, discusses ideological tensions within Fatah's commitment to Arab unity. To quell concerns of supporters further to the left, the organization often adopted a moderate socialism. MI, Direction de la surveillance du territoire, "Note d'information: Projet d'installation d'un bureau de presse du Fatah à Paris. Évolution du Fatah," 1 September 1969, 19990260, art. 23, CAC. For an example of Fatah's more leftist efforts, see "Dans un communiqué publié à Alger: L'organisation palestinienne 'El Feth' s'engage a poursuivre la lutte jusqu'à la victoire," *El Moudjahid*, 4 May 1968, p. 7.

82. Directeur central des RG to Directeur de la règlementation, 6ème bureau, "Renseignements sur l'Union générale des étudiants de Palestine," 18 August 1970, 19870799, art. 20, N° 3383, CAC. Ideological divisions ultimately threatened the UGEP. Préfecture de police, 19 February 1970, 19870799, art. 20, N° 3383; "L'Union générale des étudiants palestiniens en France," June 1972, 19990260, art. 23, CAC.

83. Préfecture de police, 1 November 1972, 19870799, art. 20, N° 3383; Préfecture de police, 12 November 1972, 19990260, art. 23, CAC.

84. Cited in Auron, *Les Juifs d'extrême gauche*, 107–10.

85. Simon, *L'immigration algérienne en France*, 24–26.

86. Gastaut, *L'immigration et l'opinion*, 282–97, points to 1971–73 as the height of anti-Arab racism.

87. Wihtol de Wenden, *Les immigrés et la politique*, 155–79.

88. Aissaoui, *Immigration and National Identity*, 153–216, and Hajjat, "L'expérience politique du Mouvement des travailleurs arabes," 76–85.

89. The GP had been weakened in 1970 after a French government ban and a controversial decision to attack the Jordanian embassy as well as after 1972 disagreements over the Palestinian resistance organization Black September's kidnapping of Israeli athletes at the Munich Olympics, which some members (primarily the Jewish leadership) condemned. Auron, *Les Juifs d'extrême gauche*, 145–46, 227–40; Jocelyne Cesari, *Être musulman en France: Associations, militants, et mosquées* (Paris: Éditions Karthala et Iremam, 1994), p. 174; Szafran, *Les Juifs dans la politique*, 177–93.

90. Posters in Marseille prior to Golda Meir's 1973 visit to France, for example, linked anti-Zionism and the immigrant struggle. Commissariat central de Marseille to Préfet de la région, 12 January 1973; Commissariat central de Marseille, "Note," 12 January 1973; Commissariat de police de la Ciotat to Contrôleur général, "Diffusion d'un tract émanant de divers mouvements gauchistes et relatif à la visite en France de Mme Golda Meir," 12 January 1973, 135W57, BdR.

91. Cited in Gastaut, *L'immigration et l'opinion*, 161. For the centrality of Palestine, see Hajjat, "Les Comités Palestines," 90; Wihtol de Wenden, *Les immigrés et la politique*, 178. Aissaoui, *Immigration and National Identity*, 156–60, 212–17, notes that MTA activists took up all issues relevant to the Arab people.

92. Ministre des armes, Bureau emploi-renseignement, "Collecte en faveur des Palestiniens," 7 May 1973, 19980547, art. 17 (extrait: Palestine), CAC. For the MTA's ethnonational politics, see Aissaoui, *Immigration and National Identity*, 156–60.

93. Cited in Hajjat, "Les Comités Palestine," 90. Mauritians and Pakistanis broke away from the MTA in 1974 complaining of its over-involvement in the struggle against Zionism and North African regimes. RG, 22 June 1974, 19900353, Article 11 (liasse 1), CAC.

94. RG, "Nervosité chez les Algériens en France," 3 July 1969, 19960311, art. 4, CAC.

95. RG, "Les activités politiques des Nord-Africains résidant en France," April 1970, 19850087, art. 39, CAC.

96. Commissariat central de Marseille, "Note: Distribution de tracts aux Ets Coder," 7 October 1970; Directeur départemental des services de sécurité publique de Bouches-du-Rhône to Directeur central de la sécurité publique, Paris, "Pénétration du milieu des travailleurs immigrés par les gauchistes," 10 July 1970, 135W124, BdR.

97. GILR, Procès-verbal de la réunion du 16 mai 1970; Directeur départemental des services de sécurité publique de Bouches-du-Rhône to Directeur central de la sécurité publique, Paris, "Pénétration du milieu des travailleurs immigrés par les gauchistes," 10 July 1970, 135W124, BdR. By July, the GP's influence had been weakened by arrests and departures. GILR, Procès verbal de la réunion du 8 juillet 1970, same file.

98. Cited in Hajjat, "Les Comités Palestine," 84–86.

99. Préfet to ME and MI, "Association dite 'Bureau d'aide en France à la révolution palestinienne' B.A.R.P.," 14 September 1971, 19990426, art. 17 (liasse 1 N° 468); RG, "Le rôle d'éléments algériens dans le terrorisme international," 26 June 1971, 19960311, art. 4, CAC.

100. GILR, Procès verbal de la réunion du 20 octobre 1970; "Un responsable de l'ex-gauche prolétarienne, à Antony envisage de s'installer définitivement dans la région de Marseille," 7 October 1970, 135W124, BdR. Direction de la réglementation, 14 September 1971, 19960311, art. 1, CAC.

101. Commissariat central de Marseille, "Note," 27 March 1972, 135W57, BdR.

102. MI, "Marseille—Manifestation gauchiste du 12-12-72," 18 December 1972, 135W57, BdR.

103. Ibid.

104. Gordon, "Immigrants," 25.

105. Annexe 3 du rapport du Préfet du police du 23 août 1971, "Activité politique des principales colonies étrangères," 19900353, art. 11 (liasse 1); Direction de la réglementation, 14 September 1971, 19960311, art. 1, CAC.

106. Annexe 3 du rapport du Préfet du police du 23 août 1971, "Activité politique des principales colonies étrangères," 19900353, art. 11 (liasse 1), CAC.

107. Direction de la réglementation, 14 September 1971, 19960311, art. 1, CAC.

108. Préfecture de police, 19 November 1969, 19900353, art. 11 (liasse 1), CAC.

109. Hajjat, "Les Comités Palestine," 86.

110. RG, "Les organisations palestiniennes en France," 20 June 1972, 19990260, art. 23, CAC.

111. "L'Union générale des étudiants palestiniens en France," June 1972, 19990260, art. 23, CAC.

112. "Les travailleurs de Suresnes-Puteaux soutiennent la révolution palestinienne," *Fedai* (1972), in Commissariat central de Marseille, "Note," 27 March 1972, 135W57, BdR.

113. Police reported apathy among Muslim workers and students for the Palestinian cause as late as 1976. "Échec de la campagne gauchiste en faveur du Liban," 29 October 1976, 19900353, Article 11 (liasse 2), CAC.

114. Préfecture de police, 5 March 1970, 19990260, art. 23, CAC. Some Algerian immigrants blamed an explosion on 4 December 1969 at the mosqué de Paris on those tyring to punish its Algerian director for refusing to support the cause. Untitled Report, 14 January 1970, La Fédération des sociétés juives de France, BA 2315, APP. A. Selmi, "L'attentat contre la Mosquée de Paris ou le Nazisme nouvelle vague," *AE*, 15 December 1969, blamed Israelis.

115. Préfet des Vosges to MI, 8 September 1969, Algériens–Activités politiques: Divers (1966–76), 19960311, art. 4, CAC.

116. Préfecture de police, Direction des renseignements généraux et des jeux, "La communauté juive dans la région parisienne" (1970?), 19900353, art. 10 (liasse1), CAC. Roger Ascot, "Quinze mille jeunes," *L'Arche*, February 1969, pp. 17–21, claimed that 10–15 percent of Jewish youth participated in organized communal life.

117. Noiriel, *Immigration, antisémitisme et racism*, 558–64; Auron, *Les Juifs d'extrême gauche*, passim. For an example of divisions, see "Jeunes Juifs de la révolte," *L'Arche*, June–July 1968, pp. 33–36, 73–77.

118. Roger Ascot, "Le mal de la jeunesse," *L'Arche*, December 1968–January 1969; Wolf, *Harnessing the Holocaust*, 55–57.

119. Simmy Epstein and Meïr Waintrater, "Université: Les étudiants juif au pied du mur," *L'Arche*, February–March 1970, p. 40.

120. Meir Yoguev, "Les héritiers de mai 68," *L'Arche*, 25 May–25 June 1973, pp. 37–42. Also see Regina Rittel, "Les écoles juives et la crise de l'enseignement," pp. 43–46, 65, in same edition.

121. Meir Yoguev, "Les héritiers de mai 68," *L'Arche*, 25 May–25 June 1973, pp. 37–42. RG, "Les comités de soutien au peuple palestinien," 29 January 1969 19990426, art. 15 (liasse 6, Nº 122), CAC.

122. He also credited the 1967 war. Lucien Poznanski, "L'UEJF aujourd'hui," *L'Arche*, February–March 1970, p. 63.

123. In May 1969, for example, Grenoble's UEJF protested an exposition on Palestinian resistance. RG, "El Fatah et les révolutionnaires français," 25 June 1969, 19990260, art. 23, CAC.

124. RG, "Les comités de soutien au peuple palestinien," 29 January 1969, 19990426, art. 15 (liasse 6 Nº 122), CAC.

125. One Jewish communal leader remarked, "such people just deserve a pistol shot in the neck." M. P. Elkouby to M. A. Loss, "UEJF," 2 May 1972, MDI 159, CJDC.

126. Front des étudiants juifs to CRIF, "Le FEJ" (August 1974?) MDI 146 B, CDJC. For organizaing among Jewish high school students, see Auron, *Les Juifs d'extrême gauche*, 131–32.

127. Interview with Françoise Tenenbaum in Robert I. Weiner and Richard E. Sharpless, eds. *An Uncertain Future: Voices of a French Jewish Community, 1940–2012* (Toronto: University of Toronto Press, 2012), p. 68.

128. Letter to CRIF, 3 November 1969, MDI 147, CJDC.

129. Posters, Semaine de la Palestine, 24–28 March 1969, 8 Fi 791/1, BdR.

130. Untitled Report, 14 January 1970, La Fédération des sociétés juives de France, BA 2315, APP.

131. Front des étudiants juifs to CRIF, "Le FEJ" (August 1974?) MDI 146 B, CJDC. The source is a review of the FEJ's prior activities beginning in 1968.

132. RG, "El Fatah et les révolutionnaires français," 25 June 1969, 19990260, art. 23, CAC; Meir Yoguev, "Les héritiers de mai 68," *L'Arche*, 25 May–25 June 1973, pp. 37–42.

133. RG, "El Fatah et les révolutionnaires français," 25 June 1969, 19990260, art. 23, CAC.

134. Some blamed violence on antisemitic orators while others accused Betar of instigating the attack. The latter denied involvement. "Incidents antisémites au centre universitaire Censier," Bureau du CRIF, 4 February 1970, MDI 1–55; "Les incidents de Censier," 15 December 1969, MDI 66, CDJC; Préfecture de police, direction des renseignements généraux et des jeux, "La communauté juive dans la région parisienne" (1970?), 19900353, art. 10 (liasse 1, Israël), CAC; "Affrontement à Censier," *L'Aurore*, 11 December 1969, p. 3. Zionist student groups published their own account in "Des mouvements sionistes condamnent l'agression de Censier," *Le Monde*, 13 December 1969, p. 4.

135. "Incidents antisémites au centre universitaire Censier," Bureau du CRIF, 4 February 1970, MDI 1–55, CDJC; Préfecture de police, direction des renseignements généraux et des jeux, "La communauté juive dans la région parisienne" (1970?), 19900353, art. 10 (liasse 1, Israël), CAC.

136. MDI 146 B, CJDC.

137. Préfecture de police, 20 June 1970, 19850087, art 39, CAC.

138. A few days before, "the Irgoun's watching" had been scrawled on the building's door.
139. "Des mouvements sionistes," 4.
140. Préfecture de police, direction des renseignements généraux et des jeux, "La communauté juive dans la région parisienne" (1970?), 19900353, art. 10 (liasse 1, Israël), CAC.
141. "Des mouvements sionistes," 4.
142. "Incidents antisémites au centre universitaire Censier," Bureau du CRIF, 4 February 1970, MDI 1–55, CDJC.
143. CRIF meeting, 13 March 1970, MDI 146 B and MDI 1–55, CDJC.
144. CRIF meeting, 11 December 1969, MDI 1–55, CDJC.
145. Epstein and Meir, "Université," 39.
146. CRIF meeting, 24 January 1969, MDI 1–55, CDJC. Discussions of the "anti-Israel campaigns" and efforts to monitor pro-Palestinian activities can be found in Bureau du CRIF, 5 December 1969, MDI 1–55; "Solidarité avec les réfugiés palestiniens: L'association de solidarité franco-arabe vend des cartes de vœux au profit des réfugiés arabes de Palestine, qui passent un 22ème hiver en exil," 22 December 1969, MDI 326, CDJC.
147. CRIF meeting, 2 July 1970, MDI 1–55, CDJC. Fears of the conflation of anti-Zionism and antisemitism circulated widely. One such reference to the Comité Palestine can be found in Journées nationales du CRIF, in October 1971 MDI 136.
148. Préfecture de police, 23 June 1971, T9 Terrenoire, APP.
149. "A l'approche du 4ème anniversaire du conflit israélo-arabe, les Algériens de Paris craignent des provocations de la part des Israélites," 18 May 1971, Comité des étudiants juifs, BA 2315, APP. Préfecture de police, 26 May 1971, 19990260, art. 23, CAC.
150. Police report, 13 January 1972, 19990260, art. 23, CAC, blamed the FEJ and the Comité de soutien aux Juifs d'URSS.
151. Préfecture de police, 8 June 1972; Police report, 28 July 1972, 19900260, art. 23, CAC, made clear that while such tactics mirrored Meir Kahne's Jewish Defense League in New York City, the culprits had no plans to follow through.
152. In Marseille, posters accusing Israeli fascists of occupying Palestine illegally blamed deaths in Munich on German police and Israeli intransigence. Commissariat central de Marseille, "Note," 11 September 1972, 135W57, BdR. For disagreements on the far left, see Auron, Les Juifs d'extrême gauche, 227–40.
153. CRIF statement, 6 September 1972, MDI 146 B, CDJC.
154. Préfecture de police, 5 September 1972, 19990260, art. 23, CDAC.
155. Préfecture de police, 16 November 1972, 19990260, art. 23, CAC.
156. Threats came from the Jewish Defense League (JDL), via the FEJ. Préfecture de police, 25 November 1972, 19990260, art. 23; "Compte-rendu de la réunion de liaison consacré aux problèmes de terrorisme," 14 December 1972, 19890576, art 4 (liasse 1), CAC. ADAE accusations of JDL terrorism appear in, "Lâche attentat sioniste contre la librairie 'Palestine' à Paris," AE, 15 October 1972, p. 34. See documents in 19980547, Article 17 (extrait: Palestine), CAC, for Palestinian requests for police protection from Zionists.
157. Kassir and Mardam-Bey, Itinéraires de Paris à Jérusalem, 106; M.B., "Attentat sioniste contre le représentant de l'O.L.P. à Paris," AE, 16–30 December 1972, pp. 28–29; "Recrudescence du contre-terrorisme en France," 11 December 1972, 19990260,

art. 23, CAC; "La 2ème conférence des jeunes d'Europe et des pays arabes: Contre l'impérialisme et le Sionisme," *AE*, 16–30 December 1972, pp. 26–27; "Menaces et injures adressées à l'ambassade d'Algérie à Paris," *AE*, 16–29 November 1972, p. 22; Direction générale de la police nationale, "Compte-rendu de la réunion de liaison consacré aux problèmes de terrorisme," 14 December 1972, 19890576, art 4 (liasse 1), CAC.

158. In June 1971, the CRIF president warned that Paris had become "a hub of actions against Israel." CRIF meeting, 2 June 1971, MDI 1–55, CDJC. While skeptical that Jewish terrorists had bombed the Librarie Palestine, the CRIF criticized all provocateurs. CRIF meeting, 5 October 1972. Several pro-Palestinian and North African student groups called for protection from Israel's "vast liquidation campaign." MI from Union générale des étudiants de Palestine, Union nationale des étudiants du Maroc, Union général des étudiants libanais en France, Association des étudiants irakiens en France, 26 April 1973, 19990260, art. 23, CAC.

159. Meir Yoguev, "Université: Une nouvelle génération antisioniste," *L'Arche*, 26 January–25 February 1973, pp. 21–22.

160. CRIF meeting, 5 October 1972; Communiqué, 9 January 1973, MDI 146 B, CDJC.

161. "L'attentat contre l'Agence juive," *L'Arche*, January–February 1973, p. 30. For another example, see Philippe Ben's "La dernière contre offensive arabe," *L'Arche*, March–April 1973, pp. 19–20, in which the terms "Arab" and "Palestinian" are nearly always accompanied by the term "terrorism."

162. Préfecture de police, 15 December 1972, 19990260, art. 23, CAC.

163. "Le terrorisme sioniste," *AE*, 16–30 September 1972, p. 5. Rare references to Jews qua Jews included articles that compared anti-Muslim sentiment in France negatively to antisemitism in *AE*,1 December 1968; 1 November 1969; and 15 March 1968. *AE*, 1 March 1969, p. 3, accused the chief rabbi of blind support for Israel and unfair representations of Jewish life in Arab lands. Articles blurring lines between Zionists and Jews include, "À la limite de l'antisémitisme," *AE*, 1 July 1969, p. 2, and "Haro sur l'embargo," *AE*, 1 February 1969, p. 17, which provided a list of pro-Israel supporters and blamed the "pressure exercised by the Jewish milieu on French affairs" for the "hysteria" in the press after the January 1969 arms embargo on Israel. Other pieces argued that Jews controlled the media and promoted racist images of Arabs and Algerians. "Le Sionisme dans la presse française," *AE*, 14 July 1969, p. 31; "Sionisme et cie," *AE*, 14–28 May 1970, p. 31. Articles on the pro-Israel bias of the French media include: September 1969, 18 September 1969, 1 November 1969 (article about anti-Arab biases in French television), 1 December 1969, 15 December 1969, 16 January 1970, 9 April 1970, 4–17 September 1970, 1–7 October 1970, 6–21 February 1971. Préfecture de police, 12 November 1972, 19960311, art. 4, CAC.

164. MI, "Marseille—Manifestation gauchistes du 12-12-72," 18 December 1972, 135W57, BdR.

165. High schools, for example, reported frequent altercations between pro-Zionist and pro-Palestinian students. Arnold Mandel, "France," *American Jewish Yearbook* (1973), p. 399; Meir Yoguev, "L'antisionisme dans les lycées," *L'Arche*, 26 December–25 January 1973, pp. 41–45.

166. Direction de la réglementation, 22 February 1973, 19990260, art. 23, CAC.

167. Gastaut, *L'immigration et l'opinion*, 290–95.

168. Cited in Noiriel, *Immigration, antisémitisme et racism*, 567.

169. Jews were occasionally targeted as well. Vacationing Tunisian Jews in Juan-les Pins, for example, were attacked for speaking Arabic and for loitering in a local café. Arnold Mandel, "France," *American Jewish Yearbook* (1974–75), p. 427.

170. Hajjat, "L'expérience politique," 84.

171. "Maoïstes et travailleurs immigrés," 22 October 1976, 19960311, art. 4, CAC. (Comité des travailleurs algériens), December 1984; "Soutenez le CTA," 1693W234, BdR.

172. "Avant la manifestation du 14 septembre: Le gauchisme français et les travailleurs immigrés," 12 September 1973, 19960311, art. 4, CAC.

173. CRIF meeting, 8 November 1973, MDI 146 B; "Attentat ambassade d'Algerie," Marseille, no date, MDI 146, CDJC.

174. Organisation des ouvriers tunisiens, section de Toulouse, "La victoire est aux peuples arabes combattants," MDI 219; Anonymous letter to the CRIF, 21 October 1973, same reel, CJDC. The CRIF also monitored the gauchiste newspaper *Libération* (which it accused of Palestinian backing), for stories on French Jewish attacks against Muslims. Note de Service, "Comment *Libération* nourrit la campagne raciste en France," 10 October 1973; MDI 222, CJDC.

175. Interventions IIIe journée nationale du CRIF, MDI 145, CDJC.

176. These funds came from over half of the Jewish families in France. "French Jewish Leaders under Fire," no date, MDI 146, CDJC. Also see the *BIL* report on the CRIF's pro-Israel activities in MDI 146B and "Depuis le 6 October" (no date), MDI 144, CDJC. Jews on the far left, however, remained highly critical of Israeli actions.

177. Guy Porte, "La quatrième guerre: En marge du conflit-à Marseille, Juifs et Arabes ont su éviter les pièges du racisme," 25 October 1973, *Le Monde*, p. 4. Three thousand demonstrators participated. Commissariat central de Marseille, "Note," 8 October 1973, 135W57, BdR.

178. "Les organisations d'opposants algériens nuisent-elles aux bonnes relations gouvernementales entre la France et l'Algérie?" 3 November 1973, 19960311, art. 4, CAC.

179. Commissariat central de Marseille, "Note," 8 October 1973, 135 W 57.

180. Porte, "La quatrième guerre," 4.

181. "Avant la manifestation du 14 septembre: Le gauchisme français et les travailleurs immigrés," 12 September 1973, 19960311, art. 4, CAC.

182. Porte, "La quatrième guerre," 4.

183. Aissaoui, *Immigration and National Identity*, 177, 214. Porte, "La quatrième guerre," 4.

184. "Lettre aux jeunes," Service de la jeunesse en coopération avec les services culturel et de l'enseignement du FSJU, MDI 219, CJDC. Thirty Jewish volunteers left for Israel on 25 October. Secteur sud de la police de l'air et des frontières, "Note d'information," 26 October 1973, 135W57, BdR.

185. For the meeting, see D. Allen and A. Pijpers, eds., *European Foreign Policy-Making and the Arab-Israeli Conflict* (The Hague: Martinus Nijhoff Publishers, 1984), pp. 4–5, 15. Numerous articles in MDI 159, CJDC document Jewish outrage.

186. Appel du Comité de Marseille du Conseil représentatif des institutions juives de France, MDI 159, CJDC, printed in *Le Provençal*, 18 December 1974; G. L., "Les étudiants sionistes-socialistes et la situation au Moyen-Orient," *Le Provençal*, 3 December 1974.

187. Marseille's Jewish community organized the demonstration without support from the Parisian CRIF, which local leaders criticized for its silence. M. P. Elkouby to M. A. Loss, "Manifestation sur la Canebière contre la politique française au Proche Orient le 7 novembre 1974," 8 November 1974, MDI 159, CJDC.

188. "Les associations juives de Marseille ont manifesté contre la reconnaissance de l'OLP par la France," Le Provençal, 8 November 1974, MDI 159, CJDC.

189. Entretien accordé le 5 novembre 1974 à une délégation du Comité de coordination des associations juives de Marseille, 135W57, BdR.

190. Romain Gary (Émile Ajar) The Life Before Us, trans. Ralph Manheim (New York: A New Directions Book, 1986), pp. 128–31.

191. Gary, The Life Before Us, 167.

192. Ibid., 31.

193. "Projet de campagne d'information en faveur de l'image d'Israel," 1976, MDI 107, CDJC.

194. ADAE efforts to suppress the MTA are in "Réorganisation de l'Amicale des Algériens en Europe pour prémunir les travailleurs algériens contre la propagande de l'ex Ligue communiste et de l'ex 'Gauche Prolétarienne,' " 10 November 1973; "Les responsables de l'Amicale des Algériens en Europe multiplient les initiatives en vue d'une plus étroite collaboration avec les autorités françaises," 26 February 1975, 19960311, art. 4, CAC. Also see Aissaoui, Immigrant and National Identity, 206–208.

195. Hajjat, "L'éxperience politique du Mouvement des travailleurs arabes," 76–85. Étude, "Maoïstes et travailleurs immigrés," 22 October 1976, 19960311, art. 4, CAC. For diminishment in pro-immigrant political movements, see Gastaut, L'immigration et l'opinion, 164; Wihtol de Wenden, Les immigrés et la politique, 216–19.

196. Some Jewish leftists, however, criticized Israel's appropriation of Jewish identity. Auron, Les Juifs d'extrême gauche, 198–200.

197. In March 1976, for example, the Comité de soutien aux Juifs d'URSS attacked attendees of a pro-Palestinian meeting. RG, 1 April 1976, 19980547, Article 17 (extrait Palestine), CAC.

198. J. Ph Levy to Steg, no date, MDI 146, CDJC.

Chapter 6. Particularism versus Pluriculturalism: The Birth and Death of the Anti-Racist Coalition

1. Paul Silverstein, Algeria in France: Transpolitics, Race, and Nation (Bloomington: Indiana University Press, 2004), pp. 151–66. The term "Beur" marked "second-generation" marginalization linguistically. Using verlan—a form of slang that inverts syllables—to transform the term "Arab" (the misappelation of their parents who were usually of Berber origin) to "Beur," "second generation" Muslims created a new identity that was neither French nor North African.

2. Gérard Noiriel, Immigration, antisémitisme et racisme en France (XIX–XX siècle): Discours publics, humiliations privées (Paris: Fayard 2007), pp. 589–664.

3. Noiriel, Immigration, antisémitisme et racisme en France, 622–24; Judith E. Vichniac, "French Socialists and Droit à la différence: A Changing Dynamic," French Politics & Society 9, 1 (1991): 410–56.

4. Joan Scott, *Politics of the Veil* (Princeton: Princeton University Press, 2007), pp. 1–2.
5. Kimberly Arkin, "'It's the French and the Arabs against the Jews': Identity Politics and the Construction of Adolescent Jewishness in France" (Ph.D. diss., University of Chicago, 2008), pp. 207–17; Pierre Birnbaum, *Jewish Destinies: Citizenship, State and Community in Modern France*, trans. Arthur Goldhammer (New York: Hill and Wang, 2000), pp. 191–213; Judith E. Vichniac, "Jewish Identity Politics and the Scarf Affairs in France," *French Politics, Culture & Society* 26, 1 (2008): 111–28.
6. Arkin, "It's the French and Arabs," 160, makes this point specifically about Jewish activism but it could be made about Beur activism as well.
7. Scholars debate the relative virulence of antisemitism and Islamophobia in the 1980s. Yvan Gastaut, *Immigration et l'opinion en France sous la Ve république* (Paris: Seuil, 2000), pp. 276–82, for example, argues that anti-Jewish attitudes—on the decline since the end of World War II—were replaced by anti-Arab hostility. In contrast, Birnbaum, *Jewish Destinies*, 185–88, downplays the specificity of anti-Arab attitudes, placing them in a longer history of French xenophobia. He nevertheless agrees that antisemitism diminished significantly. Henry Weinberg, "French Jewry: Trauma and Renewal," *Midstream* (December 1982), p. 7, denies a decrease in antisemitism.
8. Nicholas Atkin, *The Fifth French Republic* (New York: Palgrave, 2005), pp. 128–29. For an overview of the rise in such racism, see Fausto Giudice, *Arabicides, une chronique française, 1970–1991* (Paris: La Découverte, 1992).
9. Gastaut, *L'immigration et l'opinion*, 298–338.
10. Silverstein, *Algeria in France*, 106, 108; Noiriel, *Immigration, antisémitisme et racisme*, 611–13; Gastaut, *L'immigration et l'opinion*, 478–512.
11. Noiriel, *Immigration, antisémitisme et racisme*, 625–27; Gastaut, *L'immigration et l'opinion*, 133–38.
12. Birnbaum, *Jewish Destinies*, 226–27.
13. Most Jews found the FN's xenophobia too close to traditional antisemitism to be comfortable. A tiny minority nevertheless were attracted to its targeting of Muslims. Jean Charles Bloch and Robert Hemmerdinger, Comité national des français juifs, no date, MDI 188, CJDC.
14. Birnbaum, *Jewish Destinies*, 184–85. Silverstein, *Algeria in France*, 159, notes that this new wave targeted children of immigrants rather than their parents.
15. Alain Chouraqui, "Note sommaire sur les agressions antisémites en France après mai 1981," December 1982, MDI 206b, *CJDC*, reported a 31 percent rise in anti-Jewish violence from 1975 to 1980. Birnbaum, *Jewish Destinies*, 236–39, provides a compendium of attacks between 1980 and 1994. Anti-Jewish violence surged again during the 1982 war in Lebanon, most famously, with the 9 August attack on Jo Goldenberg's delicatessen. Weinberg, "French Jewry," 7–12. While this violence often originated with far-right extremist groups, some—such as the bomb at rue Copernic—was carried out by organizations based in the Middle East. Michel Wieviorka, *La tentation antisémite: Haine des Juifs dans la France d'aujourd'hui* (Paris: Robert Laffont, 2005), p. 20.
16. The MRAP changed its name to the Mouvement contre le racisme et pour l'amitié entre les peuples, while in 1979, the LICA became LICRA (the "R" for "racisme" being added to the acronym), despite some reluctance against collapsing anti-Arab racism and antisemitism. Gastaut, *L'immigration et l'opinion*, 181–84.

17. Cited in F. de Muizon, "Les Juifs de Marseille: La 'révolution' des pieds noirs," *Regard*, in (1976), MDI 159, CJDC.

18. Martine Gozlan, "Le racisme de tous les jours," *L'Arche*, February 1978, pp. 32–35.

19. Roger Ascot, "Racisme: Fantômes et réalités," December 1978, pp. 24–26. Also see "Le petit racisme de tous les jours," *L'Arche*, August 1979, pp. 96–98.

20. "Communiqué: Le CRIF face au racisme," *Tribune juive*, 22–28 June 1979.

21. Tahar Ben Jelloun, *French Hospitality: Racism and French Hospitality*, trans. Barbara Bray (New York: Columbia University Press, 1999), p. 94.

22. Doris Bensimon, *Les Juifs de France et leurs relations avec Israël: 1945–1988* (Paris: Éditions l'Harmattan, 1989), pp. 237–38; Haim Zafrani, "Le patrimoine judéo-arabe et judéo-berbère," *Cultures de France*, 11 August 1979.

23. "Festival judéo-arabe de musique," *L'Arche*, August 1979, p. 40.

24. C.G., "Racisme: Danger," *L'Arche*, February 1979, pp. 61–62.

25. For examples of the former, see Weinberg, "French Jewry under the Mitterrand Presidency," 228–41, in MDI 187, CJDC and Richard Liscia, "Le temps des terroristes," *L'Arche*, May 1982, pp. 42–44. For the latter, see Alain Chouraqui, "Note sommaire sur les agressions antisémites en France après mai 1981," December 1982, MDI 206b, CJDC.

26. Jacquot Grunewald, "La nécessité de solidarité avec les travailleurs immigrés," *Tribune juive*, 6–12 March 1980, p. 4, cited in Arkin, "It's the French and the Arabs," 199.

27. "Meeting anti-raciste du Renouveau juif à la Mutualité," *ATJ*, 26 February 1981, MDI 181, CJDC.

28. Sabine Roitman, "France" no date, MDI 187, CJDC.

29. Shmuel Trigano, "Face à la montée des périls," *L'Arche*, August 1979, pp. 99–101.

30. As Rabah Aissaoui, *Immigration and National Identity: North African Political Movements in Colonial and Postcolonial France* (London and New York: Tauris Academic Studies, 2009), pp. 181–91, makes clear, they explained bigotry as capitalism's reaction to Muslim immigrant mobilization in particular. Their approach, however, was also rooted in universalist values around class.

31. Unless noted, material on the Beur Movement is from Silverstein, *Algeria in France*, 151–66.

32. Arkin, "It's the French and Arabs," 160–217; Birnbaum, *Jewish Destinies*, 200.

33. Michel Wieviorka, "Une communauté insaisissable," *Passages*, MDI 188, CJDC.

34. By the late 1980s, 17,000 out of 100,000 Jewish school-age children (often of North African origin) were attending such schools. By 2002, the number had grown to 30,000, or one quarter of the school-age population. Arkin, "It's the French and the Arabs," 34; Birnbaum, *Jewish Destinies*, 190–94; Erik Cohen, *L'étude et l'éducation juive en France* (Paris: Le Cerf, 1991), pp. 25–27. For speculation on a Jewish vote prior to the 1980s, see *L'Arche*, January and February 1973, March 1978. Also see Sylvie Strudel, *Votes juifs: Itinéraires migratoires, religieux et politiques* (Paris: Presses de la Fondation nationale des sciences politiques, 1996).

35. As in 1967 and 1973, the CRIF proclaimed unwavering French Jewish support for Israel. Unlike previously, however, a vocal Jewish minority publicly condemned the invasion and the CRIF for claiming to speak for them. Institutional declarations of support for Israel, including the CRIF's, are found in MDI 223, CJDC. For Jewish criticism of the invasion, see "Un appel d'organisations juives progressistes pour une manifestation contre l'invasion," *Le Monde*, 15 June 1982; "Des intellectuels

juifs français dénoncent la politique de Jérusalem"; Paul Balta, "Devant l'ambassade d'Israël à Paris"; and Liliane Atlan, "Madame, c'est du poison que je voudrais," *Le Monde*, 17 June 1982, pp. 2–3. MDI 223, 224, and 225, CJDC include numerous documents attesting to the controversy. Also see Yair Auron, *Les Juifs d'extrême gauche en Mai 68*, translated from Hebrew by Katherine Werchowski (Paris: Albin Michel 1998), pp. 202–207.

36. Tahar Ben Jelloun called summer 1982 the moment Beur activists embraced the Palestinian cause in Annette Levy-Willard, "Dialogue d'en France: Marek Halter et Tahar Ben Jelloun," *Libération*, 15–16 June 1985. Also see Esther Benbassa, *La République face à ses minorités: Les Juifs hier, les Musulmans aujourd'hui* (Paris: Mille et une nuits, 2004), pp. 21–23; Jocelyne Cesari, *Être musulman en France: Associations, militants, et mosquées* (Paris: Éditions Karthala et Iremam, 1994), pp. 48–50; and Denis Sieffert, *Israël-Palestine, une passion française: La France dans le miroir du conflit israélo-palestinien* (Paris: Éditions la Decouverte, 2004), pp. 30–31.

37. Cited in Jelloun, *French Hospitality*, 93.

38. "Mobilisons-nous pour soutenir le peuple palestinien," Box Bibliothèque, UEJF. This file also holds documentation protesting Israeli actions from the Comité Liban de soutien à l'Association libanaise d'action populaire and the Centre international d'information sur les prisonniers, déportés et disparus palestiniens et libanais.

39. "Recrutement de volontaires et soutien aux Palestiniens," 7 July 1982; "Solidarité et manoeuvres frauduleuses," 9 July 1982; "Collecte de fonds et départs de volontaires," 19 July 1982 19980547, art. 17 (extrait: Palestine), CAC. Documentation of the pro-Palestinian groups that raised awareness that summer is located in Box Bibliothèque, UEJF.

40. "Motion pour la paix au proche-orient de la commnauté israélite de Belfort" (June 1982), MDI 223, CJDC. Various press accounts concurred, including "Manifestation 'contre l'agression israélienne au Liban': Les syndicats appellent à une solidarité active," *L'Est républicain*, 1 July 1982; and Luc Rosenzweig, "Les Feujs mettent la main à la pâte: Entrainée par ses étudiants, la communauté juive oublie le keffié des Beurs," *Libération*, 15–16 June 1985.

41. Appel, no date, MDI 223, CJDC.

42. Fernard I. cited in Jacques Frémontier, *L'étoile rouge de David: Les Juifs communistes en France* (Paris: Fayard, 2002), pp. 261–62.

43. J. P. Kapel, "Français, Arabe de France et fier de l'être," *Libération*, 31 July–1 August 1982. See Patrick Jarreau, "Les controverses sur la politique israélienne provoquent une crise au sein de la communauté juive française," *Le Monde*, 16–17 October 1983, for the fissures this incident created among Jews over the legitmacy of criticizing Israel.

44. "Une étrange conception du nazisme," *Le Monde*, 2 June 1982. Istiqulal denied links between the author's opinions and those of the party. Said Fatm, "Le Nazisme: Création du Sionisme," *L'Opinion*, 30 May 1982. "Non à l'amalgame," *L'Opinion*, 6 June 1982. Mhamed Douiri, Ministre du plan, de la formation des cadres, et de la formation professionnelle, Maroc, to André Azoulay, Identité et dialogue, 21 June 1982, MDI 182; Alain de Rothschild to Youssef Ben Abbes, Ambassadeur du Royaume du Maroc, 2 June 1982, MDI 182E, CJDC.

45. Brigitte Kantor, "Le 'Sabra et Chatila Tranquille' des 'Beurs,' " *Le Matin*, 4 December 1983.

46. Valeie Serfati, "Bilan antisémitisme," *Amphi J*, December 1981, Section de Strasbourg: Archives administratives/Toulouse, UEJF.

47. A focus on the links between antisemitism and anti-Zionism helped legitimize such views. See, for example, David Benizri, "L'antisionisme: Nouveau prétexte à l'antisemitisme?" *Amphi J*, December 1981.

48. Annie Kriegel, "Parler vrai," *L'Arche*, January 1984, pp. 79–83.

49. Adam Loss, "Une France pluriculturelle?" *L'Arche*, January 1984, p. 9.

50. Richard Liscia, "Nous sommes tous des Maghrébins," *L'Arche*, August–September 1984, pp. 52–53.

51. Romain Garbaie, *Getting into Local Power: The Politics of Ethnic Minorities in British and French Cities* (Malden, Mass.: Wiley-Blackwell, 2006), p. 77.

52. Cited in Eric Favereau, "SOS racisme au tournant: Des potes s'en mêlent," *Libération*, 10 May 1985.

53. Gastaut, *L'immigration et l'opinion*, 184–88.

54. Bernard-Henri Lévy as cited in Robert Solé, "SOS racisme victime de son succès: Touche pas à mon badge," *Le Monde*, 30 March 1985.

55. Cited in Annette Levy-Willard, "Dialogue d'en France: Marek Halter et Tahar Ben Jelloun," *Libération*, 15–16 June 1985.

56. Invitation, " 'Je ne suis pas raciste mais': Il n'y a pas de mais," MDI 207, CJDC. Claude Askolovitch, "Respecte l'étranger," *L'Arche*, April 1985, p. 48; Eric Favereau, "SOS racisme au tournant: des potes s'en mêlent," *Libération*, 10 May 1985. Lévy and Halter had years of involvement in French Jewish politics, and Halter had worked since the 1960s to promote dialogue between Israelis and Palestinians. Bensimon, *Les Juifs de France*, 237–38.

57. Michel Chemin, "Lifting pour l'antiracisme: SOS racisme, la dernière née des associations antiracistes veut démontrer que la société multiraciale existe," *Libération*, 20 February 1985; Roselyne Posnanski, "Racisme: SOS politique," *La Croix*, 23 February 1985.

58. Eric Ghébali, "Moi, je ne suis pas raciste mais, il n'y a pas de mais. On est raciste ou on ne l'est pas," reprinted in *Amphi J*, May–June 1985, p. 5.

59. Cited in Arkin, "It's the French and the Arabs," 172.

60. Marc Bitton, "Le sens d'un engagement," *Amphi J*, November 1985. Bitton's article was written to justify adhesion to SOS racisme for critics *within* the UEJF. The UEJF almost vetoed the iconic symbol of SOS racisme, which they found "too Beur" due to its invocation of the hand of Fatma, the palm-shaped amulet popular throughout the Middle East and North Africa as a defense against the evil eye. Eric Favereau, "La génération d'un Must," *Libération*, 13 June 1985.

61. D.J., "Étudiants juifs: Le congrès de la relance," XVIIème congrès national, Strasbourg 7–10 November 1980, UEJF. Juif en France, *Agence télégraphique juive*, 13 November 1980, XVIIème congrès national, Strasbourg 7–10 November 1980, UEJF.

62. "Exorciser la peur d'autres," no date, Section de Strasbourg, Archives administratives/Toulouse, UEJF.

63. The 1982 figure comes from "Interview avec Eric Sprung, président de UEJF," *Le Journal de l'UEJF*, March 1982, Section de Strasbourg: Archives administratives/Toulouse, UEJF. Eric Ghébali, "Ne touche pas à notre indépendance," *Amphi J*, May–June 1985, p. 2.

64. "Dossier sponsor et promotion publicitaire," Union des étudiants juifs de France, XIème congrès, Paris, 24–27 March 1988, Binder: Bitton, Marc I (06/05086-27/03/88), UEJF.

65. This commitment was clear in November 1980 at the first national congress since 1976. Motions, XVIIème congrès national, Strasbourg, 7–10 November 1980, UEJF.

66. D.J., "Étudiants juifs: Le congrès de la relance," XVIIème congrès national, Strasbourg, 7–10 November 1980, UJEF.

67. Materials in the UEJF archives point to the attack on the kosher restaurant in Paris as the impetus behind the new organizational strength. "De l'intérêt d'être syndiqué, Union générale des étudiants de Strasbourg," Section de Strasbourg: Archives administratives/Toulouse, UEJF. Materials on the first national congress come from, D.J., "Étudiants juifs: Le congrès de la relance," XVIIème congrès national, Strasbourg, 7–10 November 1980, UJEF.

68. Under his leadership, the organization held a conference on "Europe et Israël—Politique et culture" in December 1983 for eight hundred students from sixteen countries, demanded that the government denounce the PLO as a detriment to Middle East peace, and railed against Jewish passivity before rising antisemitism. Report, Colloque européen, Europe et Israël: Politique et culture, December 1983; "La France doit reconnaître le véritable visage de l'OLP," Dossier OLP, Box Ghébali; Colette Partoche, "La vie de l'UEJF: Antisémitisme," Amphi J, December 1983, Section de Strasbourg: Archives administratives/Toulouse, UEJF.

69. "Ghébali Président: Élections nationales de l'UEJF Ghébali: 17 voix," Le Journal de l'UEJF, February 1983, Box Ghébali, UEJF.

70. Katia D. Kaupp, "SOS racisme: La main magique, Le Nouvel observateur, 5 April 1985, pp. 21–22; "La France, est-elle vraiment raciste?" Le Point, 8 April 1985, p. 58.

71. Cited in Daniel Schneidermann, "Juifs et Arabes, même combat?" Le Monde, 4 April 1985, p. 8. The UEJF visually cemented this relationship on the cover of its journal in May/June 1985. The image, which carried the title, "Touche pas à mon pote," depicted the murder in Menton by showing a man holding a pistol to the head of a wounded Beur. The SOS racisme badge stood behind both, shot through with bullets and dripping blood. Chapters in the provinces similarly declared a commitment to the anti-racist agenda. Amphi J, May–June 1985; Charlie Bensemhoun, "Toulouse tient ses promesses," Amphi J, November 1985.

72. Jacquot Gruenwald, "De la rue Copernic en 1980 à la rue de Rivoli en 1985: Les étapes de l'espoir," Tribune juive, 5–11 April 1985, p. 17, cited in Arkin, "It's the French and the Arabs," 198.

73. Daniel Schneidermann, "Juifs et Arabes, même combat?" Le Monde, 4 April 1985, p. 8.

74. Robert Solé, "SOS racisme victime de son succès: Touche pas à mon badge," Le Monde, 30 March 1985.

75. Serge July, "L'antiracisme ne se partage pas," Libération, 1 April 1985.

76. Annette Levy-Willard, "Dialogue d'en France: Marek Halter et Tahar Ben Jelloun," Libération, 15–16 June 1985.

77. E.F., "Initiative spectaculaire dans un cadre précis: Des personnalités arabes appuient l'initiative anti-Bitburg de SOS racisme," Libération, 2 and 5 May 1985.

78. Cited in Agathe Logeart, "La marche des jeunes Juifs de France et de SOS racisme: 'Ni haine ni oubli,'" Le Monde, 2 May 1985.

79. Marek Halter, "Eh Gorbatchev, les Juifs d'URSS sont aussi nos potes!" *Amphi J*, November 1985. This article and several others defending Soviet Jews ran under the heading, "SOS racisme / Touche pas à mon pote."

80. SOS racisme to Mme Sabine Roitman, CRIF, 3 October (1985), MDI 207 CJDC; Philippe Bernard, "La main dans la main," *Le Monde*, 25 June 1985. Journalists documented large numbers of Jewish high school students selling SOS racisme's badge. Luc Rosenzweig, "Les Feujs mettent la main à la pâte: Entraînée par ses étudiants, la communauté juive oublie le keffié des Beurs," *Libération*, 15–16 June 1985.

81. Mylene Sebbah, "Le Juif et l'Arabe," *L'Arche*, July 1985, pp. 22–23.

82. Claude Regent, "La voix des jeunes arabes de Lyon," *Le Monde*, 2 December 1985.

83. Daniel Schneidermann, "Juifs et Arabes, même combat?" *Le Monde*, 4 April 1985, p. 8, Eric Favereau, "SOS racisme au tournant: Des potes s'en mêlent," *Libération*, 10 May 1985, and Philippe Bernard, "Une grande fête de SOS racisme le 15 Juin: La nuit de la Concorde," *Le Monde*, June 1985.

84. Cited in Eric Favereau, "Le soutien des associations juives," *Libération*, 6 December 1985.

85. Jean-Francois Moruzzi, "Incidents entre étudiants juifs et pro-palestiniens à Jussieu," *Quotidien de Paris*, clipping with no date; "Meeting de l'UEJF à la faculté de Jussieu," ATJ, 18 February 1985; "Jussieu: Des étudiants pro-palestiniens contre des étudiants juifs," *Libération*, clipping with no date, Box Amphi J, UEJF. Ongoing struggles between the UEJF and pro-Palestinian organizations on campus are documented in *Amphi J*, June/July 1988, Box Amphi J; Communiqué, 30 March 1990, Box Bensehoun, Arié, 27/3/88-00/01/90, UEJF.

86. "Racisme et Palestine vaincra," *Droit et vivre* (March 1986), MDI 211, CJDC.

87. Cited in Eric Favereau, "SOS racisme au tournant: Des potes s'en mêlent," *Libération*, 10 May 1985. Delorme also faulted SOS racisme for turning racial attacks into a media circus.

88. SIONA, B'nai Brith, Renouveau juif, Fédération des Juifs de France, Éclaireurs israélites de France, and Identité et dialogue, also offered support. Eric Favereau, "Le soutien des associations juives," *Libération*, 6 December 1985.

89. Claude Askolovitch, "Respecte l'étrangère," *L'Arche*, April 1985, p. 48.

90. Elvis Journo, "Est-ce bon pour nous?" *Journal de B'nai B'rith*, June–July 1985. Block was on record for asserting that the struggle against racism, whether targeted at Arabs or Jews was the same, although the organization directed most of its efforts to fighting antisemitism. Roger Ascot and Haïm Musicant, "Contre tous les racismes," *L'Arche*, August 1983, pp. 50–51.

91. Eric Favereau, "Le soutien des associations juives," *Libération*, 6 December 1985.

92. Richard Liscia, "Le racisme nous connaissons," *L'Arche*, May 1985, pp. 59–60.

93. Elvis Journo, "Est-ce bon pour nous?" *Journal de B'nai B'rith*, June–July 1985; Eric Favereau, "SOS racisme au tournant: Des potes s'en mêlent," *Libération*, 10 May 1985. In an October 1985 speech, Klein insisted that the Jews' experiences during World War II compelled them to fight for the rights and dignity of all, including particularly North African immigrants. Théo Klein, "Le droit de s'exprimer et la responsabilité de le faire," published in *CRIF Rencontres*, 19–20 November 1985, p. 11, MDI 133, CJDC.

94. Jean Paul Elkann, "Le Judaïsme! Une Mosaïque?" *Haboné*, August/September 1985, p. 31.

95. "Un débat sur la solidarité entre Juifs et Arabes," clipping with no title or date; "Appel judéo-arabe contre le racisme et l'antisémitisme," 9 June early 1980s, MDI 207, CJDC.

96. Elvis Journo, "Est-ce bon pour nous?" *Journal de B'nai B'rith*, June–July 1985; Eric Favereau, "Débat cartes sur table entre SOS racisme et les Beurs," *Libération*, 13 May 1985; Luc Rosenzweig, "Les Feujs mettent la main à la pâte: Entraînée par ses étudiants, la communauté juive oublie le keffié des Beurs," *Libération*, 15–16 June 1985.

97. Annette Levy-Willard, "Dialogue d'en France: Marek Halter et Tahar Ben Jelloun," *Libération*, 15–16 June 1985.

98. Philippe Bernard, "La main dans la main," *Le Monde*, 25 June 1985. Disagreements within SOS racisme nevertheless emerged, such as when Kaïssa Titous criticized Bernard-Herni Lévy—both prominent members of SOS racisme—for arguing that anti-Zionism rendered antisemitism acceptable. "Antisémitisme," *Droit et vivre* (March 1986), MDI 211, CJDC.

99. Eric Favereau, "'Divergences 85' pour les deux marches de l'anti-racisme," *Libération*, 18 October 1985. For divisions *within* the Beur Movement, see Eric Favereau and Nicolas Beau, "Loin de SOS, la marche des Beurs implose," *Libération*, 30 October 1985.

100. Eric Landal, "Julien Dray: 'SOS racisme' veut s'appuyer sur toutes les communautés," *Libération*, 22 October 1985. In late November, representatives from SOS racisme and the Beur Movement agreed to march together to the Place de la Concorde. Didier François, "Beurs et potes bras dessus bras dessous," *Libération*, 22 November 1985.

101. Eric Favereau, "Le dialogue de deux exils," *Libération*, 6 December 1985.

102. André Wormser to Théo Klein, 10 April 1985, MDI 211, CJDC. See also Jean Yves Camus, "Contre tous les racismes: Le C.E.R.A.C., la crise et la montée des périls," *L'Arche*, May 1985, p. 60.

103. A. Wormser, Centre d'études et de recherches sur l'antisémitisme contemporain, N° 9, September–October 1986, MDI 211, CJDC. The CERAC's increasing interest in France's North African population and its attitudes toward fundamentalism, Jews, and the Middle East is documented in MDI 212, CJDC, particularly André Wormser and Nelly Hansson to Cher(e) Ami(e), 4 June 1986. The CRIF also started paying closer attention to France's Muslim population, evident in numerous clippings on Islam, Muslim politics, and Beur radio stations in MDI 182, CJDC.

104. Annie Kriegel, "Juifs et Musulmans," *L'Arche*, March 1987, pp. 28–31.

105. See, for example, Ivan Levaï, "Les dessous du je: Raciste, antisémite"; and Pierre Birnbaum, "Rétro: National-populisme et antisémitisme," *L'Arche*, October 1987, pp. 22–23, 44–45.

106. Annie Kriegel, "Le vrai danger," *L'Arche*, November 1987, pp. 28–30.

107. Michel Gurfinkiel, "L'Islam contemporain et les Juifs" (Paris: Comité d'initiative pour Israël, [1987]), MDI 182, CJDC.

108. "Antisémitisme, faits et analyse" (1988), MDI 270, CJDC. An Islamic bookstore in Lyon also carried copies. "Intégrisme islamique et antisémitisme," *Le Monde*, 8 February 1987.

109. "Beurs-Feujs: Garre aux excès," *Lettre d'information: David*, September 1988. In "Le silence des intellectuels arabes," *Le Nouvel observateur*, 11 February 1985, Jean

Daniel, editor of *Nouvel obvsevateur* and of Algerian Jewish origin, spoke of radio propaganda seeking to raise questions for Arab immigrants about the Holocaust's veracity.

110. Pierre Birnbaum, "Les Beurs et la République," *L'Arche*, December 1987, pp. 84–85.

111. Gastaut, *L'immigration et l'opinion*, 133–35.

112. Ibid., 545–61. See Miriam Feldblum, *Reconstructing Citizenship: The Politics of Nationality Reform and Immigration in Contemporary France* (Albany: State University of New York Press, 1999), for the roots of this process.

113. Scott, *The Politics of the Veil*, 22–23, Silverstein, *Algeria in France*, 132–33, 139–42; Patrick Weil, *La France et ses étrangers: L'aventure d'une politique de l'immigration, 1938–1991* (Paris: Calmann-Lévy, 1991), p. 287; Noiriel, *Immigration, antisémitisme et racisme*, 628.

114. Silverstein, *Algeria in France*, 165–73.

115. *La Lettre de France plus*, 1 February 1989, MDI 181, CJDC.

116. Gastaut, *Immigration et l'opinion*, 184–88.

117. Alec G. Hargreaves, *Immigration, Race, and Ethnicity in Contemporary France* (London; New York: Routledge, 1995), pp. 144–48. Hargreaves makes clear that despite fighting for opportunities for North Africans who suffered from discrimination, France plus did not expect its political candidates to pursue an ethnic agenda and instead supported "integration." Also see, Garbaie, *Getting into Local Power*, 77.

118. "Répression en Palestine des organisations girondines réagissent," *Sud-Ouest*, 31 December 1987.

119. Farid Aïchoune, "La logique des sourds," *Le Monde*, January 1988, MDI 181, CJDC.

120. "Les Beurs de France, les Arabes de Palestine," *Libération*, 3 March 1988.

121. Farid Aïchoune, "La logique des sourds," *Le Monde*, January 1988, MDI 181, CJDC.

122. "Les Beurs de France, les Arabes de Palestine," *Libération*, 3 March 1988.

123. Jean-Michel Caradech, "Juifs de France: Le désarroi. Une communauté troublée par les images de la violence, même si la fidélité à Israël ne se discute pas," *L'Express*, 19–25 February 1988.

124. Dominique Audibert, "Juifs français: La déchirure," *Le Point*, 18 February 1988. For other examples, see Jean-Moise Brattberg, "France: Une communauté partagée entre le désarroi et l'amertume," *Quotidien de Paris*, 14 January 1988; "Juifs: Le grand désarroi," *Le Nouvel observateur*, 19–25 February 1988; "Les Juifs français face au drame israélien," *L'Événement*, 3–10 February 1988. Théo Klein, "Un peu de modération et de justice," *Le Monde*, 12 January 1988, p. 2, expressed frustration over media portrayals of Israel. While not fully condoning Israeli policies, Klein emphasized multiple "guilty parties."

125. For criticisms, see "Appel de Juifs pour la défense des droit de l'homme dans les territoires occupés et en Israël," *Le Monde*, 20 January 1988, p. 11.

126. "Appel: Arabes et Juifs pour la paix," *Le Monde*, 22 February 1988.

127. Alain Léauthier, "Palestine: Poussée de fièvre chez les Beurs," *Libération*, clipping with no date, MDI 181, CJDC.

128. "Les Beurs de France, les Arabes de Palestine," *Libération*, 3 March 1988.

129. "Bensemhoun-Dahmani: Attention aux dérapages!" *L'Express*, July 1988, reprinted in *Amphi J*, June–July 1988.

130. Alain Léauthier, "Palestine: Poussée de fièvre chez les Beurs," *Libération*, clipping with no date, MDI 181, CJDC.

131. Cited in "Désapprouvant une prise de position sur le Proche-Orient: L'Union des étudiants juifs va reconsidérer; ses relations avec SOS racisme," *Le Monde*, 26 April 1988.

132. Rafaële Rivais, "A son deuxième congrès national: SOS racisme trouve un compromis entre Juifs et Arabes," *Le Monde*, 5 April 1988.

133. Monique Ayoun, "SOS racisme: Les Feujs et les Beurs," *L'Arche*, May 1988, pp. 63–64. Jewish fears of Le Pen spiked in spring 1988 as is evident in the numerous articles in *L'Arche*. While most focused on the meaning of Le Pen's showing for France and for Jews, Richard Liscia ("Le parti du malheur," pp. 69–70) called on Jews to defend Arabs.

134. Emphasis mine. "Congrès malgré," *Amphi J*, June–July 1988.

135. "Bensemhoun-Dahmani: Attention aux dérapages!" *L'Express*, July 1988 (Reprinted in *Amphi J*, June–July 1988). Alain Léauthier, "Palestine: Poussée de fièvre chez les Beurs," *Libération*, clipping with no date, MDI 181, CJDC. A.B., "Des Juifs et des Beurs appellent au dialogue," *Le Quotidien de Paris*, 11 February 1988; N.B. "Quand les Beurs rencontrent les Sépharades," *Politis, le citoyen*, 18 February 1988.

136. Etienne Gau, "La paix maintenant: Des Juifs et des Maghrébins de France ouvrent le dialogue," *La Croix*, 18 February 1988.

137. "Une France unie pour l'intégration," *La Lettre de France plus*, 1 February 1989, MDI 181, CJDC.

138. See, for example, Benjamin Stora's interview with Arezki Dahmani and Farid Aïchone in *Passages*, 1988 (MDI 181, CJDC). The pro-dialogue context also facilitated a public debate between Théo Klein, president of CRIF, and Hamadi Essid, head of the Arab League's mission in Paris, on the Israeli/ Palestinian conflict. Hamadi Essid and Théo Klein, *Deux vérités en face: Un dialogue* (Paris: Lieu commun, 1988), p. 7.

139. "Beurs-Feujs: La rencontre événement d'octobre," *Passages*, 17 October 1988.

140. "Bensemhoun-Dahmani: Attention aux dérapages!" *L'Express*, July 1988, reprinted in *Amphi J*, June–July 1988.

141. "Première rencontre entre Arabes et Juifs en France," MDI 182, CJDC. Tegouva, Département de la jeunesse et du Héhaloutz to Chers Amis, 19 November 1988, *Amphi J*, UEJF.

142. The organization continued to work with SOS racisme *and* France plus. Nevertheless, 1987/1988 saw a shift in the UEJF's willingness to submerge its interests in the wider anti-racist movement. "Beurs-Feujs: La rencontre événement d'octobre," *Passages*, 17 October 1988.

143. After his presidency, Ghébali had a falling-out with the UEJF, resulting in the removal of his title as honorary president (awarded to all former presidents). Marc Bitton to Tous les responsables de section and toutes les institutions juives de France, 17 March 1988, MDI 188, CJDC; "Chers amis," no date, Marc I (06/05/86-27/03/88), UEJF; "Les états généraux des étudiants juifs parisiens," no date, Binder Bitton, Marc I (06/05/86-27/03/88), UEJF; Arié Behsemhoun to Mme Sabine Roitman, 1 January 1988, MDI 188 CJDC.

144. "Dialogue difficile entre Beurs et Feujs à l'occasion du premier colloque judéo-arabe en France," *AFP*, 11 October 1988.

145. David Francés, "Des Juifs et les Beurs," *L'Arche*, November 1988, pp. 56–57, accused the event of being a publicity stunt and largely inconsequential.

146. Lionel Raux, "Le dialogue des 'Beurs' et 'Feujs,'" *L'Est républicain*, 6 October 1988. Elsewhere, Touïsi emphasized even stronger links with Jews: "I grew up with Jews. When I see them beside other French men and women, they are the ones most like me." Alain Léauthier, "Palestine: Poussée de fièvre chez les Beurs," *Libération*, clipping with no date, MDI 181, CJDC.

147. Valérie Colin, "Rencontre Beurs-Feujs: La démocratie à l'endroit," *Amphi J*, January–February 1989, p. 30.

148. François Devinat, "Dialogue à haut risque entre les Beurs et les Feujs," *Libération*, 12 October 1988; Robert Solé, "Une rencontre inédite à Paris, Arabes et Juifs face à face," *Le Monde*, 13 October 1988. See also Étienne Gau, "Rencontre judéo-arabe: Premières pierres d'un dialogue," *La Croix*, 14 October 1988.

149. François Devinat, "Dialogue à haut risque entre les Beurs et les Feujs," *Libération*, 12 October 1988.

150. "Dialogue difficile entre Beurs et Feujs à l'occasion du premier colloque judéo-arabe en France," *AFP*, 11 October 1988.

151. By late 1980s, SOS racisme had moved to a similar construction. Harlem Désir and SOS racisme, *SOS désirs* (Paris: Calmann Lévy, 1987).

152. "Beurs-Feujs: La rencontre événement d'octobre," *Passages*, 17 October 1988.

153. Jean-Moïse Braitberg, "Juifs-Arabes: Un premier dialogue, *Le Quotidien de Paris*, 11 October (circa 1988), clipping in MDI 182, CJDC.

154. Report, Marc Rochman, Binder Bitton, Marc I (circa 1988) (06/05/86-27/03/88), UEJF.

155. Albert Jorevitch, "La courte échelle," *L'Arche*, November 1988, p. 57, criticized this pro-Palestinian stance.

156. Jacqueline Keller, "Rapport moral et d'activités, présenté à l'assemblée générale du 19 novembre 1989," MDI 125, CJDC. In a communiqué, 18 August 1989, same file, Kahn also decried anti-Muslim activities.

157. Arkin, "It's the French and the Arabs," 197. See, for example, Annie Kriegel, "Ça compte pour du beurre?" *L'Arche*, November 1988, pp. 26–29.

158. Scott, *Politics of the Veil*, passim.

159. Gastaut, *Immigration et l'opinion*, 512–18.

160. Unless noted, discussion of Jewish responses to the head-scarf controversy comes from Birnbaum, *Jewish Destinies*, 200–13, and Vichniac, "Jewish Identity Politics and the Scarf Affairs in France," 111–28.

161. Discours de Marc Rochman, president de l'UEJF au troisième congrès de SOS racisme, le 30 avril 1990 à Longjumeau, Rochman, M., Correspondances, 1990 (Janv.–Juin I), UEJF.

162. Annie Kriegel, "La marginalisation," *L'Arche*, December 1989, pp. 21–22, also criticized Rabbi Sitruck for drawing unsubstantiated equivalencies. Figure comes from Scott, *The Politics of the Veil*, 3.

163. The CRIF's rather equivocal position emphasized the organization's commitment to state secularism while also calling for greater compromise around individual religious commitment. Déclaration du président du CRIF, 23 October 1989; Jean Kahn, Adresse au premier ministre, 18 November 1989; Jacqueline Keller, Rapport moral et d'activités, présenté à l'assemblée générale du 19 novembre 1989, MDI 125, CJDC.

164. Richard Liscia, "De la liberté," *L'Arche*, December 1989, p. 43.

165. For a Jewish focus on Muslim "foreignness," see Arkin, "It's the French and the Arabs," 209–21.

166. Shmuel Trigano, "Notre continuité," *L'Arche*, January 1990, pp. 75–76. In the same edition, Kriegel again challenged comparisons between Arab-Muslims and Jews in France.

167. Birnbaum, *Jewish Destinies*, 231–50.

168. Noiriel, *Immigration, antisémitisme et racisme*, 323.

169. Benjamin Stora, "Dialoguer," *L'Express*, 13 October 1989.

170. "Racisme: M. Rocard a reçu le président du CRIF," *Le Monde*, 12 October 1989.

171. Discours de Monsieur Jean Kahn, président du CRIF au troisième congrès de SOS racisme, 28, 29 30 avril 1990 à Longjumeau, MDI 208, CJDC. Some of Kahn's efforts to fight racism are documented in Jacqueline Keller, directrice de CRIF, to Cher Monsieur, Chère Madame, 24 January 1990, Rochman (1990/91)—Institutions juives; Institutions publiques I, UEJF. Arezki Dahmani to CRIF, 5 April 1990; Jean Kahn to Arezki Dahmani, 23 April 1990, MDI 182; Déclaration de M. Jean Kahn, président du CRIF, 27 March 1990, MDI 208, CJDC.

172. Discours de Marc Rochman, président de l'UEJF au troisième congrès de SOS racisme, le 30 avril 1990 à Longjumeau, Rochman, M., Correspondances, 1990 (Janv.–Juin I), UEJF.

173. Pierre Birnbaum, "Les Juifs, nouveaux boucs émissaires," *L'Arche*, November 1990, p. 60, claimed that antisemitism increased as well while Annie Kriegel, "Notre après-guerre," *L'Arche*, March 1990, pp. 21–22, argued that the French public supported Israel and the Jews.

174. For French Muslim diversity on the war, see Gastaut, *L'immigration et l'opinion*, 441.

175. Gastaut, *L'immigration et l'opinion*, 436–42; Noiriel, *Immigration, antisémitisme et racisme*, 624–25.

176. "Crise du Golfe—État de l'opinion publique des Bouches-du-Rhône," 16 January 1991, 1693W239, BDR.

177. Articles by Dominique le Guilledoux, *Le Monde*, 16, 17, and 24 January 1991. See Silverstein, *Algeria in France*, 130–35, for the Plan Vigipirate's role in criminalizing Muslims later in the decade.

178. "L'entretien télévisé du chef de l'état," *Le Monde*, 22 January 1991, p. 13.

179. Gastaut, *L'immigration et l'opinion*, 438.

180. First citation from Robert P. Vigouroux and Jacques Ouaknin, *Laïcité + religions: Marseille-Espérance* (Marseille: Transbordeurs, 2004), p. 41. *L'Autre journal*, 9 February 1991, cited in Gastaut, *L'immigration et l'opinion*, 438.

181. The chief rabbi also cosigned a petition with the rector of the Mosquée de Paris calling for intercommunal calm. H.T., "Veillées de prières en France," *Le Monde*, 16 January 1991, p. 10.

182. Marc Rochman to tous les responsables, 21 January 1991, Rochman (1991)—17/10/91, Correspondances, UEJF. "Crise dans le Golfe persique: Réactions de l'opinion publique des Bouches-du-Rhône," 14 December 1990; "Réactions de l'opinion publique des Bouches-du-Rhône à la tension dans le Golfe persique et aux perspectives de guerre," 8 January 1991; "Crise du Golfe—État de l'opinion publique des Bouches-du-Rhône," 16 January 1991, 1693W239, BdR.

183. "État d'esprit de la communauté musulmane à l'approche de l'expiration de l'ultimatum du 15/1/91," 14 January 1991; "Crise du Golfe—État de l'opinion publique des Bouches-du-Rhône," 16 January 1991, 1693W239, BdR.

184. Cited in Bernard Philippe, "Les Beurs entre la fierté et la crainte," *Le Monde*, 17 January 1991, p. 9.

185. As documents in Bensehoun, Arié, 27/3/88-00/01/90 and Rochman M., Correspondances, 1990 (Janv.—Juin I), UEJF, attest, the UEJF and SOS racisme created an Observatoire de l'antisémitisme in 1989, and published a brochure on the Holocaust for secondary schools and universities in 1990. However, they clashed in May 1989 when President Mitterrand officially welcomed Yassir Arafat to Paris. See Benjamin Stora, "Dialoguer," *L'Express*, 13 October 1989. XXIème congres, 24–31 December 1989, Box Bensemoun, Arié, 27/3/88-00/01/90; UEJF.

186. SOS racisme et Fédération indépendante et démocratique lycéenne (FIDL), "Arrêtez la guerre," 21 January 1991, Rochman, M. Correspondances 1990 (Juillet–Dec.) II, UEJF. Muslim-Jewish links in SOS racisme were further undermined in 1990 when Serge Malik, one early leader, accused SOS racisme's top leadership of encouraging UEJF participation in order to marginalize Beur activists. In Malik's version, SOS racisme capitalized on Muslim-Jewish tensions as a way to seem inclusive while pushing aside those who might interfere with the leadership's ambitions. Although Malik's text was dismissed as the ramblings of a bitter man, the organization's image as a space in which Muslims and Jews could work together had been further compromised. Serge Malik, *L'histoire secrète de SOS racisme* (Paris: Éditions Albin Michel, 1990), p. 89. The UEJF's dismissal of Malik's analysis is evident in Alain Kisermann, "Résumé de l'histoire secrète de SOS racisme,'" no date, Rochman, M. Correspondances 1990 (Juillet–Décembre) II, UEJF.

187. Bernard Philippe, "Le recentrage de SOS-racisme," *Le Monde*, 2 February 1991, p. 7. Eric Ghébali and Marek Halter stayed affiliated while expressing anger at Désir's position.

188. The UEJF's relationship with Israel intensified at the end of the 1980s as documents in Bensehoun, Arié, 27/3/88-00/01/90; Rochman, M. Correspondances, 1990 (Janv.—Juin I); and Rochman (1991)—17/10/91, Correspondances, UEJF, make clear.

189. SOS racisme, Communiqué, 18 January 1991; UEJF, "Communiqué no. 1," 18 January 1991, Rochman (1991)—17/10/91, Correspondances, UEJF.

190. "Les potes penchent vers le pacifisme et perdent leurs parrains," *Actualité juive*, 21 January 1991.

191. Minutes, 3 February 1991; Marc Rochman to tous les présidents de section, 22 February 1991; Belaich, Président villetaneuse to Cher ami, 11 March 1991; Serge Vatine, Responsable national de la collecte to tous les présidents, 12 March 1991; Rochman to Jean Kahn, 17 April 1991; Marc Rochman to Raphy Bensimon, Directeur general du l'AUJF, 16 July 1991, Rochman (1991)—17/10/91, Correspondances, UEJF. Invitation, Rochman, M., J'aime Israël, Paris le 14 Avril 1991, UEJF.

192. "Premier bilan de la confrontation armée dans le Golfe pour la communauté musulmane," 6 March 1991; "Crise du Golfe—Réactions de l'opinion publique des Bouches-du-Rhône," 28 January 1991, 1693W239, BdR; Maud Mandel, "The War Comes Home: Muslim/Jewish Relations in Marseille during the 1991 Gulf War," in *Israeli-Palestinian Conflict in the Francophone World*, ed. Nathalie Debrauwere-Miller (New York: Routledge, 2010): 163–79.

193. "Crise du Golfe—État de l'opinion publique des Bouches-du-Rhône," 15 January 1991; Vigouroux and Ouaknin, *Laïcité + religions*.

194. "Conflit du Golfe—Réactions de l'opinion publique des Bouches-du-Rhône," 18 January 1991; "Conflit dans le Golfe—Réactions de la communauté juive dans

la région Provence, Alpes, Côte d'Azur," 19 January 1991; "Conflit du Golfe—Réactions de l'opinion publique de la région Provence-Alpes-Côte d'Azur," 21 January 1991, 1693W239, BdR.

195. Gastaut, *Immigration et opinion*, 441; Henri Tincq, "Selon un sondage de l'IFOP incertitude et peur chez les Musulmans en France," *Le Monde*, 30 January 1991, p. 9.

196. "Crise du Golfe—Réactions de la communauté musulmane," 26 January 1991, 1693W239, BdR.

197. Jocelyne Cesari, "Les modes d'action collective des Musulmans en France: Le cas particulier de Marseille," in Bruno Étienne, ed., *L'Islam en France: Islam, état et société* (Paris: Éditions du Centre national de la recherche scientifique, 1991): 282–94.

198. "Communauté islamique de Marseille: État d'esprit des responsables associatifs," 25 February 1991, 1693W239, BdR.

199. "Premier bilan de la confrontation armée dans le Golfe pour la communauté musulmane," 6 March 1991, 1693W239, BdR.

200. "Premier bilan de la confrontation armée dans le Golfe pour la communauté musulmane," 6 March 1991, 1693W239, BdR.

201. Annie Kriegel, "Notre après-guerre," *L'Arche*, March 1991, pp. 21–22, even attributed Muslims' relatively muted response to the war to an understanding that France stood with Jews and Israel.

202. During the Gulf War, the rare pluricultural appeal was still heard. See, for example, "Juifs et Arabes retrouvent une mémoire commune," *Libération*, 23–24 February 1991.

203. Garbaie, *Getting into Local Power*, 77.

204. Silverstein, *Algeria in France*, 173–74.

205. Arkin, "It's the French and the Arabs," passim.

206. Relevant documents in 1992, Vive émotion dans la communauté juive; Cohen, Francis 1992: Correspondances I, UEJF.

207. Documents in Pinto S. 05/1993-09/1993 and Pinto S. 03/1993-04/1993; *Entre nous*, 1 October 1993, Pinto S. 10/1993-11/1993, UEJF. Controversy surrounded the conference, but the debate was internal, focusing on the legitimacy of Jewish criticism of Israel.

208. Manifs (July 1999–June 2001), UEJF. The file "Subvention 1999" makes clear the UEJF began thinking of these issues prior to the violence in September 2000. After 2000, SOS racisme rejoined the struggle against antisemitism. Wieviorka, *La tentation antisémite*, 29.

Conclusion

1. Michel Wieviorka's, *La tentation antisémite: Haine des Juifs dans la France d'aujourd'hui* (Paris: Robert Lafont, 2005).

2. Jacques Tarnero, "Les territoires occupés de l'imaginaire Beur," *Observatoire du monde juif*, Bulletin No.1, November 2001, pp. 39–40, cited in Pierre-André Taguieff, *La nouvelle judéophobie* (Paris: Mille et une nuits, 2002), pp. 178-79, discusses a 1997/1998 survey in which French-born Muslim youth made these links.

3. Denis Sieffert, *Israël-Palestine, une passion française: La France dans le miroir du conflit israélo palestinien* (Paris: Éditions la Decouverte 2004), pp. 212–15.

4. Esther Benbassa, *La République face à ses minorités: Les Juifs hier, les Musulmans aujourd'hui* (Paris: Mille et une nuits, 2004).

5. Kimberly Arkin, " 'It's the French and the Arabs against the Jews': Identity Politics and the Construction of Adolescent Jewishness in France" (Ph.D. diss., University of Chicago, 2008). Sieffert, *Israël-Palestine*, 217–30, discusses the way the fight against antisemitism has itself served to polarize.

6. Taguieff's focus in *La nouvelle judéophobie* and other work on fusions between radical Islam and third-worldism is useful for understanding a discursive shift in anti-Jewish thought. It is limited, however, in explaining transitions in social practice. Nor does such a framework help explain evolving Jewish positions on Muslims.

7. Benjamin Stora, *Les trois exils: Juifs d'Algérie* (Paris: Éditions Stock, 2006), pp. 177–81, makes a similar point.

8. "Réactions des responsables de la communauté juive des Bouches-du-Rhône, après l'attentat par explosif d'un foyer Sonacotra à Cagnes-sur Mer et sa revendication par un 'groupe Massada,' " 22 December 1988, 1693W233, BdR.

9. Alain Goldman to Monsieur le Grand Rabbin Haik, Toulouse, 19 April 1989; Alain Goldman to Fernand Tarraube, Directeur abattoire municipale, St Gaudens; Monsieur Fuzere, Vétérinaire abattoir municipal, St Gaudens, 19 April 1989; "Dissensions au sein de la communauté juive dans les Bouches-du-Rhône," 16 June 1989; "La communauté juive dans les Bouches-du-Rhône," 17 November 1989,1693W233, BdR.

10. In 2000, as Paris and other large French cities saw Muslim youth lash out against their Jewish neighbors, Marseille also experienced its share of violence, including the March 2002 arson of the Or Aviv synagogue. Unlike elsewhere in France, however, such attacks diminished rapidly, and Marseille saw very little social unrest in 2005 when banlieues throughout France were burning. Claire Berlinski, "The Hope of Marseille," *Azure* 19 (Winter 5765/2005), p. 33–34. Social commentators and scholars have disagreed over the cause for the relative calm in Marseille, focusing on everything from its sunny weather to its cohesive urban geography. For the range of explanations, see Jocelyne Cesari, Alain Moreau and Alexandra Schleyer-Lindenmann, *"Plus marseillais que moi, tu meurs!" Migrations identités et territoires à Marseille* (Paris: L'Harmattan, 2001), p. 11–26. For a recent analysis, see Katharyne Mitchell, "Marseille's Not for Burning: Comparative Networks of Integration and Exclusion in Two French Cities," *Annals of the Association of American Geographers* 101, 2 (2011): 404–23, who argues that Marseille's ethnically networked capitalist system combined with the city's urban development help explain its relatively peaceful ethnic landscape.

Abbas, Ferhat, 51, 52
Abderrahmane, Dahmane, 134
Abdjellil, Omar, 42
Abromovitch, Stanley, 46, 47
ADAE (Amicale des Algériens en Europe):
anti-Jewish rhetoric of, 115; on Aubervil-
liers shooting (December 1968), 115;
Belleville riots, 103, 104; Croissant-
rouge, 109, 218n70; FLN support for, 88,
89, 110; government relations with, 88,
90–91; Palestinian nationalism supported
by, 22, 88–89, 94, 105, 123, 219n77;
recruitment for combat volunteers to
Palestine, 22, 89, 94; as social services
provider, 88–89, 90
l'affaire foulard. See head-scarf controversy
Al Afif (Egyptian newspaper), 21
Aïchoune, Farid, 140
Aissaoui, Rabah, 228n30
AIU (Alliance israélite universelle), 3, 36, 38,
40, 41, 60, 62, 166n44
Ajar, Émile (pseud. for Romain Gary), 122–
23, 124
AJDC (American Jewish Joint Distribution
Committee), 30, 36, 40, 45, 46–47, 53, 54
AJOA (Association des Juifs originaires
d'Algérie), 94
Algeria: anti-Jewish violence, 45, 46, 47,
51; Arab identity of, 20; Berbers in, 20,
68, 151, 163n36; French presence in,
37, 43, 47, 48–49, 53, 181n68, 182n90;
GPRA (Gouvernement provisoire de la
république algérienne), 52, 53, 54; Kabyle
migration from, 163n36; nationalist
movement in, 16, 20, 22, 26, 48–49, 50,
67, 109; nationalization of Algerian
oil/gas companies (1971), 111; Palestinian
movement supported by, 89, 94; State
of Israel relations with, 52, 58, 63, 78,
89; suspension of immigration to
France, 120

Algerian independence movement: Évian
Accords, 53, 54; Fatah support for, 89;
GPRA (Gouvernement provisoire de la
république algérienne), 52, 53, 54; Israel
independence, 63, 78; Jewish ambivalence
towards, 45, 48–51, 55, 57, 62–63, 108;
leadership of, 58, 89; MTLD (Mouvement
pour le triomphe des libertés démocratiques), 17, 26; PPA (Parti du peuple
algérien), 20, 22, 26. See also FLN (Front
de libération nationale)
Algerian Jews: acculturation of, 3–4, 63, 67,
147, 161n19, 162n20; anti-Jewish sentiments in, 45; CJAES (d'études sociales),
39, 43, 45, 46–47, 50–51, 53; communal
aid for, 72–73, 75, 120; emigration of, 35,
45–46, 46–47, 52, 58, 67, 175n3; ethnic
identity of, 53, 64; French citizenship, 3,
43, 51–52, 57, 69, 72–73, 74–75; Jewish
social service agencies assisting, 29–30;
leadership of, 43; support for French presence in Algeria, 43, 47, 48–49, 53, 181n68,
182n90; violence and vulnerability narrative of, 181n68
Algerian Muslims: arrival in France, 3;
citizenship, 4, 19, 25, 29, 33, 182n90; discrimination against, 4, 25–26, 29, 162n23,
171n24, 171n71; employment, 25–26, 119,
171n71, 171n72; on French colonialism
in Algeria, 25, 26; harkis, 42–43, 76–77,
180n64, 199n123, 199n124; immigration reforms for, 19; internment of, 25;
Jews and, 30, 45–47, 51, 53, 58, 66; living
conditions in France, 70; marginalization
of, 29; political activity of, 20; political
engagement of, 26; political recognition
of, 29; post-World War II era, 25; pro-
Palestinian sentiments, 88; recruitment
for military duty in Palestine, 22, 89, 94,
114; support for Arab cause in Palestine,
31–32, 90–91; xenophobic attacks on, 119.

Algerian Muslims (cont'd)
  See also ADAE (Amicale des Algériens
    en Europe)
Algerian Muslim workers: aid organizations
  for, 70, 89, 111–13, 120–21, 123–24;
  employment, 25–26, 171n71, 171n72;
  engagement with the Palestinian cause,
  112; in Grand Arénas transit camp, 70–71;
  labor unions, 89
Algerian nationalist movement, 16, 20, 22, 26,
  48–49, 50, 67, 109
L'Algérien en Europe (ADAE newspaper), 89,
  90, 91, 104, 119
Algiers synagogue bombing, 45, 46, 51
Alliance France-Israël, 97, 116
Altelena (ship), 30–31
Amara, Saliha, 134
AMF (Association des Marocains en France),
  134, 218n71
Amicale des Algériens en France (later Amicale des Algériens en Europe), 88, 90
Amitiés France-Israël, 97
Ammar, Mejid Daboussi, 137
Amsellem, Rolland, 78
anti-Jewish violence, 1, 5, 129; at Algerian
  synagogues, 45, 46, 47, 51; in Constantine,
  45, 49, 53, 55, 181n68; and the decision
  to emigrate, 46, 55; Jewish film festival
  bombing, 133, 134; Munich Olympics
  massacre (September 1972), 118, 119,
  220n89, 223n152; Oujda riots (Morocco),
  27, 28, 38, 39, 40, 61, 172n86; Petitjean
  murders, 27, 28, 39; rue de Copernic
  synagogue bombing, 5, 128, 130; in
  Tlemcen, 65
anti-Muslim violence, 87, 128; after Gerlache
  murder in Marseille, 119; anti-racism
  rally (September 14, 1973), 120; death of
  Nourredine Daouadji in Marseille, 133;
  FEJ attack on Iraqi and Syrian airlines offices, 119; at Gerlache funeral, 119; Jewish
  condemnation of anti-Muslim violence,
  66–67; Jews as perpetrators of, 117, 118;
  in Marseille, 119–20; murder in Menton,
  133; murder of Mahmoud Hamchari, 118,
  119; murder of Moroccan immigrant in
  Menton, 133, 231n71; Nazi oppression
  compared with, 66–67; relations between
  Jews and Arabs, 120; xenophobic attacks,
  111, 119, 127, 227n13
antisemitism: ADAE, 104, 209n115; after
  Lebanon invasion, 130–31; allegations of

Jewish imperialism, 24, 108–9; antiracism
  initiatives, 131–33, 136–37; Arab-Israeli
  conflict, 94, 96; Arabs and, 62, 97, 128,
  227n7; CERAC (Centre d'études et de
  recherches sur l'antisémitisme contemporain), 137, 233n103; in contemporary
  France, 159n3; ethnic identity, 63, 64–65;
  European antisemitism linked with
  Arab nationalism, 61; MRAP (Mouvement contre le racisme, l'antisémitisme,
  et pour la paix), 66, 86, 98, 128, 206n69,
  227n16; Muslims and, 64, 65, 66, 127–28,
  224n163; perceptions of increase, 64–
  66; racism, 147–48; support for Israel,
  168n29; on university campuses, 116,
  222n134; Zionism, 97, 115–17, 143. See
  also anti-Jewish violence; hate crimes;
  racism; SOS racisme
anti-war demonstrations (17 October 1961),
  66
Arab (use of term), 2, 9, 22, 59–61, 63, 65, 67,
  118–19, 164n45, 169n49
Arabic language, 5, 68, 163n28
Arab League, 87–88, 97
Arafat, Yassir, 86, 101, 121
L'Arche, 64, 66, 72, 85, 97, 114; "Arab" used
  in, 118–19; on contemporary racism,
  128; criticism of Muslim-Jewish relations,
  137–38; on head scarf controversy, 147;
  mention of mounting anti-Arab violence
  absent from, 120; responses to Marche
  pour l'égalité, 131; on rise of violence,
  117–19; SOS racisme supported by, 135;
  UEJF-Beur alliance, 135
Arkin, Kimberly, 162n20
Aron, Raymond, 34
Ascot, Roger, 128
Ashkenazim, 75
Aspects de la France (newspaper), 87
Association des amis de la Palestine, 21–22
Association des étudiants musulmans nord-
  africains, 96, 98–99, 109, 116
Association des Juifs de gauche, 135
Association des Musulmans algériens, 32
Association de solidarité Franco-Arabe, 117
Atlan, Henri, 63–64
ATOM (Association d'aide travailleurs
  d'outre-mer), 70
Attal, Jacques, 45
Aubervilliers shooting (December 1968), 115
Aulnay-sous-Bois, 68
Auron, Yair, 018

L'Autre Journal, 149
Azoulay, André, 128–29

Badinter, Robert, 134
Bahad (Jewish religious organization), 173n109
Beckelman, Moses, 40–41
Belkacem, Krim, 52
Belleville, 10; Jewish-Muslim relations in, 100, 102; riots in, 6, 100, 102, 114, 117, 153, 154; settlement patterns in, 71; Tunisian Jewish refugees in, 103
Belleville riots (June 1968), 6, 100, 102, 104, 114, 117, 153, 154
Ben Ali, Djelali, 111
Ben Bachir, Mohammed, 64
Ben Bella, Ahmed, 58, 89
Ben Jelloun, Abderkader, 42
Ben Jelloun, Tahar, 134, 229n36
Benkhedda, Benyoucef, 52
Bennani, Souad, 134
Bensemhoun, Arié, 141, 142, 143, 144
Bensemhoun-Dahmani dialogues, 142, 143, 144
Bensimon, Jean, 46, 57, 58
Berbers, 20, 68, 151, 163n36
Bernheim, Gilles, 147
Betar, 94, 211n141, 222n134
Beurs and Beur Movement: about, 226n1; antisemitism among, 130–31; criticism of, 143; disbanding of, 151; France plus, 140; harkis, 42–43, 76–77, 140, 180n64, 199n123, 199n124; integration into French society, 145; isolation of, 139; on Israel's response to first intifada (1987), 140–41; Jews compared with, 144–45; kaffiyehs, 131, 135, 154; political voice for, 125, 136–37; pro-Palestinian sentiment among, 130, 131, 135, 154; protest against Ronald Reagan's visit to Bitburg, 134; rabeus, 151; racism opposed by, 125, 129, 131–32, 136–37, 226n1; right to be different, 126, 129–30; Kaïssa Titous, 141, 233n98; UEJF alliance with, 135, 136
Bismuth, Gérard, 92
Bitburg, Ronald Reagan visit to, 134, 137
Bitton, Marc, 132–33, 141, 144
Bizerte naval base, 54
Black September (expulsion of Palestinians from Jordan), 109, 112
Black September (Palestinian organization), 220n89

Bloch, Jean-Pierre, 104, 135–36
Blum, Isi, 66
Blum, Léon, 22
Blumel, André, 41
Boghari, Algeria synagogue bombing, 45
Bône, Algeria, 45, 46, 53
Bouches-du-Rhône, 69, 76
Boudiaf, Mohamed, 52
Boudjemma, Hayette, 140
Bouhali, Larbi, 26
Boumediene, Houari, 89
Bourguiba, Habib, 54

Cahen, Janine, 63
Calamaro, Paul, 60–61
Carpentras cemetery, desecration of, 5, 146, 147–48
Cassin, Fedia, 25
Cassin, René, 22
Cazes-Benatar, Hélène, 40
Censier incidents, 116–17, 222n134
Centre de liaison et d'informations, 93
CERAC (Centre d'études et de recherches sur l'antisémitisme contemporain), 137, 233n103
Cercle Bernard Lazare, 135
CGT (Confédération générale du travail), 26
Chanderli, Abdelkader, 51, 52, 57
Chemouilli, Henri, 45–46, 52
Chibi, Abdelbaki Mosbah, 54
Chirac, Jacques, 139
Choukroun, Moise, 56
Cinema Chavé, 93
Cinema Colibri, 26, 33
Cinema Rivoli, anti-Jewish violence at, 133, 134, 136
cinema rue Canebière, 29
circulaire Fontanet, 127
cité de transit, 74, 77, 197n104
Cité Universitaire, 98, 109, 115–16
citizenship: for Algerian Jews, 3, 43, 51–52, 57, 69, 72–73, 74–75; for Algerian Muslims, 4, 19, 25, 29, 33, 182n90; for children of foreigners, 139; Jews in France, 25; as source of Jewish-Muslim conflict, 4
CJAES (Comité juif algérien d'études sociales), 39, 43, 45, 46–47, 50–51, 53
Cohen, David, 46
Cohn, Lionel, 64
Cohn-Bendit, Daniel, 85, 107

colonialism: anti-Zionism as anti-colonialism, 21, 24, 26–28, 115–17, 224n163
Comité anti-colonialiste (University of Strasbourg), 99
Comité d'action contre la guerre mondiale, 118
Comité de coordination (Lyon), 83
Comité de coordination de la jeunesse juive, 92, 99
Comité de liaison des étudiants arabes, 105–6
Comité democrate socialiste pour le droit d'Israël, 82
Comité d'entente de la jeunesse juive, 116
Comité des étudiants juif antisionistes, 86, 108
Comité de soutien aux luttes anti-impérialistes des peuples arabes, 92, 93–94, 106
Comité d'initiative pour Israël, 138
Comité hébreu de la libération nationale, 22
Comité national de coordination, 83, 84, 85, 202n25
Comité Palestine de France, 130
Comité Palestine ouvrier nanterre, 109
Comité permanent d'action pour la Palestine, 108
Comité pour la paix negocié au Moyen-Orient, 115–16
Comités d'action Palestine, 106, 108, 110
Comités Palestine, 109, 112, 121, 218n72
Comité unifié de soutien á Israël, 92, 93–94
Communist Party, 85, 86–87, 93, 101, 106, 108, 168n29
Conseil national des français d'origine arabe, 149
Consistoire, 20, 61, 95, 211n144
Consistoire de France, 136
Constantine, 45, 46, 49, 53, 55, 181n68
Crémieux Decree, 3
CRIF (Conseil représentatif des israélites de France): on anti-Arab racism, 129; on anti-Jewish violence on university campuses, 116–17; Carpentras cemetery desecration protested by, 147; impact of North African Jewish immigration on communal life in 1967, 82; Israel supported by, 83, 86–87, 228n35; on Jewish settlement in Palestine, 20; murder of African workers condemned by, 128; on Muslim antisemitism, 65; on OAS

violence, 66, 193n48, 193n50; persecution of Iraqi Jews protested by, 20, 61, 2061; republican universalism of, 66; state secularism and Jewish integration, 147
Croissant-rouge, 109, 218n70
Cultuelle de Maison-Carée, 56

Dahmani, Arezki, 140, 142–43, 145
Dalsheim, Joyce, 8
Daniel, Pierre, 62
DAVID (Décider agir avec vigilance pour Israël et la diaspora), 138
Davidson, Naomi, 8
Débra, Sylvain Cahn, 39
Décider agir avec vigilance pour Israël et la diaspora (DAVID), 138
Defferre, Gaston: influence of, 12, 69; Jewish constituency of, 60, 78, 92, 95; pieds noirs' relations with, 95–96; support for Israel, 78–79, 92–94, 120, 201n141
de Gaulle, Charles: Algerian policies of, 18, 47, 50; Defferre's criticism of, 95; on Jewish elitism, 95, 211n147; Middle East policies of, 81, 93, 202n12, 207n80; Palestinian support for, 110; support for federated Algerian state, 50; visit to Algeria, 46, 95
Delorme, Christian, 135
Désir, Harlem, 131, 132, 135, 141
Djérada riots, 28, 40, 61
dockworkers, 15, 27, 28, 29, 31
Dray, Julien, 131, 132, 137
Dreyfus, Jacques, 83
droit á la différence, 126, 129–30, 144

Easterman, Alexander, 42
Eastern European Jews. See FSJF (Fédération des sociétés juives de France)
Egyptian Jews, 44–45, 61
el Fasi, Allal, 42
Elkan, Jean-Paul, 136
El Moudjahid (FLN newspaper), 89, 103, 115
El-Nadi, Bahgat (Mahmoud Hussein), 101
El Samman, Aly, 96–97
L'Emigré (MTLD-PPA newspaper), 26
employment, 25–26, 72, 75, 119, 127, 171n71, 171n72
Essid, Hamadi, 143–44
Évian Accords, 53, 54
Exodus Affair (July 1947), 24

Faculté des Sciences (Marseille), 115–16

Fatah: al-Assifa (Fatah military branch), 108; Algerian support for, 89; Belleville riots, 103, 104; commitment to Arab unity, 110, 219n81; French support for, 101, 105–6; gauchistes, 106, 107, 108–9, 110; Jewish support for, 108; Maoist attraction to, 101, 216n47; PFLP (Popular Front for the Liberation of Palestine), 216n47, 217n72, 218n72; UGEP cooperation with, 113; on university campuses, 105–6

FDGS (Fédération de la gauche démocrate et socialiste), 93

Fedai (Comités Palestine and MTA newspaper), 112, 113

Fedayin (Fatah newspaper), 105

Fédération des étudiants révolutionnaires, 106

Fédération sioniste d'Algérie, 43

Fédération sioniste de France, 203n25

FEJ (Front des étudiants juifs), 103, 104, 115, 119

feujs (Jewish students), 133, 135

Le Figaro, 75, 148

film festival bombing, Paris, 133, 134

Finkielkraut, Alain, 147

Fischer, Joseph, 21

FLN (Front de libération nationale): ADAE (Amicale des Algériens en Europe), 88, 90; on anti-Jewish violence in Oran, 35, 36, 37, 54 ; Congrès de la Soummam, 49, 50; *El Moudjahid*, 89; Evian Accords, 88, 90; GPRA (Gouvernement provisoire de la république algérienne), 52; Jewish relations with, 45, 48–51, 55, 57, 62–63, 108; leadership of, 58, 89; links with Egyptian government, 44; in Marseille, 73; relations with State of Israel, 41, 52; on self-determination, 53

FN (Front nationale), 6, 126, 127–28, 139, 227n13

Fofana, Youssouf, 159n1

Fond social juif unifié, 84

France plus (anti-racism organization), 140, 142, 143–44, 147, 152

François, Didion, 131

Francos, Ania, 108

French colonialism: anti-war demonstrations (17 October 1961), 66; and domestic minority policies, 20–21; group identities and loyalties after, 45, 48–51, 55,

57, 62–64, 97–99, 108, 142–44; Jewish emigration from North Africa, 35, 38–42, 175n3; Jewish support for, 49–50, 55, 62–63; ordinance of 7 March 1944, 19

French government: Arab nationalism as danger to, 16; Evian negotiations with GPRA, 53, 54; Gauche prolétarienne banned by, 123; head-scarf controversy, 126, 146–47; immigration restrictions, 111, 139; Mitterrand administration (François Mitterrand), 6, 125, 126, 129–30, 139, 148, 228n34; on Moroccan independence movement, 39–40, 178n40; Muslim-Jewish tensions, 29; PLO relations with, 121, 133; relations with *harkis*, 42–43, 76–77, 180n64, 199n123, 199n125; relations with Israel, 17, 20–24, 32–33, 41, 81–82, 150, 178n30, 202n12, 204n35; relations with post–World War II Jewish community, 25; support for Palestine, 33, 90. *See also* Algeria; de Gaulle, Charles

French Jews: Algerian militarism opposed by, 60, 62, 144; "Arabs" as term used by, 2–3, 61; Ashkenazic-Sephardic division among, 7–8, 163n39; and the construction of Frenchness, 3–4, 8, 21, 55, 57, 74, 161n19; as *israélites*, 9; 1947 Partition Plan in Palestine supported by, 22, 169n44; political influence of, 21–22, 169n41, 169n44; on pro-Palestinian sentiments of Muslim youth, 130–31; support for Zionism, 19–20, 80, 82; vocal politicization of, 82–84, 202n12. *See also* Israel

French Muslims: civic rights of, 140; conservative agenda against, 6; criminalization of, 148–49, 150; on Gulf War (1991), 148; heterogeneity of, 7, 163n36; isolation of, 127; marginalization of, 146–51; Plan Vigipirate, 148, 150; political influence of, 21–22; reaction to alleged pro-Arab positons of, 148; suffrage for, 19; surveillance of, 73–74, 148, 150

FSFR (Fédération sud de français rapatrié), 95–96

FSJF (Fédération des sociétés juives de France): aid for co-religionists in Palestine, 22, 30–31, 32, 43, 44; condemnation of pro-Palestine rally by Algerian students, 97; 1967 Arab-Israeli War, 86; persecution of Iraqi Jews protested by,

FSJF (cont'd)
61; on resettlement of Algerian Jews in France, 75; support for Algerian anti-war protestors, 66

Gary, Romain, 122–23, 124
Gastaut, Yvan, 87
gauchistes: anti-Zionism of, 107–9, 114, 116, 118; dissent among, 110, 112, 219n81; Fatah's appeal to, 106; FDGS (Fédération de la gauche démocrate et socialiste), 93; GP (La Gauche prolétarienne), 62–63, 107–9, 108–9, 110, 112, 220n89; on immigrant rights, 107; Jewish leftists, 62–63, 107–8, 107–9, 108, 110, 114, 116; relations with Israel, 86, 114, 116, 202n4, 206n69
Geismar, Alain, 62–63, 107, 108, 119
Gerlache murder in Marseille, 119
Gérmont, Felix, 147
Ghébali, Eric, 132, 133, 136, 141, 143, 231n68
Gorbachev, Mikhail, 134
GP (La Gauche prolétarienne), 62–63, 107, 108–9, 110, 112, 220n89
GPRA (Gouvernement provisoire de la république algérienne), 52, 53, 54
Grand Arénas transit camp, 31–32, 69–71, 77–78
Grunewald, Jacques, 129, 134
Guérin, Daniel, 106
Gulf War (1991), 13, 126, 146, 148–50
Gurfinkiel, Michel, 138

Habash, George, 216n47
Haber, Samuel, 41
Hachaloutz, 173n109
Haddad, Charles, 93
Hajjat, Abdellali, 218n73
Halimi, Ilan, 1, 159n1
Hallouss, Mimoun, 112
Halter, Marek, 132, 134, 135, 136
Hamchari, Mahmoud, 105, 118, 119
Hargreaves, Alex, 234n117
harkis, 42–43, 76–77, 140, 180n64, 199n123, 199n124
hate crimes: at Algerian synagogues, 35, 36, 37, 45, 46, 47, 51, 54, 55; anti-Jewish riots in Tunisia, 103; bombing of Jewish Agency, 118; cemeteries, 128; in Constantine, 45, 49, 53, 55, 181n68; defacement of Tourtille synagogue, 104; film festival

bombing, Paris, 133, 134; at Jewish school in Toulouse, 1; Librairie Palestine bombing, 118; in Marseille, 118; monitoring of, 45, 53; Munich Olympics massacre (September 1972), 118, 119, 220n89, 223n152; murder of Mahmoud Hamchari, 118, 119; against Muslims, 66–67, 111, 127, 128, 129, 227n13; in Oran, 35, 36, 37, 45, 54, 54, 55; Or Aviv synagogue arson, 240n10; Oujda riots (Morocco), 27, 28, 38, 39, 40, 61, 172n86; rue de Copernic synagogue bombing, 5, 128, 130, 227n15; Sétif massacre, 19, 26. See also anti-Jewish violence; anti-Muslim violence
Hawatmeh, Nayef, 216n47
head-scarf controversy, 126, 146–47
Hechaloutz (Zionist youth organization), 173n109
Heler, Benjamin, 45
Herscho, Tsilla, 169n41
HLM (Habitations á loyer modéré), 74, 77, 198n116
Holocaust: anti-Arab rhetoric, 94, 119; concentration camps, 135; denial of, 131, 133; descendents of survivors, 102, 105, 107–8, 114; imagery of, 82, 85, 92, 97, 212n159; in Israeli/Palestinian debate, 97, 212n159; Jewish identity, 84–85, 114; Muslims and, 24, 135; oppression of Jews in Arab lands linked with, 61, 117, 119; re-bonding of French Jews with the Republic after, 21; survivor resettlement, 35–36, 41; La Vie devant soi (Émil Ajar), 122–23
housing shortages, 11–12, 23, 68, 70–71, 74–77, 197n104, 198n116
Hussein, Mahmoud (Bahgat El-Nadi), 101
Hussein, Saddam, 149

Identité et dialogue, 128–29
identity politics: Arab (use of term), 2, 9, 22, 59–61, 63, 65, 67, 118–19, 164n45, 169n49; Beur generation, 125, 127; construction of Frenchness, 3–4, 21, 29, 33, 48, 50–51, 146–47, 161n19; construction of identity, 7–10, 24, 35, 118–19, 125; contesting, 8, 63, 94, 127; ethnic identity and antisemitism, 63, 64–65; head-scarf controversy, 126, 146–47; in 1980s France, 127, 130; young people and, 84–85, 114, 125
Information juive (Algerian Jewish newspaper), 44, 45

internment camps, 30, 31–32, 33, 69–71, 74, 77–78, 197n104
intifada (1987), 139–41, 154
Iran, 9, 127
Iraqi Jews, persecution of, 61
Irgun (Ha'Irgun HaTzva'i haLe'umi BeEretz Yisra'el), 30, 94, 211n141
Islam française, 8
Islamophobia, 127–28
Israel: anti-Jewish hostilities, 27, 172n86; commando attacks in France, 118; declaration of independence, 15–17, 22, 30; as defense against antisemitism, 136; Defferre's support for, 78–79, 92–94, 120, 201n141; first intifada (1987), 139–41, 154; French diplomatic support of, 27, 32; French Jewish support of, 32, 84; Gulf War (1991), 13, 146, 148–50; independence movements in North African countries, 62; invasion of Lebanon (1982), 130; Jewish students' support for, 114; Lebanon invasion (1982), 130, 131; leftists' relations with, 86, 114, 202n4, 206n69; Marseille alliance with Jewish population, 93–94; media reports on, 1, 78–79, 85, 86, 92, 93, 141; migration to, 15–17, 19, 22, 27–28, 30–32, 38, 40–42, 69–70, 178n30, 178n40; 1947 Partition Plan, 21–22, 169n44; 1948 War, 16–17, 24, 27–28, 32, 38; Operation Susannah, 61; rallies in support of, 61, 92, 93–94, 95, 113, 121; relations with Algeria, 52, 58, 63, 78, 89; scud attacks on, 149, 150; UEJF support for, 114–15, 133, 149, 231n68; volunteers to, 85, 121. *See also* migration to Israel; 1967 Arab-Israeli War; Zionism
Istiqlal, 17, 27, 28, 39–40, 41, 42

JALB (Jeunes Arabes de Lyon et banlieue), 135
Jazouli, Adil, 134
JDL (Jewish Defense League), 223n156
Le Jeune Afrique, 103
Jeunesse communiste révolutionnaire, 106
Jewish Agency, 30–32, 52, 69–70, 118, 169n41
Jewish-Arab dialogue (11 October 1988), 143–44
Jewish identity: Algerianness, 48–52; construction of, 4, 8, 9, 36, 48–50, 55, 57, 74, 176n13; as European, 74; Frenchness, 147; Holocaust, 84–85; identification with

Israel, 82, 85; invisibility of, 56; Jewish particularity, 44–45, 48–52, 54, 56; of Jewish youth, 84–85, 114; as *pied noirs*, 43, 54, 55, 56, 180n65; visibility of, 543; Zionism, 39
Jewish particularity, 44–45, 49, 50, 52, 54, 56
Jordan, 109
Jordan, M., 56
Joxe, Louis, 51
Judaïsme contre sionisme (Levyne), 107–8
Judaism et socialisme, 135
Juin, Alphonse, 27, 28, 38, 172n93
July, Serge, 134

Kabyles, 163n36
Kadimah (UEJF publication), 63, 64
kaffiyehs, 131, 135, 154
Kahn, Jean, 145, 147–48
Kapel, J. P., 130–31
Kaplan, Jacob, 83
Kateb, Yacine, 64
Katz, Ethan, 18, 103, 160n8, 181n68, 181n70, 183n98, 184n124, 187n163, 196n93, 208n87, 209n109
Katzki, Herb, 40
Kelman, Claude, 84
Keren Kayemet LeIsrael (KKL), 29–30, 120
Kettane, Nacer, 140
Klein, Théo, 83, 136, 232n93, 234n124
Kochmann, René, 63
Korcaz, Sylvie, 87
kosher butchers, 155–56
Kriegel, Annie, 131, 138
Krivine, Alain, 107
Kupfer, Jacques, 116
Kuwait invasion (1991), 148

laborers: aid organizations for, 111, 112, 113, 120–21, 123–24; labor unions, 26, 89; 1968 uprisings, 106; strikes against anti-Arab violence, 120; support for Palestinian cause, 89, 106–7, 108, 109, 110, 112, 118
Lacoste, Francis, 37–38, 41
Ladj, Lounès, assassination of, 120
Lanzman, Claude, 62, 82
Lapides, Max, 52
Laurence, Jonathan, 7
Lazarus, Jacques, 39, 43, 45, 47–48, 51, 53, 94
Lebanon invasion by Israel (1982), 130, 131
leftists: anti-Muslim violence, 117–20; anti-Zionism of, 107–9, 114, 116, 118;

leftists: anti-Muslim violence (*cont'd*)
confrontational politics of, 115–
16; FDGS (Fédération de la gauche
démocrate et socialiste), 93; GP (La
Gauche prolétarienne), 107–9, 108–9,
110, 112, 220n89; on immigration, 139;
Jewish leftists, 62–63, 107–8, 107–9, 108,
110, 114, 116; Munich Olympics massa-
cre (September 1972), 118, 119, 220n89,
223n152; relations with Israel, 86, 114,
116, 202n4, 206n69
Le Pen, Jean Marie, 6, 127–28, 131, 142
Lévy, Benny, 86, 107, 108
Lévy, Bernard-Henri, 132, 149 233n98
Lévy, Catherine, 108
Lévy, Léo, 108
Lévy, Tony, 86, 108
Lévyne, Emmanuel, 107–8
Libération, 130–31, 134
Librairie Palestine bombing, 118
LICA (Ligue international contre
l'antisémitisme). *See* LICRA
LICRA (Ligue international contre le racism
et l'antisémitisme), 97, 104, 107, 123, 128,
135, 138, 227n16
Ligue des droits de l'homme, 128
Liscia, Richard, 135–36, 147
Lyons rodeos (July/August 1981), 127

Maoists, 62–63, 100, 107, 108, 109, 112,
216n47. *See also* leftists
Marche pour l'égalité (October–November
1983), 129
La Marseillaise (Communist paper), 93
Marseille: anti-colonialist demonstrations,
26; demographics of, 10–11, 24, 25, 69,
74, 164n49, 164n50; discrimination
against Algerian Muslims, 25–26, 171n24,
171n71; ethnic violence in, 24, 94–95, 119,
120, 133, 150, 240n10; FLN activities in,
73; housing shortages in, 11–12, 23, 68,
70–71, 74–77, 197n104, 198n116; impact
of French decolonization on, 69; inequities in city politics, 78; Jewish fundraising
for October 1973 Arab-Israeli War, 120;
Jewish settlement patterns in, 75–76,
198n116; Jewish welfare agencies in, 29–
30, 33; kosher butchers in, 155–56; map
of, 14; paramilitary groups in, 30; post–
World War II reconstruction, 23; PPA
(Parti du peuple algérien) in, 26; profile of,
10–11, 23, 27, 33; pro-Palestinian appeals

in, 26–27; proximity to North Africa,
27, 60; reaction to 1948 war declaration
of Israeli independence, 15–17. *See also*
Deferre, Gaston; port of Marseille
Marseille-Espérance, 150
Le Matin, 131
Mayer, Daniel, 22
Mayer, Muhammad Abou, 105
Mayer, René, 22
MCRA (Section française du mouvement
contre racisme anti-arabe), 106, 107
media: anti-Arab rhetoric in, 87, 119,
224n163; anti-Jewish rhetoric in, 119,
130–31, 186n157, 224n163; anti-Zionist
rhetoric in, 26, 104; Arab-language press
in Algeria on, 24; attacks on Algerian
Muslims, 119; Belleville riots in, 103, 104;
on Beur French identity, 140; on French
Muslim insecurity, 150–51; head-scarf
controversy in, 146; Holocaust denial in,
131; inclusion of Algerian Jews in the
national project, 50; inter-ethnic tensions
in Marseille in the wake of 1967 War, 92;
Israel in, 1, 78–79, 85, 86, 92, 93, 141; on
Jewish migration, 24, 41; Lyons rodeos
(July/August 1981), 127; Muslim identity
in, 8; Muslim-Jewish relations in, 103,
134, 137–38, 149; on Muslim loyalty, 148;
on North African Muslim workers' political activism, 112–13; Palestinian cause
in, 89, 90, 96–97, 106, 114; *pieds noirs* in,
95; on racial violence, 134, 137; responses
to Marche pour l'égalité, 131; Ronald
Reagan's visit to Bitburg, 134, 137; SOS
racisme in, 132
media, Jewish: anti-Arab discourse in, 61;
criticism of Muslim-Jewish relations in,
137–38; French Middle Eastern policies,
202n4; Holocaust imagery in, 61; Israel's
impact on youth's Jewish identity, 85;
Jewish-Muslim cooperative initiatives
against racism, 136; Jewish social mobility,
72; particularism in articles in, 129; on
racial violence, 134; SOS racisme supported by, 135; Yiddish press on Israel, 86.
See also *L'Arche*
Meir, Golda, 118
Meiss, Léon, 61–62
Melhaa, Khaled, 140
Memmi, Albert, 64, 103
Mèndes-France, Pierre, 37
Merah, Mohammed, 1

Le Méridional–La France (center-right paper), 93, 119, 150–51

Messali Hadj, 20, 26, 73

migration to Israel: accusations of Muslim antisemitism, 40–42, 178n40; ambivalence toward, 42; anti-Jewish violence as catalyst, 46; criticism of, 37–39, 38, 42, 177n20, 177n26; as disruptive, 38; French decolonization, 37; impact on indigenous communities, 179n52; international Jewish agencies on, 37; opposition to, 42; as sign of French duplicity, 38; as sparking hostility, 41–42

Minute (newspaper), 87

Mischmar, 116

Mitterrand administration (François Mitterrand), 6, 125, 126, 129–30, 139, 148, 228n34

Le Monde, 50, 96, 104, 131, 134, 137, 140

Morin, Jean, 57

Moroccan Jews: anti-Jewish violence, 27–28, 38, 39–40, 50, 82, 172n86; migration of, 28, 35, 37–39, 42, 44, 69–70, 82, 172n91, 175n3; on Moroccan independence movement, 39–41, 178n40; safety of, 39–40, 177n26

Morocco: AMF (Association des Marocains en France), 134, 218n71; anti-Jewish violence, 27–28, 38, 39–40, 50, 82, 172n86; associations of Moroccans in France, 109, 130, 134, 218n71; construction of Jewish identity in, 36; identification with Arab world, 44; independence movement, 39–41, 42, 178n40; Muslim control of, 3; nationalist movement, 27–28, 37; naturalization guidelines, 3, 162n20; opposition groups in, 109, 218n71

Mouvement démocratique féminin, 93

MRAP (Mouvement contre le racisme, l'antisémitism, et pour la paix), 66, 86, 98, 128, 206n69, 227n16

MTA (Mouvement des travailleurs arabes), 111, 112, 113, 120–21, 123–24

MTLD (Mouvement pour le triomphe des libertés démocratiques), 17, 26, 33

Munich Olympics massacre (September 1972), 118, 119, 220n89, 223n152

murder of Mahmoud Hamchari, 118, 119

murder of Moroccan immigrant in Menton, 133, 231n71

Muslim identity: construction of, 8–9, 164n45

Muslim-Jewish relations: anti-Arab rhetoric's impact on, 94–95; Belleville riot, 100; calls for dialogue, 63–64, 97–99, 142, 143–44; citizenship as source of conflict, 4, 74; Constantine riots (1934), 181n68; first intifada (1987), 139–41; French presence, 45–46; immigrant experience in France, 7–8, 31–32, 67–74, 76, 77–78, 128; Jewish migration to Palestine as source of tension, 16–17, 24, 41–42; Jewish radicalism, 117–18; Jewish support for anti-war protestors, 66; Lebanon invasion by Israel (1982), 130; Marseille Jewish community, schism within, 155–56; neighborhood relations in Marseille, 67–71; particularism vs. pluriculturalism in, 135–39, 144–45; question of Palestine, 20–22; and relationships to the French state, 59; tensions in, 2–3, 79, 94–95, 103, 118–20, 201n144, 201n146; unemployment, 119; *La Vie devant soi* (Émil Ajar), 122–23; volatility of, 45–47, 48–50, 135–39; during World War II, 24. *See also* anti-Arab violence; anti-Jewish violence; hate crimes; Israel; Palestinian movement

Muslim-Jewish riots in Constantine (1934), 181n68

Muslims: anti-Zionism conflated with antisemitism, 143; foreignness of, 126, 137–38, 142, 147; French diplomatic support for Israel, 166n7; French minority policies, 20–21; impact of decolonization on, 2, 3, 160n8; integration into French society, 144; *Islam française*, 8; political legitimacy asserted by, 21, 169n41; as political symbol, 2; in post–World War II era, 24; use of term, 7–9, 10

Muslim students, 97–98, 109, 140, 218n72

Muslim workers: aid organizations for, 70, 89, 111–13, 120–21, 123–24; dockworkers, 15, 27, 28, 29, 31; employment, 25–26, 171n71, 171n72; engagement with the Palestinian cause, 112, 121; GP recruitment of, 112–13; in Grand Arénas transit camp, 70–71; housing for, 73–74; strike, 120

musulman (use of term), 9

Narboni, André, 43, 57

Nasser, Gamal Abdel, 44, 52, 61, 82

nationalist movement in Algeria, 16, 20, 22, 26, 48–49, 50, 67, 109

Naye Presse, 86

Nazism: anti-Muslim violence compared with, 66–67; anti-war demonstrations (17 October 1961) compared with, 66; empathy for Jewish victims of, 16, 21; France under, 21, 24; in Israel-Palestine issue, 97, 104, 115, 144, 212n159; in Jewish-Muslim discourse, 66; Jews in propaganda images, 24; racialized discourse of, 9, 18, 97; State of Israel, 82, 86, 96

Neher, André, 83

Neo Destour, 17, 41, 42

1948 War, 16–17, 24, 27–28, 32, 38

1956 declaration, 50

1967 Arab-Israeli War: Belleville riots (June 1968), 102; French government neutrality, 81, 87, 93; French Jewish activism during, 82–84, 85, 202n12, 204n35; Holocaust imagery, 82, 85, 92; Muslim-Jewish tensions during, 80, 87, 91–92, 94–96; North African immigrant identification with the Palestinians, 80; North African immigrants, 80–82; opposition to Israel during, 85, 86–87, 88

1968 student uprising, 100, 101, 106–7

OAS (Organisation de l'armée secrète), 55–56, 66, 115

October 1970 demonstration, 112

October 1971 murder of Algerian Muslims, 111

October 1973 Arab-Israeli War, 119, 120

Office palestinien d'immigration (later, Office d'immigration de l'État d'Israël), 31

oil crisis (1973), 127

Operation Susannah, 61

L'Opinion (Istiqlal publication), 131

Oran, Algeria, anti-Jewish violence in, 35, 36, 37, 45, 54, 55

Or Aviv synagogue arson, 240n10

ORT (Organization for Rehabilitation and Training), 47

OSF (Organisation sioniste de France), 21

Oujda riots (Morocco), 27, 28, 38, 39, 40, 61, 172n86

Ozar Hatorah murders, 1

Palant, Charles, 98

Palestine: Algerian nationalist recruitment for combat volunteers in Palestine, 22; commando attacks in France, 118; CRIF support for Jewish home in, 20; French diplomatic support for, 16, 166n7; Jewish migration to, 15–16, 17, 19, 22, 27–28;

1947 Partition Plan, 21–22; recruitment for combat volunteers in, 22, 89; as source of interethnic tensions, 18

La Palestine vaincra, 116, 135

Palestinian movement: activism, 26, 96–97, 104, 115–16, 121, 130, 131–32; ADAE (Amicale des Algériens en Europe), 88–89, 105; Beur activism on behalf of, 130; demonstrations in support of, 112–13; Fatah, 89, 101, 104, 105; first intifada (1987), 139–41, 154; fundraising for, 90, 130; Israel's right to exist, 114–15; Jewish support for, 102, 107–8, 116; leftist support for, 106, 107, 108–9; organizational representation of, 21–22, 87; Palestinian diplomacy in France, 105; PDFLP (Popular Democratic Front for the Liberation of Palestine), 108, 216n47, 218n73; PFLP (Popular Front for the Liberation of Palestine), 113–14, 115, 216n47, 217n72, 218n72, 218n73; publications of, 105, 109, 112, 113; rallies for, 26, 96–97, 104, 115–16, 121, 131–32; recruitment for combat volunteers, 22, 89; student support for, 6, 96–97, 101, 106, 109, 116, 218n72; worker recruitment for, 109–10, 118

Paris, 10, 24, 68, 71–72, 95, 109, 116, 121, 133–34, 222n134. See also Belleville

Paris-Presse, 95

Passages (Jewish monthly), 143

PDFLP (Popular Democratic Front for the Liberation of Palestine), 108, 216n47, 218n73

Peace Now, 152

Perlzweig, Maurice, 39–40, 48

Petitjean murders, 27, 28, 39–40

PFLP (Popular Front for the Liberation of Palestine), 113–14, 115, 216n47, 217n72, 218n72, 218n73

pied noirs, 11, 43, 54, 55, 56, 77, 95–96, 180n65, 212n153

Plan Vigipirate, 148, 150

PLO (Palestinian Liberation Organization), 87, 101, 121, 152; French government relations with, 121, 133

pluriculturalism: and call for dialogue, 63–64, 142, 143–44; criticism of, 137–38; Gulf War (1991), 148–50; head-scarf ban as challenge to, 146; Jews on, 135, 137–38; in Muslim-Jewish relations, 135–39, 144–45; particularism compared with, 126, 146–51; use of term, 125–26

police-immigrant relations, 16, 20, 32, 113, 121, 127, 129
port of Marseille: dockworkers, 15, 27, 28, 29, 30, 31; Jewish migration to Palestine through, 15–16, 17, 23, 27–30, 172n91; military arms transfers through, 11, 15, 23, 29, 30
PPA (Parti du peuple algérien), 20, 22, 26, 31, 33
La Provençal, 78, 93

Rabi, Wladimir, 62, 79, 96
Rabiaz, Patrick, 108
racism: anti-Arab violence, 119–20, 128, 148; Beur Movement, 125, 129, 131–32, 136–37, 226n1; coalitions against, 6, 120–21, 125, 142–43, 144; FN (Front nationale), 6, 126, 127–28, 139, 227n13; France plus, 140, 142, 143–44, 147; interethnic cooperation in opposing, 128–29, 133–35; Jewish-Muslim cooperation, 96, 98; restrictions on immigration, 111, 139; similarities between Muslim and Jewish experiences in France, 132–33; strike in against, 120; violence against North African Muslim immigrants, 111. See also antisemitism; hate crimes; SOS racisme
Reagan, Ronald, 134, 137
Rebois, Charles, 148
refugee camps, 30, 31–32, 33, 69–71, 74, 77–78, 197n104
Résistance populaire (Comité de soutien aux luttes anti-impérialistes des peuples arabes), 106, 107
Rifaat, Adel, 101, 108
right to be different, 126, 129–30, 144
Robinson, Nehemiah, 47
Rochman, Marc, 145, 148
rodeo riots, 127, 129
Rodinson, Maxime, 96, 107
Roosevelt-Churchill Atlantic Charter, 18–19
Rothschild, Alain de, 61
Rothschild, Guy de, 83, 84
rue Copernic synagogue, 5, 128, 130, 227n15
Rushdie, Salman, 146

Sabra and Shatila massacre, 130
Safrani, Robert, 78
Salomon, Michel, 97
Salzer, Israel, 73
Sans frontières (Beur newspaper), 134, 137, 140

Sarcelles, 10, 68, 71–72
Sayigh, Yezid, 219n81
Schneiderman, Daniel, 134
Sebbar, Leïla, 134
second generation (French-born children of immigrants). See Beurs and Beur Movement
Secretariat d'état aux affaires algérienne, 51
Section Marseille Provence du mouvement démocratique féminin, 93
self-defense organizations, 45, 54, 223n156
Service social de l'association consistoire israélite, 46
Sétif massacre, 19, 26
Shepard, Todd, 8, 35, 55, 56
Sibony, Simon, 85
Signoret, Simone, 122
Simon, Jean, 103
Sinclair, Anne, 85
Sirat, René, 66
Sitruk, Joseph, 146
Smaïn (Algerian comedian), 149
Solomon, Michel, 98
SOS racisme: anti-racism alliance, 147–48; criticism of, 135–36; founding of, 131–33; on Israel's response to first intifada (1987), 140, 141–42; marches in support of antiracism, 136–37; media events of, 132, 232n87; multiculturalist perspective of, 131–32; Muslim-Jewish collaborative efforts against racism, 134; pluricultural approach of, 136; Soviet Jewry, 134–35; Kaïssa Titous, 141, 233n98; "Touche pas á mon pote" (SOS racisme badge), 132, 135, 136, 231n71; UEJF alliance with, 132–33, 135, 141–42, 149, 230n60
Soviet Jewry, 134–35
Statute of Algeria (1947), 25
Stein, Herman, 40
Stillman, Norman, 172n86
Stora, Benjamin, 58, 142
students: anti-American propaganda, 101, 115; Arab activism in, 98–99; associations of, 86, 105–6, 108, 109, 218n71; on Israel, 85, 98–99, 101, 114–15; Jewish-Muslim dialogues, 63–64, 143–44; Jewish students, 63, 114, 133, 135; Muslim students, 97–98, 109, 140, 218n72; Palestinians supported by, 6, 96–97, 101, 106, 109, 116, 218n72; student uprising (1968), 100, 101, 106–7. See also UEJF (Union des étudiants juif de France); university campuses

Suez crisis, 44, 61, 209n115
Syndicat des ouvriers musulmans de Port-de-Bouc, 31, 174n119
Syria, 117–18

Talmoudi, Mohamed, 31
Tenenbaum, Françoise, 85, 115
Terrenoire, Louis, 117
La Terre retrouvé (French Zionist newspaper), 39
Thau, Frédéric, 30
Timsit, Daniel, 46
Titous, Kaïssa, 141, 233n98
Torres, Abdelkhalek, 42
Touati, Emile, 72
"Touche pas á mon pote" (SOS racisme badge), 132, 135, 136, 231n71
Touïsi, Rabeh (France plus), 143–44, 236n146
Tribune juive, 129, 134, 135
Trigano, Shmuel, 129, 147
Trotskyists, 100, 106, 108, 131, 216n47, 217n62, 218n73
Tsur, Yaron, 41
Tunisia: AIU (Alliance israélite universelle) in, 36; anti-Jewish hostilities, 50, 82; clashes with French, 54; construction of Jewish identity in, 36; identification with Arab world, 44; Jewish migration patterns, 3, 35, 38, 42, 82, 103, 175n3, 177n23; Muslim control of, 3; nationalist resistance in, 37

UEJF (Union des étudiants juifs de France): anti-racist demonstration, 132; Belleville riots, 102, 104; Arié Bensemhoun, 141, 142, 143, 144; Beur alliances with, 135, 136; dialogues with North African nationalists, 63–64, 99, 143–44; France plus, 143, 145; fundamentalist secularism criticized by, 146; and Eric Ghébali, 132, 133, 136, 141, 143, 231n68; Israel supported by, 114–15, 133, 149, 231n68; Palestinian movement relations with, 114–15, 116, 152, 231n68; panel on Middle East at Jussieu campus, 135; particularism of, 142, 151–52; pluri-culturalism of, 126, 135, 141–42, 149, 151–52; racism opposed by, 66; on repression in Algeria, 62; response to Jewish-Muslim tensions, 149; SOS racisme alliance with, 132–33, 135, 141–42, 149, 152, 230n60; Zionism supported by, 114–15, 133, 135, 136, 141

UGEP (Union générale des étudiants palestiniens), 87, 96, 98, 109, 110, 117–18
UGTA (Union générale des travailleurs algériens), 89
UJRE (Union juifs pour la résistance et l'entraide), 30, 33
UMEJ (Union mondiale des étudiants juifs), 99
UNEF (Union nationale des étudiants français), 101, 114
Union des engagés volontaires et anciens combattants juifs, 66
Union des étudiants communistes, 108
Union des étudiants juifs (University of Strasbourg), 99
Union des jeunesses communistes marxistes-léninistes, 101, 108
Union générale des étudiants libanais de France, 106
Union générale des étudiants tunisiens, 109
Union nationale des étudiants algériens, 109
Union nationale des étudiants marocains, 109, 130
university campuses: anti-American propaganda at, 101, 115; anti-Israel rhetoric on, 98–99, 101, 114, 115, 116, 118; Arab activism in, 98–99, 106, 109; Censier incidents, 116–17, 222n134; Cité Universitaire, 98, 109, 115–16; Jews on, 81, 98, 99, 115–17; Muslim-Jewish relations, 81, 98; Palestinian presence on, 87, 96, 98, 105–6, 109–10, 115–16, 117–18, 218n71, 218n72; Sciences Po (Paris) incident (4 December 1969), 116, 222n134; student uprising (1968), 100, 101, 106–7

Vaïsse, Justin, 7
Vidal-Naquet, Pierre, 62
La Vie devant soi (Émil Ajar), 122–23
Vigouroux, Robert, 150

"We cannot solve the Israel/Palestinian problem on the banks of the Seine," 136
Weissberg, Jean-Louis, 108
WJC (World Jewish Congress), 39, 47
Wolf, Joan, 82
workers: aid organizations for, 111, 112, 113, 120–21, 123–24; labor unions, 26, 89; 1968 uprisings, 106; strikes against anti-Arab violence, 120; support for

Palestinian cause, 89, 106–7, 108, 109, 110, 112, 118, 119

World War II. *See* Holocaust

Wormser, André, 137–38, 233n103

youth and youth organizations: Comité de coordination de la jeunesse juive, 92; Jewish-Muslim cooperation, 96, 98; pro-Palestinian sentiments of Muslims, 130–31, 153; response to pro-Israel campaign, 84–85; student uprising (1968), 100, 101, 106–7; support for Israel, 93

Zionism: Algerian nationalist movement, 26; as anti-Arab, 41, 119, 224n163; anti-Zionist protests, 21, 24, 26–27, 115–17, 119, 143, 224n163; Defferre's support for Israel, 78–79, 92–94, 120, 201n141; French diplomatic support for, 17, 166n7; French Jews, 19–20, 168n29; and French minority policies, 21–22; gauchistes on, 107–9, 114, 116, 118; Jewish opposition to, 86, 96, 107–9, 206n69; Judaism compared with, 99; migration to Israel, 15–17, 19, 22, 27–28, 30–32, 38–42, 69–70, 178n30, 178n40; Muslim opposition to, 20, 21; nationalist movements, 27–28, 37; opposition to, 26–28, 38, 41, 135; organizational support for, 21–22, 86, 108, 203n25; PPA (Parti du peuple algérien), 20, 26; pro-Israel rallies, 27, 61, 92, 93–94, 95, 113, 121; rhetoric of Arab nationalism, 88–89

FRENCH BA
Centre for Language Studies and
Applied Linguistics
Canterbury Christ Church University
Canterbury, Kent
CT1 1QU